ASSASSINATION CLASSROOM

YUSEI MATSUI

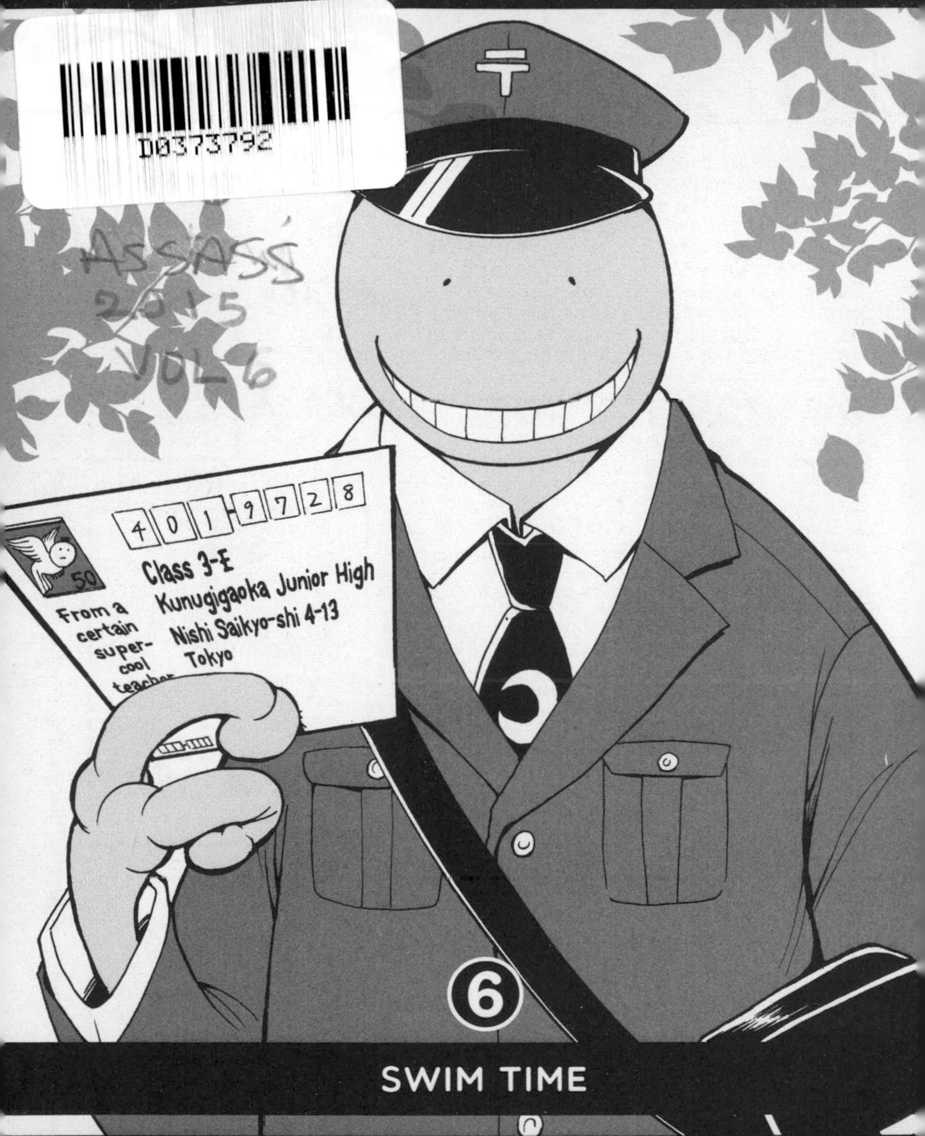
4 0 1 - 9 7 2 8
50
Class 3-E
Kunugigaoka Junior High
Nishi Saikyo-shi 4-13
Tokyo
From a
certain
super-
cool

6

SWIM TIME

SHONEN JUMP ADVANCED

Koro Tribune

July Issue

Published by: Class 3-E Newspaper Staff

Our new teacher is a creature who plans to destroy the world...?!

Story Thus Far

One day, something destroyed 70% of the moon.

I'M THE ONE WHO DISINTEGRATED PART OF THE MOON.
AND NEXT YEAR AT THIS TIME I'M GOING TO DO THE SAME THING TO YOUR PLANET EARTH.
ALSO, I'M YOUR NEW TEACHER. I HOPE WE

A mysterious creature showed up in our junior high classroom claiming that he had attacked the moon and promising to destroy the earth next March. And then...he took over as our teacher. What the—?! Faced with a creature beyond human understanding that no army could kill, the leaders of the world had no choice but to rely on the students of Kunugigaoka Junior High, Class 3-E, to do the job. For a reward of ten million dollars... SIGN ME UP!! Will the students of the so-called End Class, filled with losers and rejects, be able to kill their target Koro Sensei by graduation...?!

Koro Sensei

A mysterious octopus-like creature whose nickname is a play on the words "koro senai," which means "can't be killed." He is capable of flying at Mach 20 and his versatile tentacles protect him from attacks and aid him in everyday activities. Nobody knows why he wants to teach Class 3-E, but he has proven to be an extremely capable teacher.

His weakness is water?! What is he...the Wicked Witch?

Kaede Kayano

Class E student. She's the one who named Koro Sensei. Sits at the desk next to Nagisa, and they seem to get along well.

Nagisa Shiota

Class E student. Skilled at information gathering, he has been taking notes on Koro Sensei's weaknesses.

If we nurture his gifts as an assassin... will it be of any use to him in the future...?
SNKK

Karma Akabane

Class E student. A quick thinker skilled at surprise attacks. Succeeded in injuring Koro Sensei a few times.

Takuya Muramatsu

The best cook out of the boys of 3-E. He often competes against Hara, the best cook out of the girls, in home economics class.

pick up!

Meg Kataoka

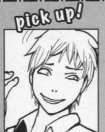

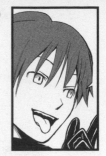

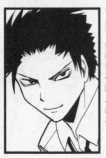

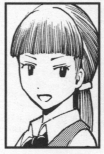

The Female Class Representative for Class E. She is very responsible and trusted by her classmates. Will she be the one to plot Koro Sensei's water assassination...?

Tadaomi Karasuma

Member of the Ministry of Defense and the Class E students' P.E. teacher. Also in charge of managing visiting assassins.

Irina Jelavich

A sexy assassin hired as an English teacher. She's known for using her "womanly charms" to get close to a target but has failed to kill Koro Sensei—yet.

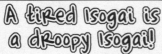

A tired Isogai is a droopy Isogai!

All work and no play makes Isogai's antennae wilt. His classmates brush them back up for him.

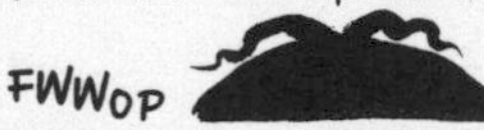

FWWOP

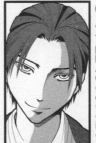

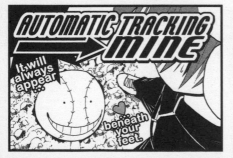

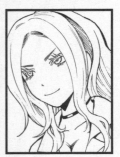

Gakuho Asano

The principal of Kunugigaoka Academy, who built this academically competitive school based on his faith in rationality and hierarchy.

AUTOMATIC TRACKING MINE
It will always appear...
...beneath your feet.

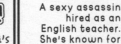

ASSASSINATION CLASSROOM 6 CONTENTS

(ANSWER SHEET)

Grade 3 | Class E | Name CONTENTS | Score

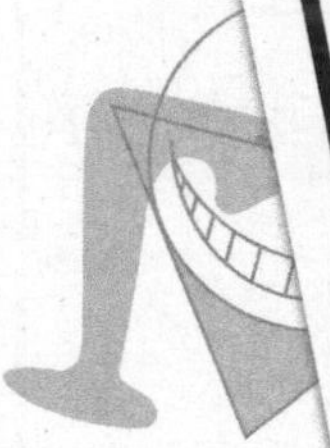

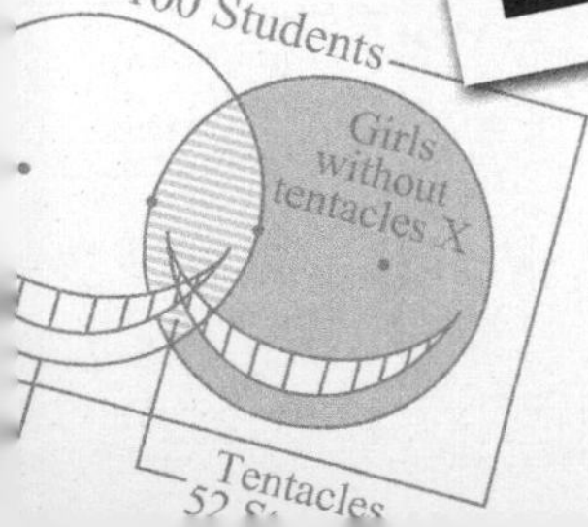

100 Students
Girls without tentacles X
Tentacles

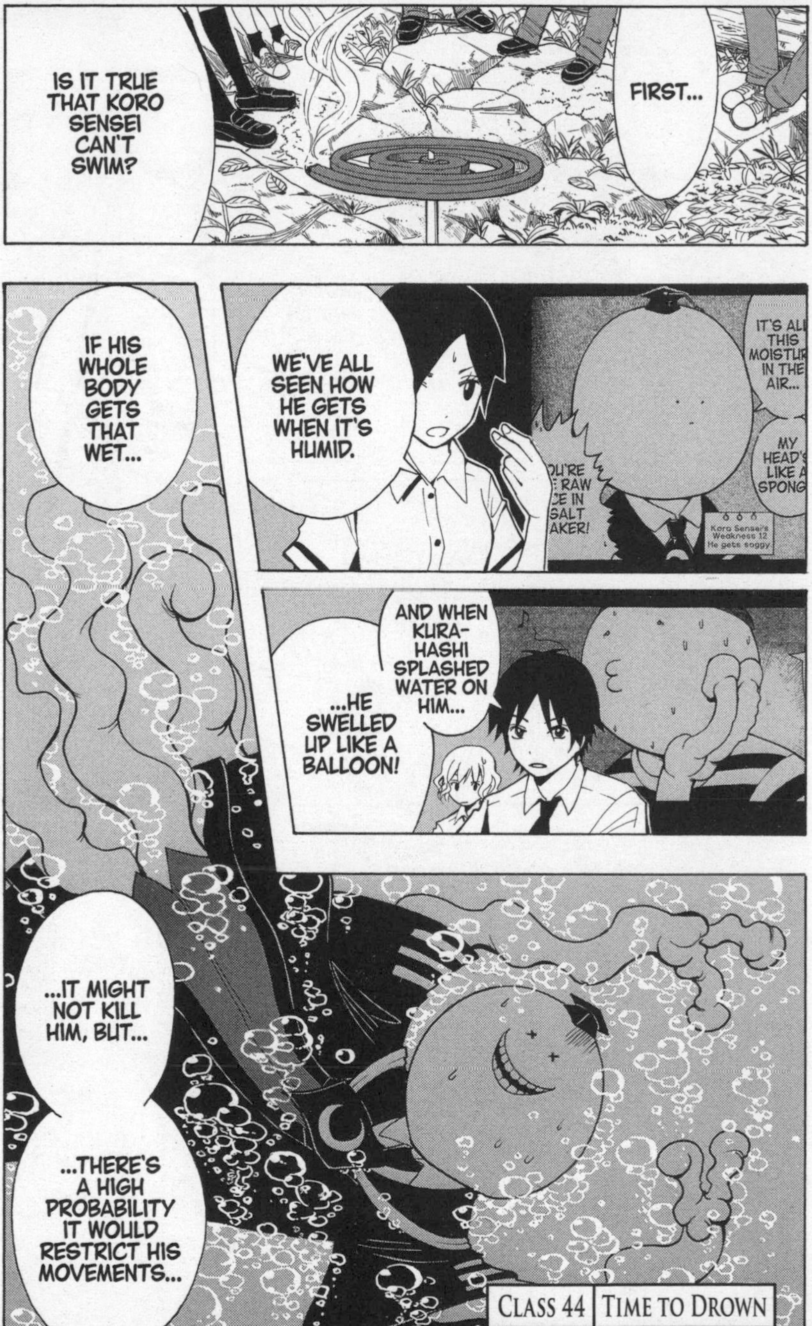
FIRST...
IS IT TRUE THAT KORO SENSEI CAN'T SWIM?
IT'S ALL THIS MOISTUR IN THE AIR...
MY HEAD'S LIKE A SPONG
RAW CE IN SALT AKER!
Koro Sensei's Weakness 12 He gets soggy
WE'VE ALL SEEN HOW HE GETS WHEN IT'S HUMID.
AND WHEN KURA-HASHI SPLASHED WATER ON HIM...
...HE SWELLED UP LIKE A BALLOON!
IF HIS WHOLE BODY GETS THAT WET...
...IT MIGHT NOT KILL HIM, BUT...
...THERE'S A HIGH PROBABILITY IT WOULD RESTRICT HIS MOVEMENTS...
CLASS 44 TIME TO DROWN

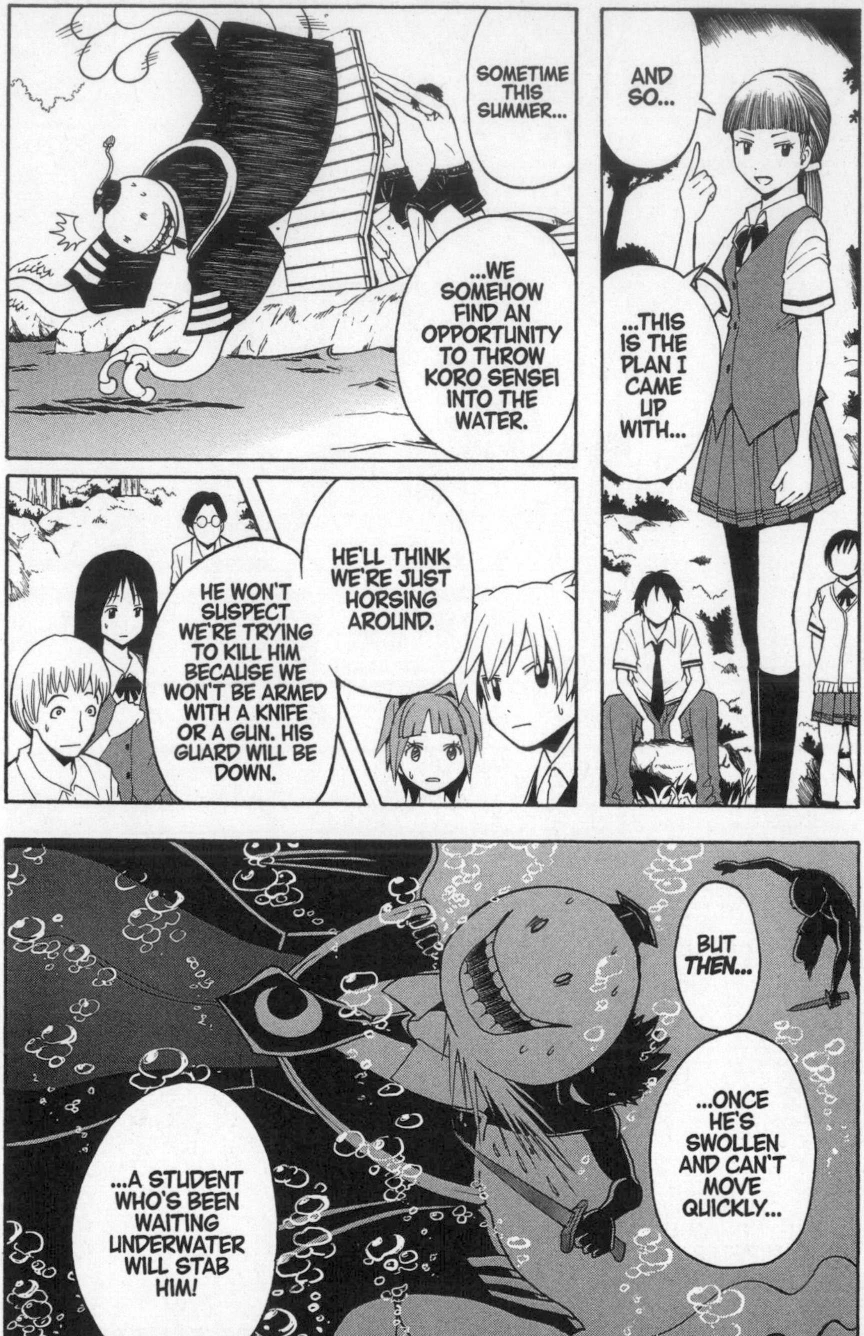
AND SO...
...THIS IS THE PLAN I CAME UP WITH...
SOMETIME THIS SUMMER...
...WE SOMEHOW FIND AN OPPORTUNITY TO THROW KORO SENSEI INTO THE WATER.
HE'LL THINK WE'RE JUST HORSING AROUND.
HE WON'T SUSPECT WE'RE TRYING TO KILL HIM BECAUSE WE WON'T BE ARMED WITH A KNIFE OR A GUN. HIS GUARD WILL BE DOWN.
BUT THEN...
...ONCE HE'S SWOLLEN AND CAN'T MOVE QUICKLY...
...A STUDENT WHO'S BEEN WAITING UNDERWATER WILL STAB HIM!

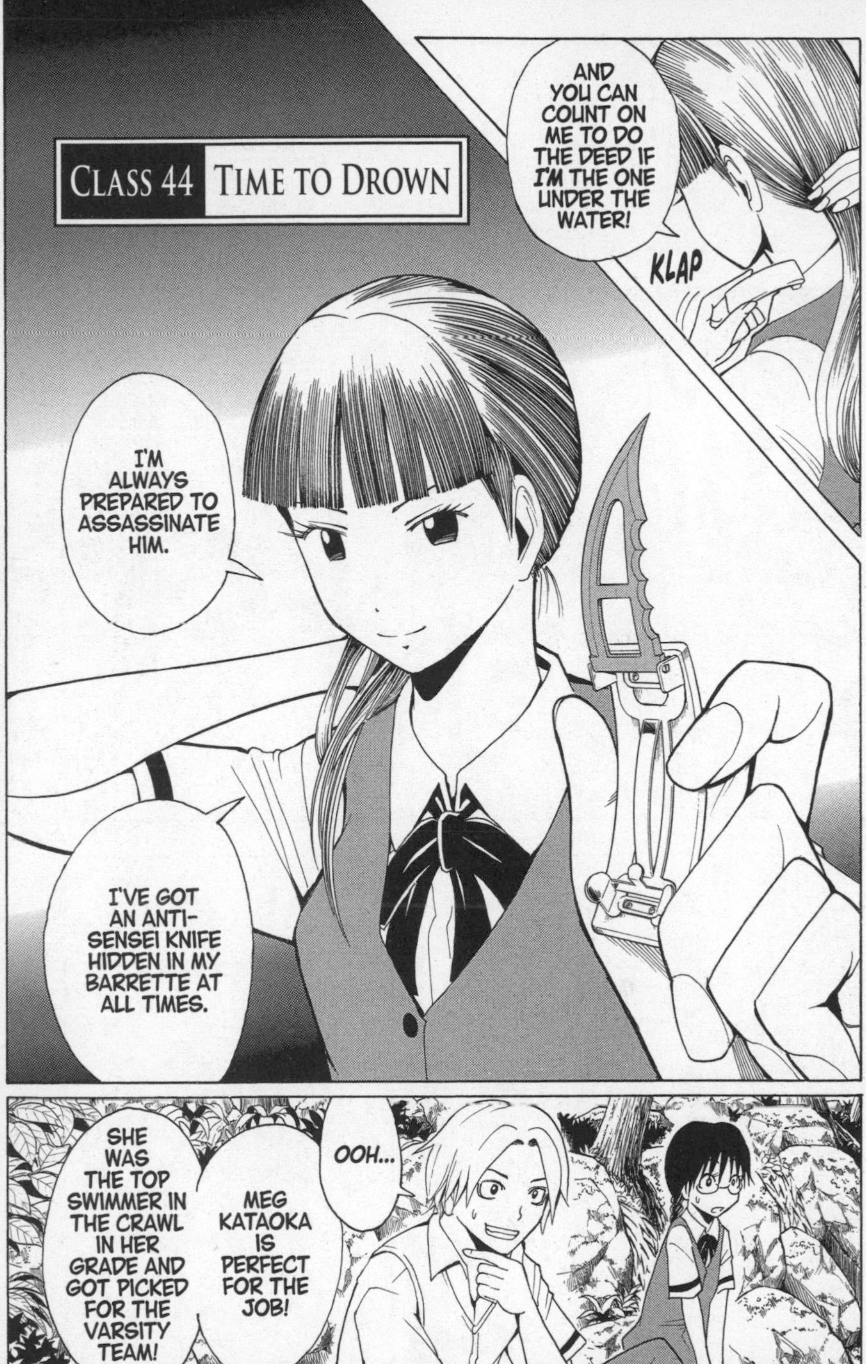
CLASS 44 TIME TO DROWN
AND YOU CAN COUNT ON ME TO DO THE DEED IF I'M THE ONE UNDER THE WATER!
KLAP
I'M ALWAYS PREPARED TO ASSASSINATE HIM.
I'VE GOT AN ANTI-SENSEI KNIFE HIDDEN IN MY BARRETTE AT ALL TIMES.
OOH...
MEG KATAOKA IS PERFECT FOR THE JOB!
SHE WAS THE TOP SWIMMER IN THE CRAWL IN HER GRADE AND GOT PICKED FOR THE VARSITY TEAM!

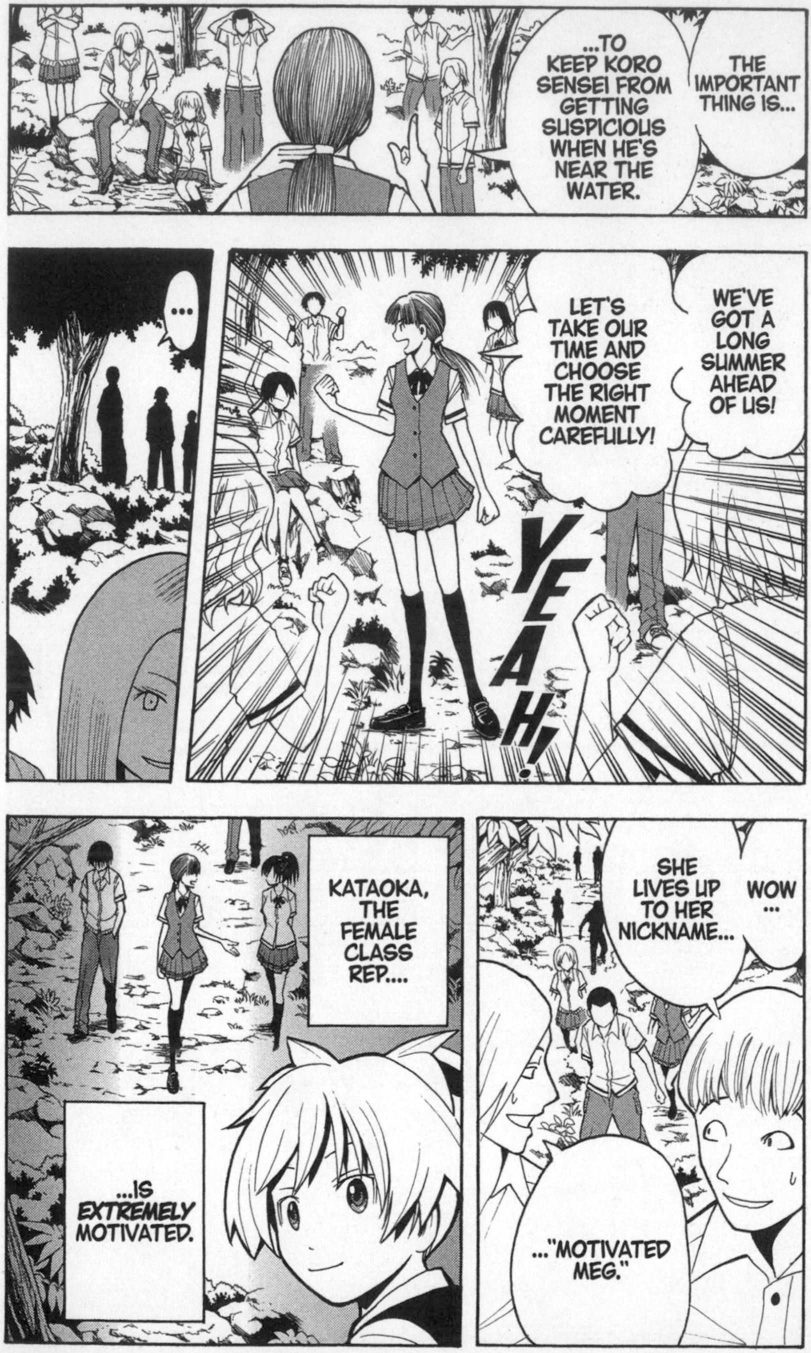
THE IMPORTANT THING IS...
...TO KEEP KORO SENSEI FROM GETTING SUSPICIOUS WHEN HE'S NEAR THE WATER.
WE'VE GOT A LONG SUMMER AHEAD OF US!
LET'S TAKE OUR TIME AND CHOOSE THE RIGHT MOMENT CAREFULLY!
YEAH!
...
WOW...
SHE LIVES UP TO HER NICKNAME...
..."MOTIVATED MEG."
KATAOKA, THE FEMALE CLASS REP....
...IS *EXTREMELY* MOTIVATED.

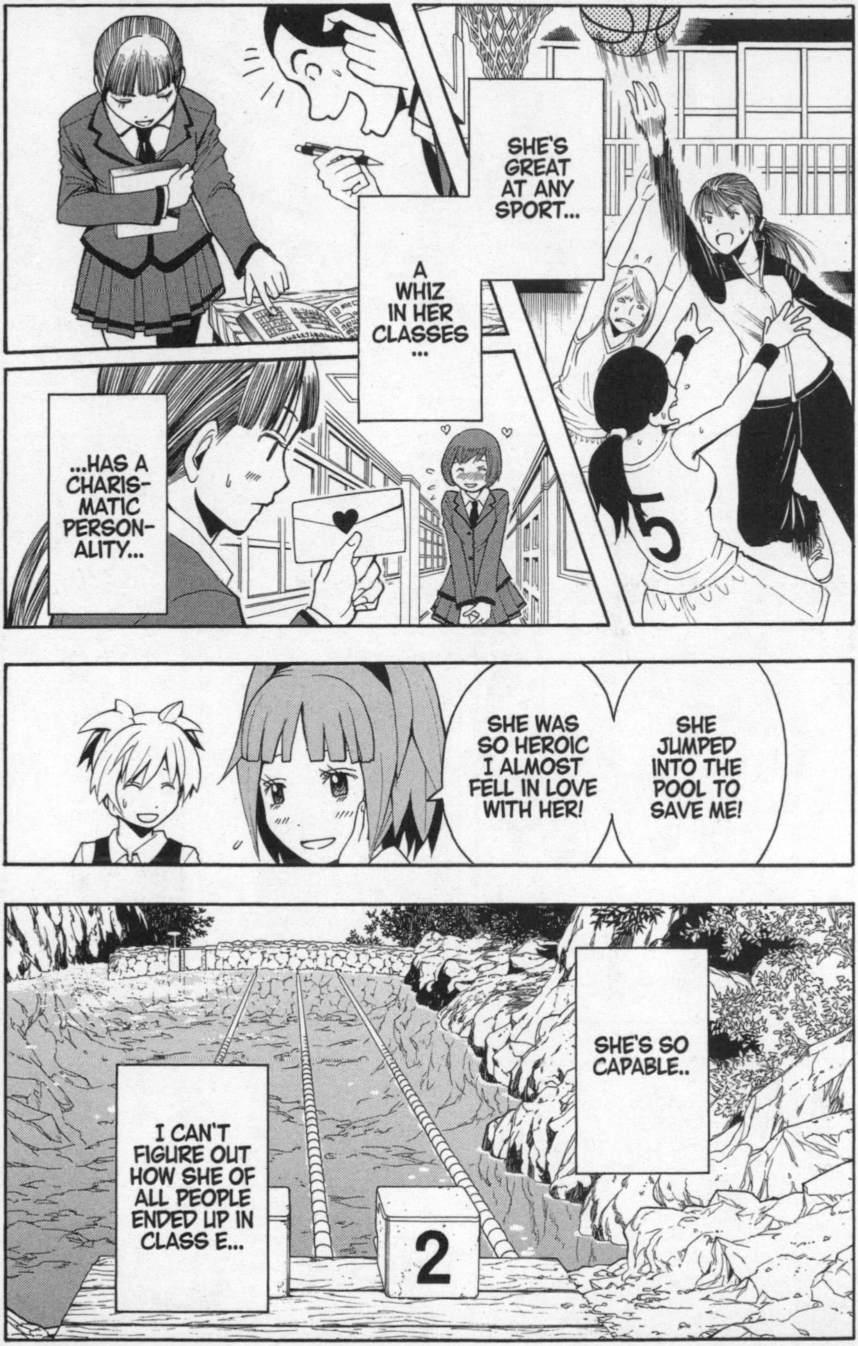
SHE'S GREAT AT ANY SPORT...
A WHIZ IN HER CLASSES ...
...HAS A CHARIS-MATIC PERSON-ALITY...
5
SHE JUMPED INTO THE POOL TO SAVE ME!
SHE WAS SO HEROIC I ALMOST FELL IN LOVE WITH HER!
SHE'S SO CAPABLE..
I CAN'T FIGURE OUT HOW SHE OF ALL PEOPLE ENDED UP IN CLASS E...
2

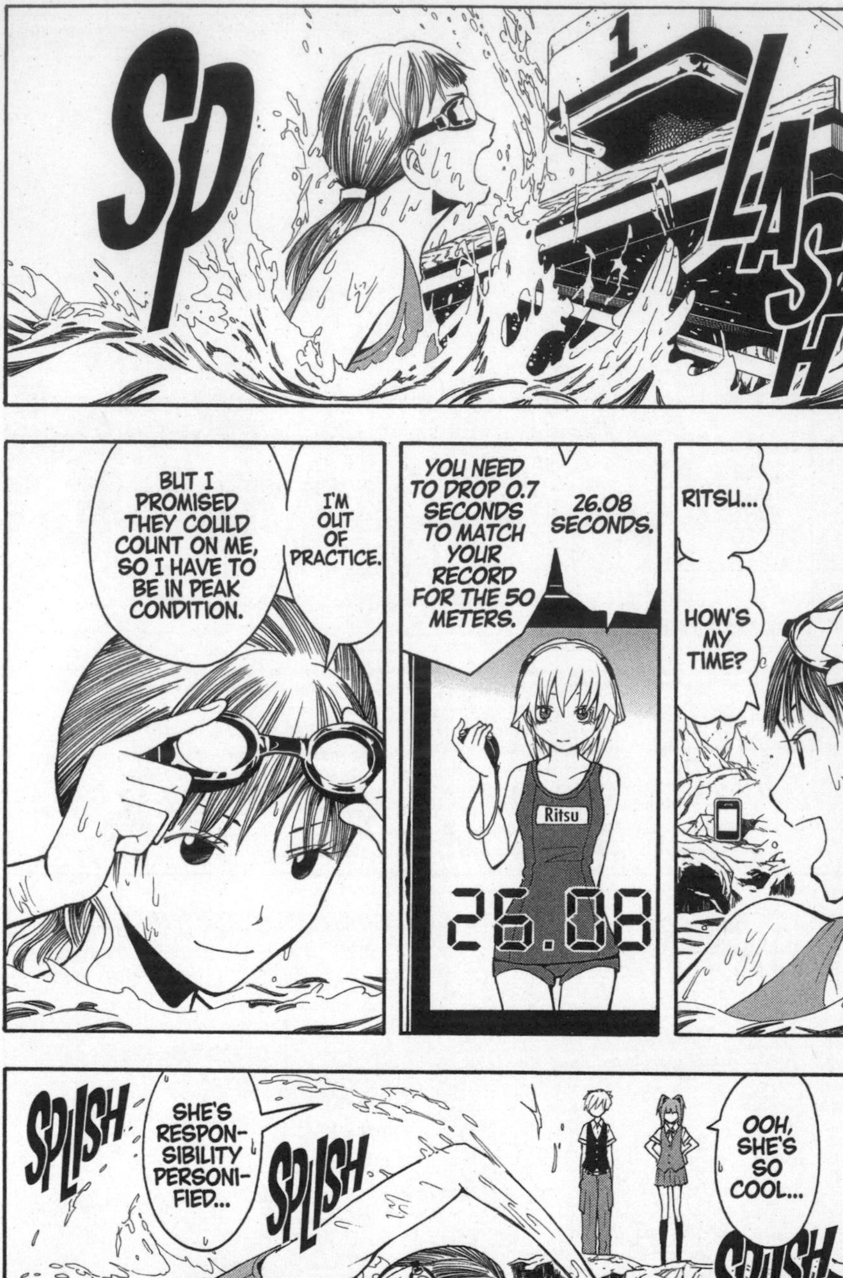
1
SPLASH
RITSU...
HOW'S MY TIME?
26.08 SECONDS.
YOU NEED TO DROP 0.7 SECONDS TO MATCH YOUR RECORD FOR THE 50 METERS.
Ritsu
26.08
I'M OUT OF PRACTICE.
BUT I PROMISED THEY COULD COUNT ON ME, SO I HAVE TO BE IN PEAK CONDITION.
OOH, SHE'S SO COOL...
SPLISH
SPLISH
SHE'S RESPON-SIBILITY PERSONI-FIED...
SPLISH

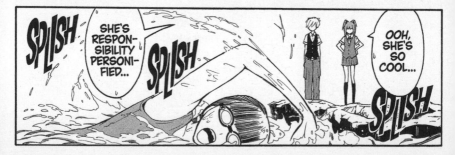

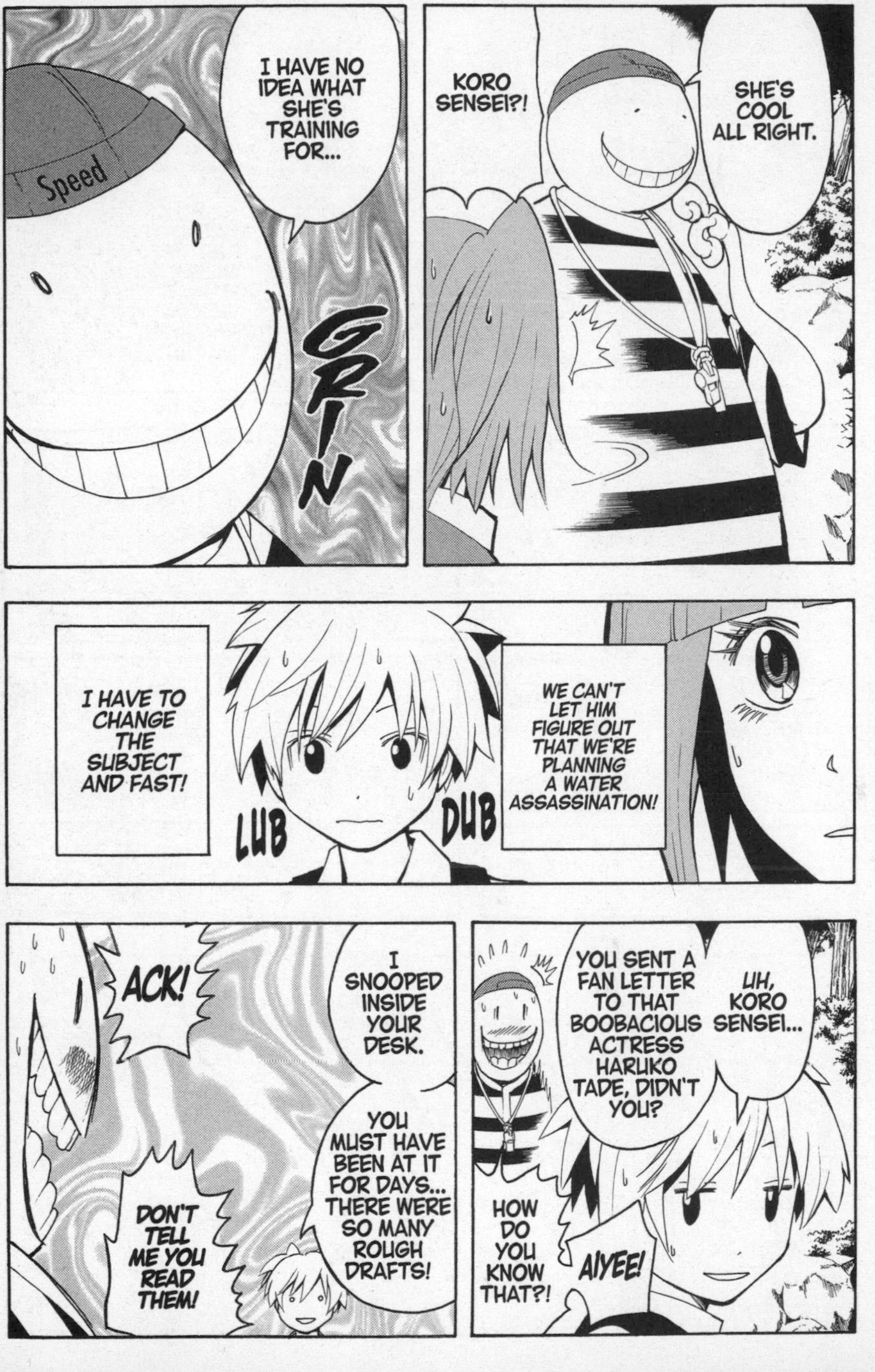
SHE'S COOL ALL RIGHT.
KORO SENSEI?!
I HAVE NO IDEA WHAT SHE'S TRAINING FOR...
Speed
GRIN
WE CAN'T LET HIM FIGURE OUT THAT WE'RE PLANNING A WATER ASSASSINATION!
I HAVE TO CHANGE THE SUBJECT AND FAST!
LUB
DUB
UH, KORO SENSEI...
YOU SENT A FAN LETTER TO THAT BOOBACIOUS ACTRESS HARUKO TADE, DIDN'T YOU?
AIYEE!
HOW DO YOU KNOW THAT?!
I SNOOPED INSIDE YOUR DESK.
ACK!
YOU MUST HAVE BEEN AT IT FOR DAYS... THERE WERE SO MANY ROUGH DRAFTS!
DON'T TELL ME YOU READ THEM!

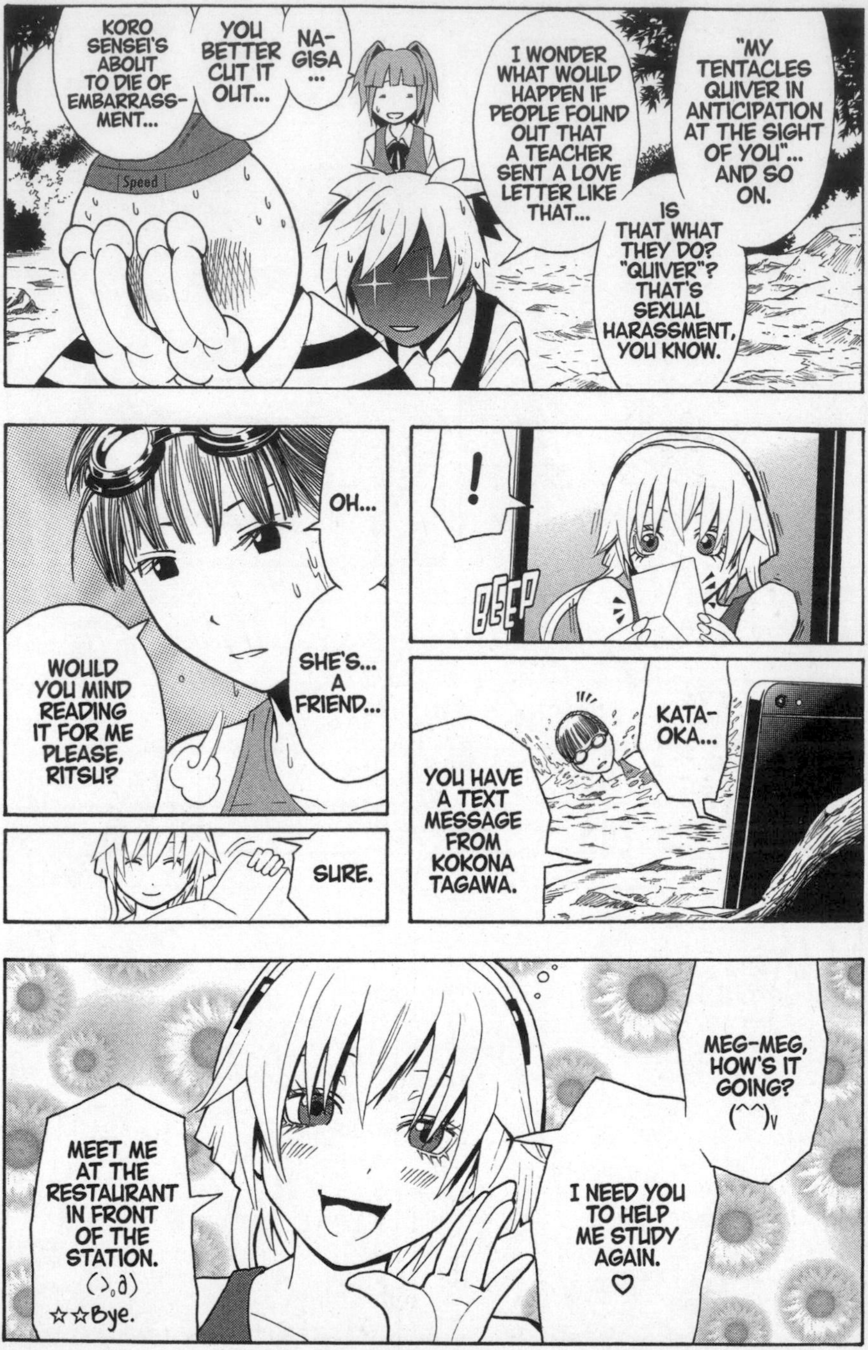
"MY TENTACLES QUIVER IN ANTICIPATION AT THE SIGHT OF YOU"... AND SO ON.
IS THAT WHAT THEY DO? "QUIVER"? THAT'S SEXUAL HARASSMENT, YOU KNOW.
I WONDER WHAT WOULD HAPPEN IF PEOPLE FOUND OUT THAT A TEACHER SENT A LOVE LETTER LIKE THAT...
NA-GISA...
YOU BETTER CUT IT OUT...
KORO SENSEI'S ABOUT TO DIE OF EMBARRASS-MENT...
Speed
!
BEEP
KATA-OKA...
YOU HAVE A TEXT MESSAGE FROM KOKONA TAGAWA.
OH...
SHE'S... A FRIEND...
WOULD YOU MIND READING IT FOR ME PLEASE, RITSU?
SURE.
MEG-MEG, HOW'S IT GOING? (^^)v
I NEED YOU TO HELP ME STUDY AGAIN. ♡
MEET ME AT THE RESTAURANT IN FRONT OF THE STATION. (ↄ。∂) ☆☆Bye.

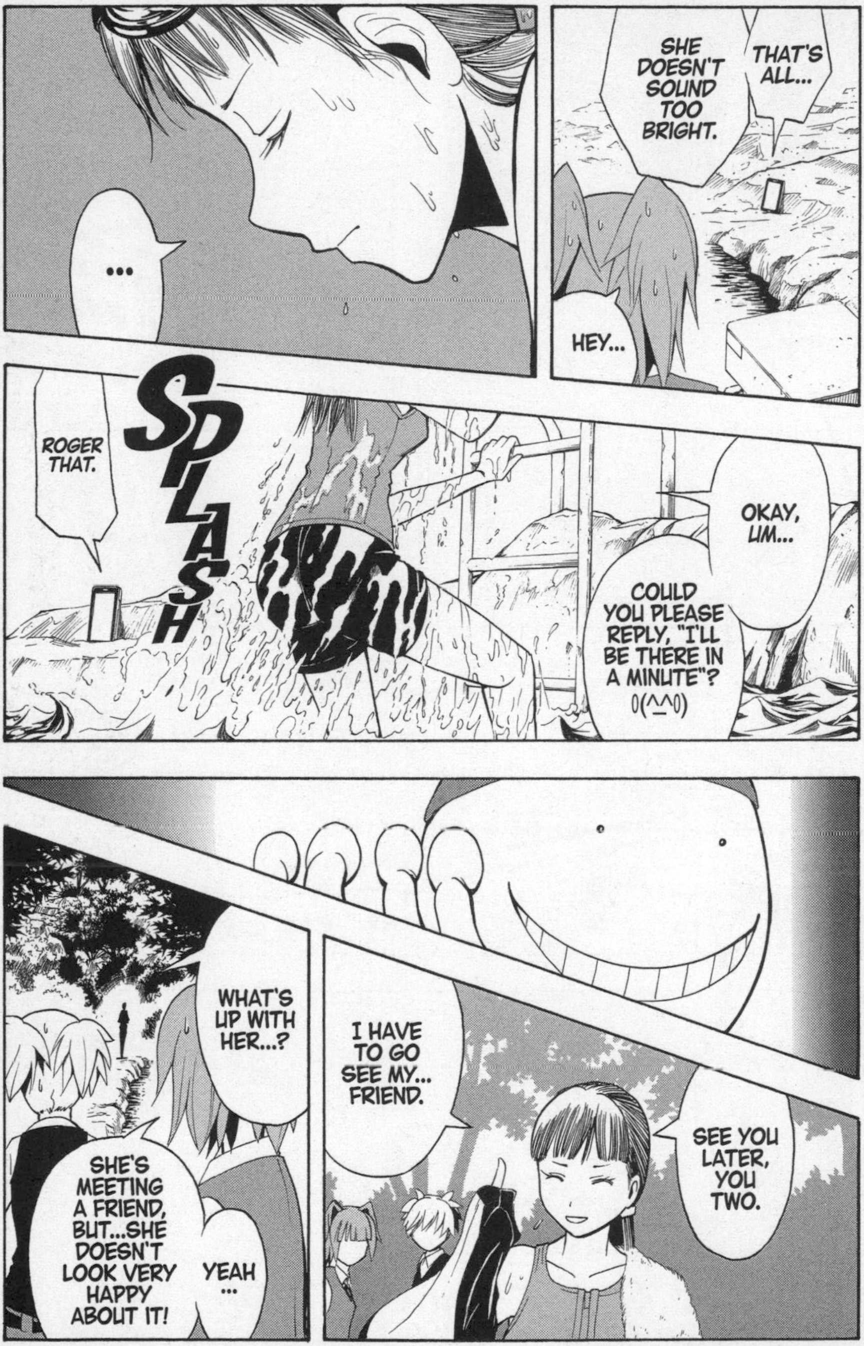
THAT'S ALL...
SHE DOESN'T SOUND TOO BRIGHT.
HEY...
...
OKAY, UM...
COULD YOU PLEASE REPLY, "I'LL BE THERE IN A MINUTE"? O(^_^O)
SPLASH
ROGER THAT.
SEE YOU LATER, YOU TWO.
I HAVE TO GO SEE MY... FRIEND.
WHAT'S UP WITH HER...?
SHE'S MEETING A FRIEND, BUT...SHE DOESN'T LOOK VERY HAPPY ABOUT IT!
YEAH ...

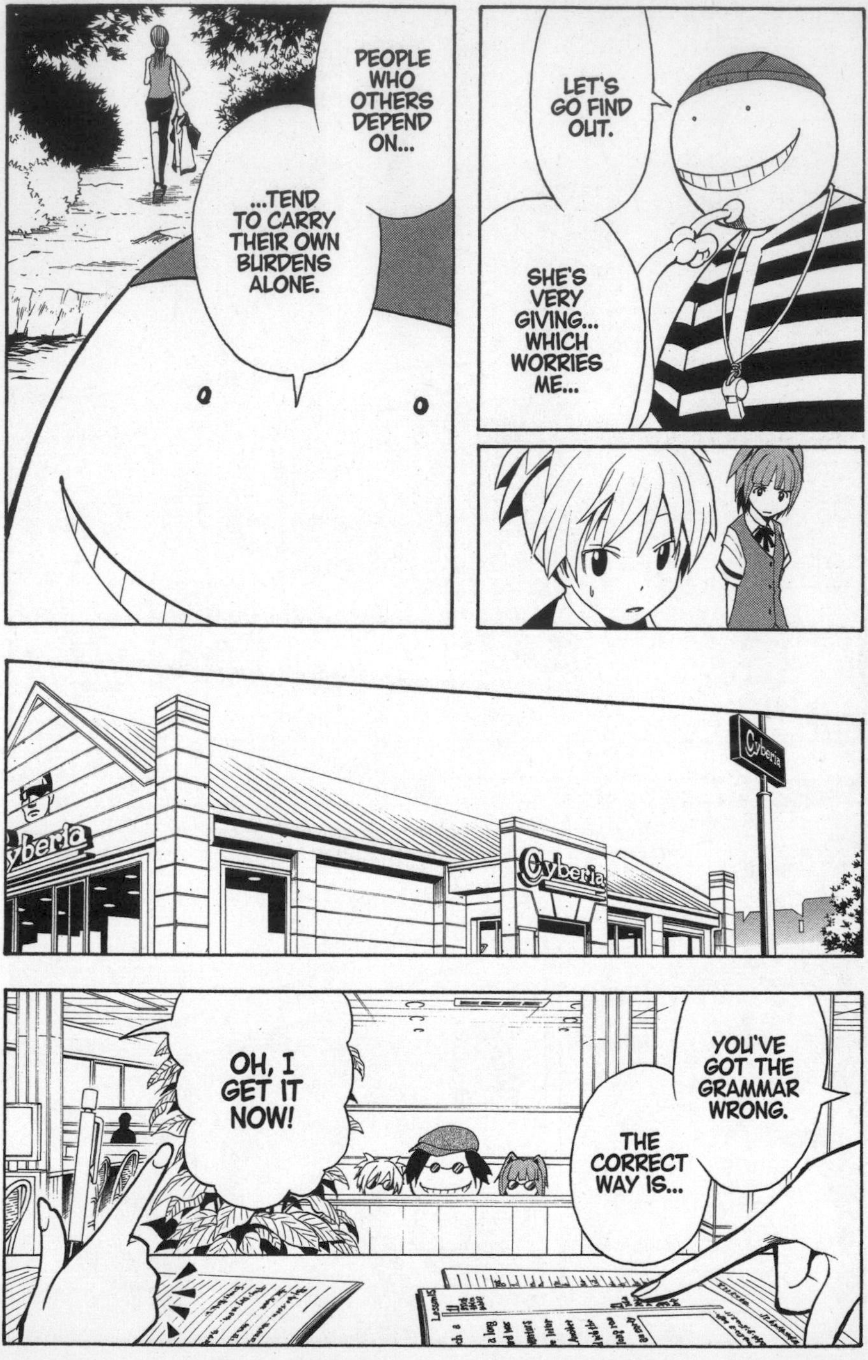
LET'S GO FIND OUT.
SHE'S VERY GIVING... WHICH WORRIES ME...
PEOPLE WHO OTHERS DEPEND ON...
...TEND TO CARRY THEIR OWN BURDENS ALONE.
Cyberia
Cyberia
yberia
YOU'VE GOT THE GRAMMAR WRONG.
THE CORRECT WAY IS...
OH, I GET IT NOW!

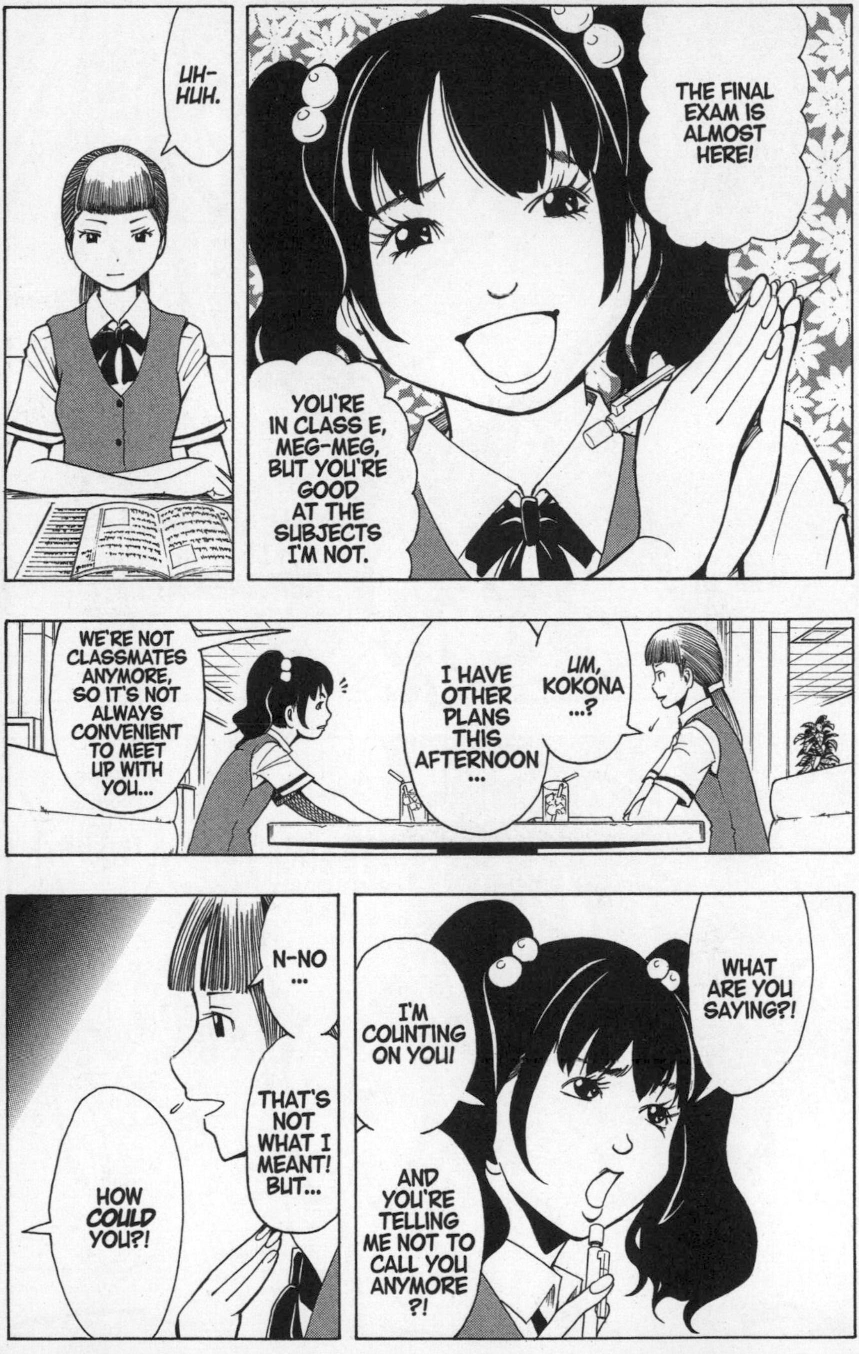
THE FINAL EXAM IS ALMOST HERE!
YOU'RE IN CLASS E, MEG-MEG, BUT YOU'RE GOOD AT THE SUBJECTS I'M NOT.
UH-HUH.
UM, KOKONA ...?
I HAVE OTHER PLANS THIS AFTERNOON ...
WE'RE NOT CLASSMATES ANYMORE, SO IT'S NOT ALWAYS CONVENIENT TO MEET UP WITH YOU...
WHAT ARE YOU SAYING?!
I'M COUNTING ON YOU!
AND YOU'RE TELLING ME NOT TO CALL YOU ANYMORE ?!
N-NO ...
THAT'S NOT WHAT I MEANT! BUT...
HOW COULD YOU?!

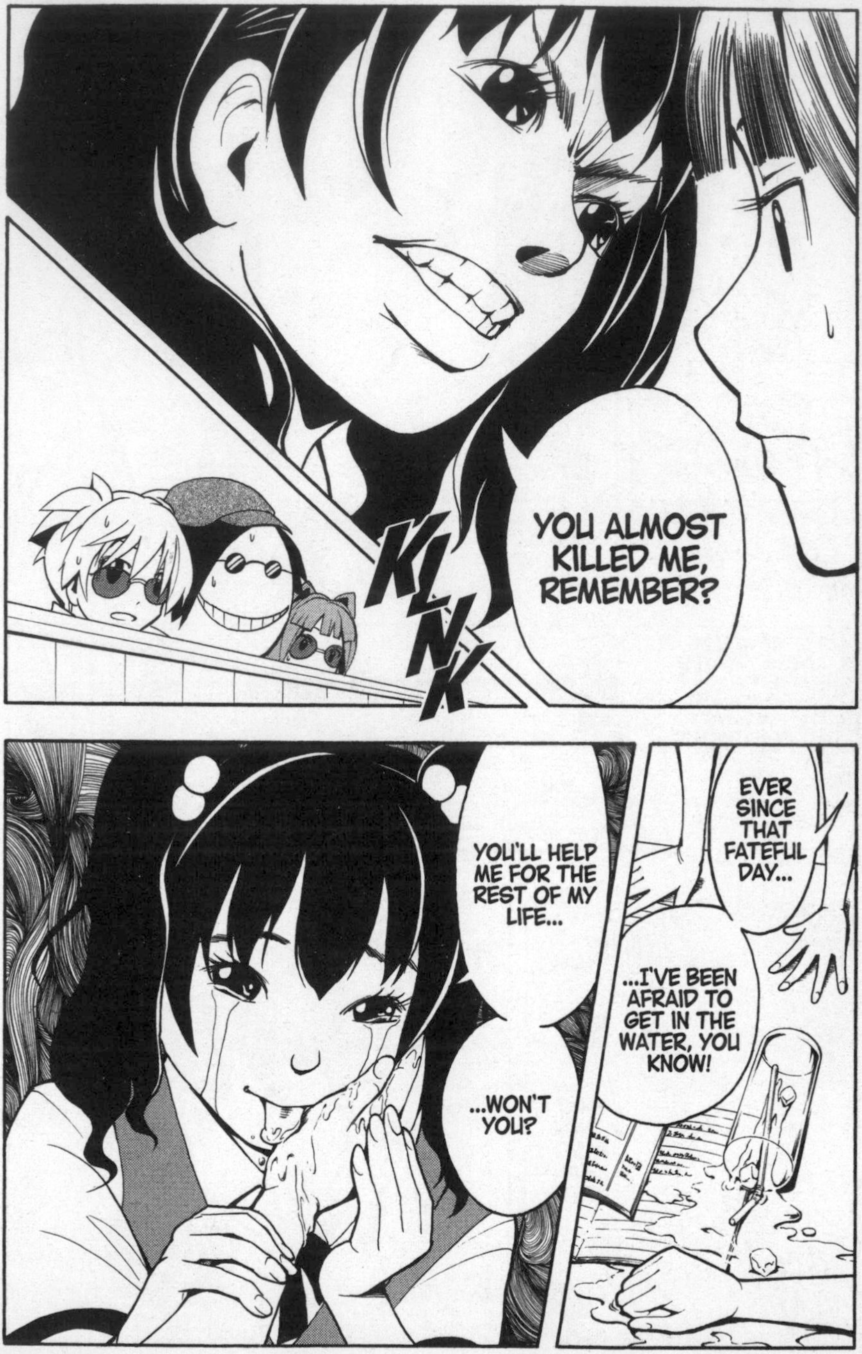
YOU ALMOST KILLED ME, REMEMBER?
KLNK
EVER SINCE THAT FATEFUL DAY...
...I'VE BEEN AFRAID TO GET IN THE WATER, YOU KNOW!
YOU'LL HELP ME FOR THE REST OF MY LIFE...
...WON'T YOU?

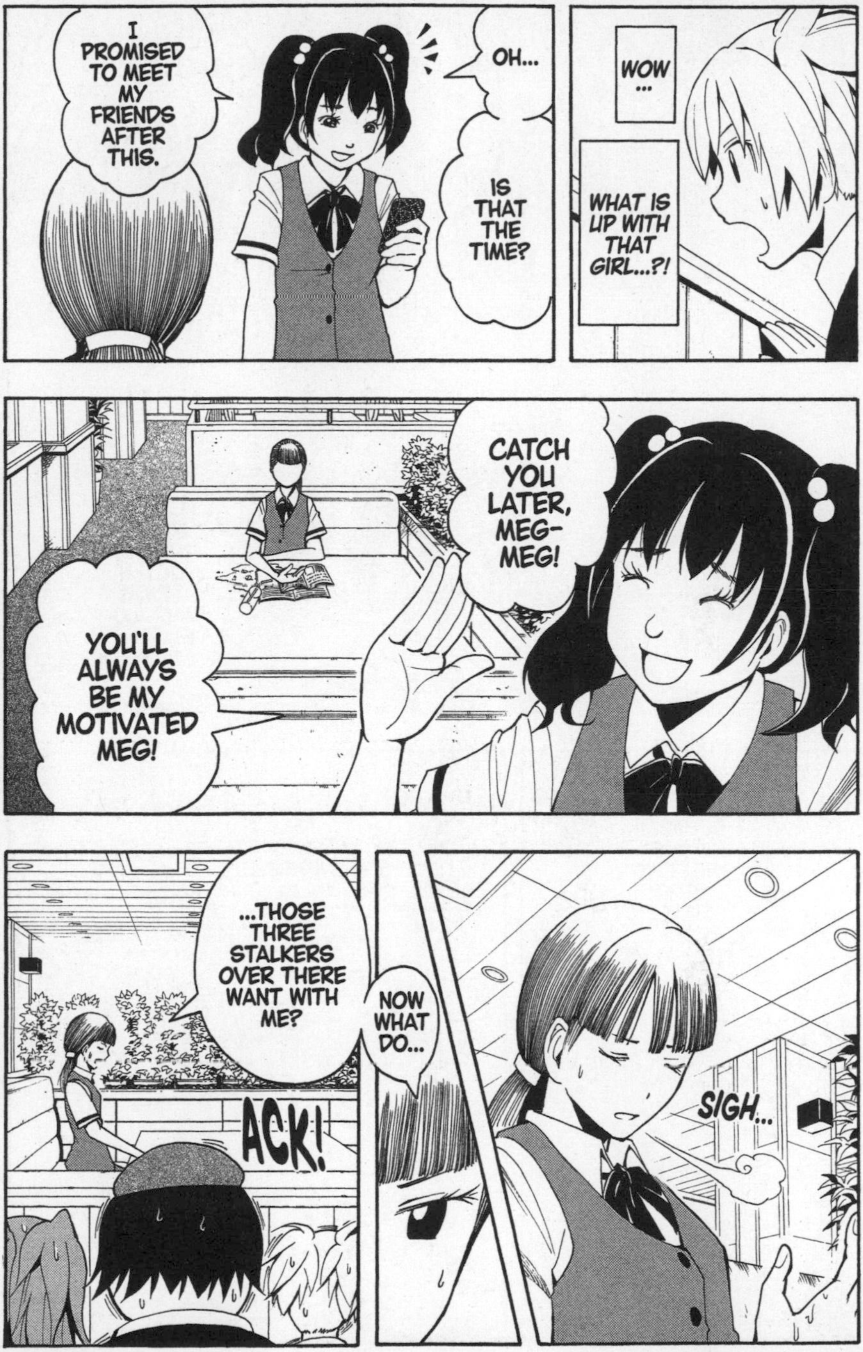
WOW ...
WHAT IS UP WITH THAT GIRL...?!
OH...
IS THAT THE TIME?
I PROMISED TO MEET MY FRIENDS AFTER THIS.
CATCH YOU LATER, MEG-MEG!
YOU'LL ALWAYS BE MY MOTIVATED MEG!
SIGH...
NOW WHAT DO...
...THOSE THREE STALKERS OVER THERE WANT WITH ME?
ACK!

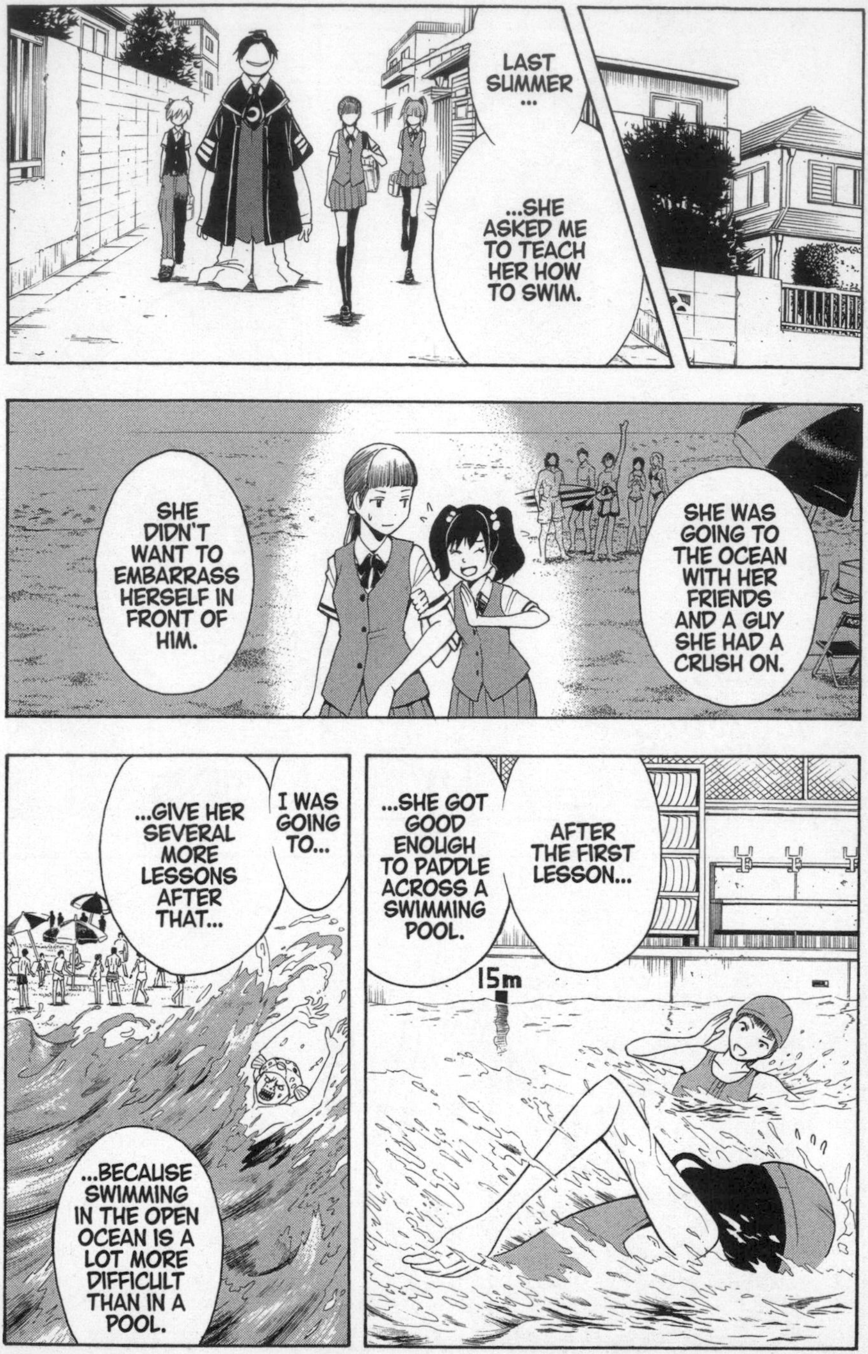
LAST SUMMER...
...SHE ASKED ME TO TEACH HER HOW TO SWIM.
SHE WAS GOING TO THE OCEAN WITH HER FRIENDS AND A GUY SHE HAD A CRUSH ON.
SHE DIDN'T WANT TO EMBARRASS HERSELF IN FRONT OF HIM.
AFTER THE FIRST LESSON...
...SHE GOT GOOD ENOUGH TO PADDLE ACROSS A SWIMMING POOL.
15m
I WAS GOING TO...
...GIVE HER SEVERAL MORE LESSONS AFTER THAT...
...BECAUSE SWIMMING IN THE OPEN OCEAN IS A LOT MORE DIFFICULT THAN IN A POOL.

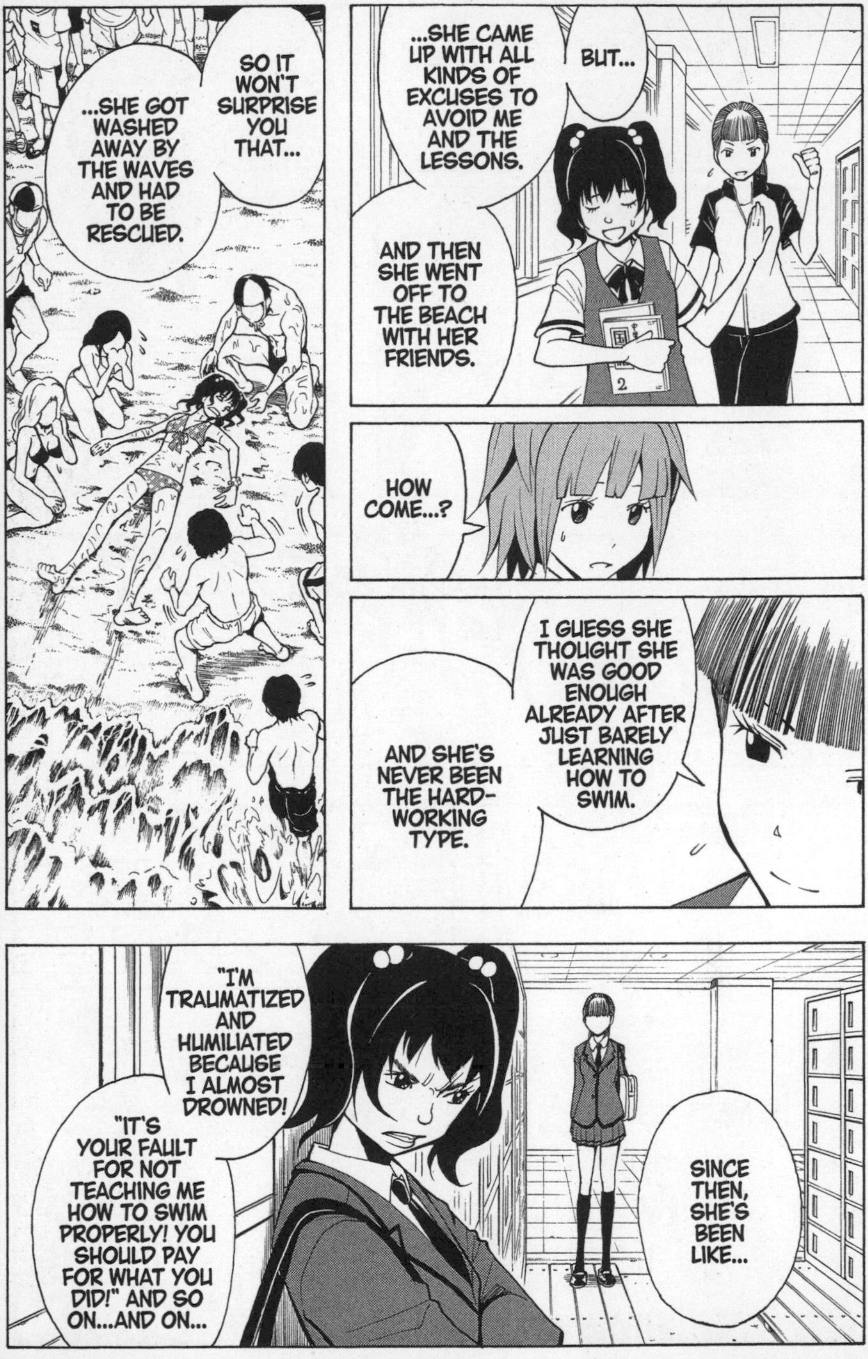
BUT...
...SHE CAME UP WITH ALL KINDS OF EXCUSES TO AVOID ME AND THE LESSONS.
AND THEN SHE WENT OFF TO THE BEACH WITH HER FRIENDS.
HOW COME...?
I GUESS SHE THOUGHT SHE WAS GOOD ENOUGH ALREADY AFTER JUST BARELY LEARNING HOW TO SWIM.
AND SHE'S NEVER BEEN THE HARD-WORKING TYPE.
SO IT WON'T SURPRISE YOU THAT...
...SHE GOT WASHED AWAY BY THE WAVES AND HAD TO BE RESCUED.
SINCE THEN, SHE'S BEEN LIKE...
"I'M TRAUMATIZED AND HUMILIATED BECAUSE I ALMOST DROWNED!
"IT'S YOUR FAULT FOR NOT TEACHING ME HOW TO SWIM PROPERLY! YOU SHOULD PAY FOR WHAT YOU DID!" AND SO ON...AND ON...

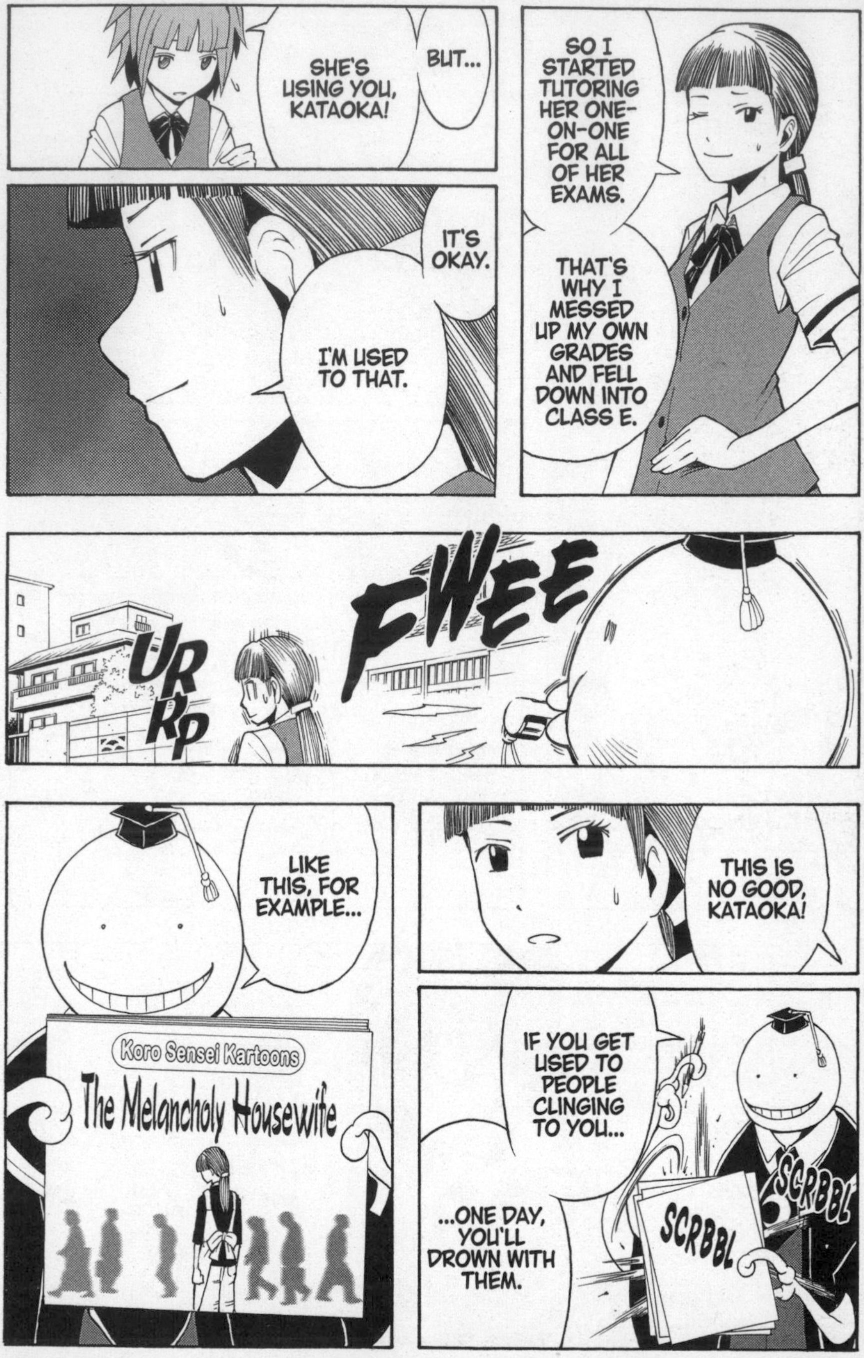
SO I STARTED TUTORING HER ONE-ON-ONE FOR ALL OF HER EXAMS.
THAT'S WHY I MESSED UP MY OWN GRADES AND FELL DOWN INTO CLASS E.
BUT...
SHE'S USING YOU, KATAOKA!
IT'S OKAY.
I'M USED TO THAT.
FWEE
URRP
THIS IS NO GOOD, KATAOKA!
IF YOU GET USED TO PEOPLE CLINGING TO YOU...
SCRBBL
SCRBBL
...ONE DAY, YOU'LL DROWN WITH THEM.
LIKE THIS, FOR EXAMPLE...
Koro Sensei Kartoons
The Melancholy Housewife

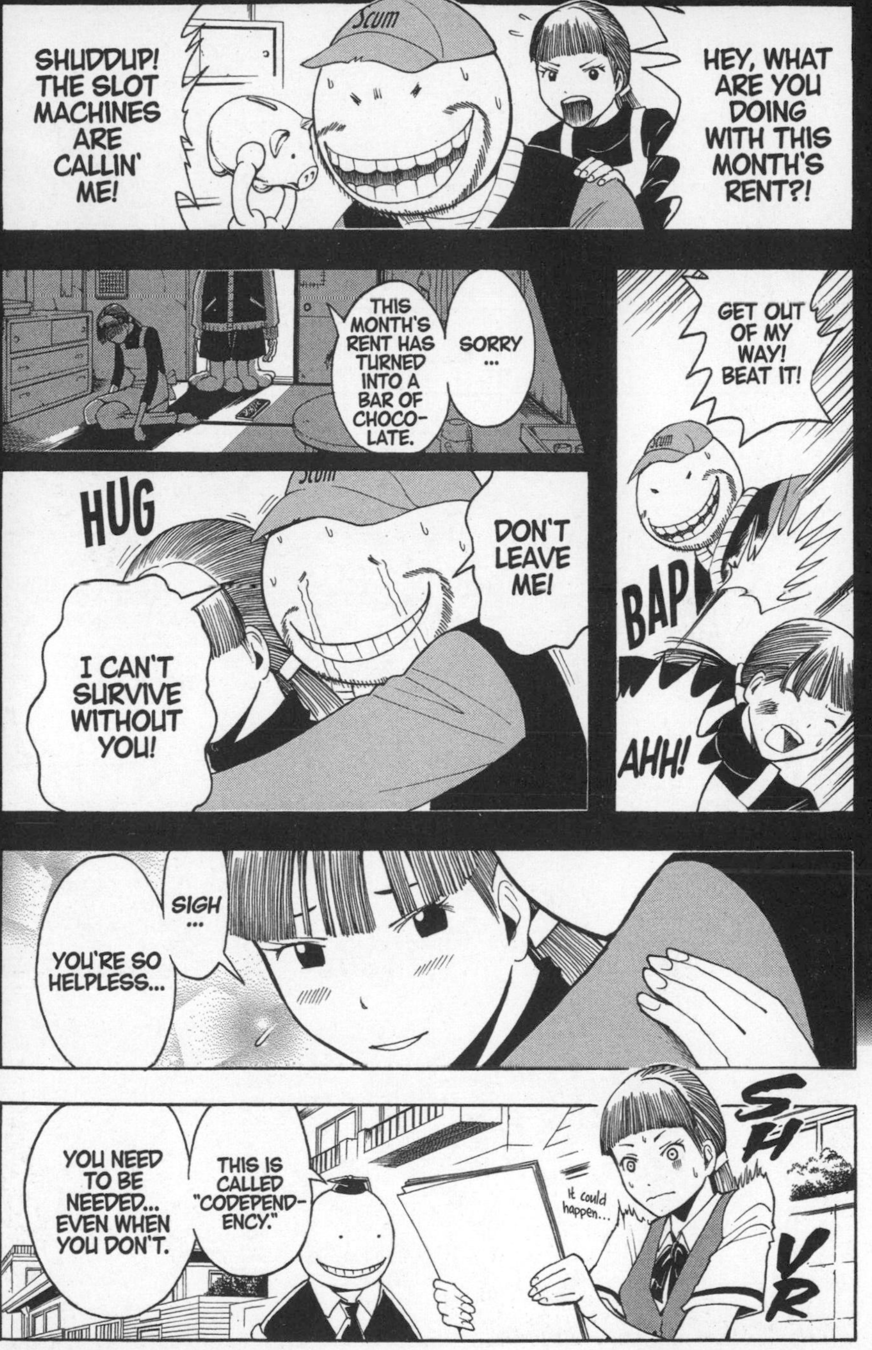
HEY, WHAT ARE YOU DOING WITH THIS MONTH'S RENT?!
SHUDDUP! THE SLOT MACHINES ARE CALLIN' ME!
GET OUT OF MY WAY! BEAT IT!
BAP
AHH!
SORRY...
THIS MONTH'S RENT HAS TURNED INTO A BAR OF CHOCO-LATE.
HUG
DON'T LEAVE ME!
I CAN'T SURVIVE WITHOUT YOU!
SIGH...
YOU'RE SO HELPLESS...
SHVR
It could happen...
THIS IS CALLED "CODEPENDENCY."
YOU NEED TO BE NEEDED... EVEN WHEN YOU DON'T.

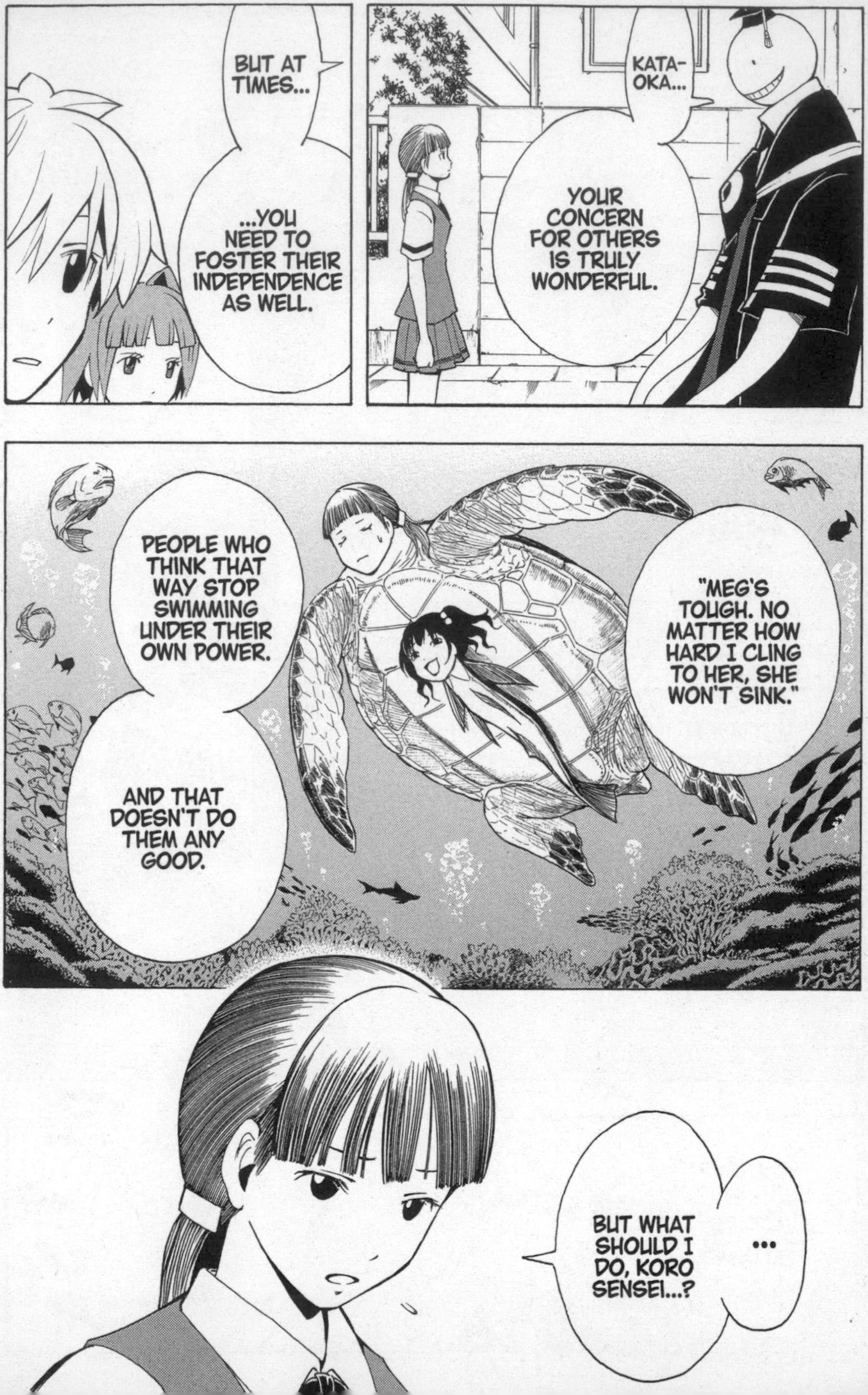
KATA-OKA...
YOUR CONCERN FOR OTHERS IS TRULY WONDERFUL.
BUT AT TIMES...
...YOU NEED TO FOSTER THEIR INDEPENDENCE AS WELL.
"MEG'S TOUGH. NO MATTER HOW HARD I CLING TO HER, SHE WON'T SINK."
PEOPLE WHO THINK THAT WAY STOP SWIMMING UNDER THEIR OWN POWER.
AND THAT DOESN'T DO THEM ANY GOOD.
...
BUT WHAT SHOULD I DO, KORO SENSEI...?

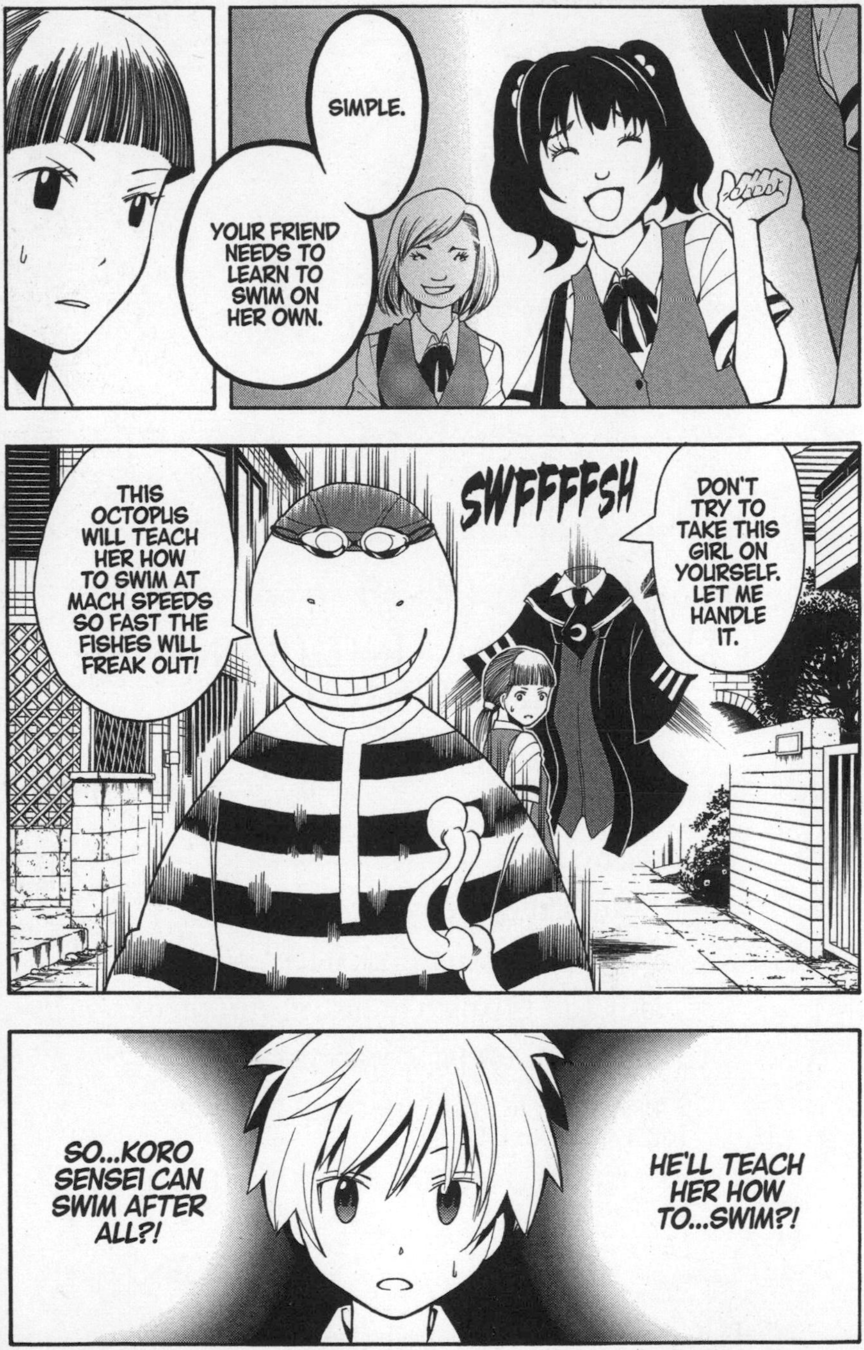
SIMPLE.
YOUR FRIEND NEEDS TO LEARN TO SWIM ON HER OWN.
DON'T TRY TO TAKE THIS GIRL ON YOURSELF. LET ME HANDLE IT.
SWFFFFSH
THIS OCTOPUS WILL TEACH HER HOW TO SWIM AT MACH SPEEDS SO FAST THE FISHES WILL FREAK OUT!
HE'LL TEACH HER HOW TO...SWIM?!
SO...KORO SENSEI CAN SWIM AFTER ALL?!

E-27 Autonomous Intelligence Fixed Artillery

- 😊 Birthday: January 1
- 😊 Height: 5' 7"
- 😊 Weight: 1,100 lbs.
- 😊 Favorite Subject: Mathematics
- 😊 Least Favorite Subject: Physical Education
- 😊 Hobby/Skill: Creating Clothing-Shaped Objects
- 😊 Future Goal: 100% Indoor Shooting Accuracy
- 😊 Top Priority of her Interpersonal Exchange Software: Honesty
- 😊 Top Priority of her Graphics Display Software: Cuteness

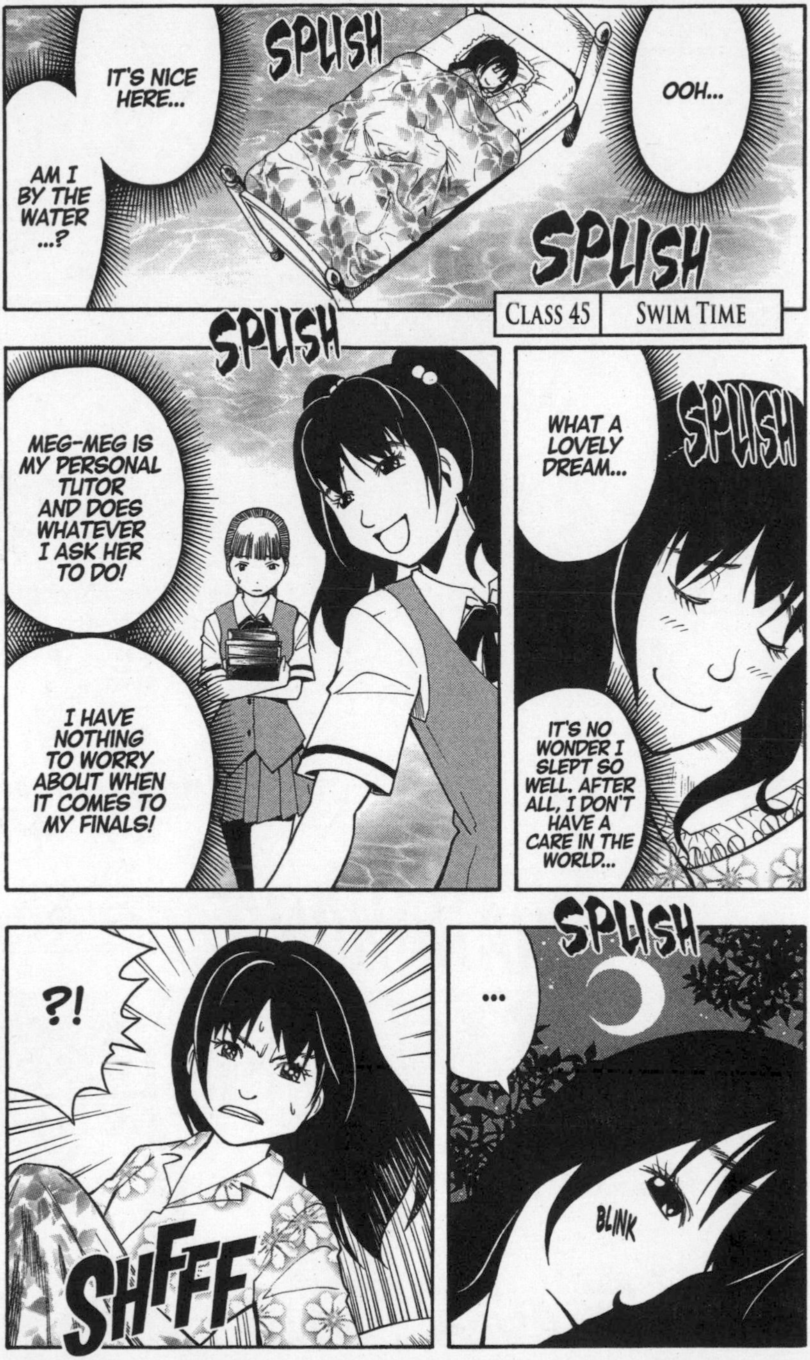
SPLISH
OOH...
IT'S NICE HERE...
AM I BY THE WATER ...?
SPLISH
CLASS 45 SWIM TIME
SPLISH
SPLISH
WHAT A LOVELY DREAM...
IT'S NO WONDER I SLEPT SO WELL. AFTER ALL, I DON'T HAVE A CARE IN THE WORLD...
MEG-MEG IS MY PERSONAL TUTOR AND DOES WHATEVER I ASK HER TO DO!
I HAVE NOTHING TO WORRY ABOUT WHEN IT COMES TO MY FINALS!
SPLISH
...
BLINK
?!
SHFFF

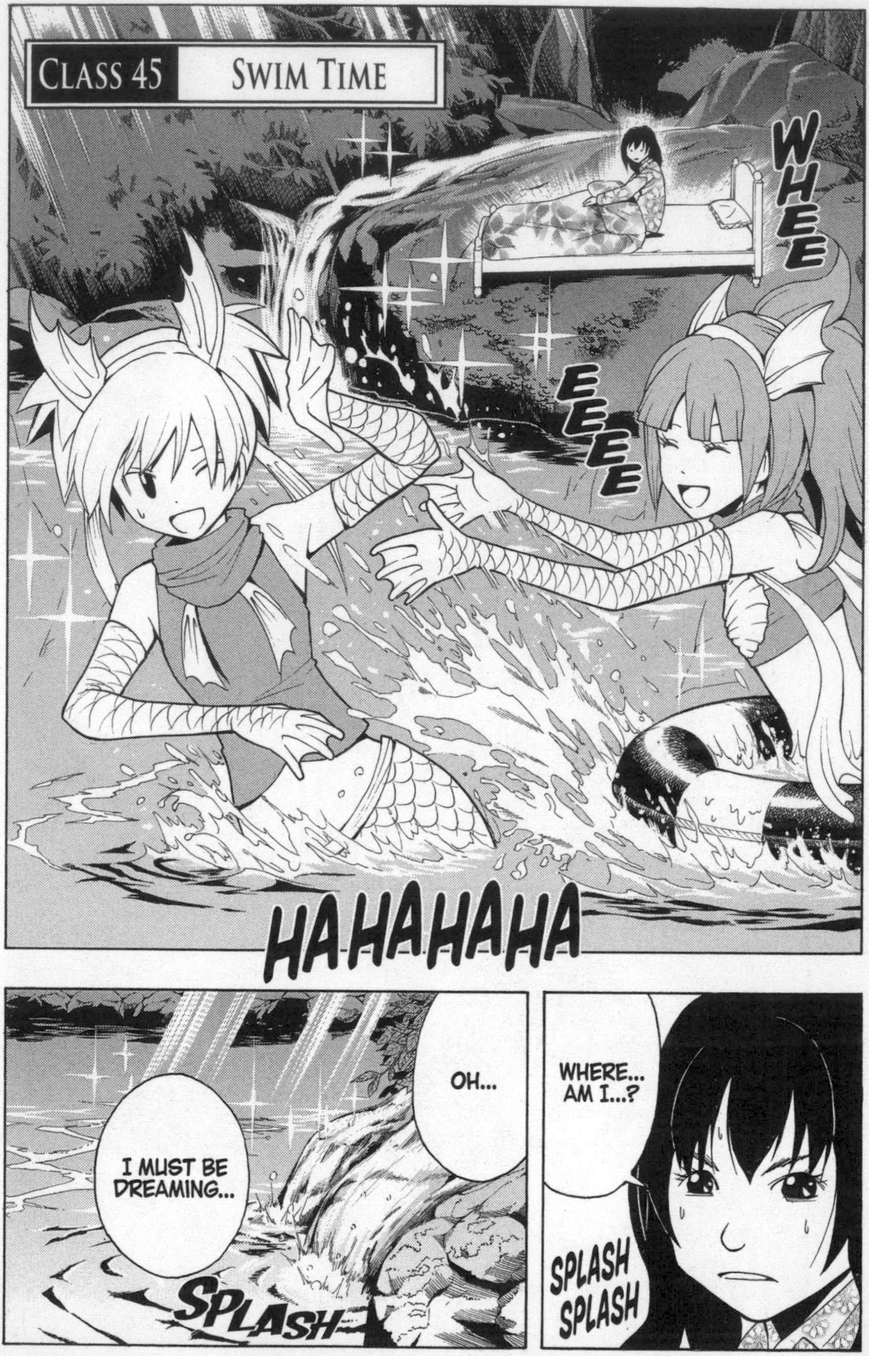

Class 45 Swim Time
WHEEEEEE
HAHAHAHA
WHERE... AM I...?
SPLASH SPLASH
OH...
I MUST BE DREAMING...
SPLASH

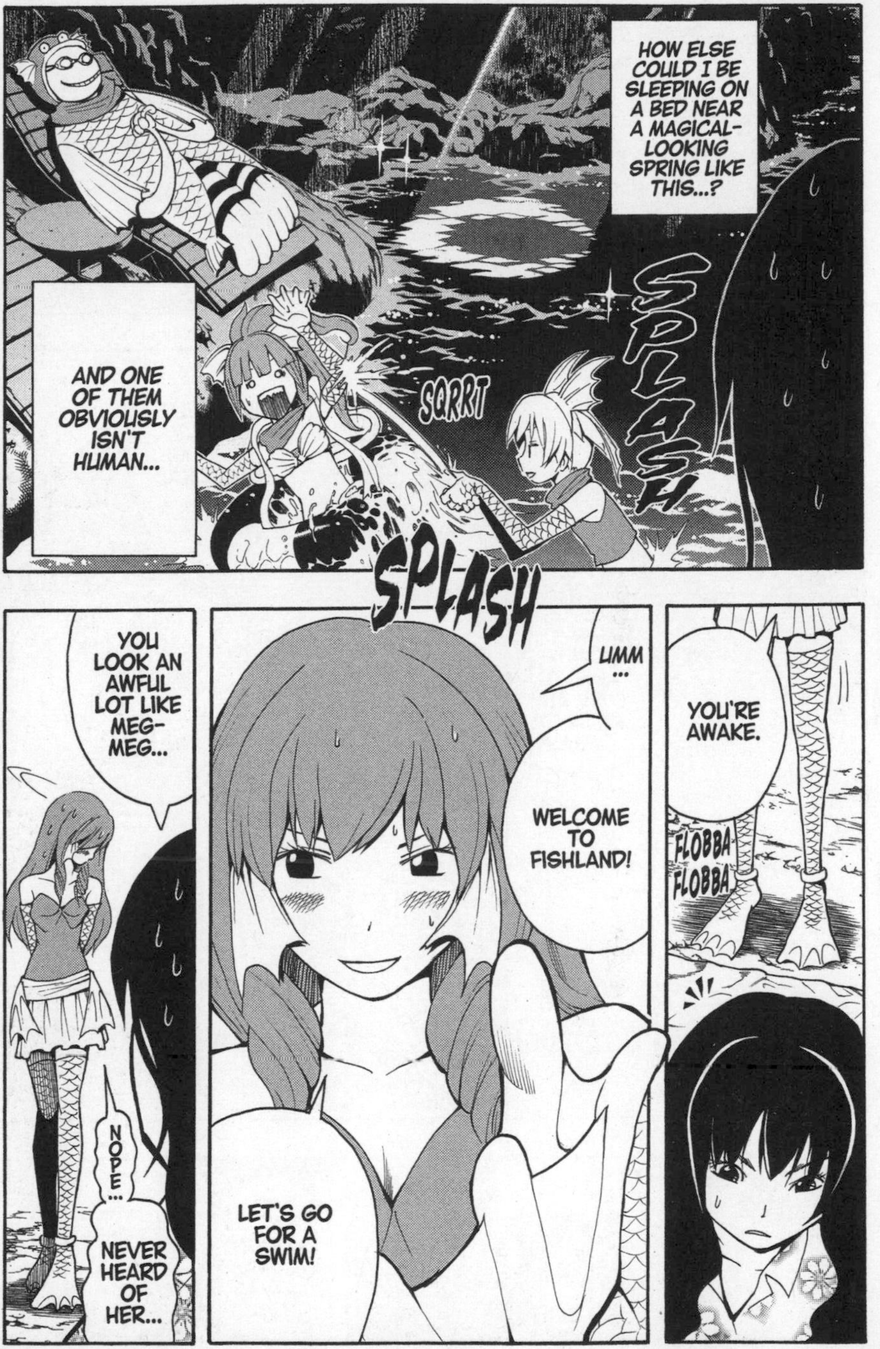
HOW ELSE COULD I BE SLEEPING ON A BED NEAR A MAGICAL-LOOKING SPRING LIKE THIS...?
SPLASH
SQRRT
AND ONE OF THEM OBVIOUSLY ISN'T HUMAN...
SPLASH
YOU'RE AWAKE.
FLOBBA FLOBBA
UMM...
WELCOME TO FISHLAND!
LET'S GO FOR A SWIM!
YOU LOOK AN AWFUL LOT LIKE MEG-MEG...
NOPE...
NEVER HEARD OF HER...

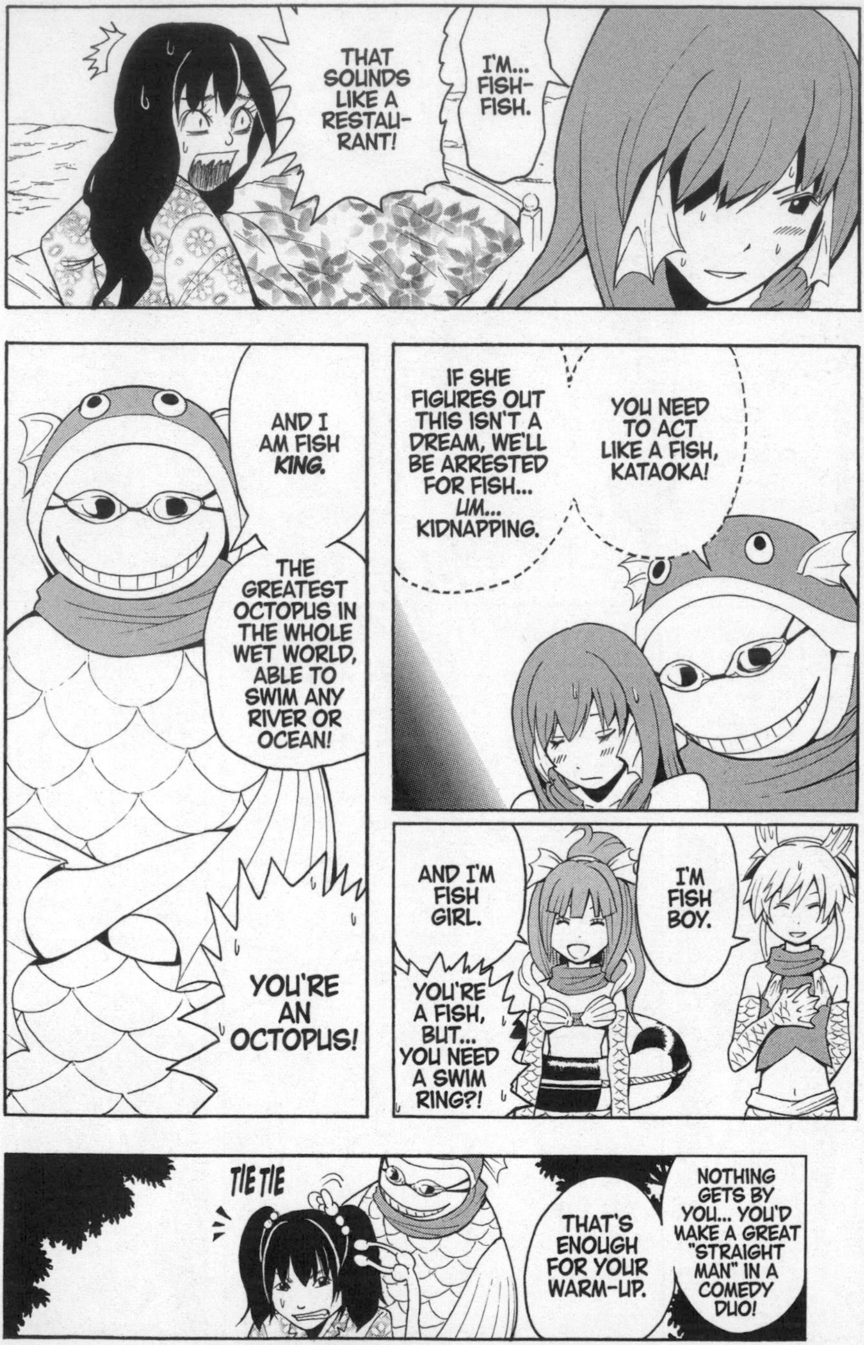
I'M... FISH-FISH.
THAT SOUNDS LIKE A RESTAURANT!
YOU NEED TO ACT LIKE A FISH, KATAOKA!
IF SHE FIGURES OUT THIS ISN'T A DREAM, WE'LL BE ARRESTED FOR FISH... UM... KIDNAPPING.
I'M FISH BOY.
AND I'M FISH GIRL.
YOU'RE A FISH, BUT... YOU NEED A SWIM RING?!
AND I AM FISH KING.
THE GREATEST OCTOPUS IN THE WHOLE WET WORLD, ABLE TO SWIM ANY RIVER OR OCEAN!
YOU'RE AN OCTOPUS!
NOTHING GETS BY YOU... YOU'D MAKE A GREAT "STRAIGHT MAN" IN A COMEDY DUO!
THAT'S ENOUGH FOR YOUR WARM-UP.
TIE TIE

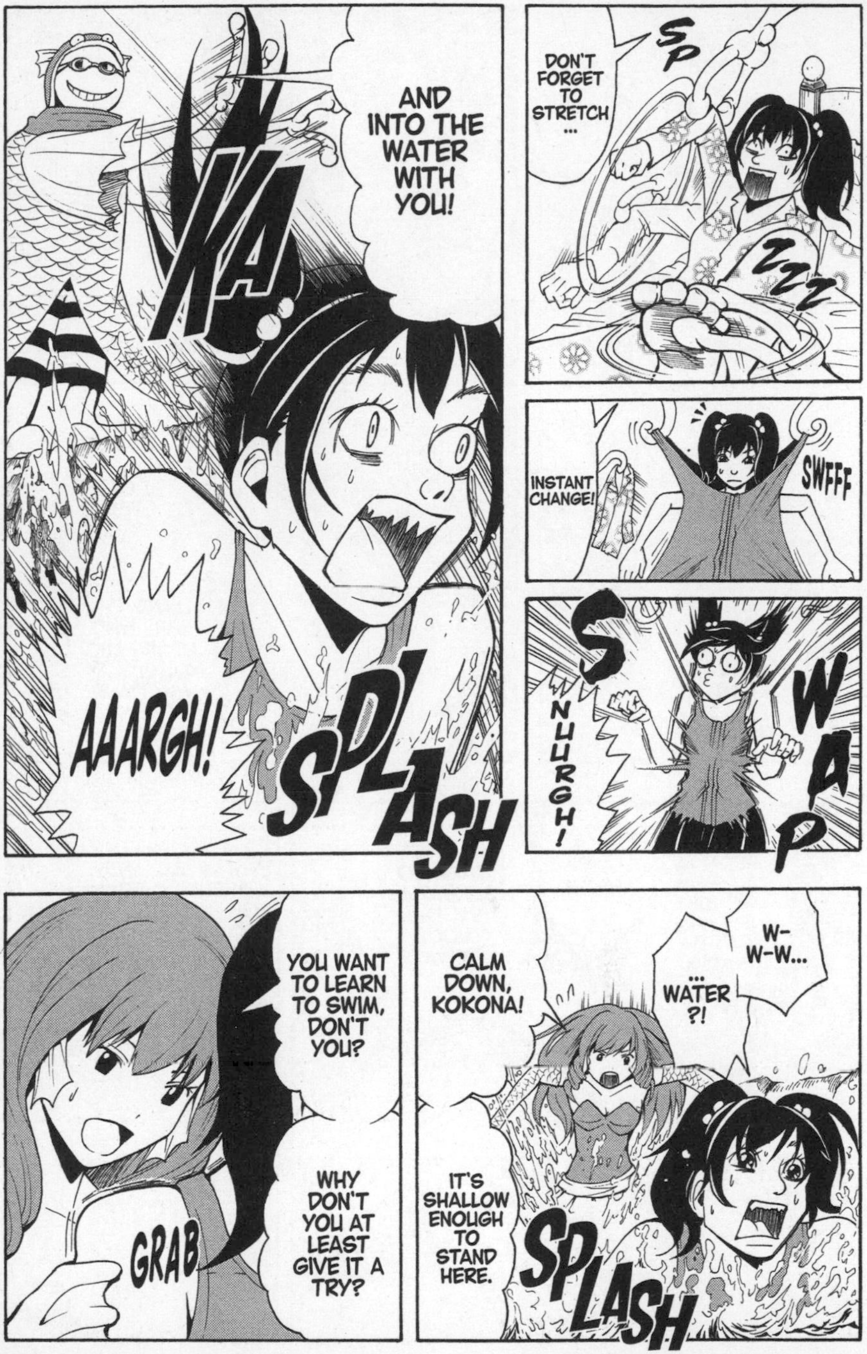
SP
DON'T FORGET TO STRETCH ...
INSTANT CHANGE!
SWFFF
NUURGH!
SWAP
AND INTO THE WATER WITH YOU!
AAARGH!
SPLASH
W- W-W...
... WATER ?!
CALM DOWN, KOKONA!
IT'S SHALLOW ENOUGH TO STAND HERE.
SPLASH
YOU WANT TO LEARN TO SWIM, DON'T YOU?
WHY DON'T YOU AT LEAST GIVE IT A TRY?
GRAB

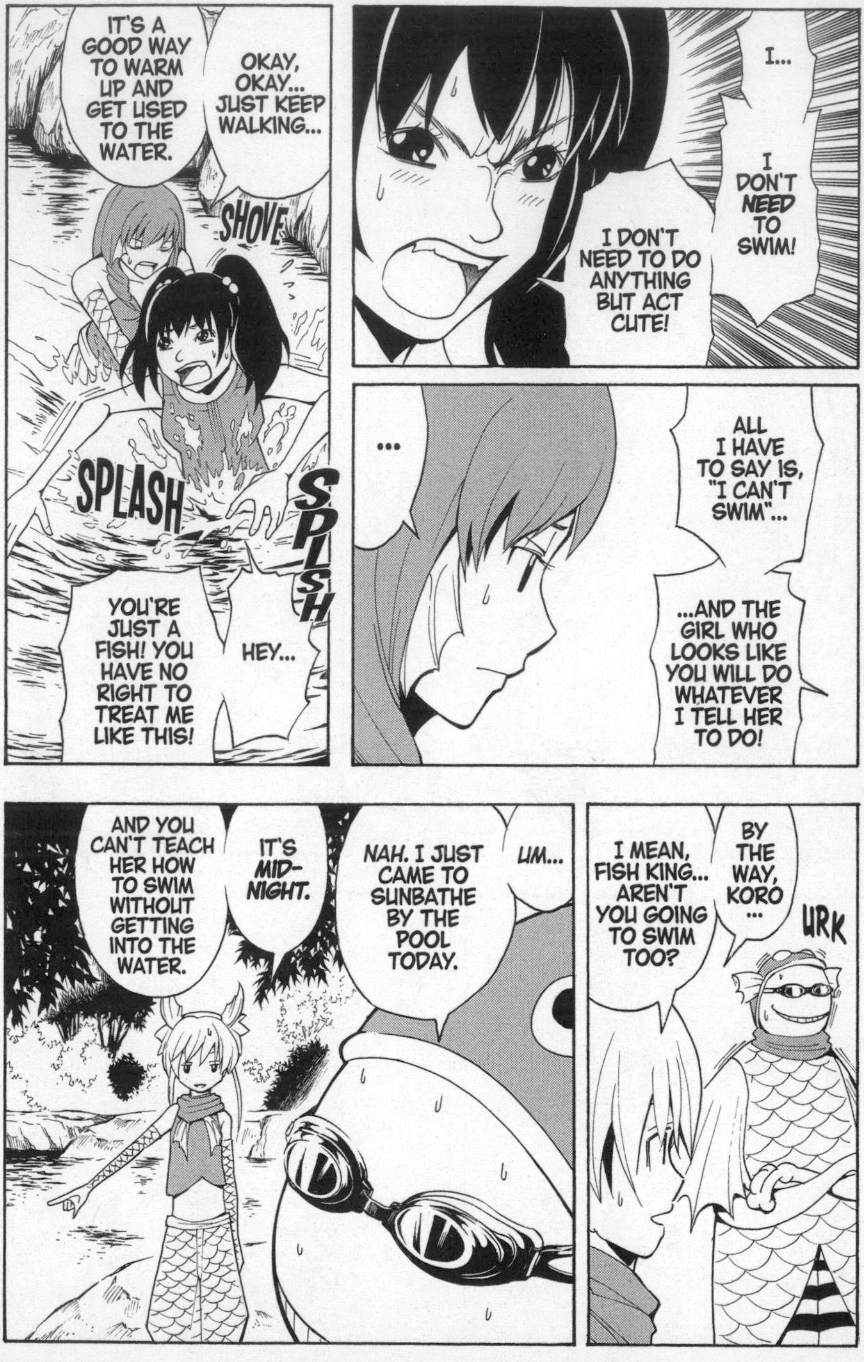
I...
I DON'T NEED TO SWIM!
I DON'T NEED TO DO ANYTHING BUT ACT CUTE!
ALL I HAVE TO SAY IS, "I CAN'T SWIM"...
...AND THE GIRL WHO LOOKS LIKE YOU WILL DO WHATEVER I TELL HER TO DO!
...
OKAY, OKAY... JUST KEEP WALKING...
IT'S A GOOD WAY TO WARM UP AND GET USED TO THE WATER.
SHOVE
SPLSH
SPLASH
HEY...
YOU'RE JUST A FISH! YOU HAVE NO RIGHT TO TREAT ME LIKE THIS!
BY THE WAY, KORO...
URK
I MEAN, FISH KING... AREN'T YOU GOING TO SWIM TOO?
UM...
NAH. I JUST CAME TO SUNBATHE BY THE POOL TODAY.
IT'S MIDNIGHT.
AND YOU CAN'T TEACH HER HOW TO SWIM WITHOUT GETTING INTO THE WATER.

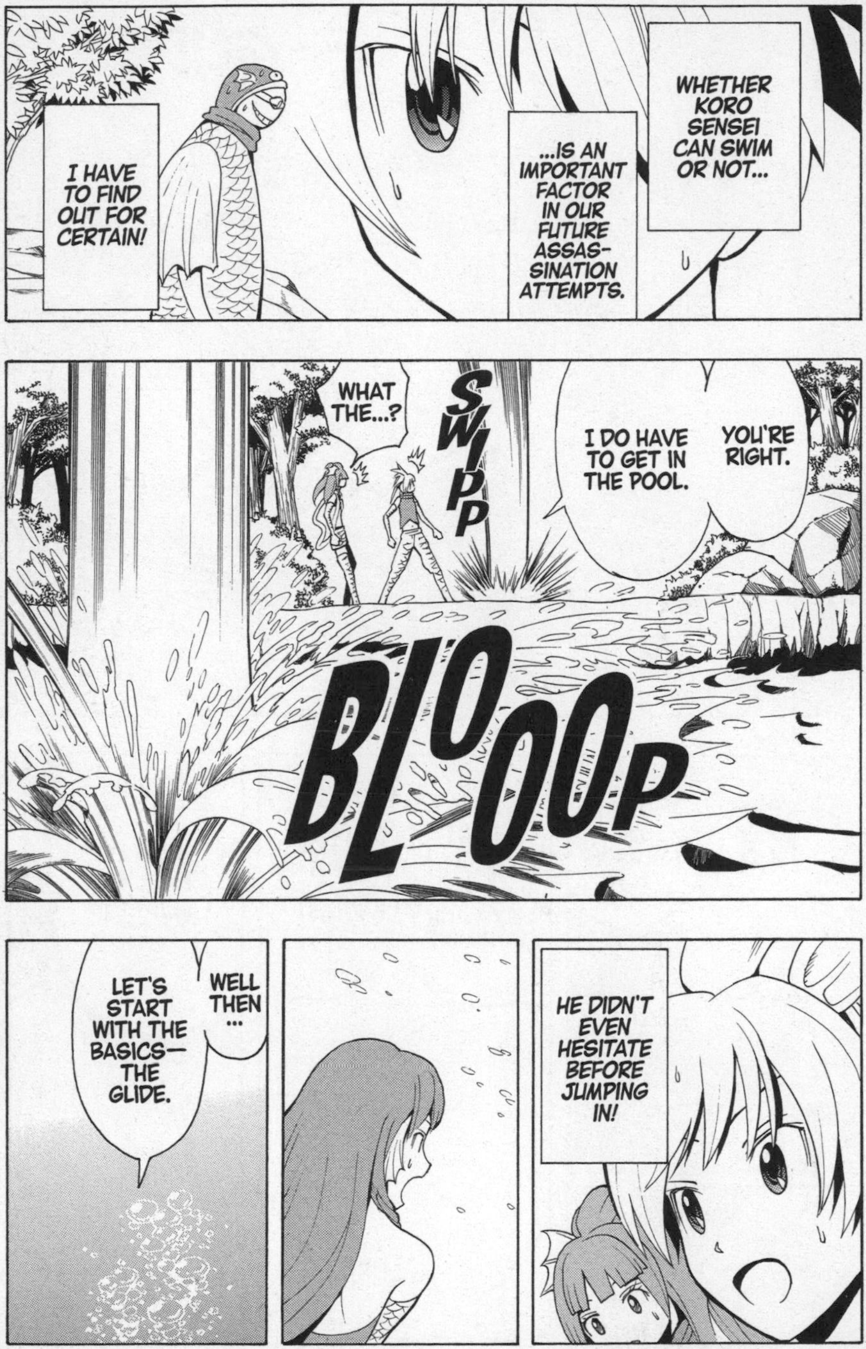
WHETHER KORO SENSEI CAN SWIM OR NOT...
...IS AN IMPORTANT FACTOR IN OUR FUTURE ASSAS-SINATION ATTEMPTS.
I HAVE TO FIND OUT FOR CERTAIN!
YOU'RE RIGHT.
I DO HAVE TO GET IN THE POOL.
SWIPP
WHAT THE...?
BLOOOP
HE DIDN'T EVEN HESITATE BEFORE JUMPING IN!
WELL THEN ...
LET'S START WITH THE BASICS—THE GLIDE.

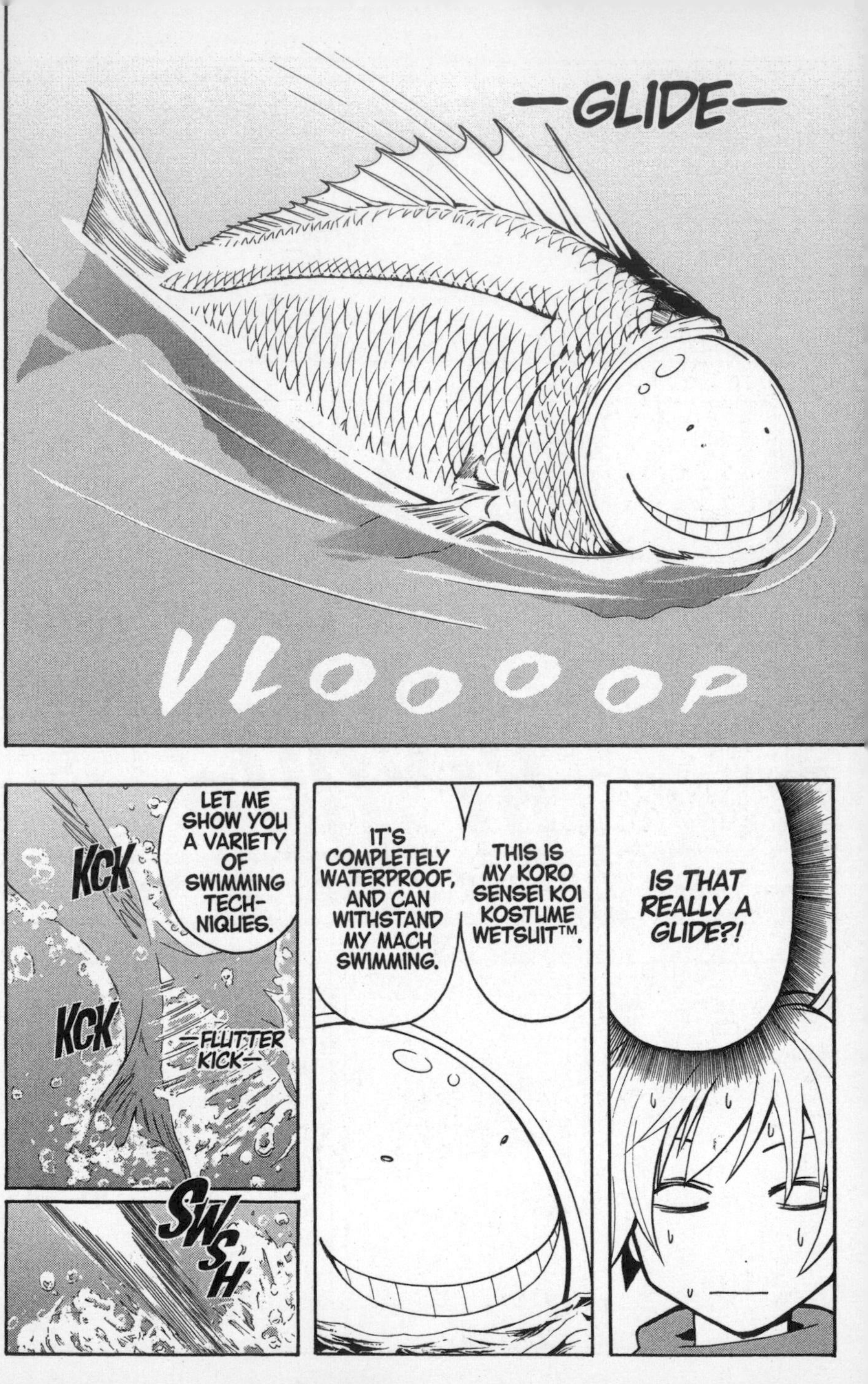
—GLIDE—
VLOOOOP
IS THAT REALLY A GLIDE?!
THIS IS MY KORO SENSEI KOI KOSTUME WETSUIT™.
IT'S COMPLETELY WATERPROOF, AND CAN WITHSTAND MY MACH SWIMMING.
LET ME SHOW YOU A VARIETY OF SWIMMING TECHNIQUES.
KCK
KCK
—FLUTTER KICK—
SWSH

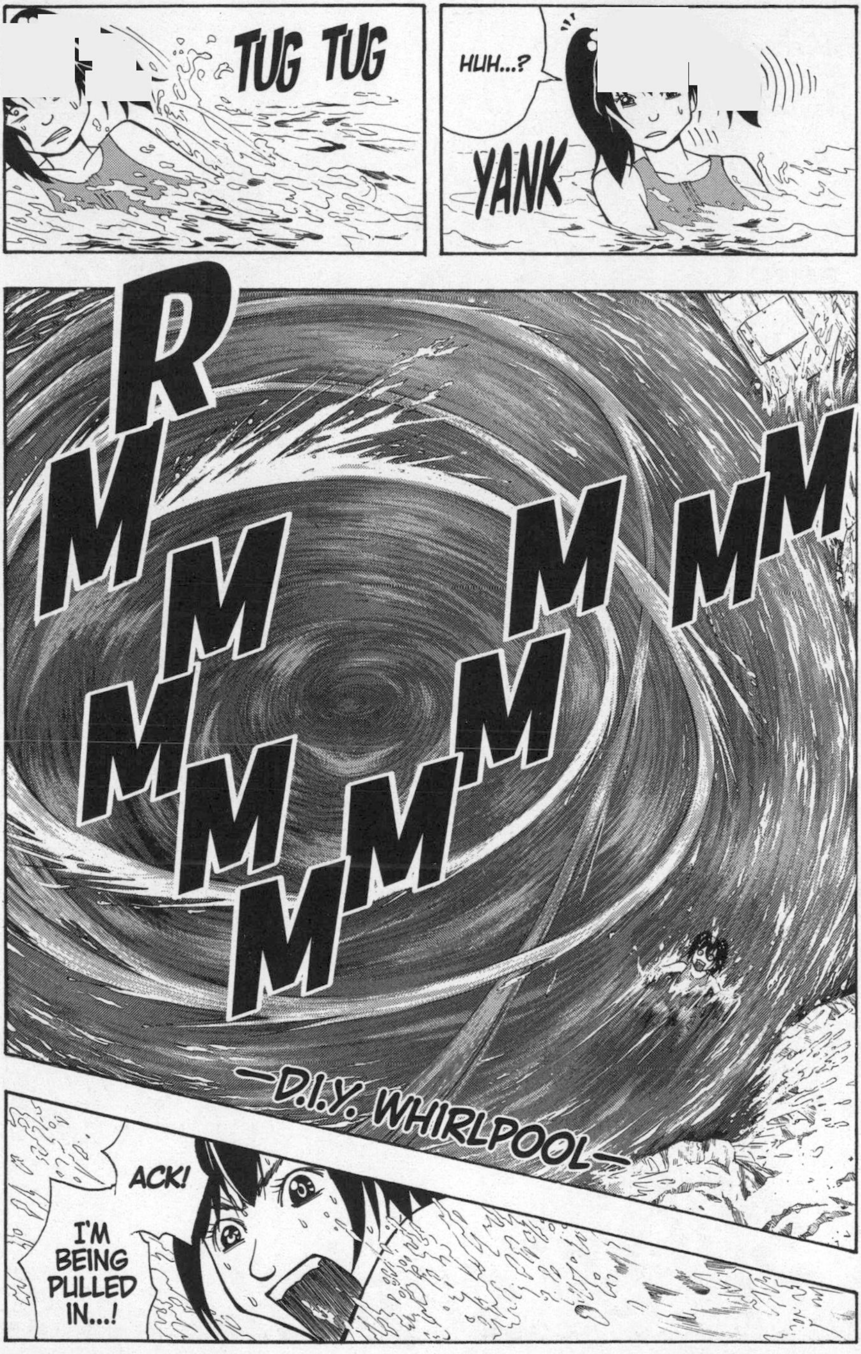
HUH...?
YANK
TUG TUG
RMMMMMMMMMMM
—D.I.Y. WHIRLPOOL—
ACK!
I'M BEING PULLED IN...!

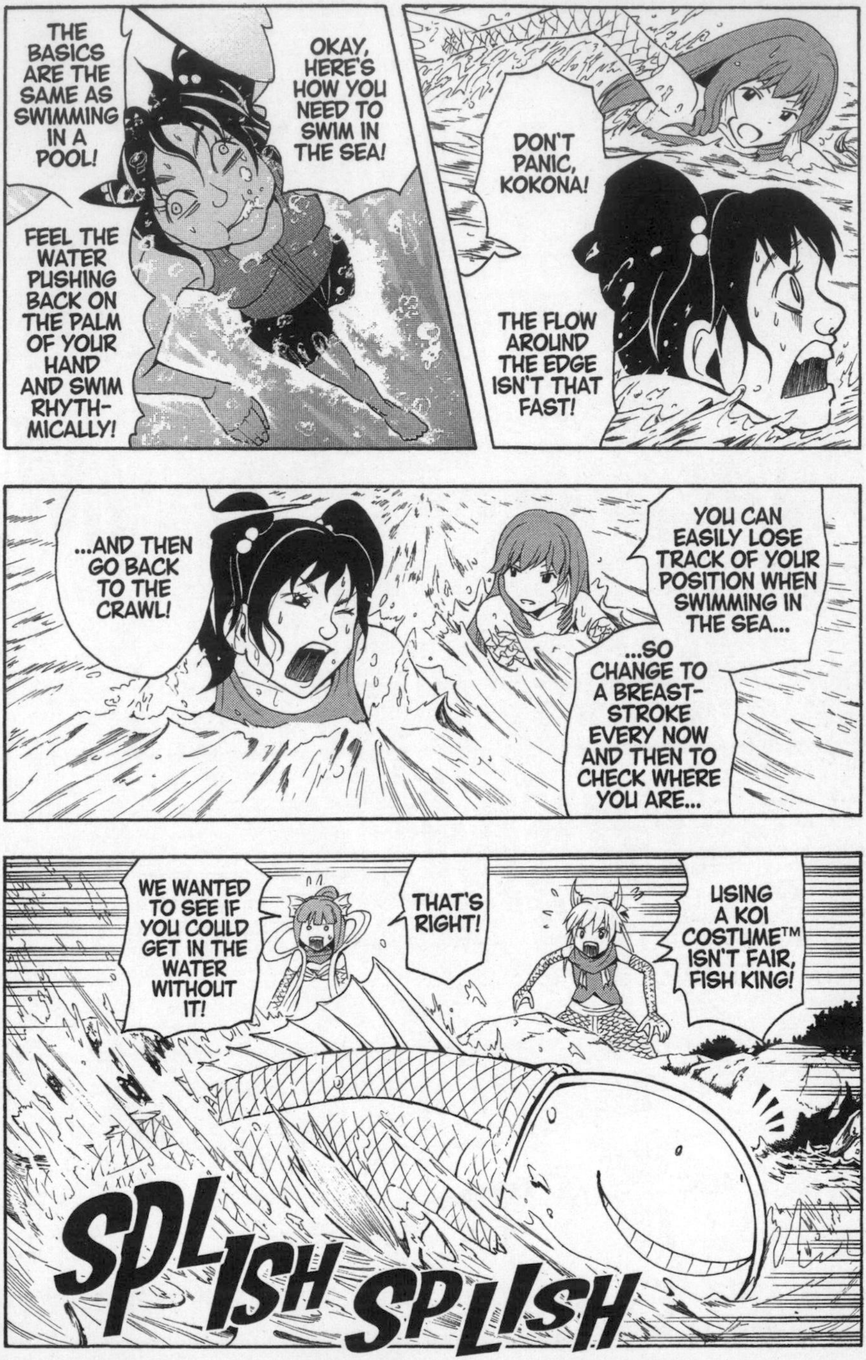
DON'T PANIC, KOKONA!
THE FLOW AROUND THE EDGE ISN'T THAT FAST!
OKAY, HERE'S HOW YOU NEED TO SWIM IN THE SEA!
THE BASICS ARE THE SAME AS SWIMMING IN A POOL!
FEEL THE WATER PUSHING BACK ON THE PALM OF YOUR HAND AND SWIM RHYTHMICALLY!
YOU CAN EASILY LOSE TRACK OF YOUR POSITION WHEN SWIMMING IN THE SEA...
...SO CHANGE TO A BREASTSTROKE EVERY NOW AND THEN TO CHECK WHERE YOU ARE...
...AND THEN GO BACK TO THE CRAWL!
USING A KOI COSTUME™ ISN'T FAIR, FISH KING!
THAT'S RIGHT!
WE WANTED TO SEE IF YOU COULD GET IN THE WATER WITHOUT IT!
SPLISH SPLISH

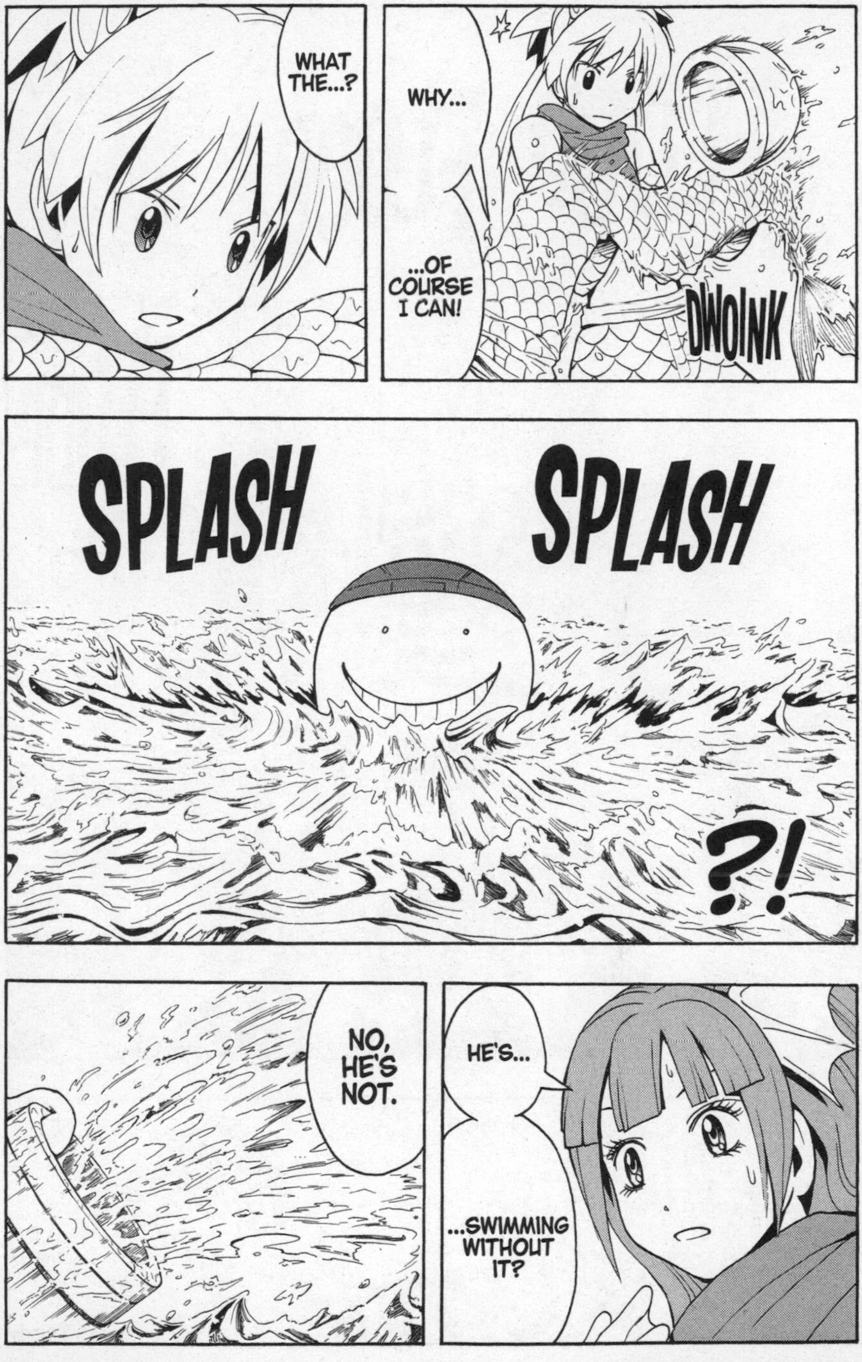
WHY...
...OF COURSE I CAN!
DWOINK
WHAT THE...?
SPLASH
SPLASH
?!
HE'S...
...SWIMMING WITHOUT IT?
NO, HE'S NOT.

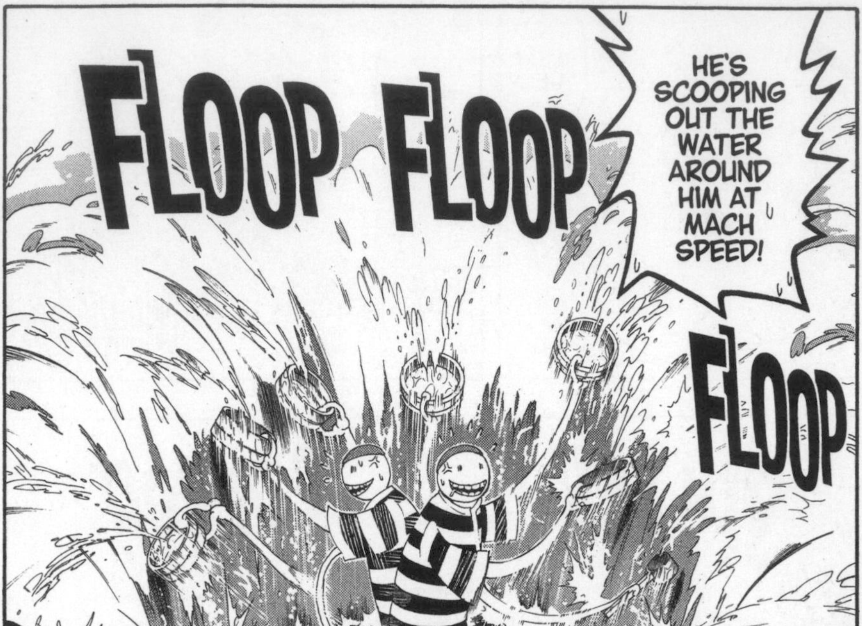
HE'S SCOOPING OUT THE WATER AROUND HIM AT MACH SPEED!
FLOOP FLOOP
FLOOP
—D.I.Y. WAVE POOL—

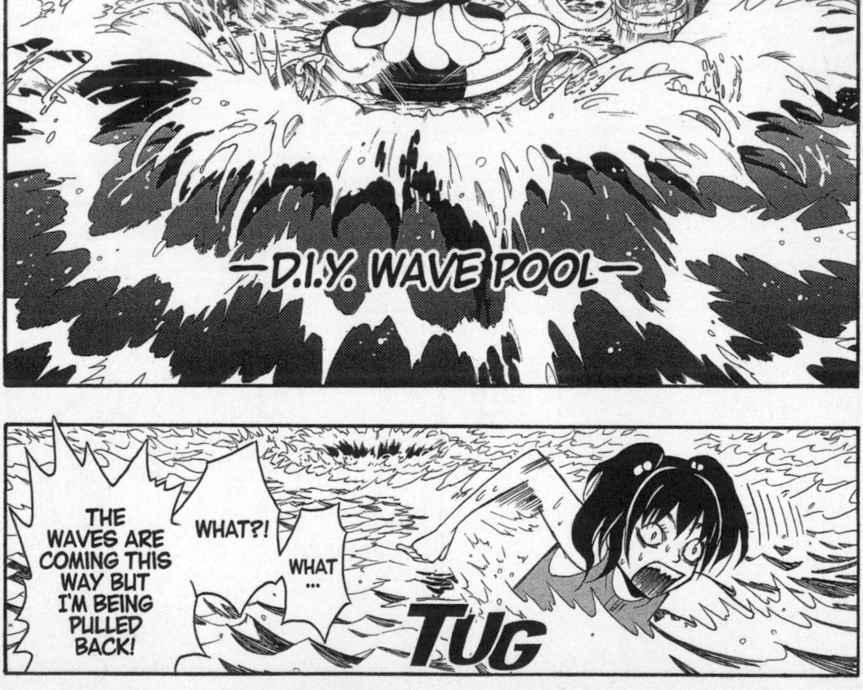
WHAT ...
WHAT?!
THE WAVES ARE COMING THIS WAY BUT I'M BEING PULLED BACK!
TUG

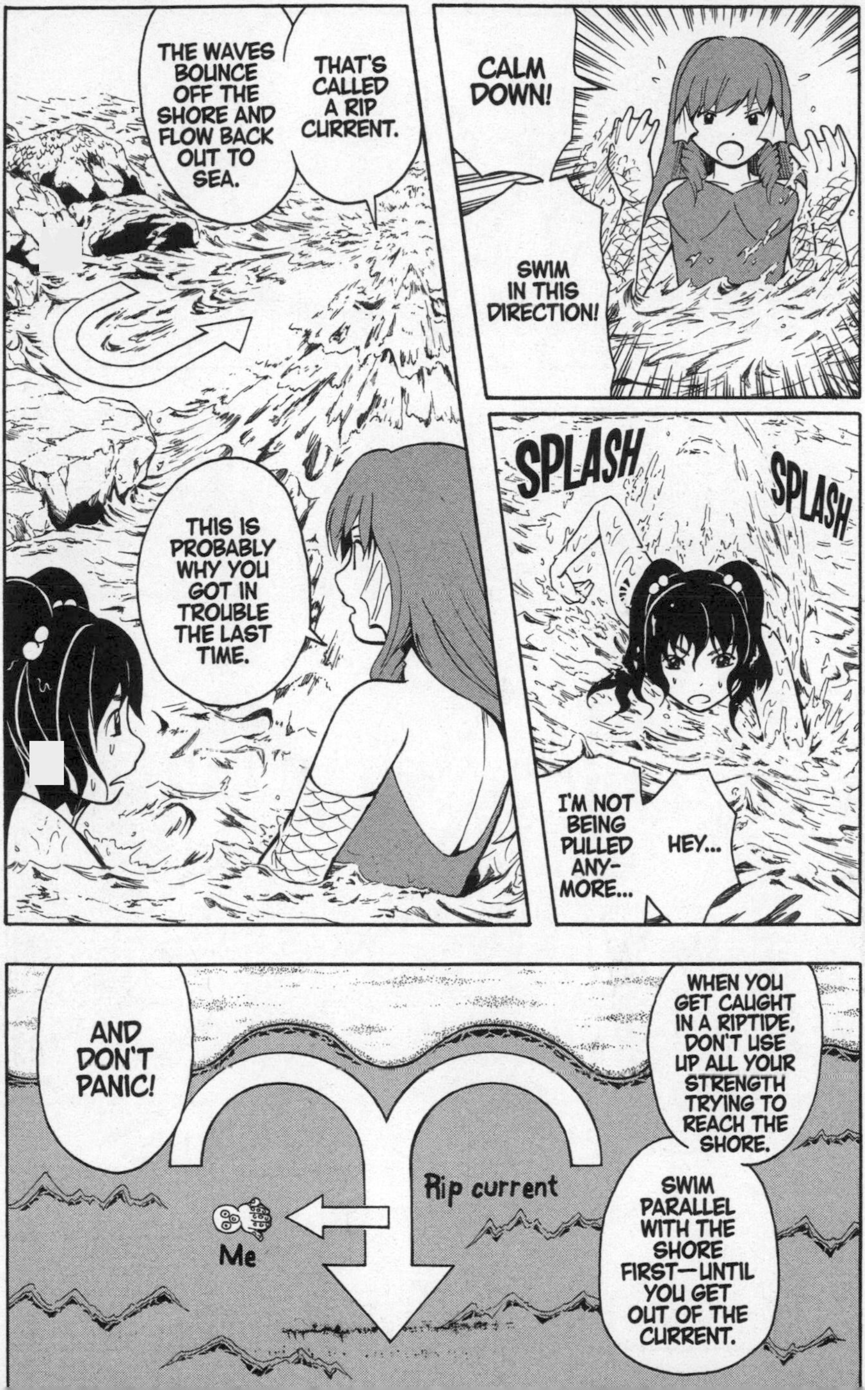
CALM DOWN!
SWIM IN THIS DIRECTION!
SPLASH
SPLASH
HEY...
I'M NOT BEING PULLED ANYMORE...
THAT'S CALLED A RIP CURRENT.
THE WAVES BOUNCE OFF THE SHORE AND FLOW BACK OUT TO SEA.
THIS IS PROBABLY WHY YOU GOT IN TROUBLE THE LAST TIME.
WHEN YOU GET CAUGHT IN A RIPTIDE, DON'T USE UP ALL YOUR STRENGTH TRYING TO REACH THE SHORE.
SWIM PARALLEL WITH THE SHORE FIRST—UNTIL YOU GET OUT OF THE CURRENT.
AND DON'T PANIC!
Rip current
Me

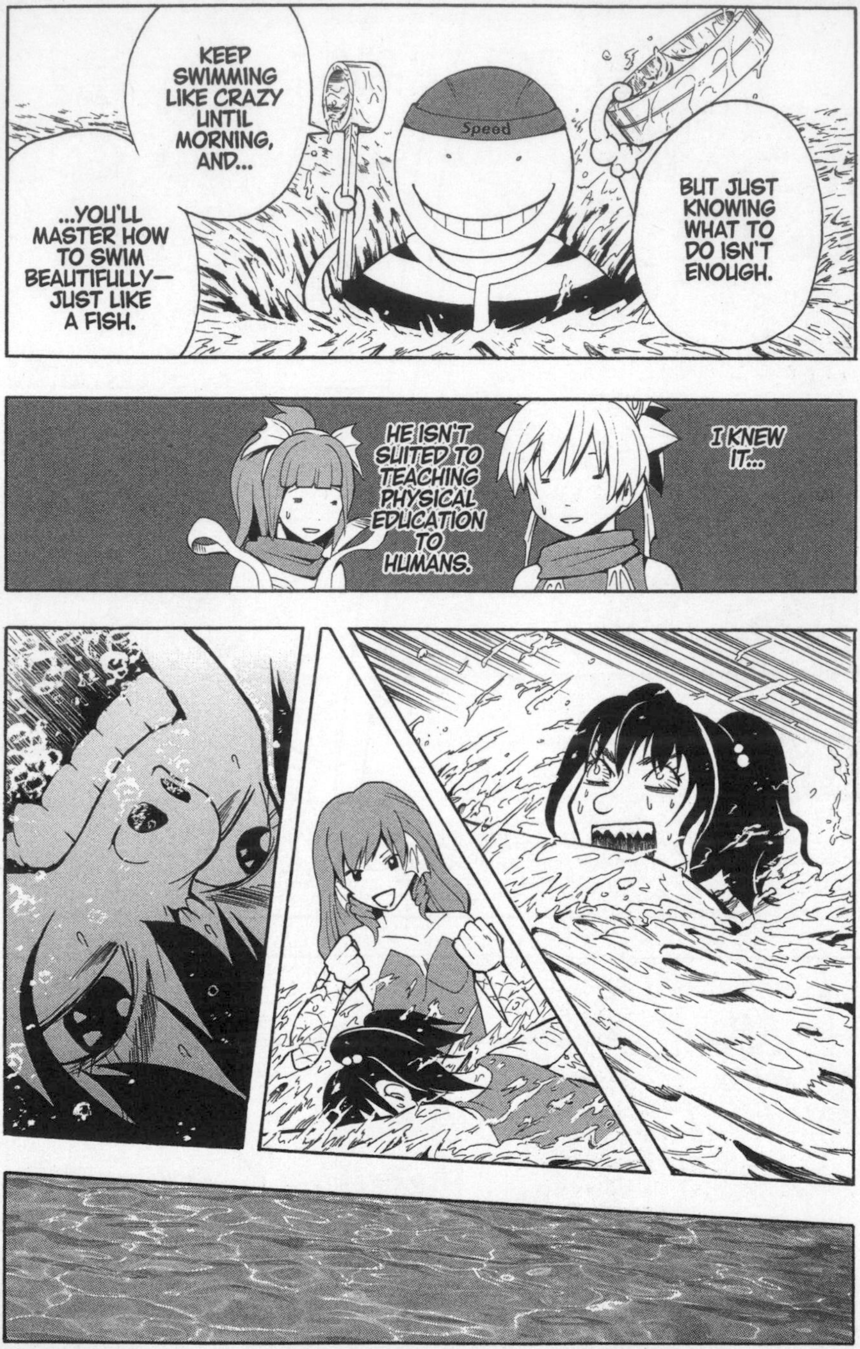
BUT JUST KNOWING WHAT TO DO ISN'T ENOUGH.
KEEP SWIMMING LIKE CRAZY UNTIL MORNING, AND...
...YOU'LL MASTER HOW TO SWIM BEAUTIFULLY—JUST LIKE A FISH.
Speed
I KNEW IT...
HE ISN'T SUITED TO TEACHING PHYSICAL EDUCATION TO HUMANS.

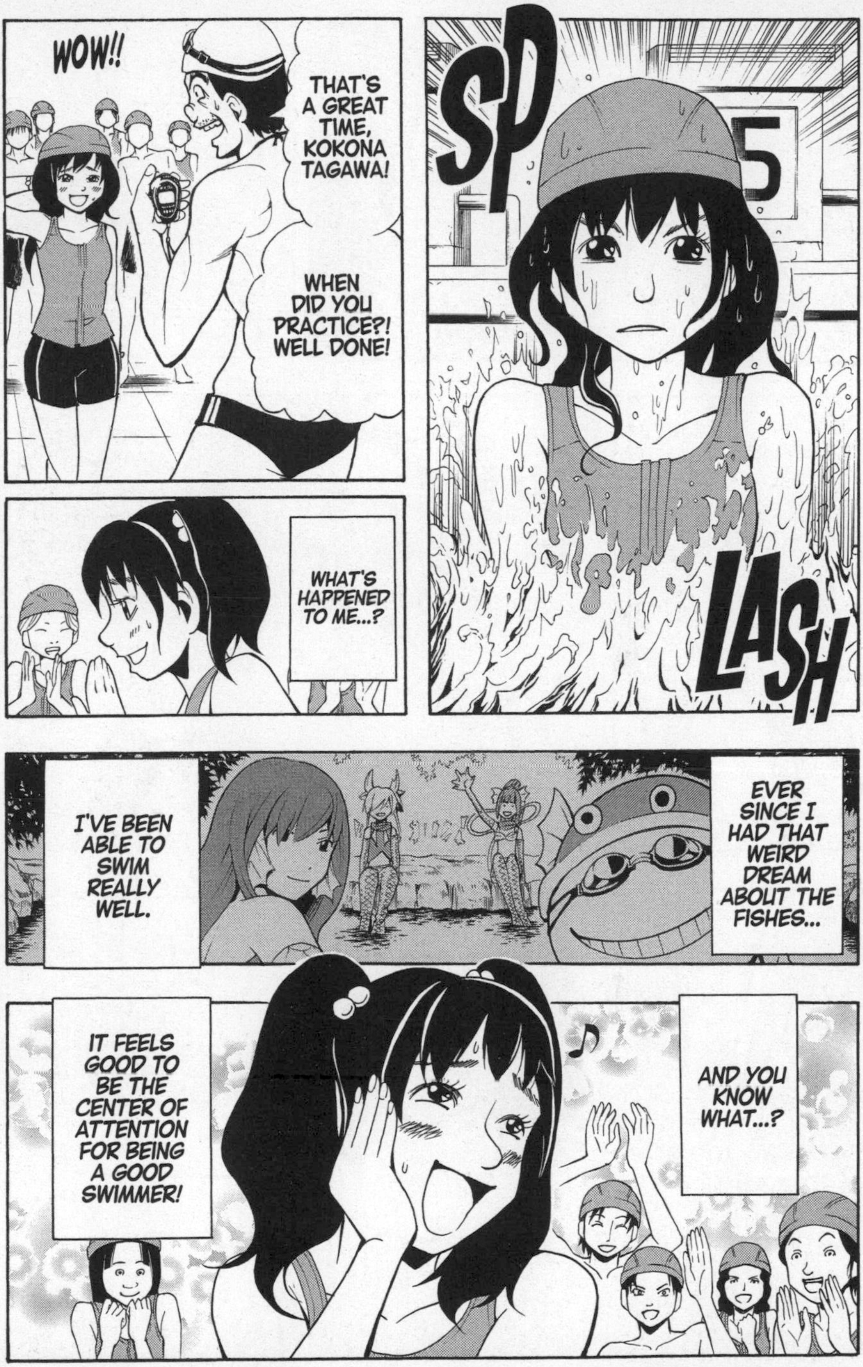
SP
LASH
THAT'S A GREAT TIME, KOKONA TAGAWA!
WOW!!
WHEN DID YOU PRACTICE?! WELL DONE!
WHAT'S HAPPENED TO ME...?
EVER SINCE I HAD THAT WEIRD DREAM ABOUT THE FISHES...
I'VE BEEN ABLE TO SWIM REALLY WELL.
AND YOU KNOW WHAT...?
IT FEELS GOOD TO BE THE CENTER OF ATTENTION FOR BEING A GOOD SWIMMER!

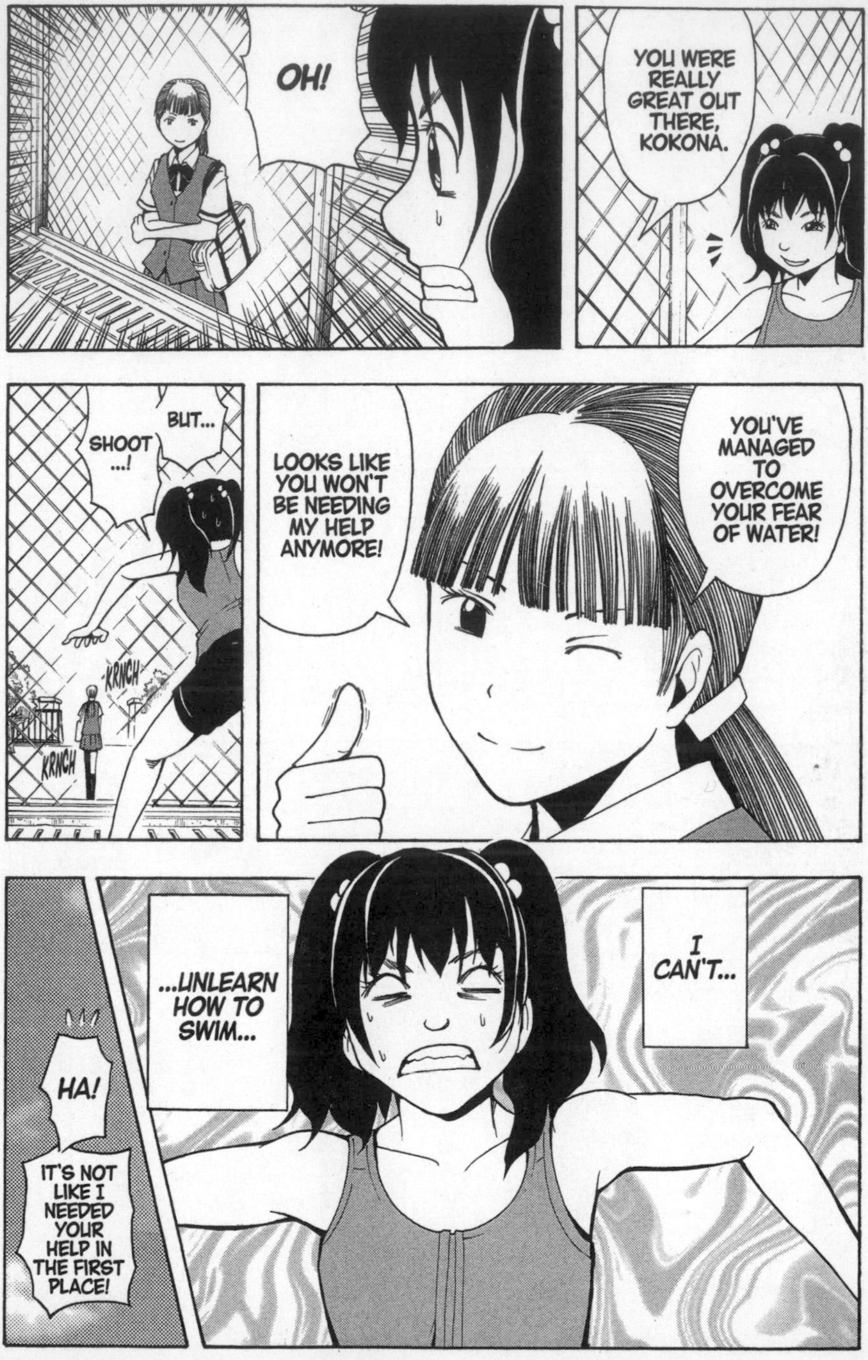
YOU WERE REALLY GREAT OUT THERE, KOKONA.
OH!
YOU'VE MANAGED TO OVERCOME YOUR FEAR OF WATER!
LOOKS LIKE YOU WON'T BE NEEDING MY HELP ANYMORE!
BUT...
SHOOT ...!
KRNCH
KRNCH
I CAN'T...
...UNLEARN HOW TO SWIM...
HA!
IT'S NOT LIKE I NEEDED YOUR HELP IN THE FIRST PLACE!

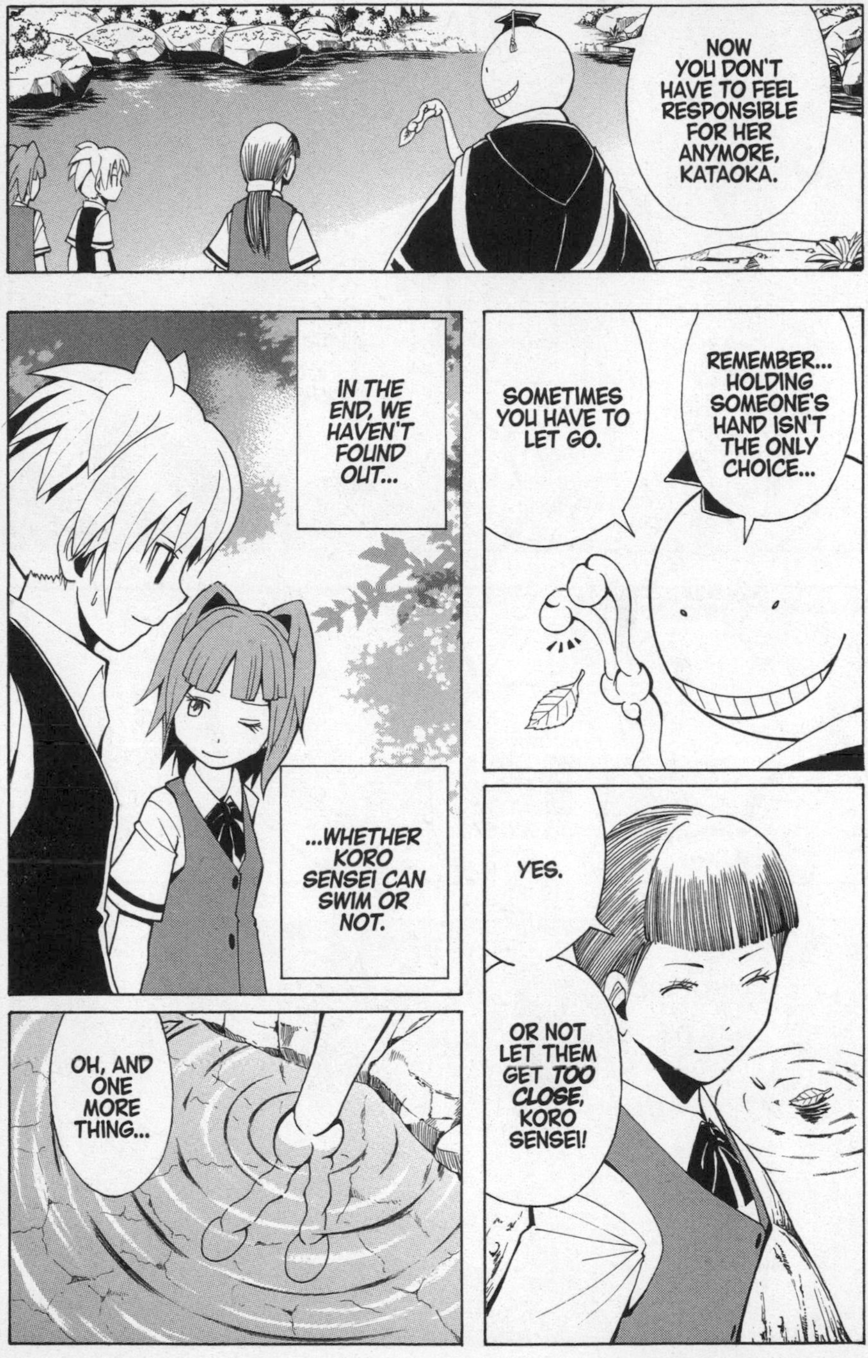
NOW YOU DON'T HAVE TO FEEL RESPONSIBLE FOR HER ANYMORE, KATAOKA.
REMEMBER... HOLDING SOMEONE'S HAND ISN'T THE ONLY CHOICE...
SOMETIMES YOU HAVE TO LET GO.
YES.
OR NOT LET THEM GET *TOO CLOSE*, KORO SENSEI!
IN THE END, WE HAVEN'T FOUND OUT...
...WHETHER KORO SENSEI CAN SWIM OR NOT.
OH, AND ONE MORE THING...

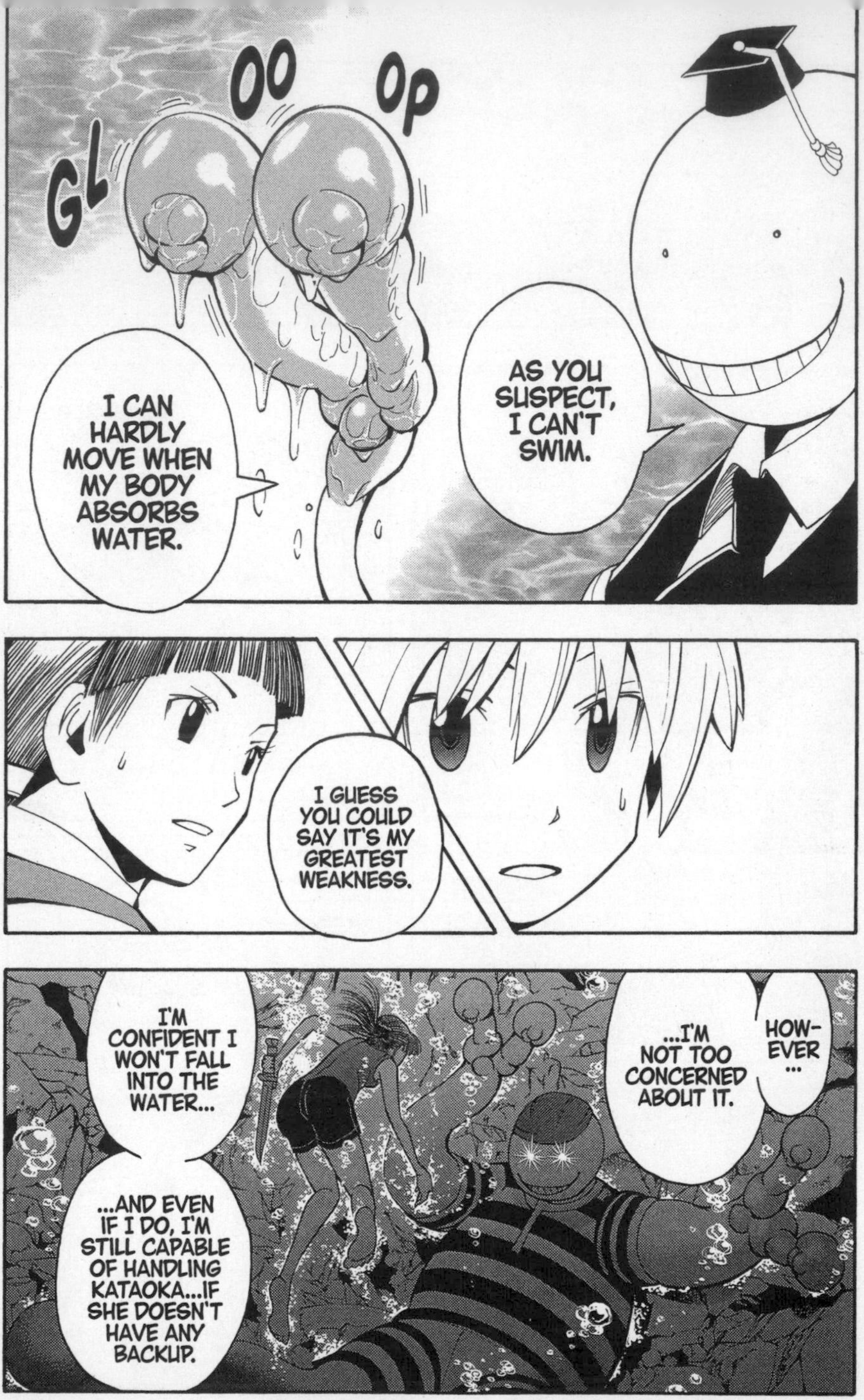
AS YOU SUSPECT, I CAN'T SWIM.
GLOOOP
I CAN HARDLY MOVE WHEN MY BODY ABSORBS WATER.
I GUESS YOU COULD SAY IT'S MY GREATEST WEAKNESS.
HOW-EVER...
...I'M NOT TOO CONCERNED ABOUT IT.
I'M CONFIDENT I WON'T FALL INTO THE WATER...
...AND EVEN IF I DO, I'M STILL CAPABLE OF HANDLING KATAOKA...IF SHE DOESN'T HAVE ANY BACKUP.

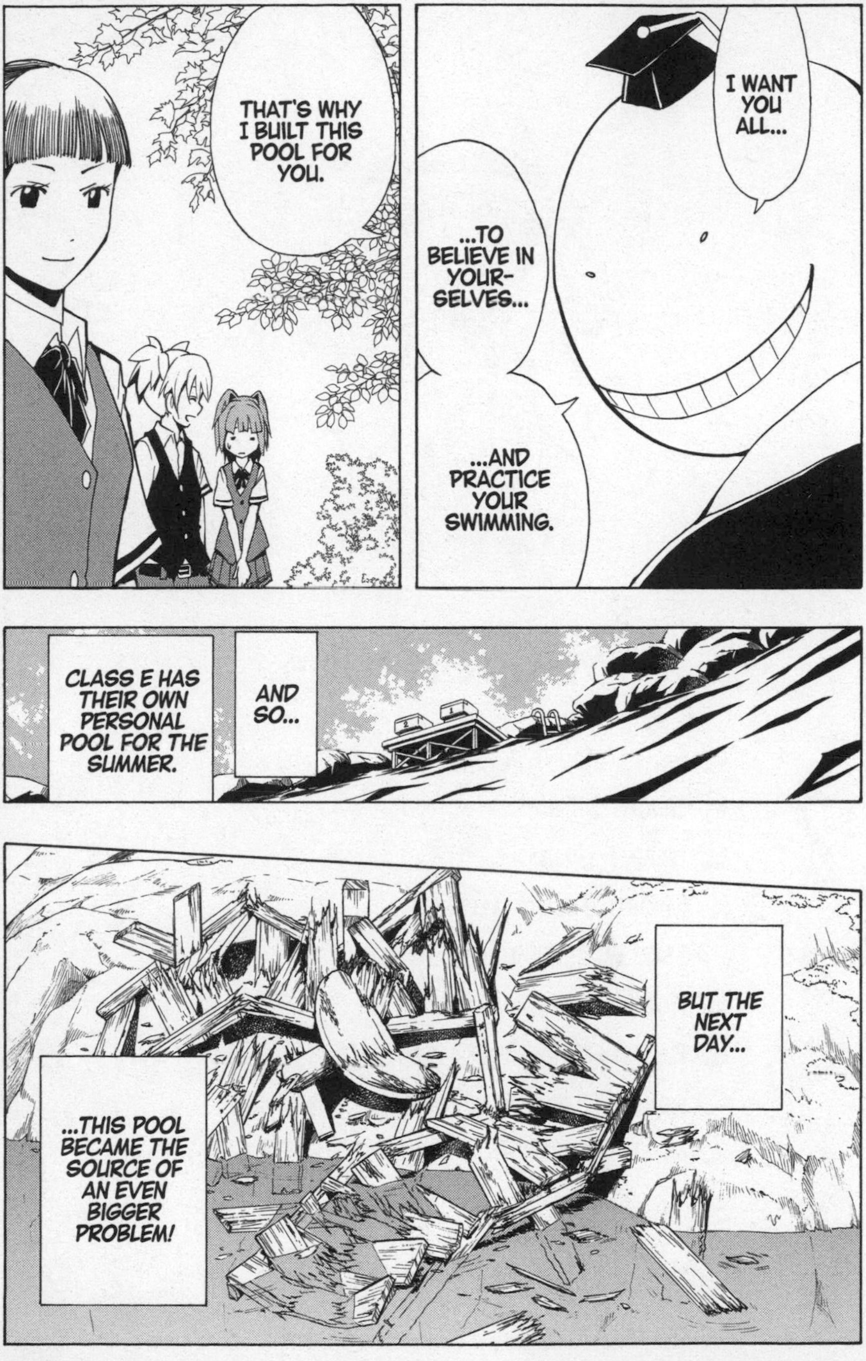
I WANT YOU ALL...
...TO BELIEVE IN YOURSELVES...
...AND PRACTICE YOUR SWIMMING.
THAT'S WHY I BUILT THIS POOL FOR YOU.
AND SO...
CLASS E HAS THEIR OWN PERSONAL POOL FOR THE SUMMER.
BUT THE NEXT DAY...
...THIS POOL BECAME THE SOURCE OF AN EVEN BIGGER PROBLEM!

E-6 MEG KATAOKA

- 😊 BIRTHDAY: JUNE 15
- 😊 HEIGHT: 5' 7"
- 😊 WEIGHT: 110 LBS.
- 😊 FAVORITE SUBJECT: JAPANESE
- 😊 LEAST FAVORITE SUBJECT: HISTORY
- 😊 HOBBY/SKILL: SWIMMING
- 😊 FUTURE GOAL: FLIGHT ATTENDANT
- 😊 DREAM: TO BE CARRIED OVER THE THRESHOLD
- 😊 MOST PEOPLE THINK *SHE* WANTS TO DO THE CARRYING...

CLASS 46 TIME FOR TERASAKA

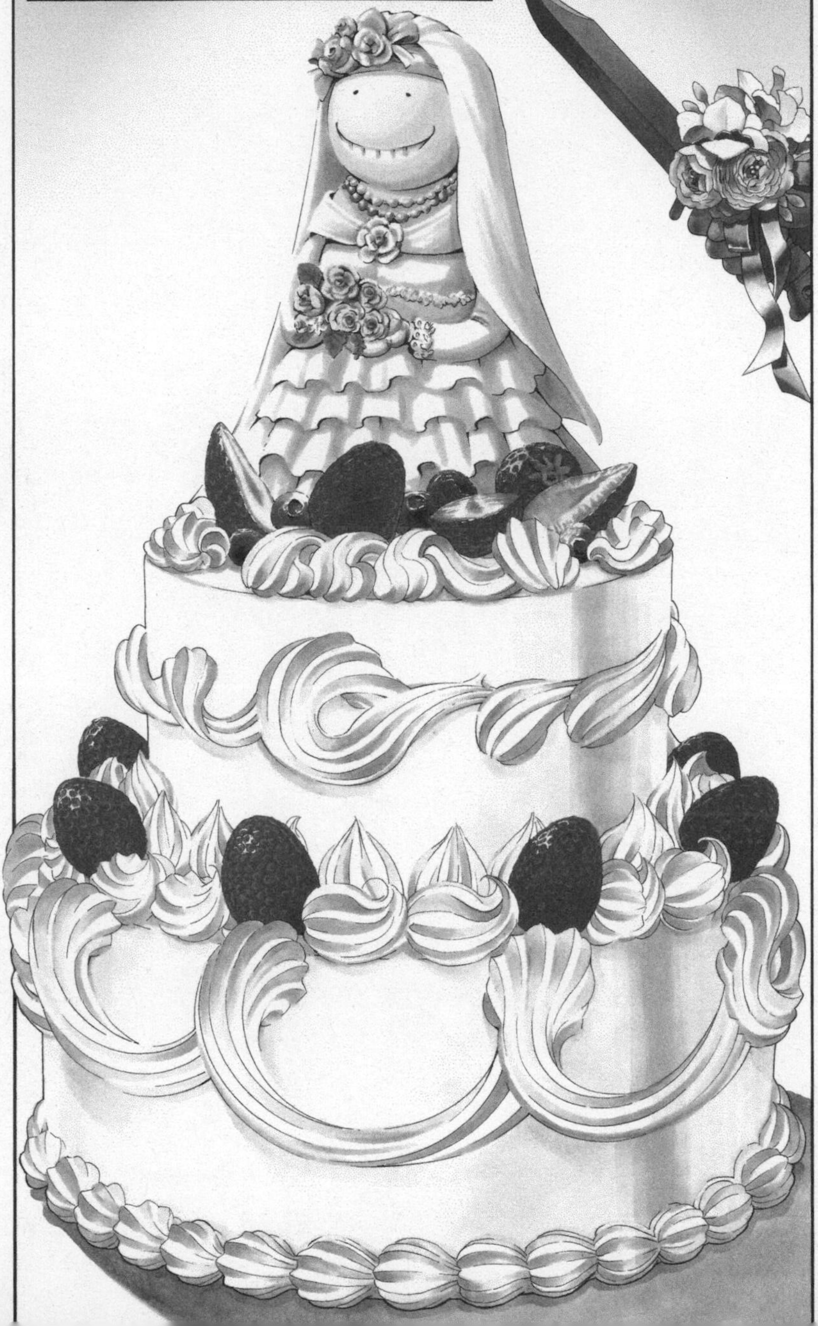

Stood up at the altar.

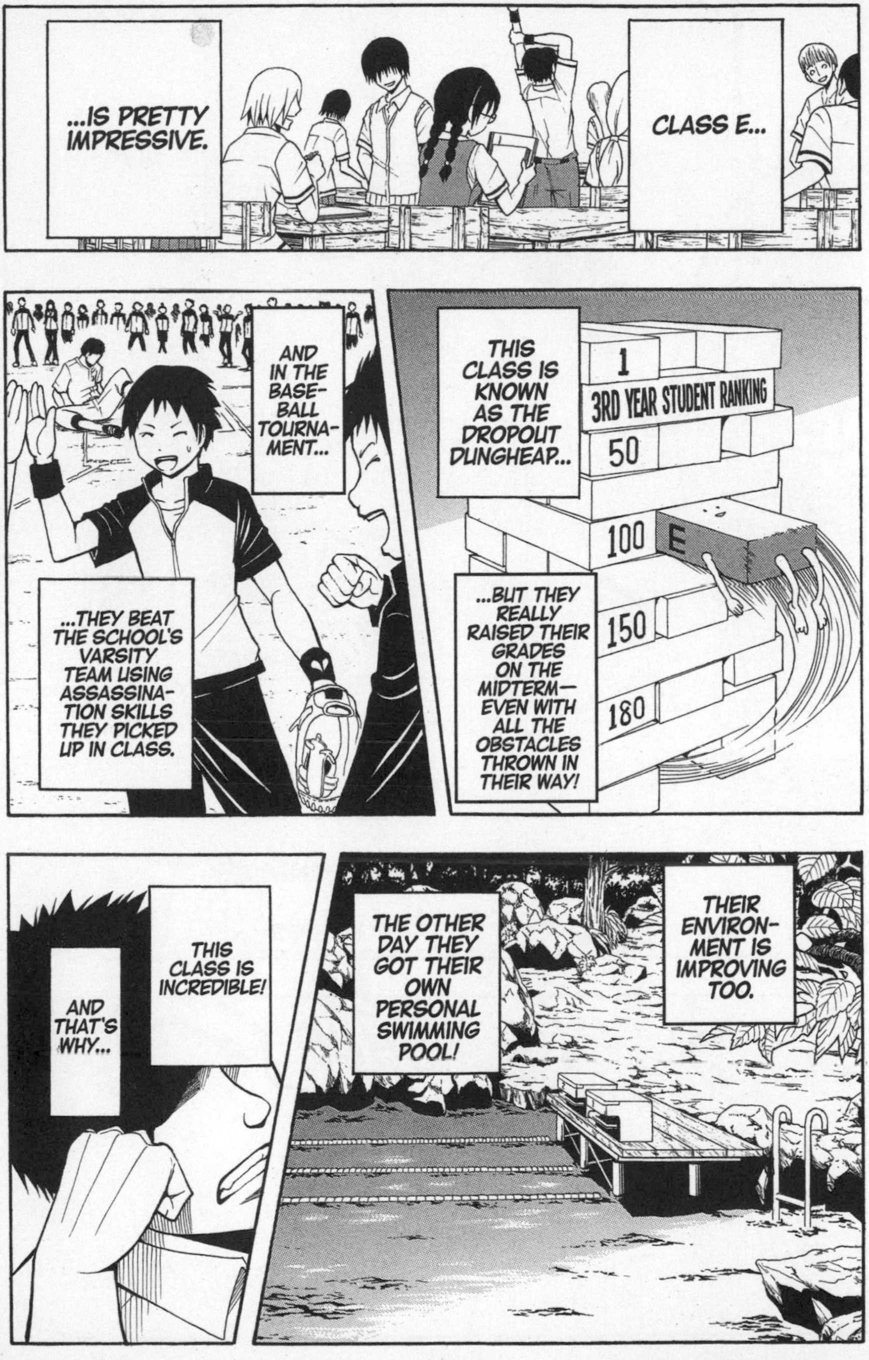
CLASS E...
...IS PRETTY IMPRESSIVE.
THIS CLASS IS KNOWN AS THE DROPOUT DUNGHEAP...
1
3RD YEAR STUDENT RANKING
50
100
E
150
180
...BUT THEY REALLY RAISED THEIR GRADES ON THE MIDTERM—EVEN WITH ALL THE OBSTACLES THROWN IN THEIR WAY!
AND IN THE BASEBALL TOURNAMENT...
...THEY BEAT THE SCHOOL'S VARSITY TEAM USING ASSASSINATION SKILLS THEY PICKED UP IN CLASS.
THEIR ENVIRONMENT IS IMPROVING TOO.
THE OTHER DAY THEY GOT THEIR OWN PERSONAL SWIMMING POOL!
THIS CLASS IS INCREDIBLE!
AND THAT'S WHY...

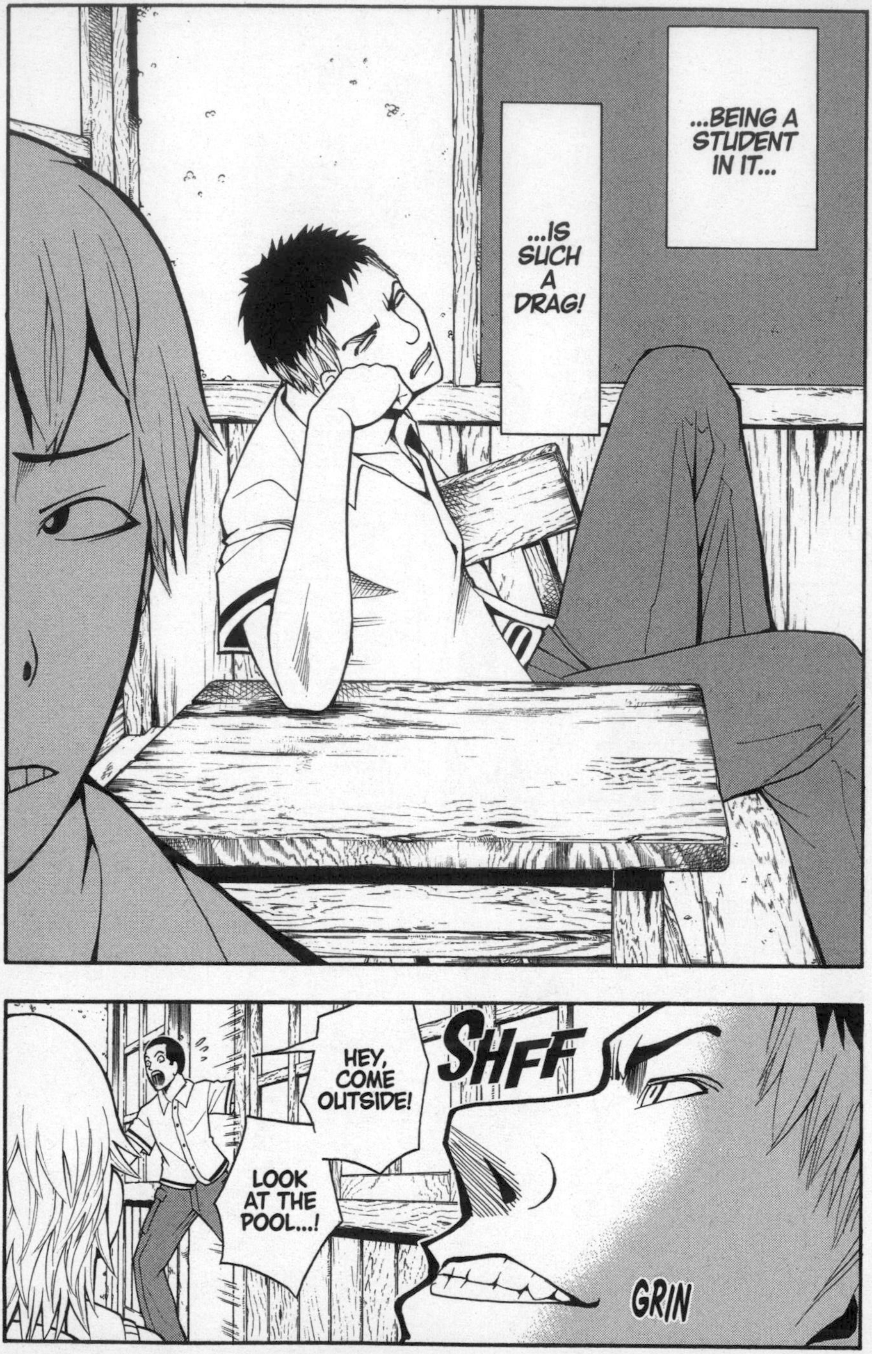
...BEING A STUDENT IN IT...
...IS SUCH A DRAG!
SHFF
HEY, COME OUTSIDE!
LOOK AT THE POOL...!
GRIN

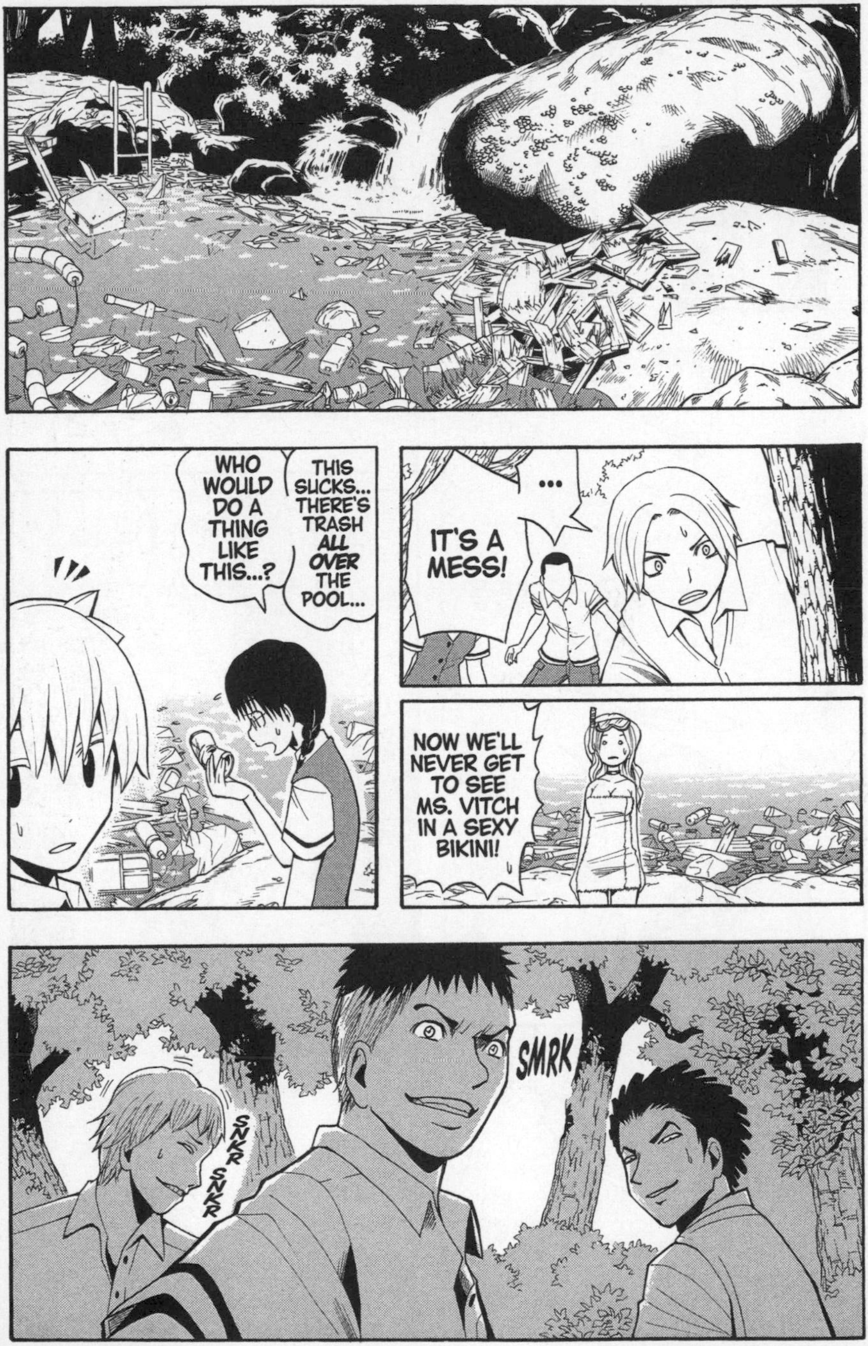
...
IT'S A MESS!
NOW WE'LL NEVER GET TO SEE MS. VITCH IN A SEXY BIKINI!
THIS SUCKS... THERE'S TRASH ALL OVER THE POOL...
WHO WOULD DO A THING LIKE THIS...?
SMRK
SNKR SNKR

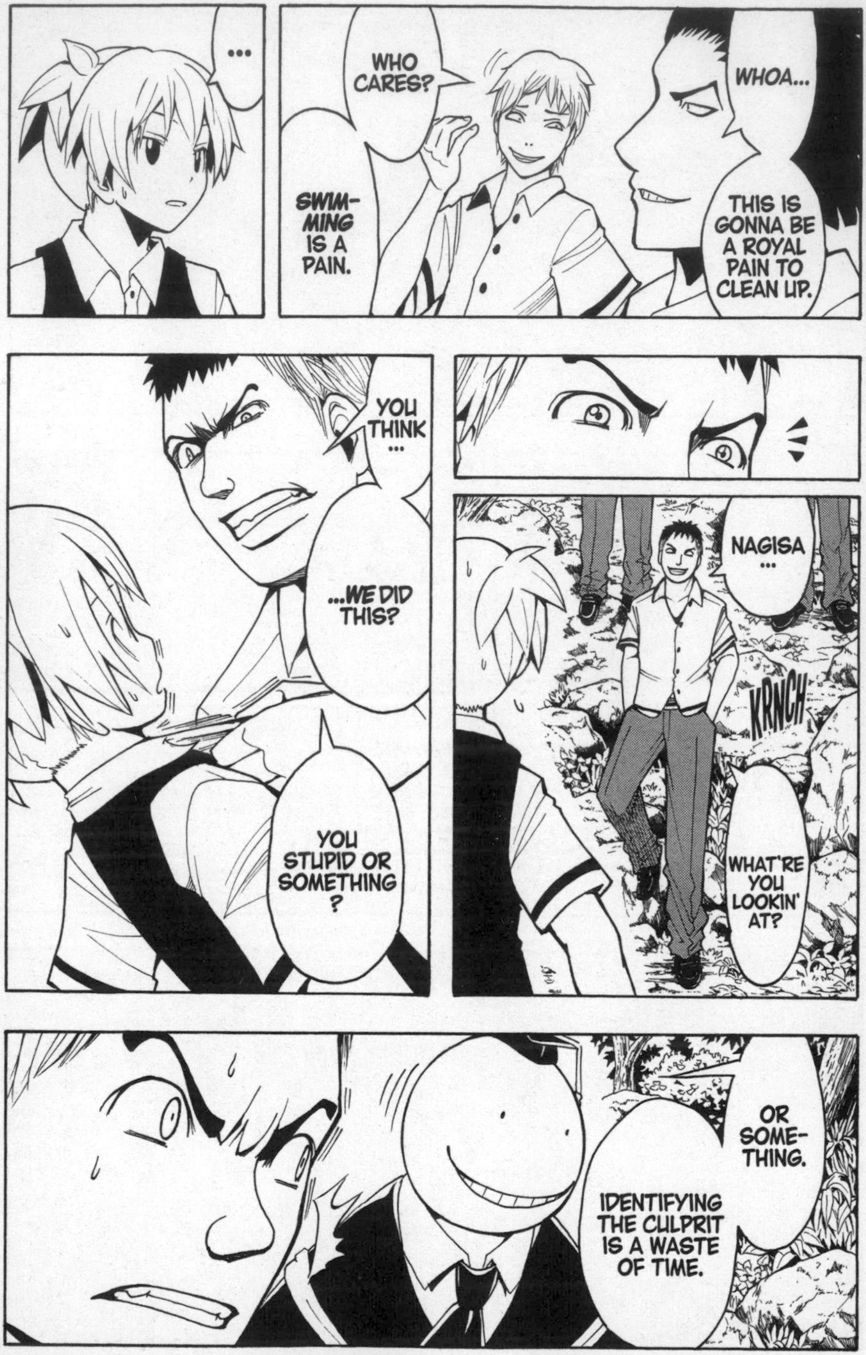
WHOA...
THIS IS GONNA BE A ROYAL PAIN TO CLEAN UP.
WHO CARES?
SWIMMING IS A PAIN.
...
NAGISA...
KRNCH
WHAT'RE YOU LOOKIN' AT?
YOU THINK...
...WE DID THIS?
YOU STUPID OR SOMETHING?
OR SOMETHING.
IDENTIFYING THE CULPRIT IS A WASTE OF TIME.

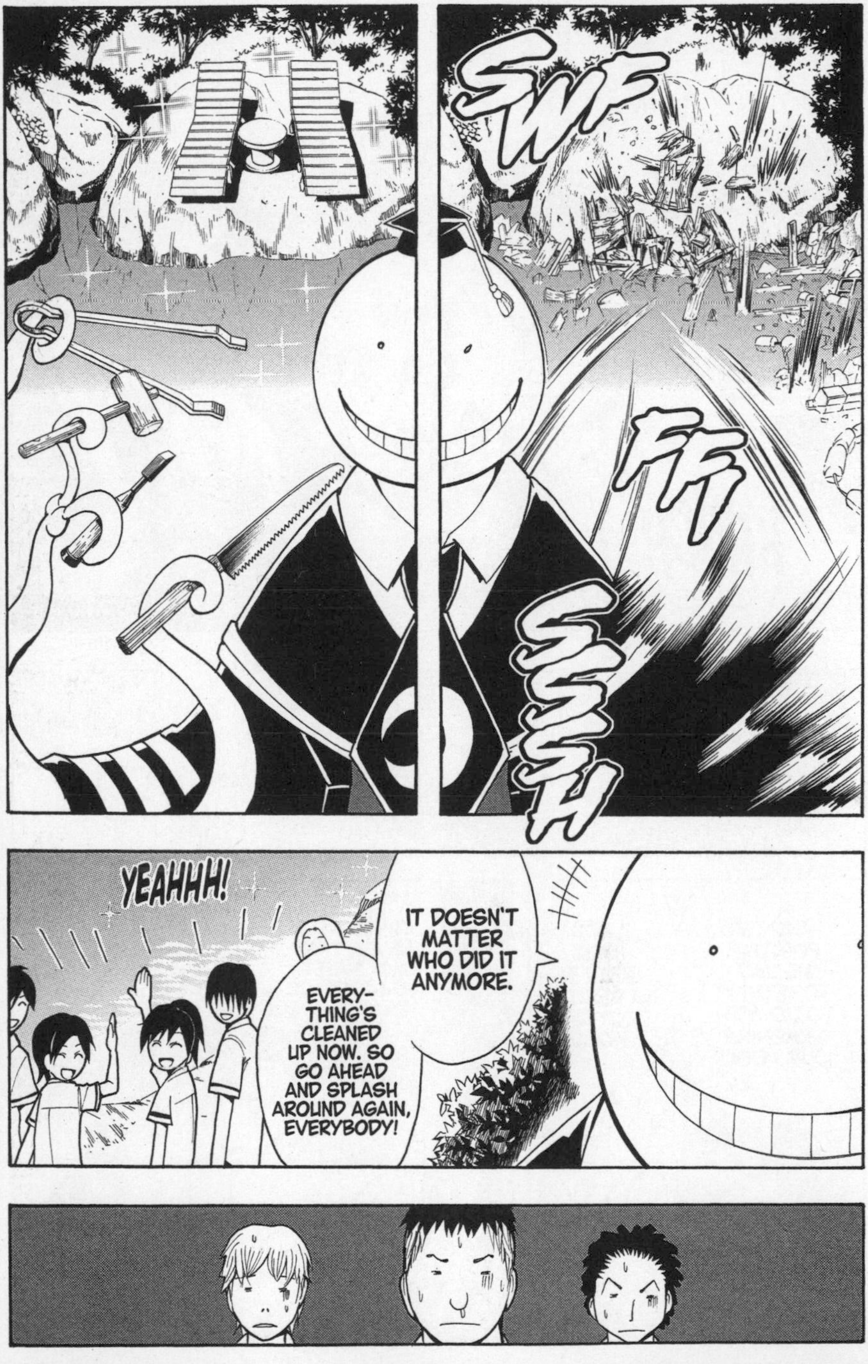
SWF
FF
SSSSH
IT DOESN'T MATTER WHO DID IT ANYMORE.
EVERY-THING'S CLEANED UP NOW. SO GO AHEAD AND SPLASH AROUND AGAIN, EVERYBODY!
YEAHHH!

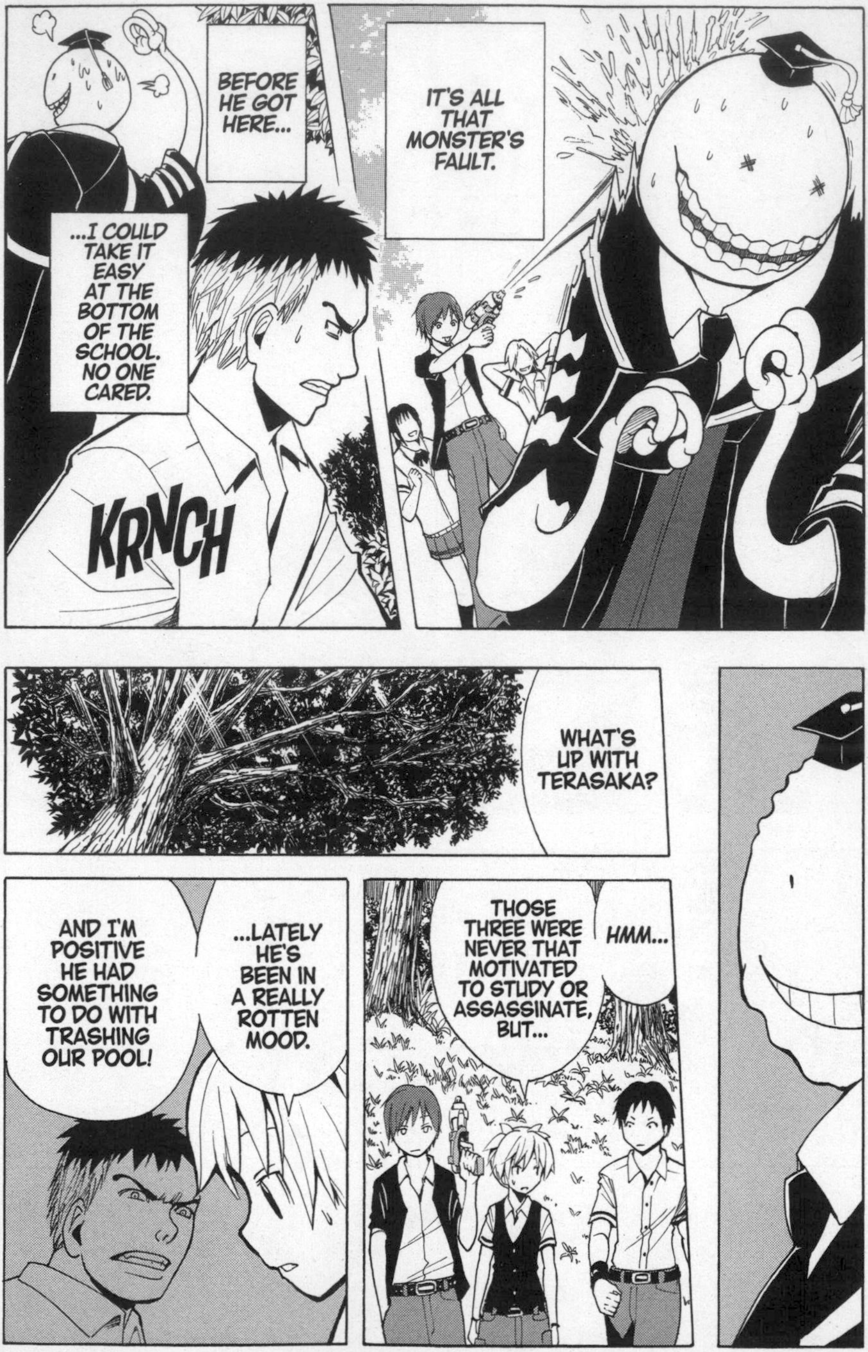
IT'S ALL THAT MONSTER'S FAULT.
BEFORE HE GOT HERE...
...I COULD TAKE IT EASY AT THE BOTTOM OF THE SCHOOL. NO ONE CARED.
KRNCH
WHAT'S UP WITH TERASAKA?
HMM...
THOSE THREE WERE NEVER THAT MOTIVATED TO STUDY OR ASSASSINATE, BUT...
...LATELY HE'S BEEN IN A REALLY ROTTEN MOOD.
AND I'M POSITIVE HE HAD SOMETHING TO DO WITH TRASHING OUR POOL!

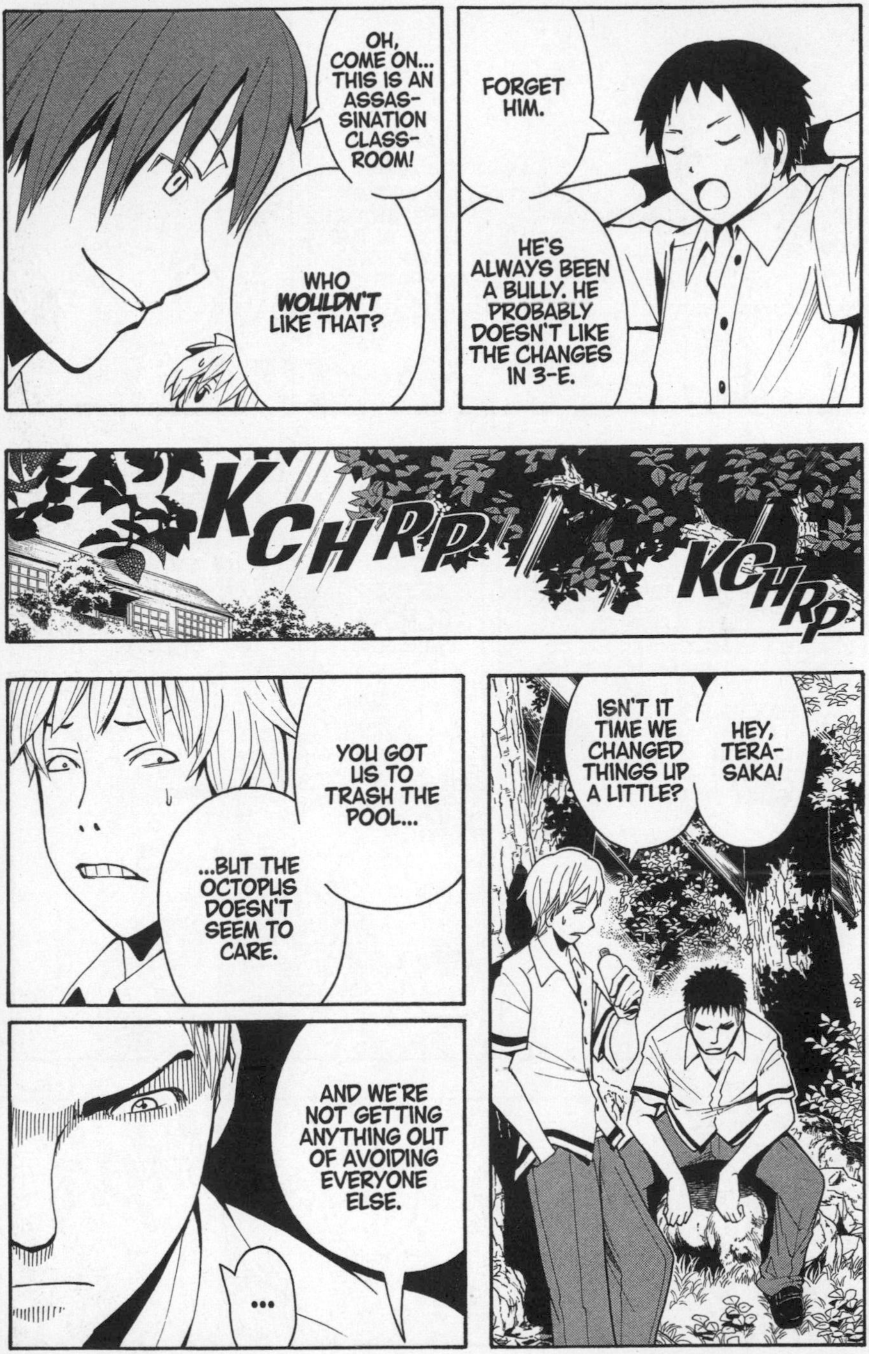
FORGET HIM.
HE'S ALWAYS BEEN A BULLY. HE PROBABLY DOESN'T LIKE THE CHANGES IN 3-E.
OH, COME ON... THIS IS AN ASSASSINATION CLASSROOM!
WHO *WOULDN'T* LIKE THAT?
KCHRP
KCHRP
HEY, TERASAKA!
ISN'T IT TIME WE CHANGED THINGS UP A LITTLE?
YOU GOT US TO TRASH THE POOL...
...BUT THE OCTOPUS DOESN'T SEEM TO CARE.
AND WE'RE NOT GETTING ANYTHING OUT OF AVOIDING EVERYONE ELSE.
...

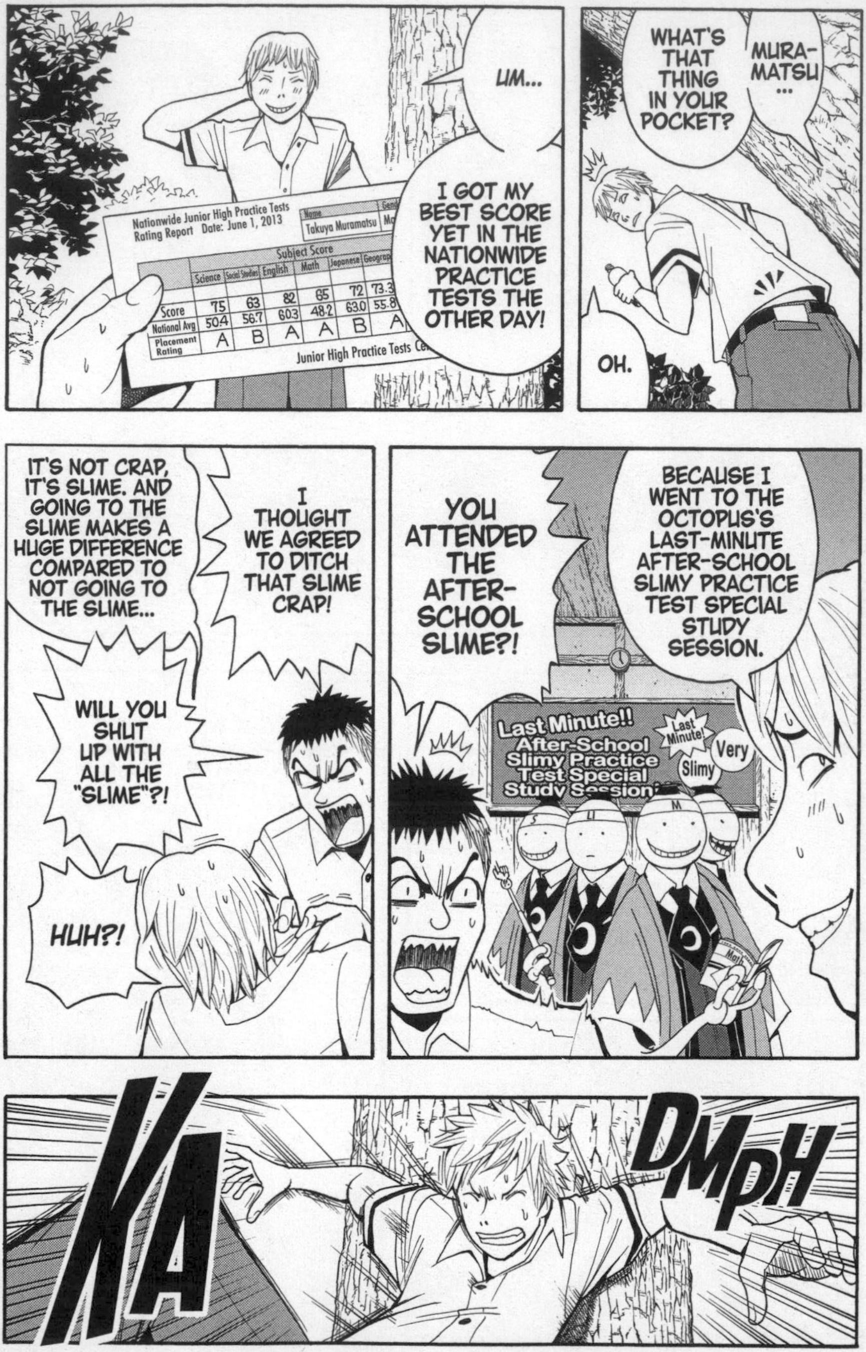
MURA-MATSU...
WHAT'S THAT THING IN YOUR POCKET?
OH.
UM...
I GOT MY BEST SCORE YET IN THE NATIONWIDE PRACTICE TESTS THE OTHER DAY!
Nationwide Junior High Practice Tests
Rating Report Date: June 1, 2013
Name
Takuya Muramatsu
Subject Score
Science Social Studies English Math Japanese
Score 75 63 82 65 72 73.3
National Avg 50.4 56.7 60.3 48.2 63.0 55.8
Placement Rating A B A A B A
Junior High Practice Tests
BECAUSE I WENT TO THE OCTOPUS'S LAST-MINUTE AFTER-SCHOOL SLIMY PRACTICE TEST SPECIAL STUDY SESSION.
YOU ATTENDED THE AFTER-SCHOOL SLIME?!
Last Minute!! After-School Slimy Practice Test Special Study Session!
Last Minute!
Very
Slimy
Math
I THOUGHT WE AGREED TO DITCH THAT SLIME CRAP!
IT'S NOT CRAP, IT'S SLIME. AND GOING TO THE SLIME MAKES A HUGE DIFFERENCE COMPARED TO NOT GOING TO THE SLIME...
WILL YOU SHUT UP WITH ALL THE "SLIME"?!
HUH?!
DMPH
KA

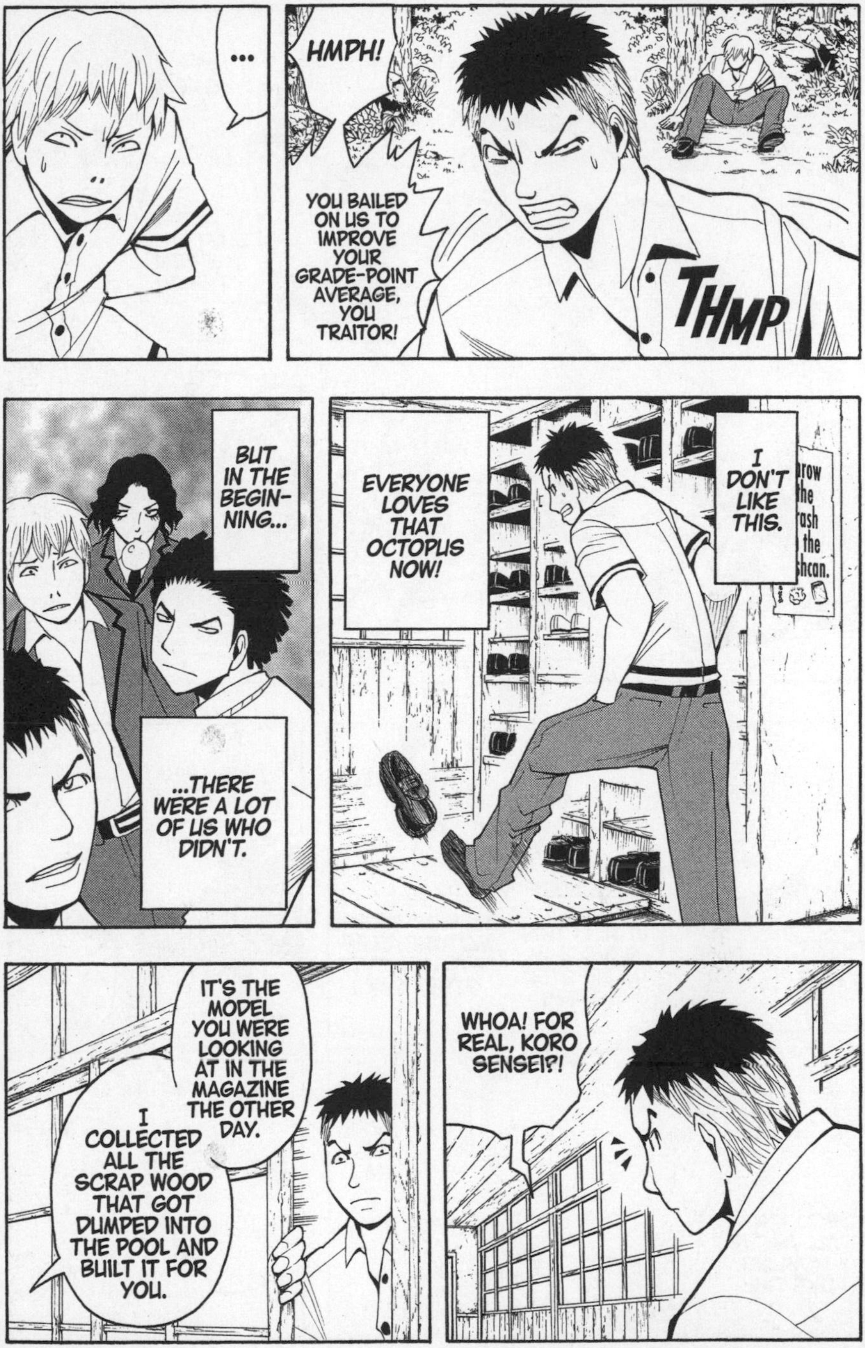
HMPH!
YOU BAILED ON US TO IMPROVE YOUR GRADE-POINT AVERAGE, YOU TRAITOR!
THMP
...
I DON'T LIKE THIS.
EVERYONE LOVES THAT OCTOPUS NOW!
BUT IN THE BEGIN-NING...
...THERE WERE A LOT OF US WHO DIDN'T.
WHOA! FOR REAL, KORO SENSEI?!
IT'S THE MODEL YOU WERE LOOKING AT IN THE MAGAZINE THE OTHER DAY.
I COLLECTED ALL THE SCRAP WOOD THAT GOT DUMPED INTO THE POOL AND BUILT IT FOR YOU.

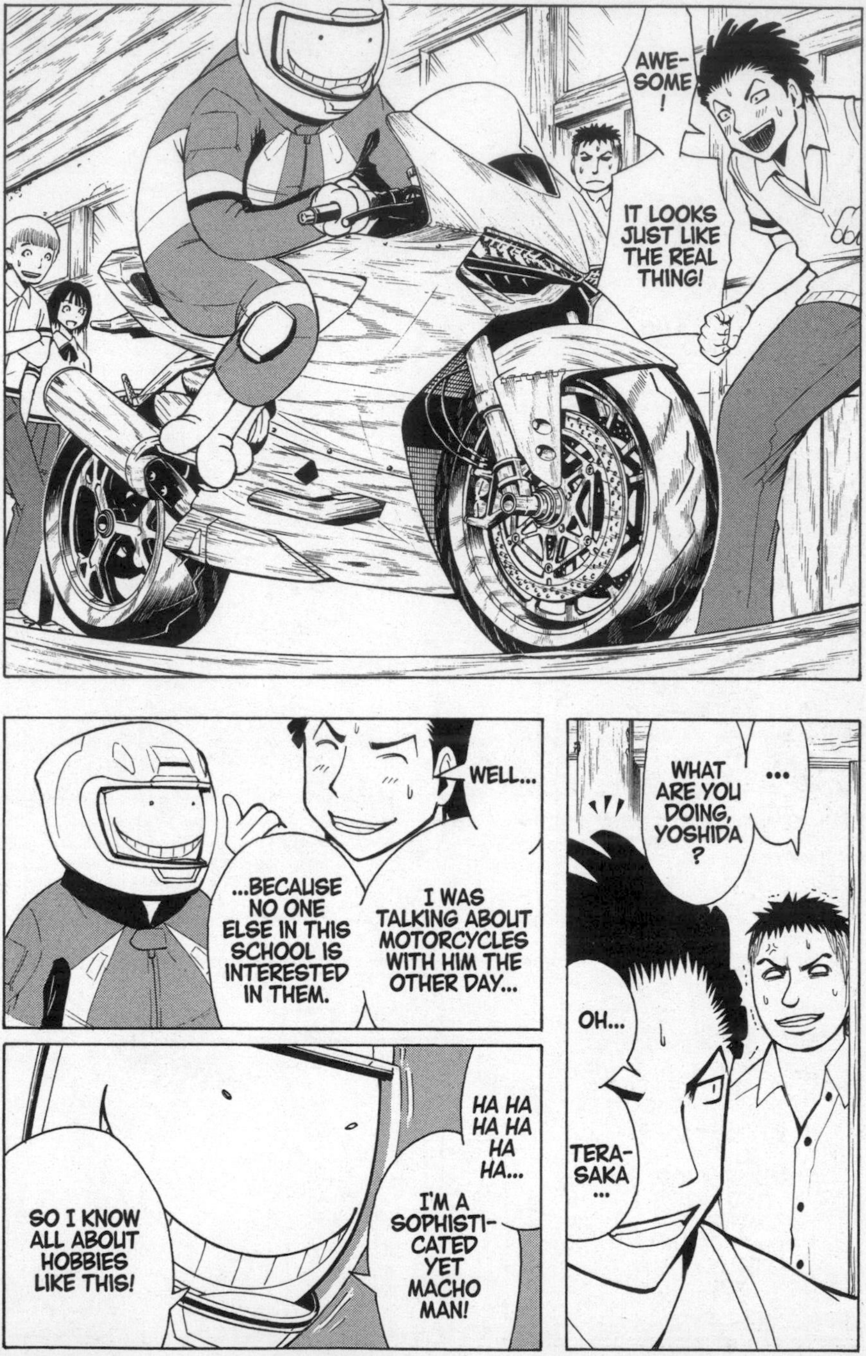
AWE-SOME!
IT LOOKS JUST LIKE THE REAL THING!
...
WHAT ARE YOU DOING, YOSHIDA?
OH...
TERA-SAKA...
WELL...
I WAS TALKING ABOUT MOTORCYCLES WITH HIM THE OTHER DAY...
...BECAUSE NO ONE ELSE IN THIS SCHOOL IS INTERESTED IN THEM.
HA HA HA HA HA HA...
I'M A SOPHISTI-CATED YET MACHO MAN!
SO I KNOW ALL ABOUT HOBBIES LIKE THIS!

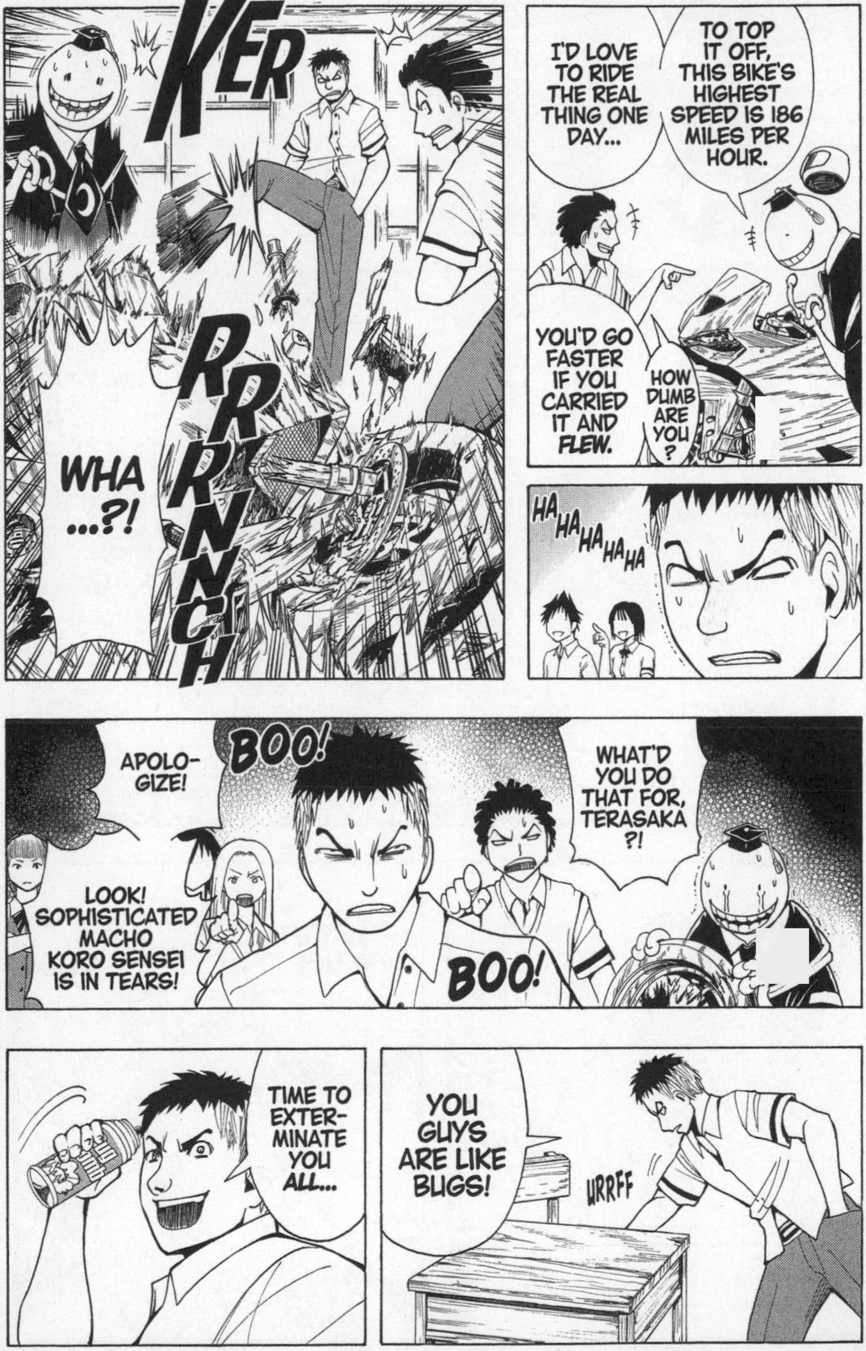
TO TOP IT OFF, THIS BIKE'S HIGHEST SPEED IS 186 MILES PER HOUR.
I'D LOVE TO RIDE THE REAL THING ONE DAY...
HOW DUMB ARE YOU?
YOU'D GO FASTER IF YOU CARRIED IT AND FLEW.
HA HA HA HA HA
KER
RRRRNCH
WHA...?!
WHAT'D YOU DO THAT FOR, TERASAKA?!
BOO!
APOLO-GIZE!
BOO!
LOOK! SOPHISTICATED MACHO KORO SENSEI IS IN TEARS!
YOU GUYS ARE LIKE BUGS!
URRFF
TIME TO EXTER-MINATE YOU ALL...

FS

KLNK KLNK

SSST

WHAT IS THAT STUFF?!

PFFSSS PP FFT

WHOA!

INSECTI-CIDE?!

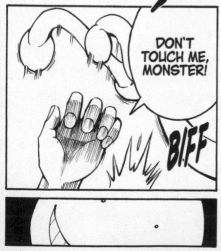

DON'T TOUCH ME, MONSTER!

BIFF

THAT'S ENOUGH.

TERA-SAKA!

GRAB

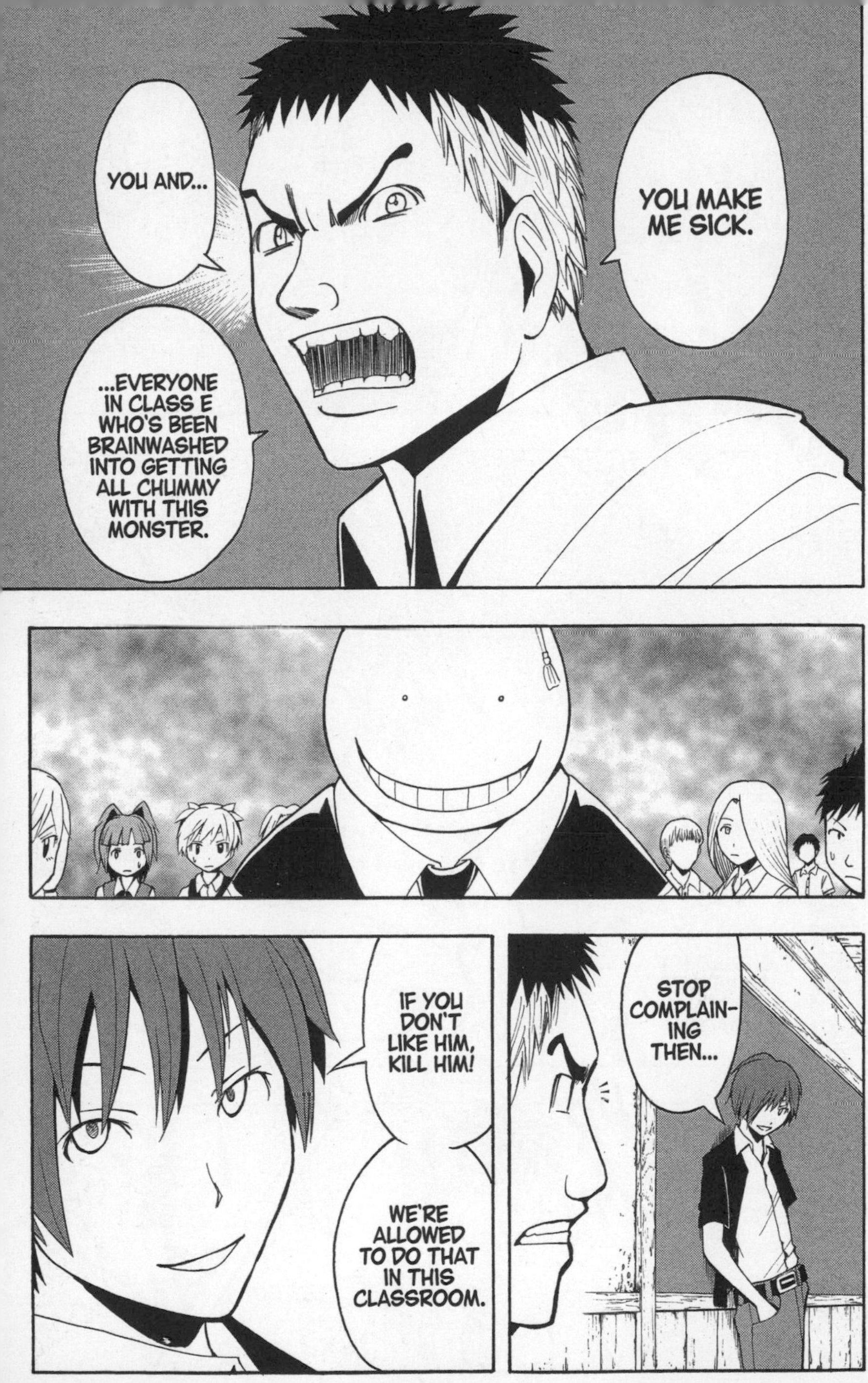
YOU MAKE ME SICK.
YOU AND...
...EVERYONE IN CLASS E WHO'S BEEN BRAINWASHED INTO GETTING ALL CHUMMY WITH THIS MONSTER.
STOP COMPLAIN-ING THEN...
IF YOU DON'T LIKE HIM, KILL HIM!
WE'RE ALLOWED TO DO THAT IN THIS CLASSROOM.

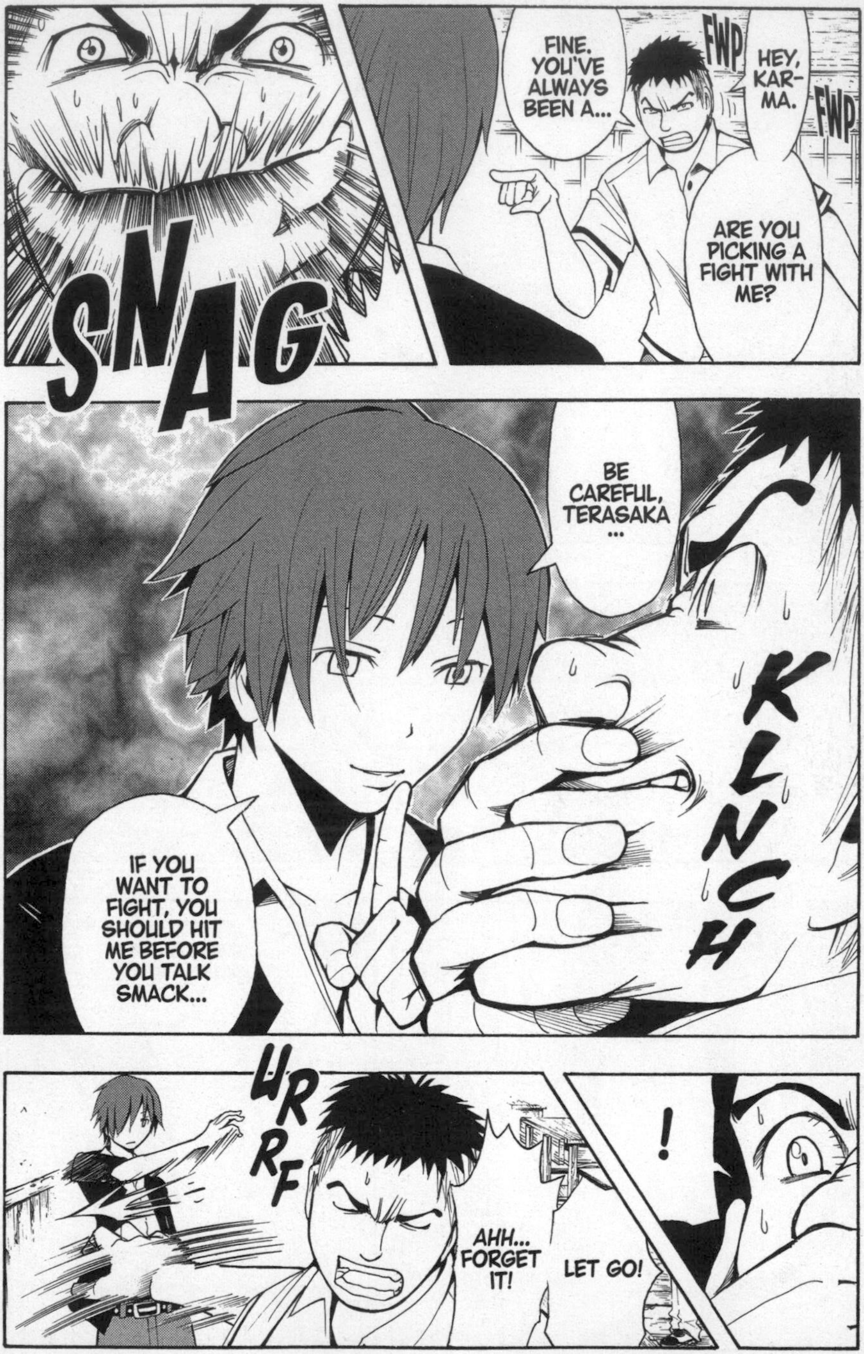
HEY, KAR-MA.
FWP
FWP
FINE. YOU'VE ALWAYS BEEN A...
ARE YOU PICKING A FIGHT WITH ME?
SNAG
BE CAREFUL, TERASAKA ...
KLINCH
IF YOU WANT TO FIGHT, YOU SHOULD HIT ME BEFORE YOU TALK SMACK...
!
LET GO!
AHH... FORGET IT!
URRF

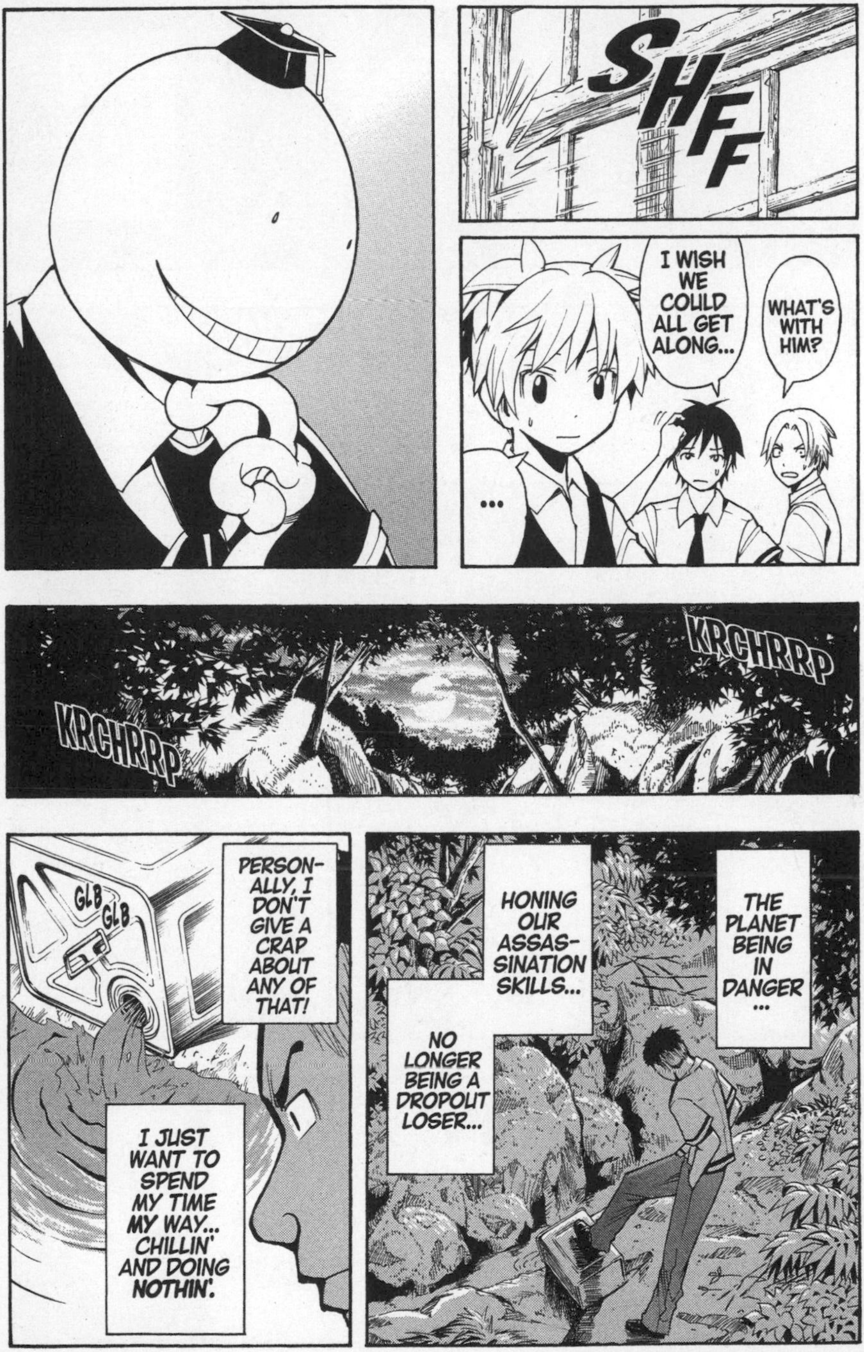
SHFF
WHAT'S WITH HIM?
I WISH WE COULD ALL GET ALONG...
...
KRCHRRP
KRCHRRP
THE PLANET BEING IN DANGER...
HONING OUR ASSAS-SINATION SKILLS...
NO LONGER BEING A DROPOUT LOSER...
PERSON-ALLY, I DON'T GIVE A CRAP ABOUT ANY OF THAT!
GLB GLB
I JUST WANT TO SPEND MY TIME MY WAY... CHILLIN' AND DOING NOTHIN'.

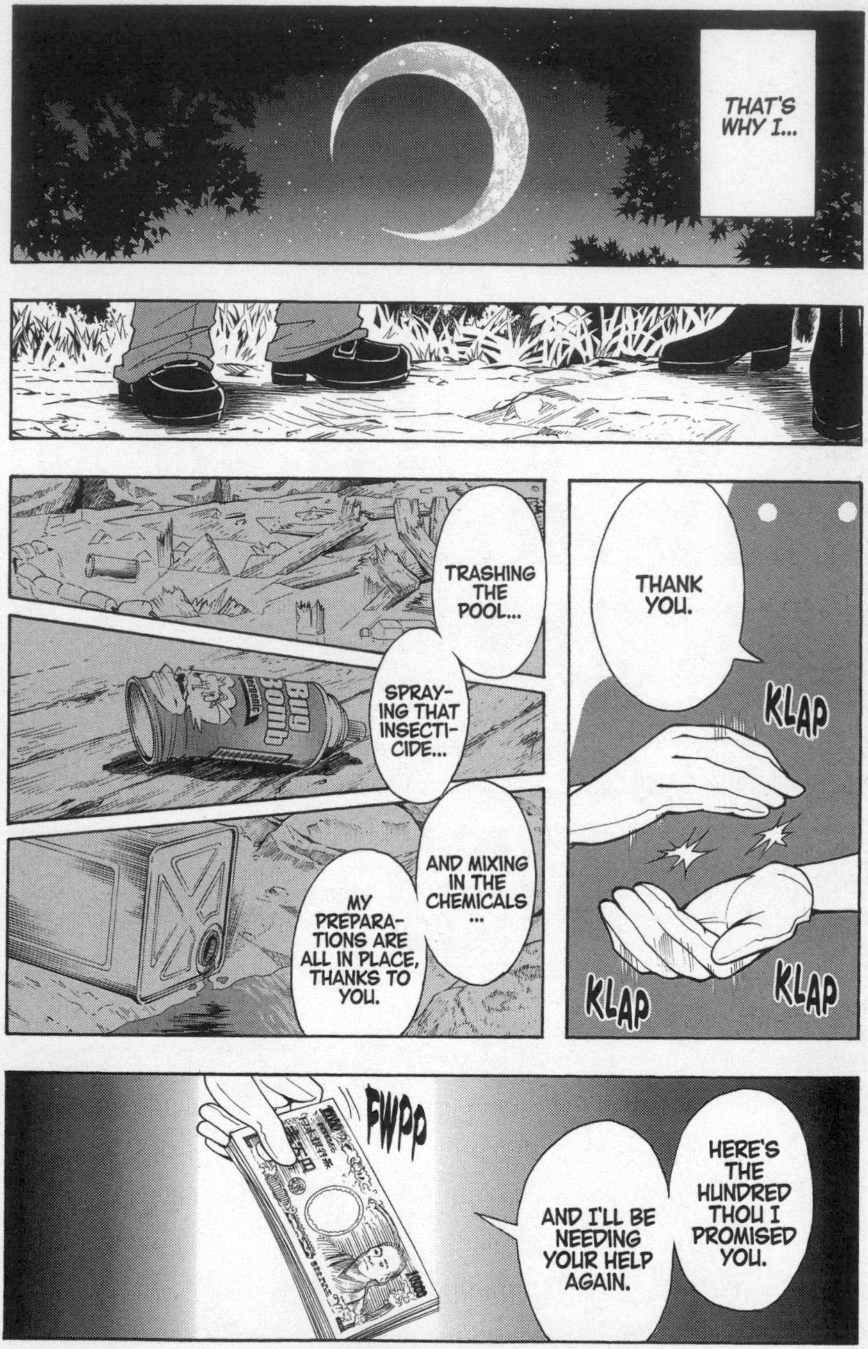
THAT'S WHY I...
THANK YOU.
KLAP
KLAP
KLAP
TRASHING THE POOL...
SPRAY-ING THAT INSECTI-CIDE...
AND MIXING IN THE CHEMICALS...
MY PREPARA-TIONS ARE ALL IN PLACE, THANKS TO YOU.
HERE'S THE HUNDRED THOU I PROMISED YOU.
AND I'LL BE NEEDING YOUR HELP AGAIN.
FWPP

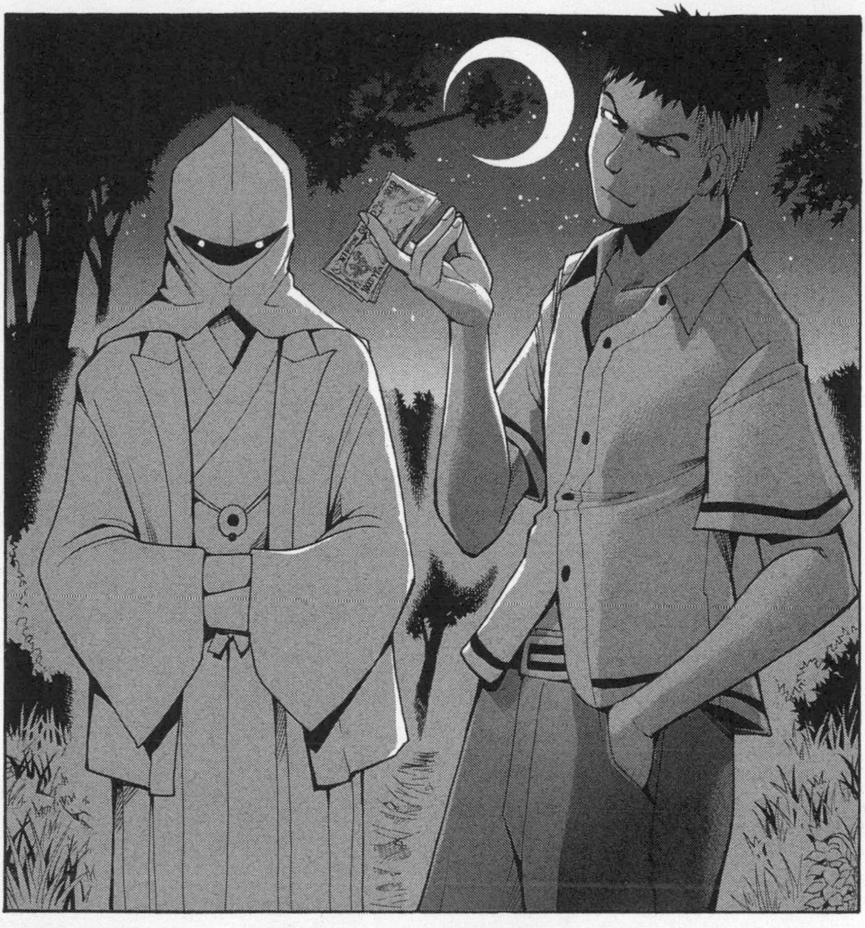

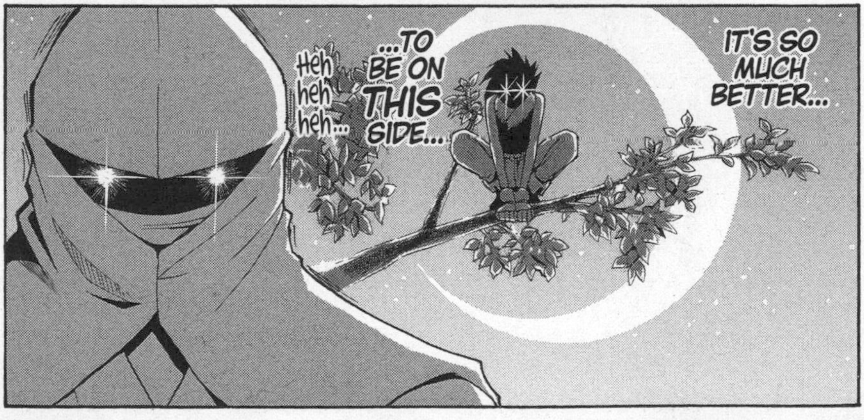
IT'S SO MUCH BETTER...
...TO BE ON THIS SIDE...
Heh heh heh...

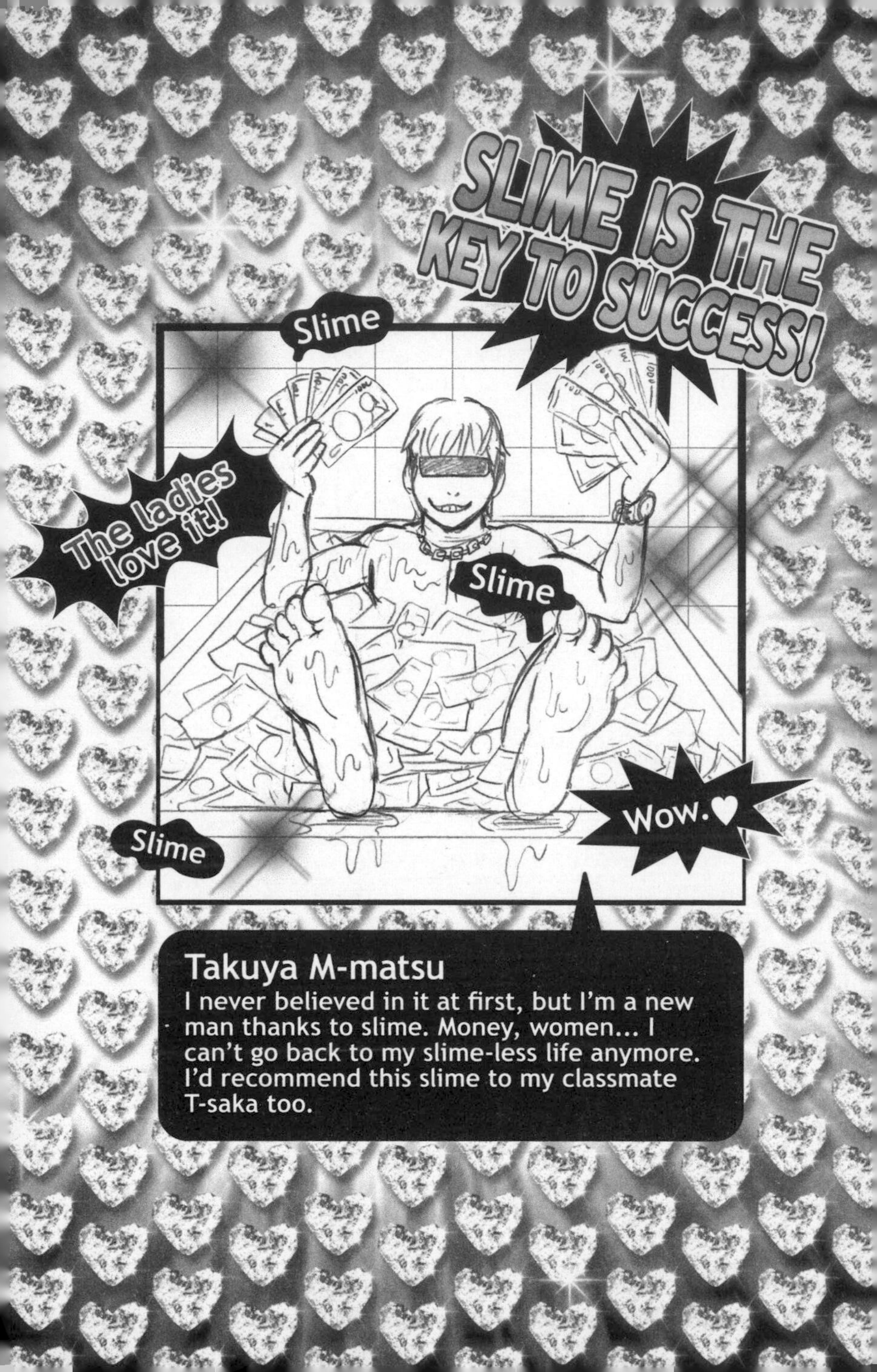
SLIME IS THE KEY TO SUCCESS!
Slime
The ladies love it!
Slime
Wow.♥
Slime
Takuya M-matsu
I never believed in it at first, but I'm a new man thanks to slime. Money, women... I can't go back to my slime-less life anymore. I'd recommend this slime to my classmate T-saka too.

CLASS 47 TIME FOR A VISION

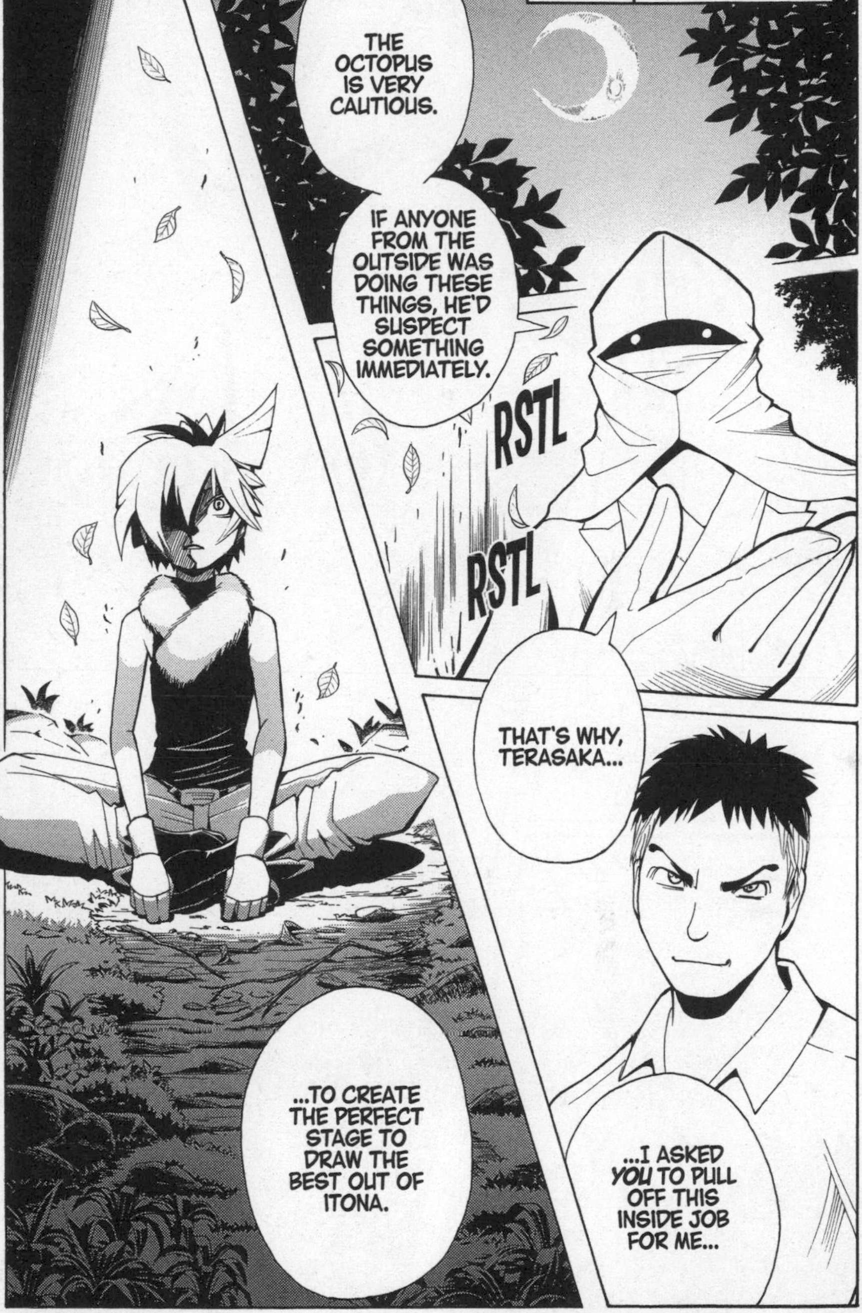

THE OCTOPUS IS VERY CAUTIOUS.
IF ANYONE FROM THE OUTSIDE WAS DOING THESE THINGS, HE'D SUSPECT SOMETHING IMMEDIATELY.
RSTL
RSTL
THAT'S WHY, TERASAKA...
...I ASKED *YOU* TO PULL OFF THIS INSIDE JOB FOR ME...
...TO CREATE THE PERFECT STAGE TO DRAW THE BEST OUT OF ITONA.

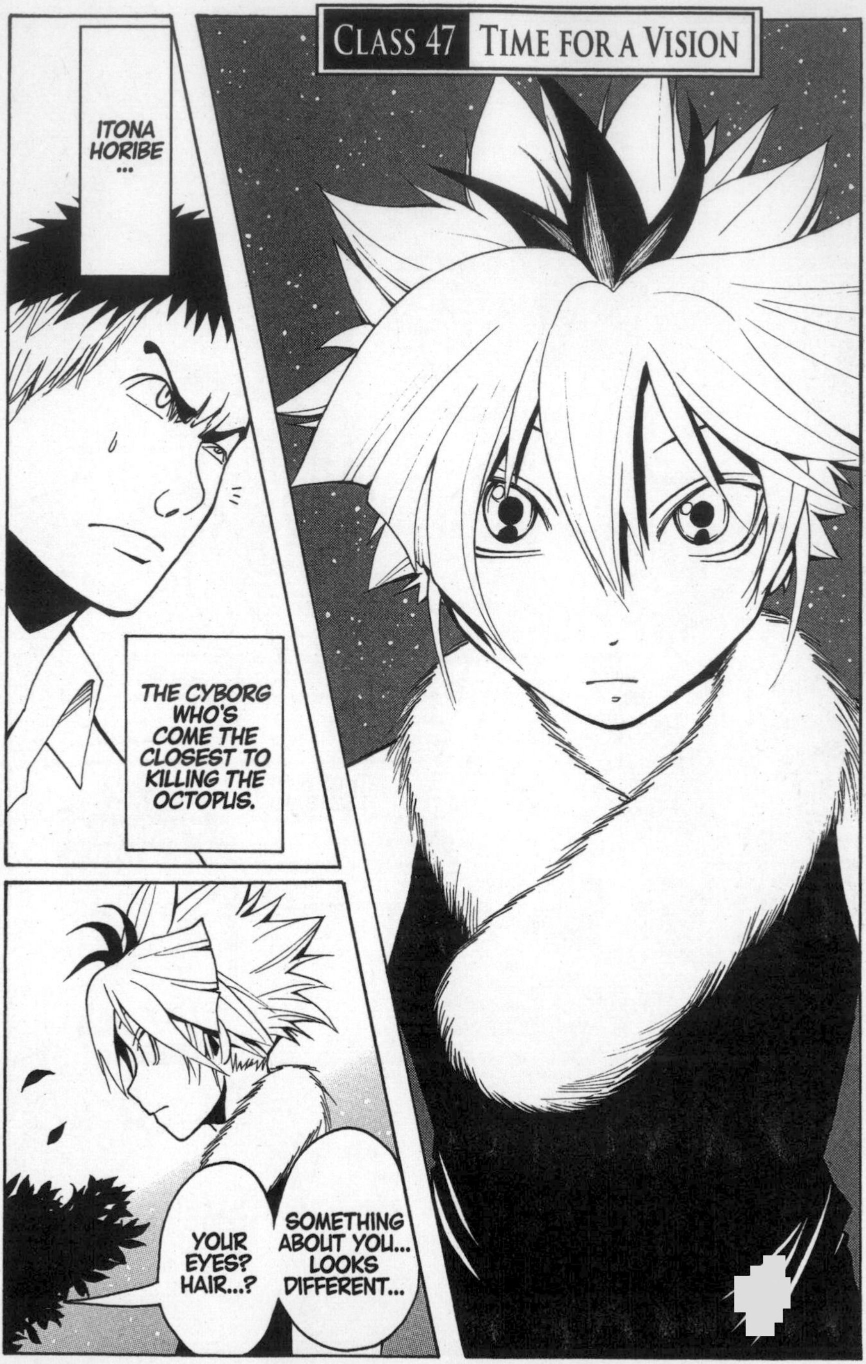
CLASS 47 TIME FOR A VISION
ITONA HORIBE ...
THE CYBORG WHO'S COME THE CLOSEST TO KILLING THE OCTOPUS.
SOMETHING ABOUT YOU... LOOKS DIFFERENT...
YOUR EYES? HAIR...?

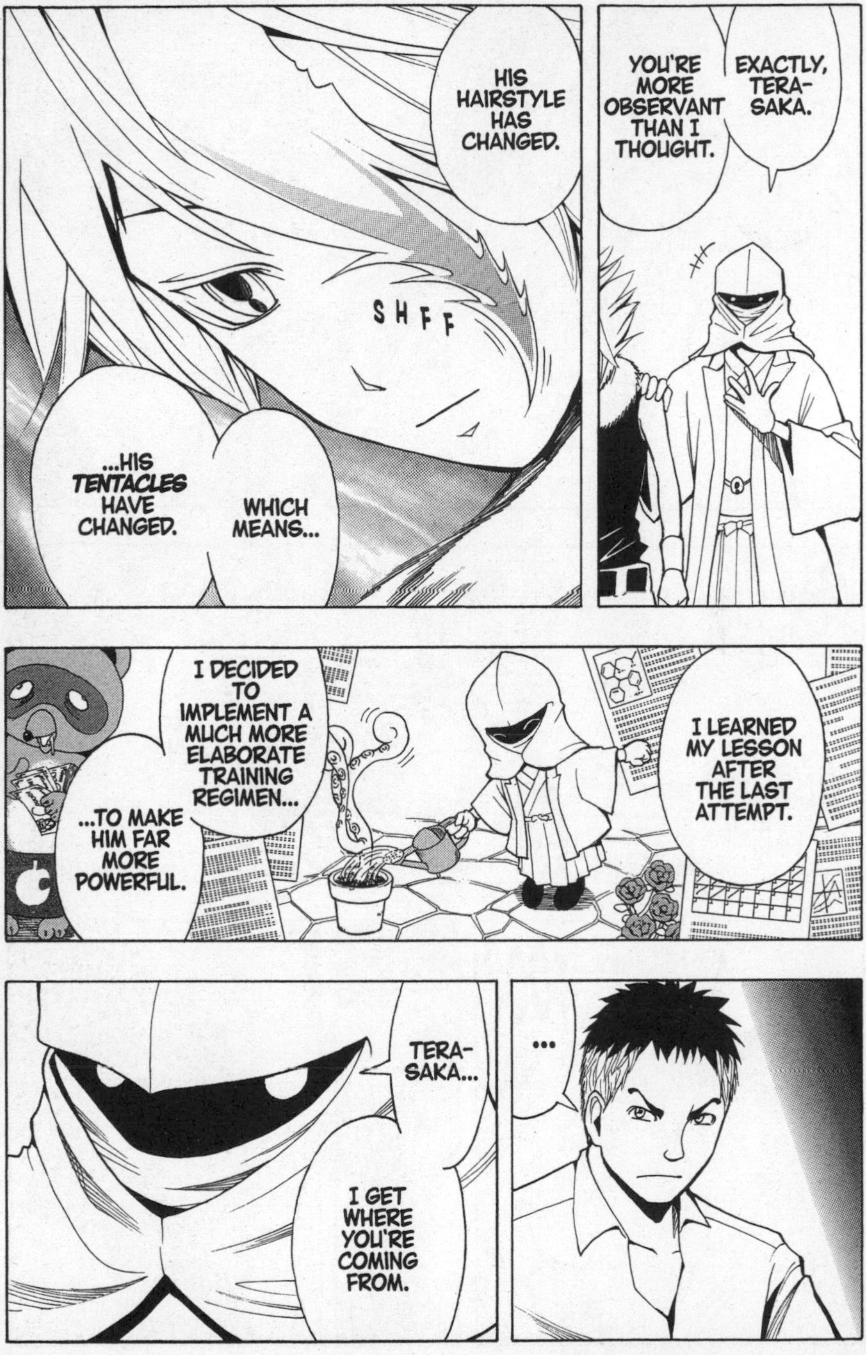
EXACTLY, TERA-SAKA.
YOU'RE MORE OBSERVANT THAN I THOUGHT.
HIS HAIRSTYLE HAS CHANGED.
SHFF
WHICH MEANS...
...HIS *TENTACLES* HAVE CHANGED.
I LEARNED MY LESSON AFTER THE LAST ATTEMPT.
I DECIDED TO IMPLEMENT A MUCH MORE ELABORATE TRAINING REGIMEN...
...TO MAKE HIM FAR MORE POWERFUL.
...
TERA-SAKA...
I GET WHERE YOU'RE COMING FROM.

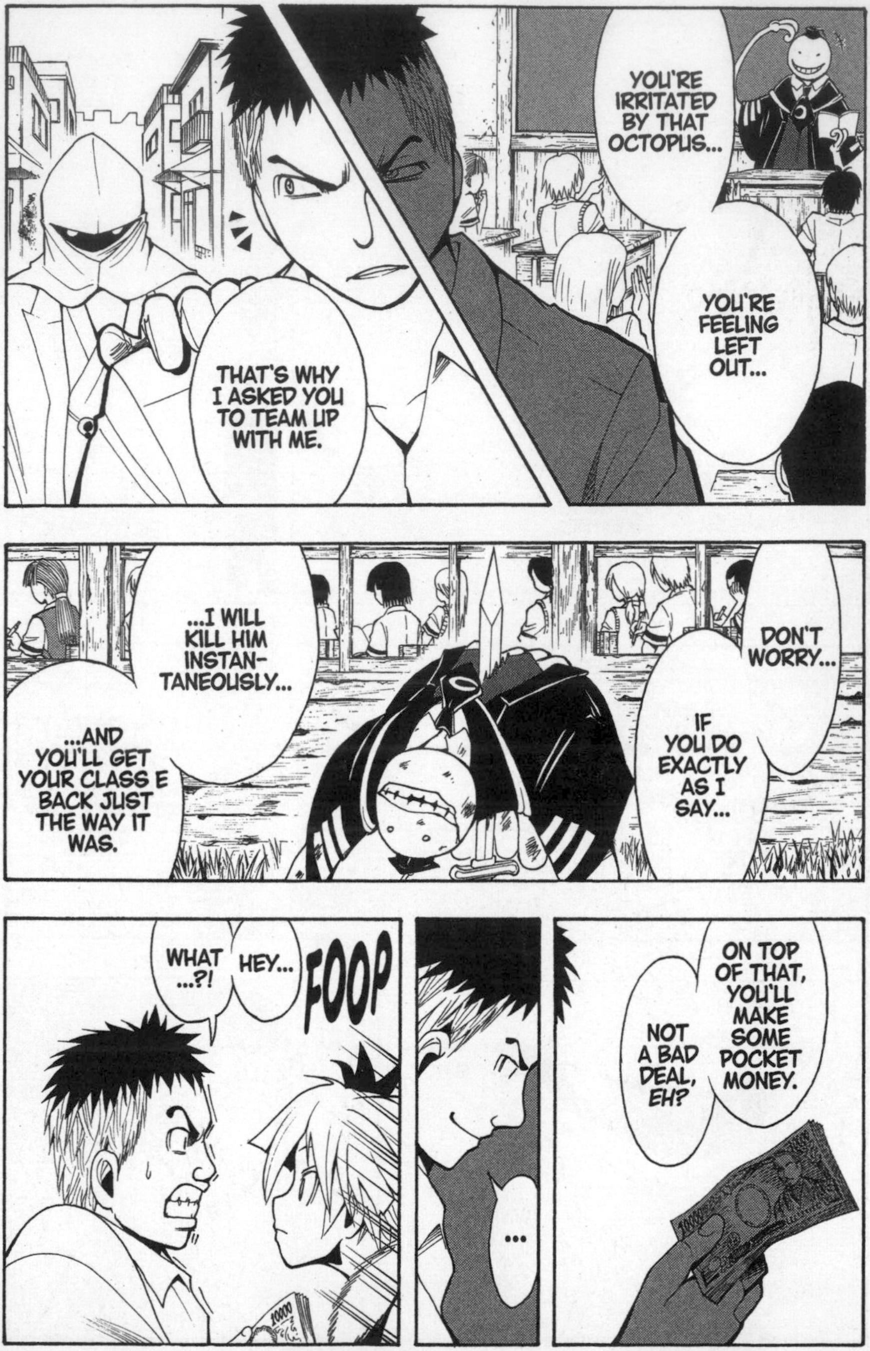
YOU'RE IRRITATED BY THAT OCTOPUS...
YOU'RE FEELING LEFT OUT...
THAT'S WHY I ASKED YOU TO TEAM UP WITH ME.
DON'T WORRY...
IF YOU DO EXACTLY AS I SAY...
...I WILL KILL HIM INSTAN-TANEOUSLY...
...AND YOU'LL GET YOUR CLASS E BACK JUST THE WAY IT WAS.
ON TOP OF THAT, YOU'LL MAKE SOME POCKET MONEY.
NOT A BAD DEAL, EH?
...
FOOP
HEY...
WHAT...?!

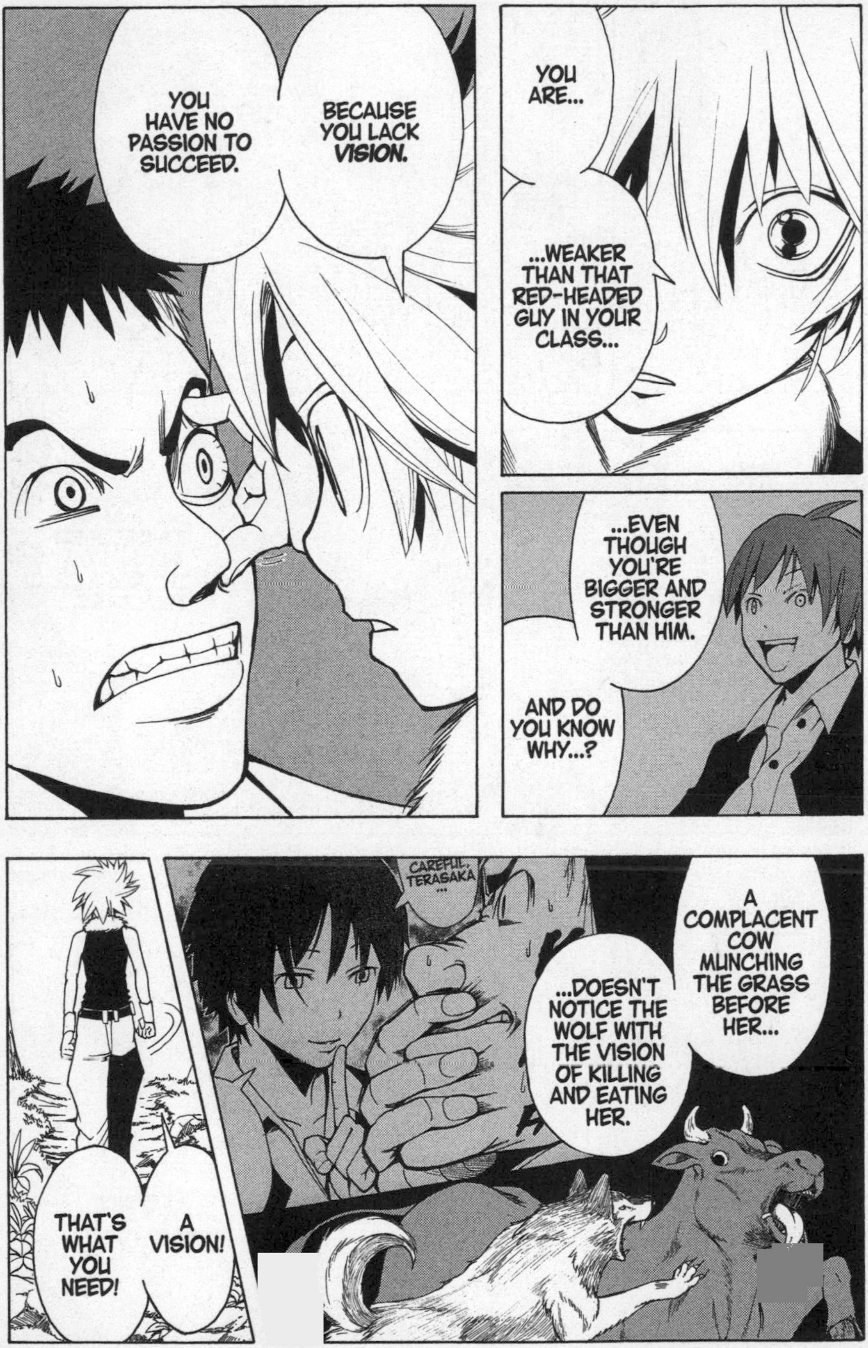
YOU ARE...
...WEAKER THAN THAT RED-HEADED GUY IN YOUR CLASS...
...EVEN THOUGH YOU'RE BIGGER AND STRONGER THAN HIM.
AND DO YOU KNOW WHY...?
BECAUSE YOU LACK **VISION.**
YOU HAVE NO PASSION TO SUCCEED.
A COMPLACENT COW MUNCHING THE GRASS BEFORE HER...
...DOESN'T NOTICE THE WOLF WITH THE VISION OF KILLING AND EATING HER.
CAREFUL, TERASAKA...
A VISION!
THAT'S WHAT YOU NEED!

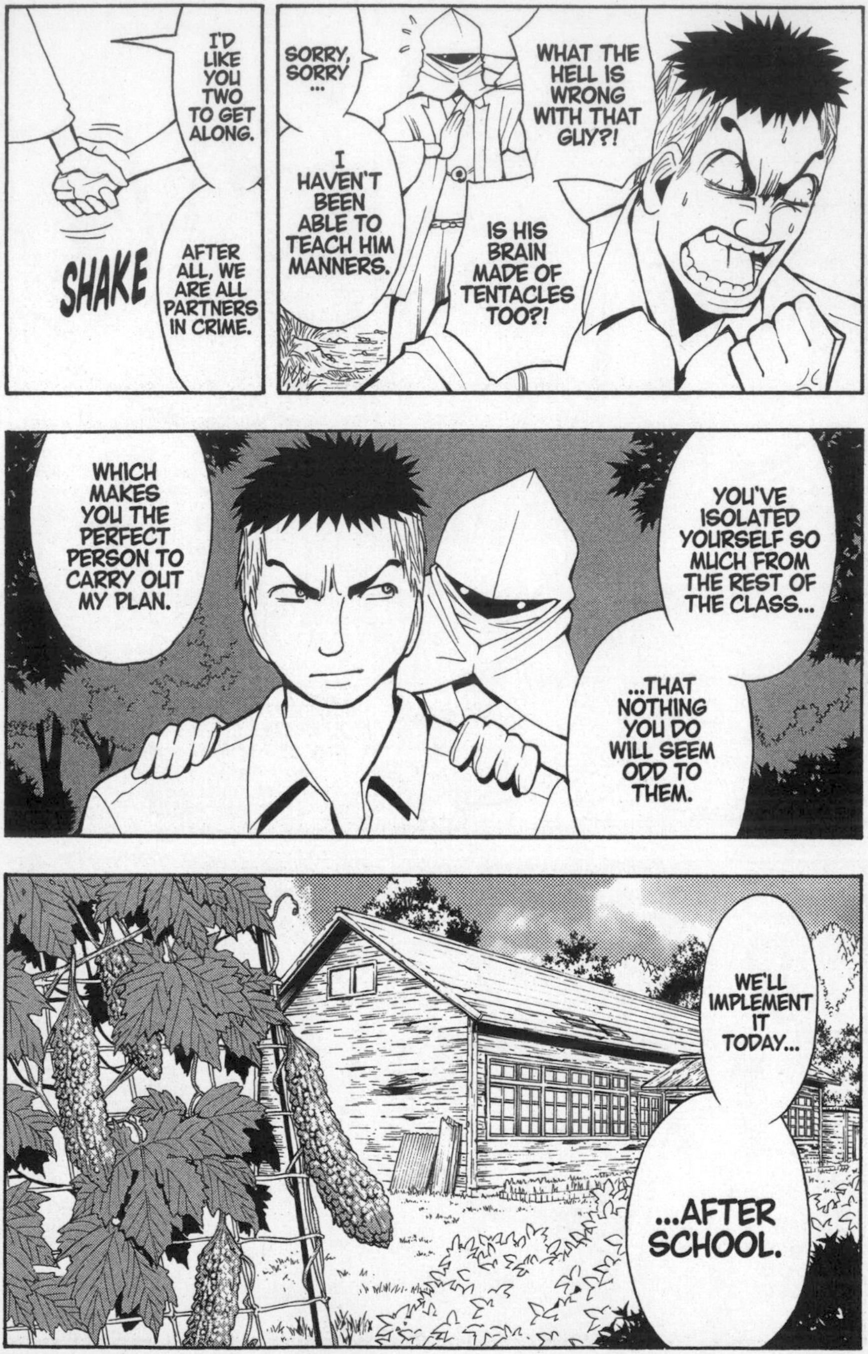
WHAT THE HELL IS WRONG WITH THAT GUY?!
IS HIS BRAIN MADE OF TENTACLES TOO?!
SORRY, SORRY...
I HAVEN'T BEEN ABLE TO TEACH HIM MANNERS.
I'D LIKE YOU TWO TO GET ALONG.
AFTER ALL, WE ARE ALL PARTNERS IN CRIME.
SHAKE
YOU'VE ISOLATED YOURSELF SO MUCH FROM THE REST OF THE CLASS...
...THAT NOTHING YOU DO WILL SEEM ODD TO THEM.
WHICH MAKES YOU THE PERFECT PERSON TO CARRY OUT MY PLAN.
WE'LL IMPLEMENT IT TODAY...
...AFTER SCHOOL.

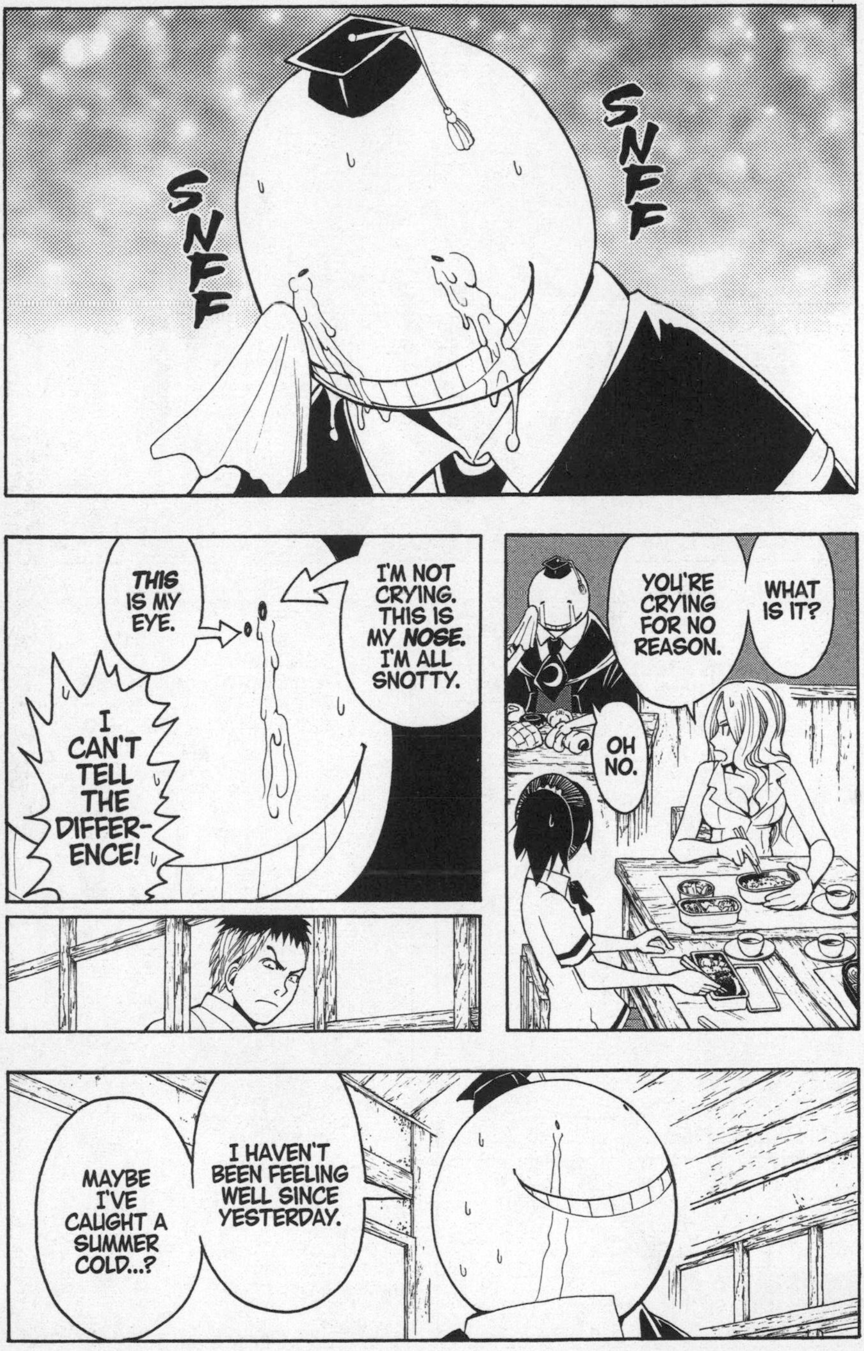
SNFF
SNFF
WHAT IS IT?
YOU'RE CRYING FOR NO REASON.
OH NO.
I'M NOT CRYING. THIS IS MY *NOSE*. I'M ALL SNOTTY.
THIS IS MY EYE.
I CAN'T TELL THE DIFFERENCE!
I HAVEN'T BEEN FEELING WELL SINCE YESTERDAY.
MAYBE I'VE CAUGHT A SUMMER COLD...?

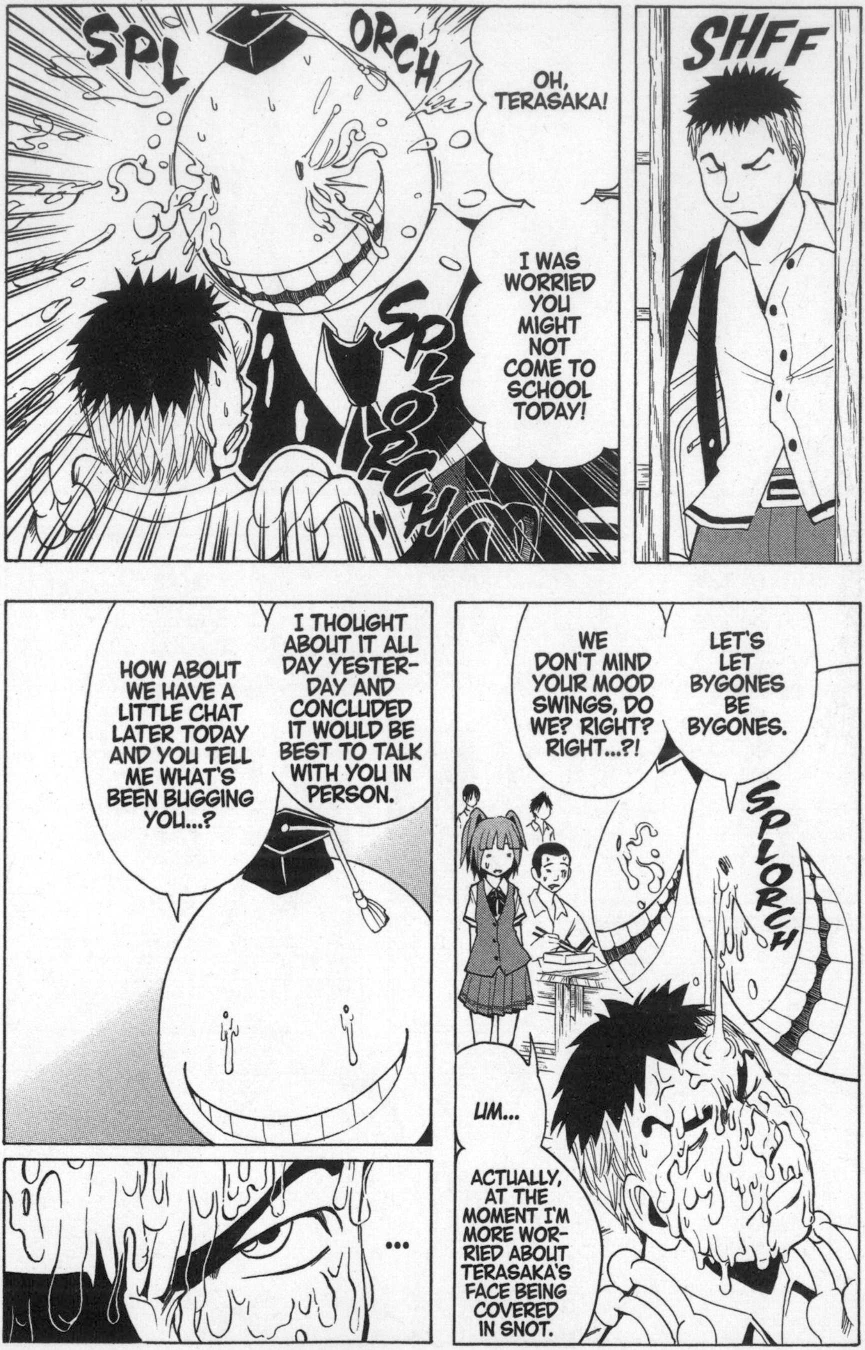
SHFF
OH, TERASAKA!
I WAS WORRIED YOU MIGHT NOT COME TO SCHOOL TODAY!
SPL
ORCH
SPLORCH
LET'S LET BYGONES BE BYGONES.
WE DON'T MIND YOUR MOOD SWINGS, DO WE? RIGHT? RIGHT...?!
SPLORCH
UM...
ACTUALLY, AT THE MOMENT I'M MORE WORRIED ABOUT TERASAKA'S FACE BEING COVERED IN SNOT.
I THOUGHT ABOUT IT ALL DAY YESTERDAY AND CONCLUDED IT WOULD BE BEST TO TALK WITH YOU IN PERSON.
HOW ABOUT WE HAVE A LITTLE CHAT LATER TODAY AND YOU TELL ME WHAT'S BEEN BUGGING YOU...?
...

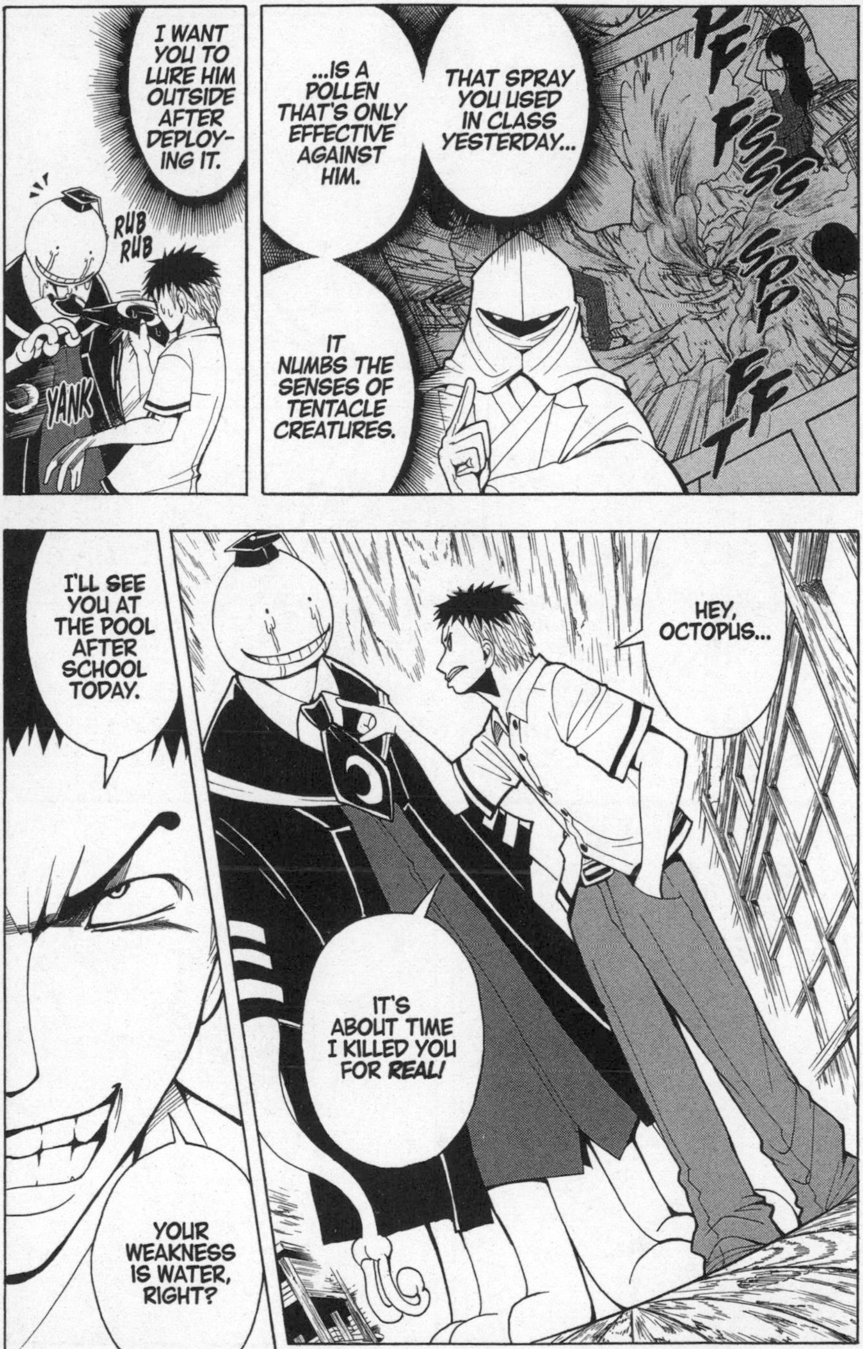
PFFFSSSSPPFFT
THAT SPRAY YOU USED IN CLASS YESTERDAY...
...IS A POLLEN THAT'S ONLY EFFECTIVE AGAINST HIM.
IT NUMBS THE SENSES OF TENTACLE CREATURES.
I WANT YOU TO LURE HIM OUTSIDE AFTER DEPLOYING IT.
RUB RUB
YANK
HEY, OCTOPUS...
IT'S ABOUT TIME I KILLED YOU FOR REAL!
I'LL SEE YOU AT THE POOL AFTER SCHOOL TODAY.
YOUR WEAKNESS IS WATER, RIGHT?

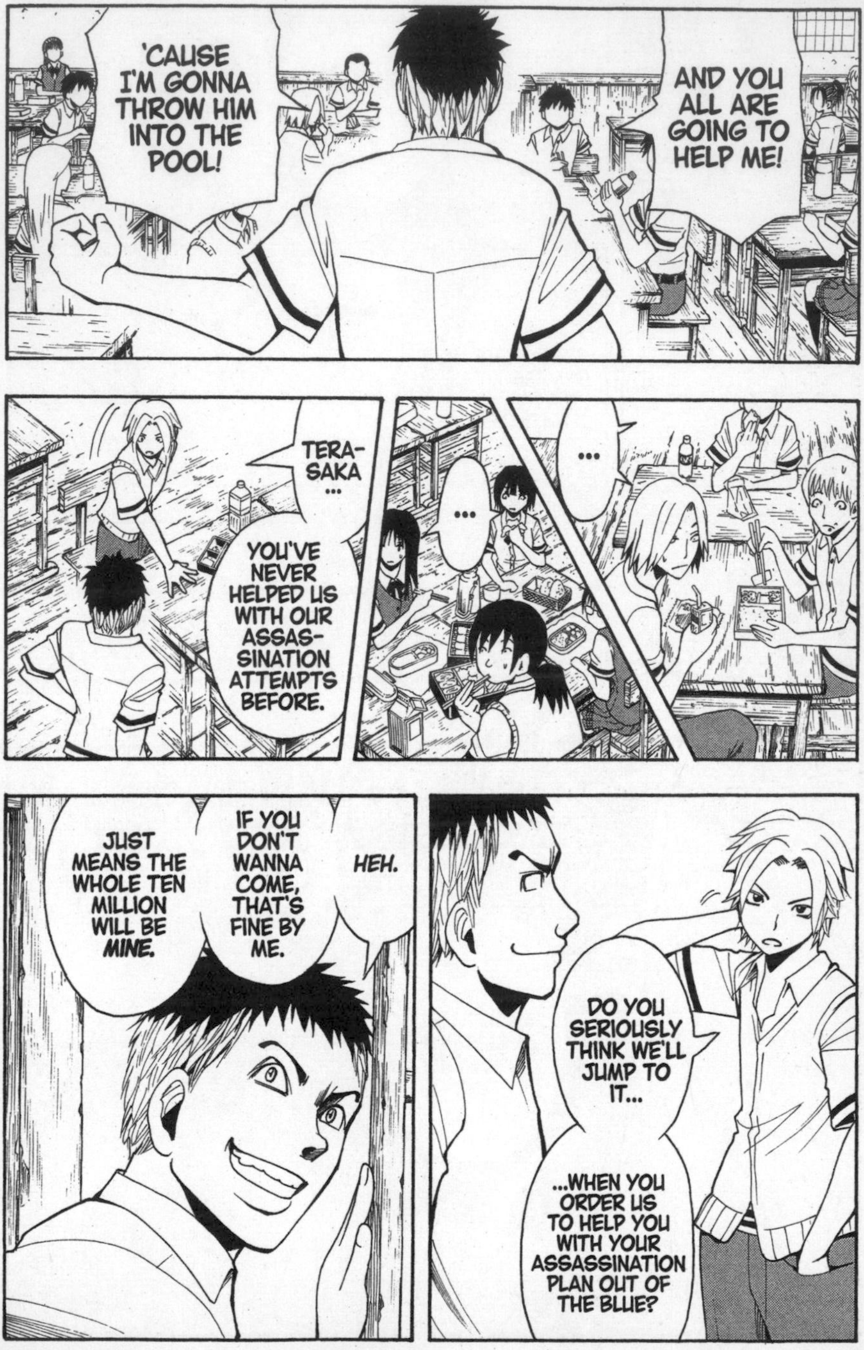
AND YOU ALL ARE GOING TO HELP ME!
'CAUSE I'M GONNA THROW HIM INTO THE POOL!
...
...
TERA-SAKA...
YOU'VE NEVER HELPED US WITH OUR ASSAS-SINATION ATTEMPTS BEFORE.
DO YOU SERIOUSLY THINK WE'LL JUMP TO IT...
...WHEN YOU ORDER US TO HELP YOU WITH YOUR ASSASSINATION PLAN OUT OF THE BLUE?
HEH.
IF YOU DON'T WANNA COME, THAT'S FINE BY ME.
JUST MEANS THE WHOLE TEN MILLION WILL BE *MINE.*

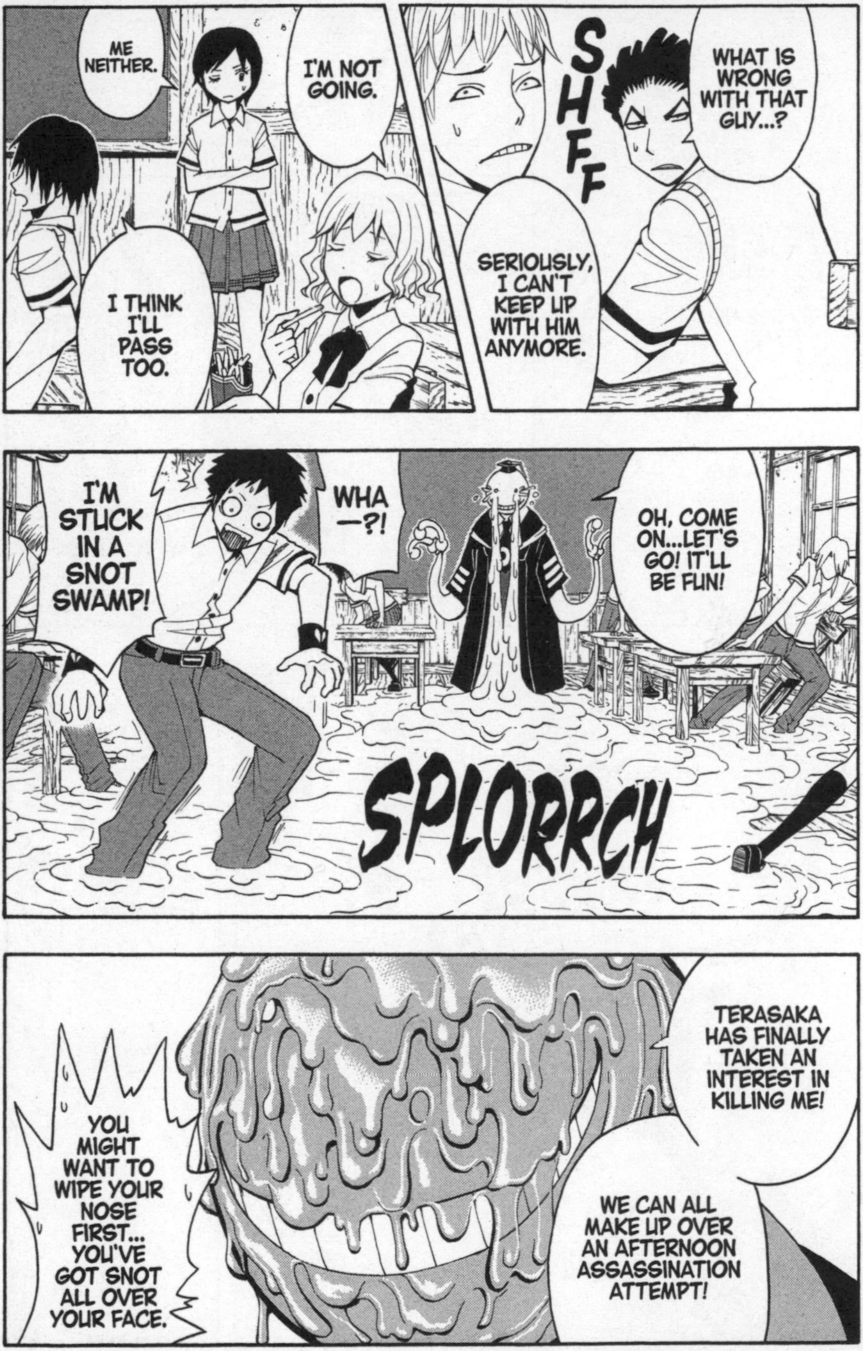
WHAT IS WRONG WITH THAT GUY...?
SHFF
SERIOUSLY, I CAN'T KEEP UP WITH HIM ANYMORE.
I'M NOT GOING.
ME NEITHER.
I THINK I'LL PASS TOO.
OH, COME ON...LET'S GO! IT'LL BE FUN!
SPLORRCH
WHA—?!
I'M STUCK IN A SNOT SWAMP!
TERASAKA HAS FINALLY TAKEN AN INTEREST IN KILLING ME!
WE CAN ALL MAKE UP OVER AN AFTERNOON ASSASSINATION ATTEMPT!
YOU MIGHT WANT TO WIPE YOUR NOSE FIRST... YOU'VE GOT SNOT ALL OVER YOUR FACE.

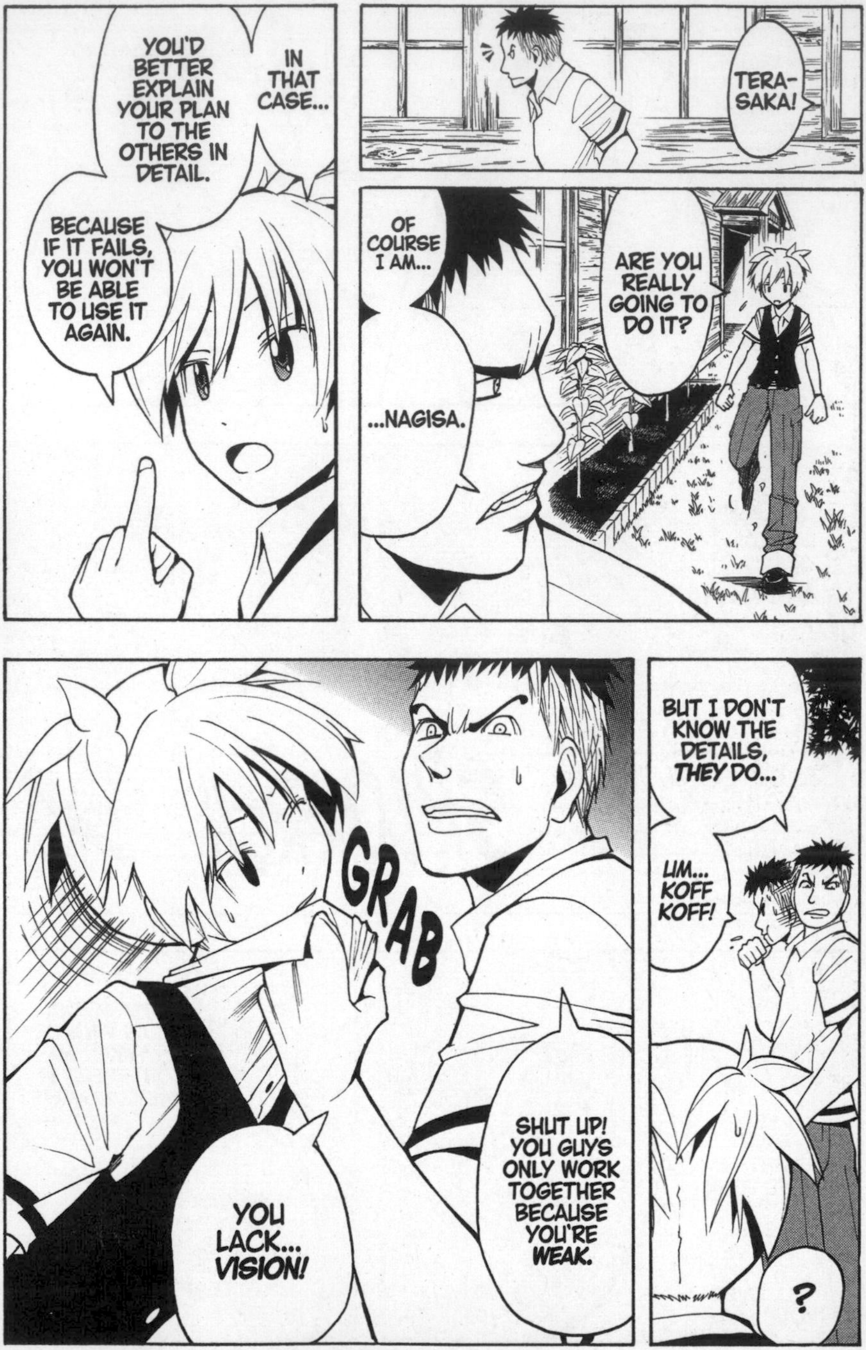
TERA-SAKA!
ARE YOU REALLY GOING TO DO IT?
OF COURSE I AM...
...NAGISA.
IN THAT CASE...
YOU'D BETTER EXPLAIN YOUR PLAN TO THE OTHERS IN DETAIL.
BECAUSE IF IT FAILS, YOU WON'T BE ABLE TO USE IT AGAIN.
BUT I DON'T KNOW THE DETAILS, *THEY DO*...
UM... KOFF KOFF!
?
GRAB
SHUT UP! YOU GUYS ONLY WORK TOGETHER BECAUSE YOU'RE *WEAK*.
YOU LACK... *VISION*!

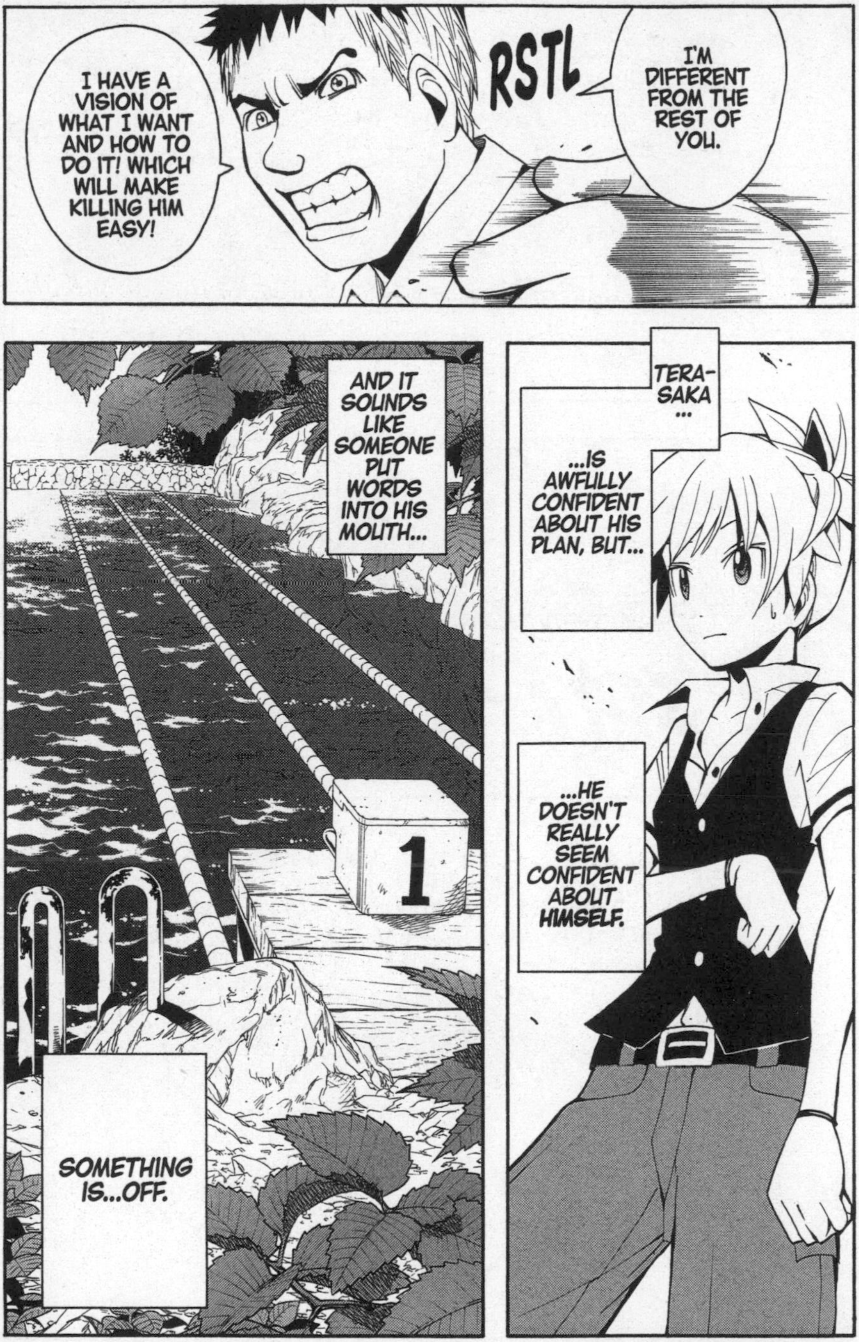
I'M DIFFERENT FROM THE REST OF YOU.
RSTL
I HAVE A VISION OF WHAT I WANT AND HOW TO DO IT! WHICH WILL MAKE KILLING HIM EASY!
TERA-SAKA ...
...IS AWFULLY CONFIDENT ABOUT HIS PLAN, BUT...
...HE DOESN'T REALLY SEEM CONFIDENT ABOUT HIMSELF.
AND IT SOUNDS LIKE SOMEONE PUT WORDS INTO HIS MOUTH...
1
SOMETHING IS...OFF.

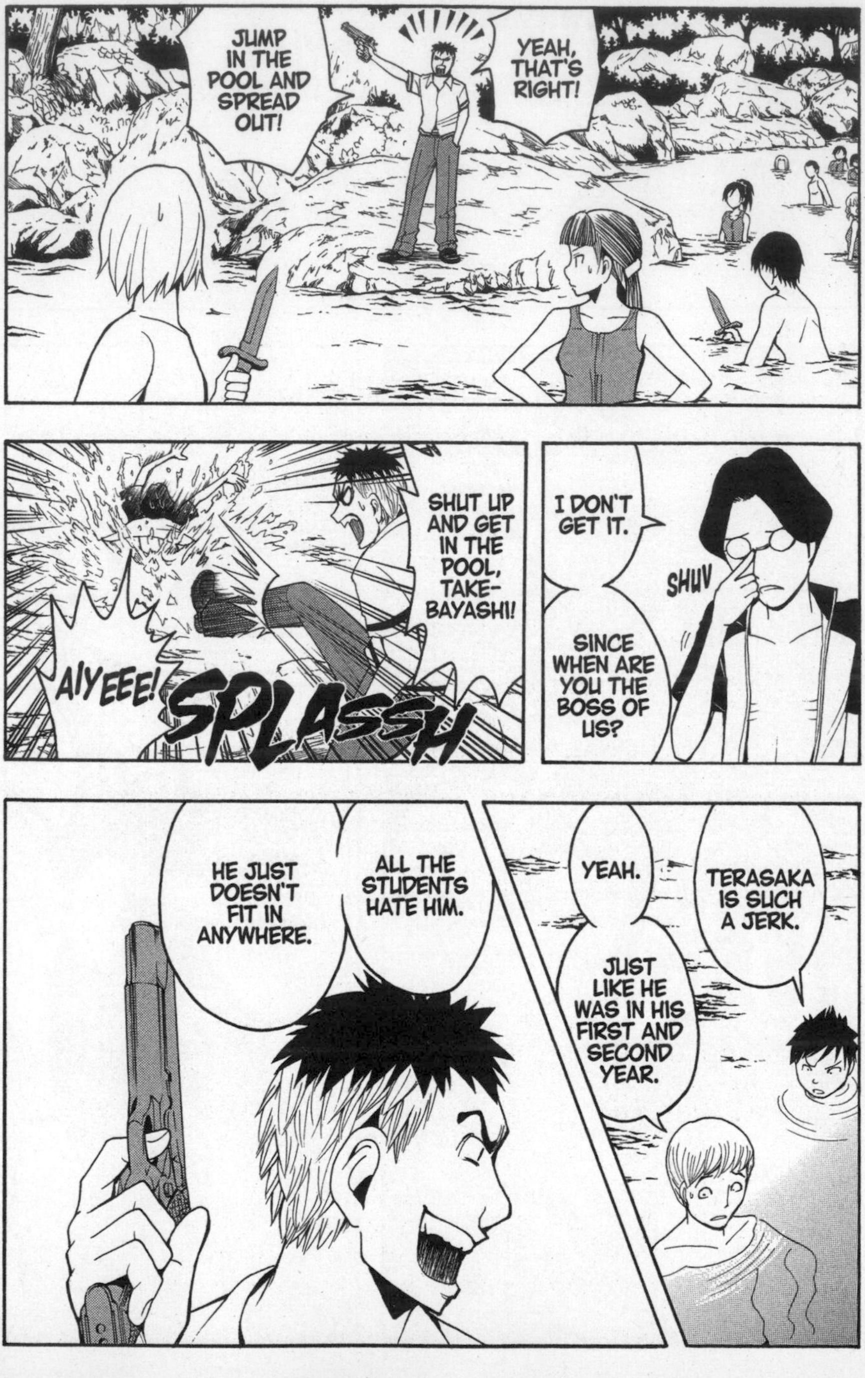
YEAH, THAT'S RIGHT!
JUMP IN THE POOL AND SPREAD OUT!
I DON'T GET IT.
SHUV
SINCE WHEN ARE YOU THE BOSS OF US?
SHUT UP AND GET IN THE POOL, TAKE-BAYASHI!
AIYEEE!
SPLASSH
TERASAKA IS SUCH A JERK.
YEAH.
JUST LIKE HE WAS IN HIS FIRST AND SECOND YEAR.
ALL THE STUDENTS HATE HIM.
HE JUST DOESN'T FIT IN ANYWHERE.

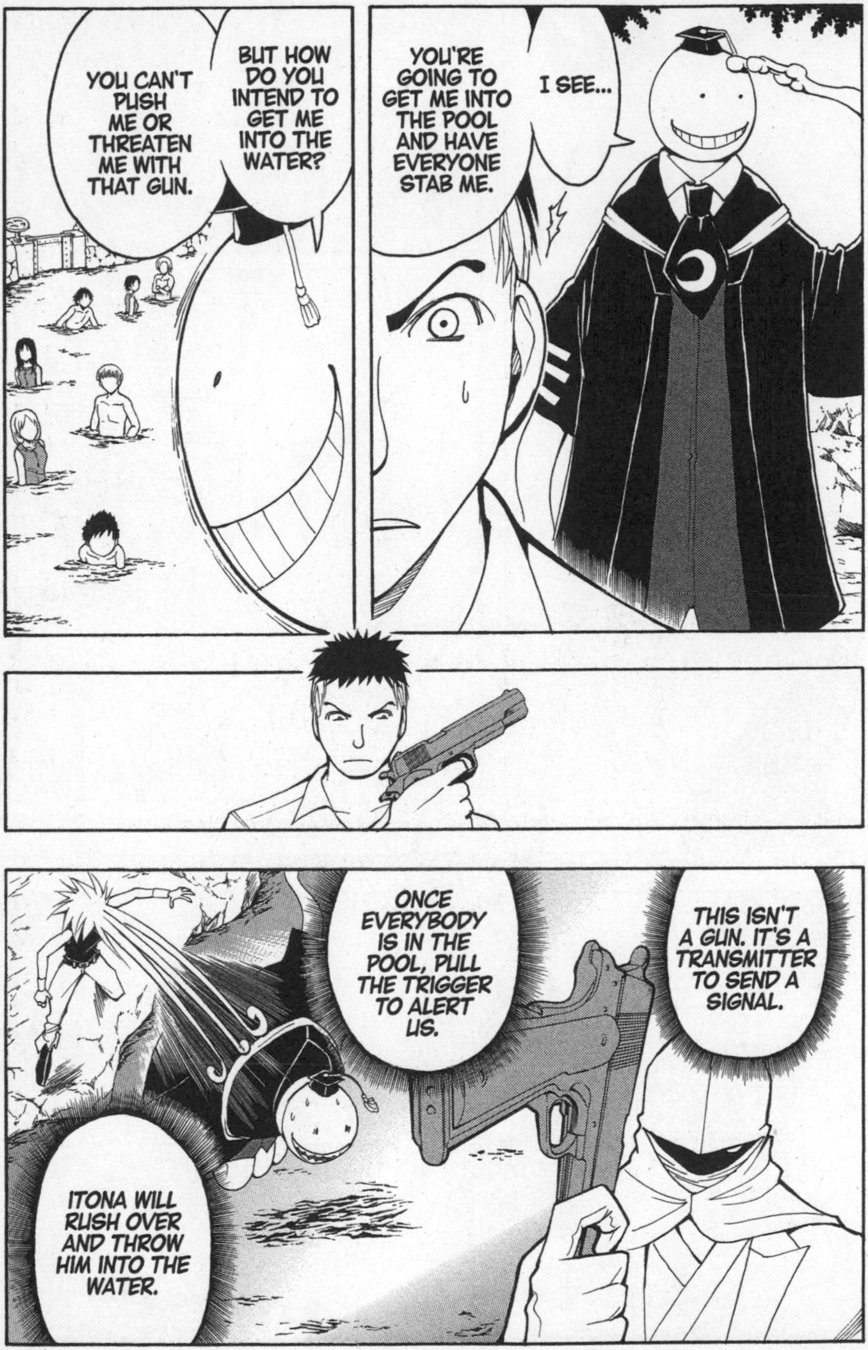
I SEE...
YOU'RE GOING TO GET ME INTO THE POOL AND HAVE EVERYONE STAB ME.
BUT HOW DO YOU INTEND TO GET ME INTO THE WATER?
YOU CAN'T PUSH ME OR THREATEN ME WITH THAT GUN.
THIS ISN'T A GUN. IT'S A TRANSMITTER TO SEND A SIGNAL.
ONCE EVERYBODY IS IN THE POOL, PULL THE TRIGGER TO ALERT US.
ITONA WILL RUSH OVER AND THROW HIM INTO THE WATER.

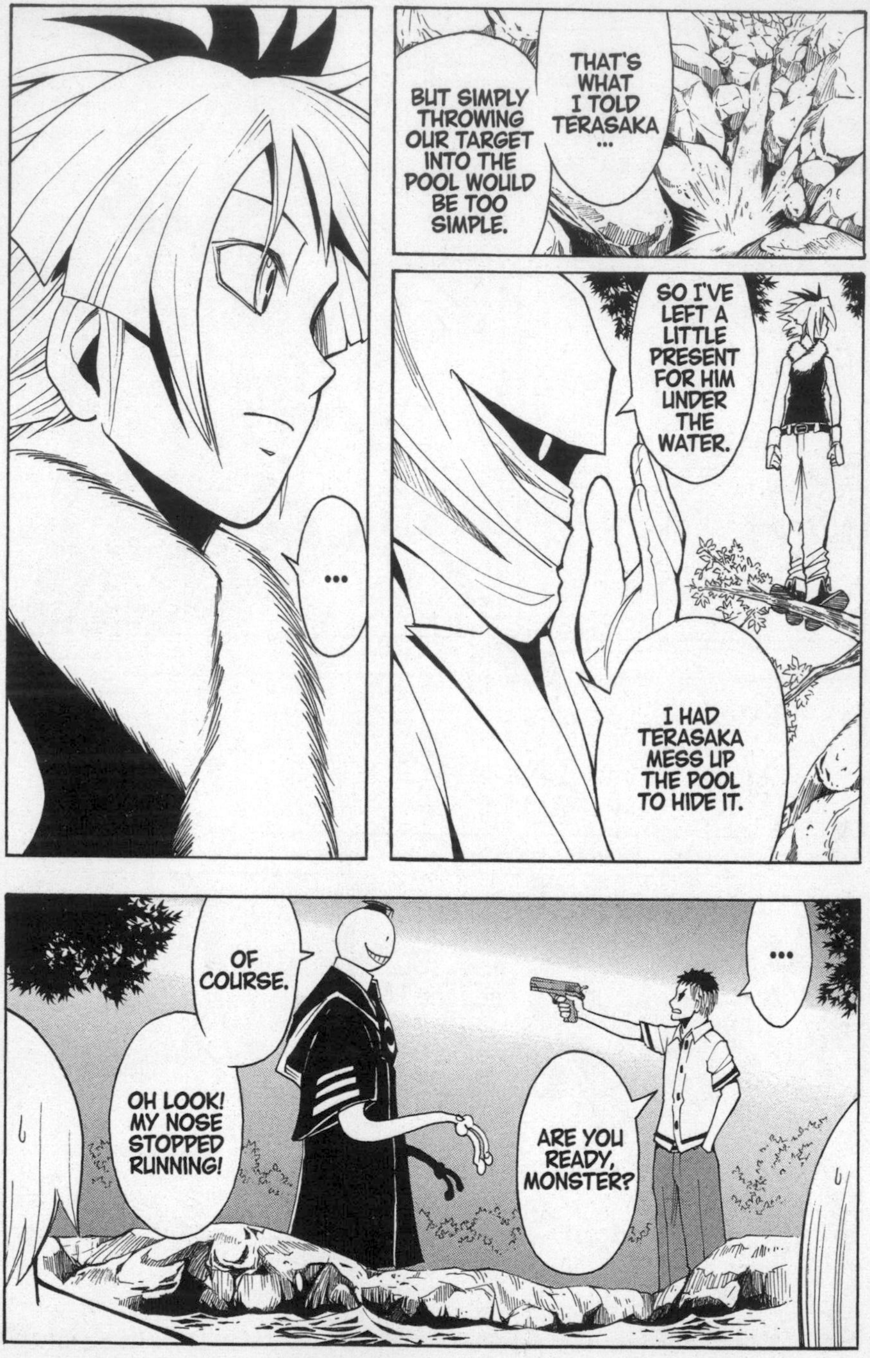
THAT'S WHAT I TOLD TERASAKA...
BUT SIMPLY THROWING OUR TARGET INTO THE POOL WOULD BE TOO SIMPLE.
SO I'VE LEFT A LITTLE PRESENT FOR HIM UNDER THE WATER.
I HAD TERASAKA MESS UP THE POOL TO HIDE IT.
...
...
ARE YOU READY, MONSTER?
OF COURSE.
OH LOOK! MY NOSE STOPPED RUNNING!

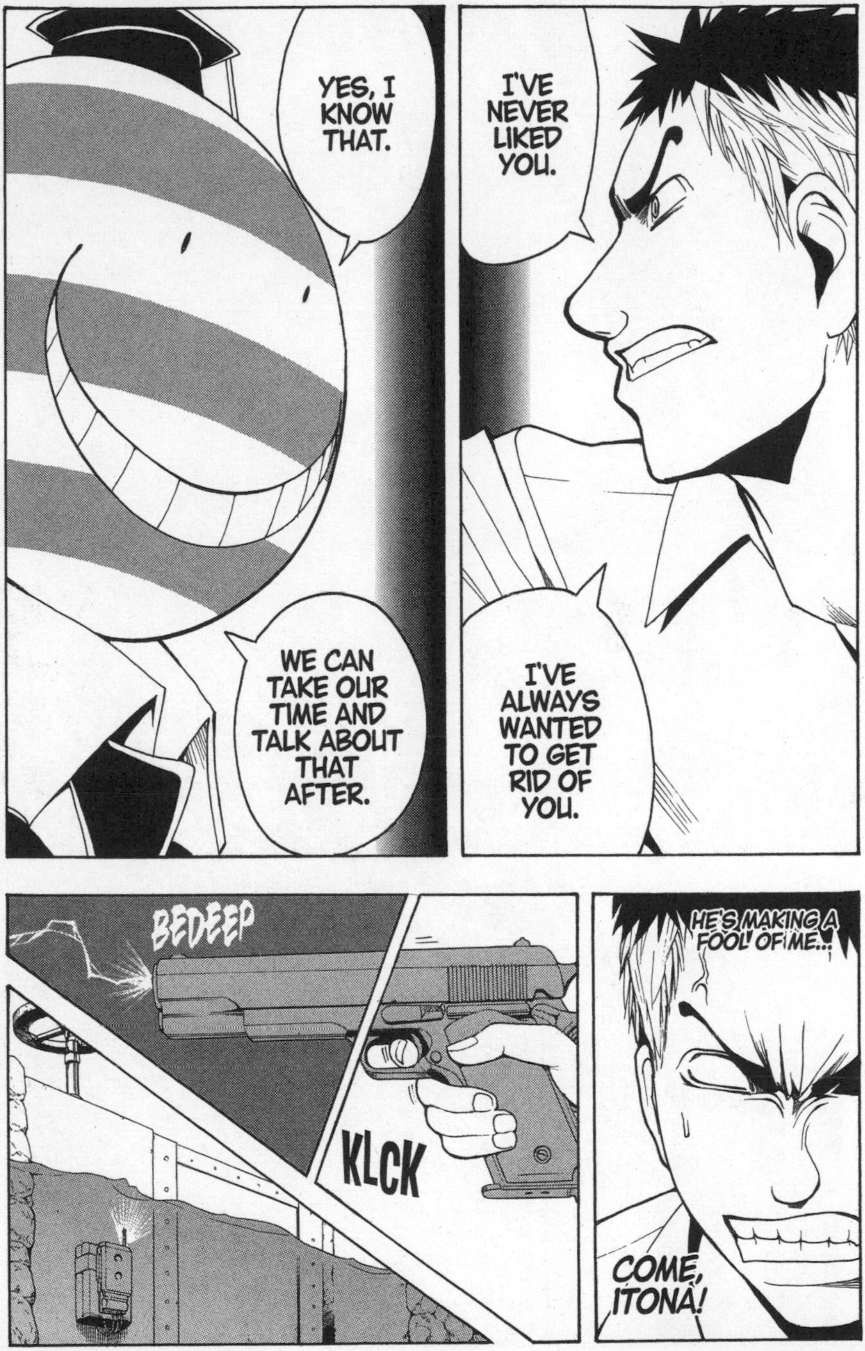
I'VE NEVER LIKED YOU.
I'VE ALWAYS WANTED TO GET RID OF YOU.
YES, I KNOW THAT.
WE CAN TAKE OUR TIME AND TALK ABOUT THAT AFTER.
HE'S MAKING A FOOL OF ME...
COME, ITONA!
BEDEEP
KLCK

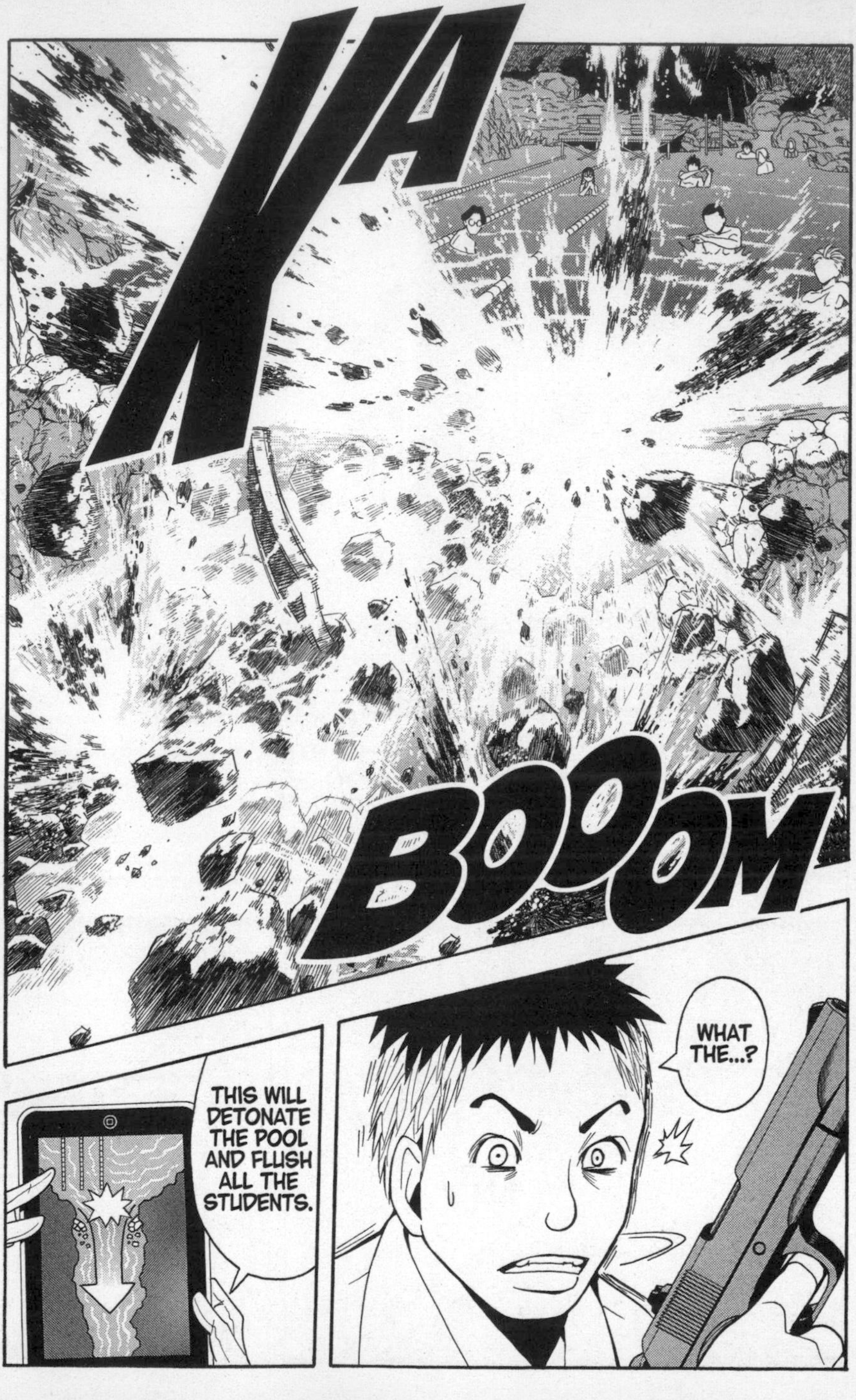
KA
BOOOM
WHAT THE...?
THIS WILL DETONATE THE POOL AND FLUSH ALL THE STUDENTS.

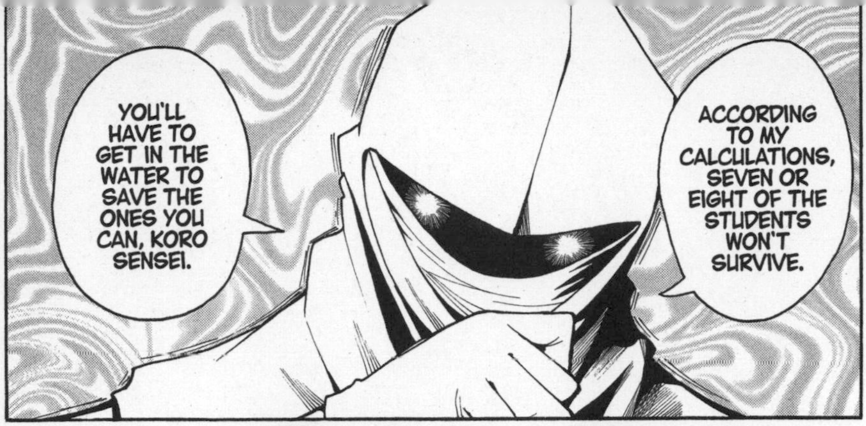
ACCORDING TO MY CALCULATIONS, SEVEN OR EIGHT OF THE STUDENTS WON'T SURVIVE.
YOU'LL HAVE TO GET IN THE WATER TO SAVE THE ONES YOU CAN, KORO SENSEI.
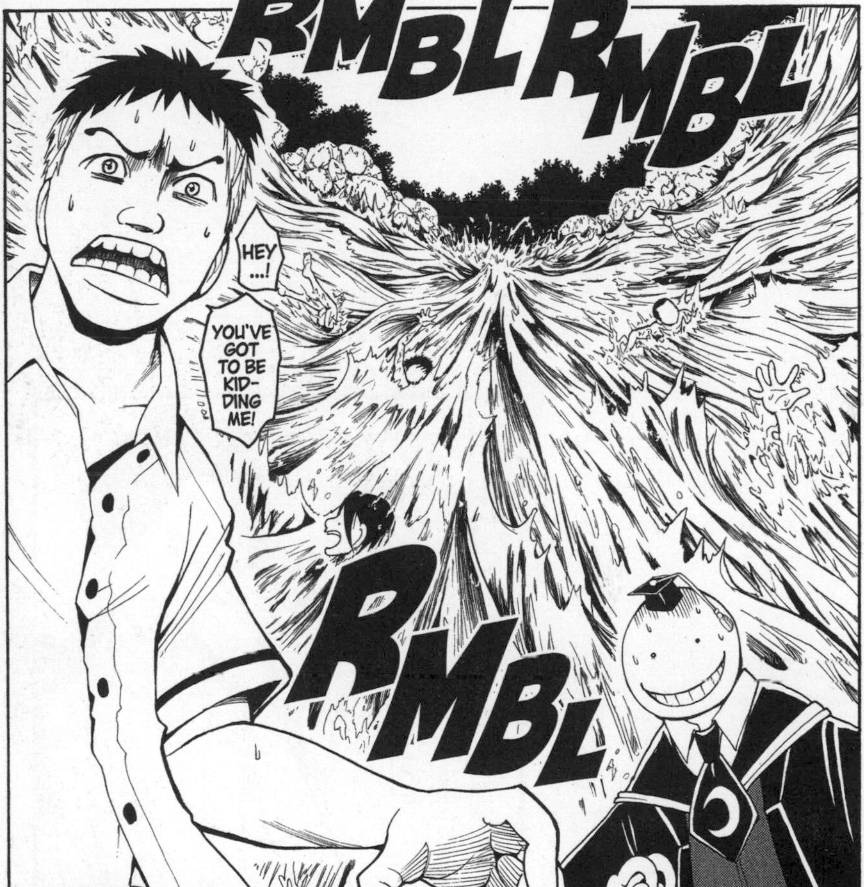
RMBL RMBL
HEY ...!
YOU'VE GOT TO BE KID-DING ME!
RMBL

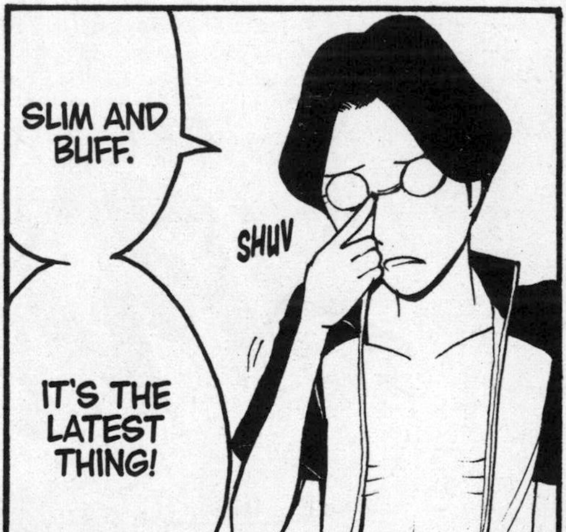
SLIM AND BUFF.
IT'S THE LATEST THING!
SHUV

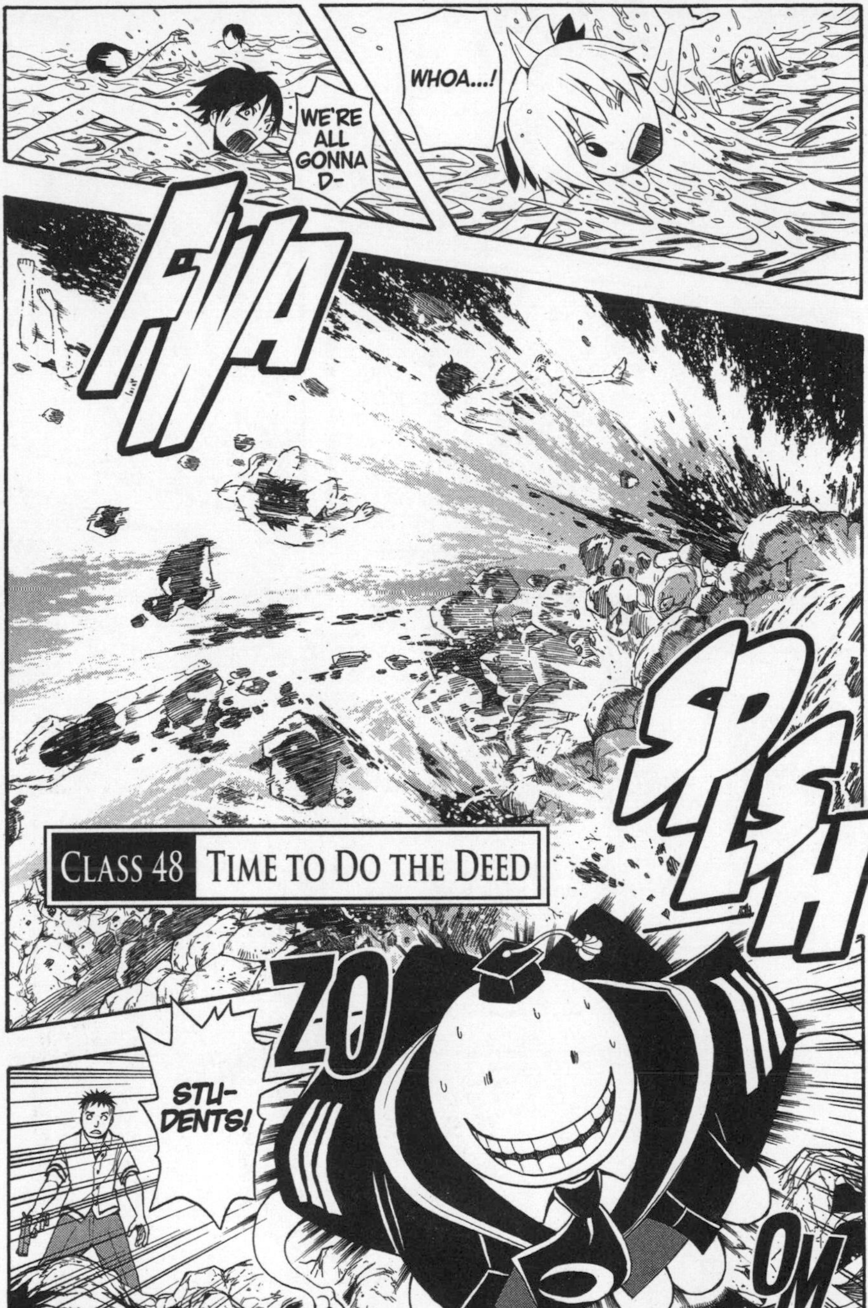
WHOA...!
WE'RE ALL GONNA D-
FWA
SPLSH
CLASS 48 TIME TO DO THE DEED
ZOOM
STU-DENTS!

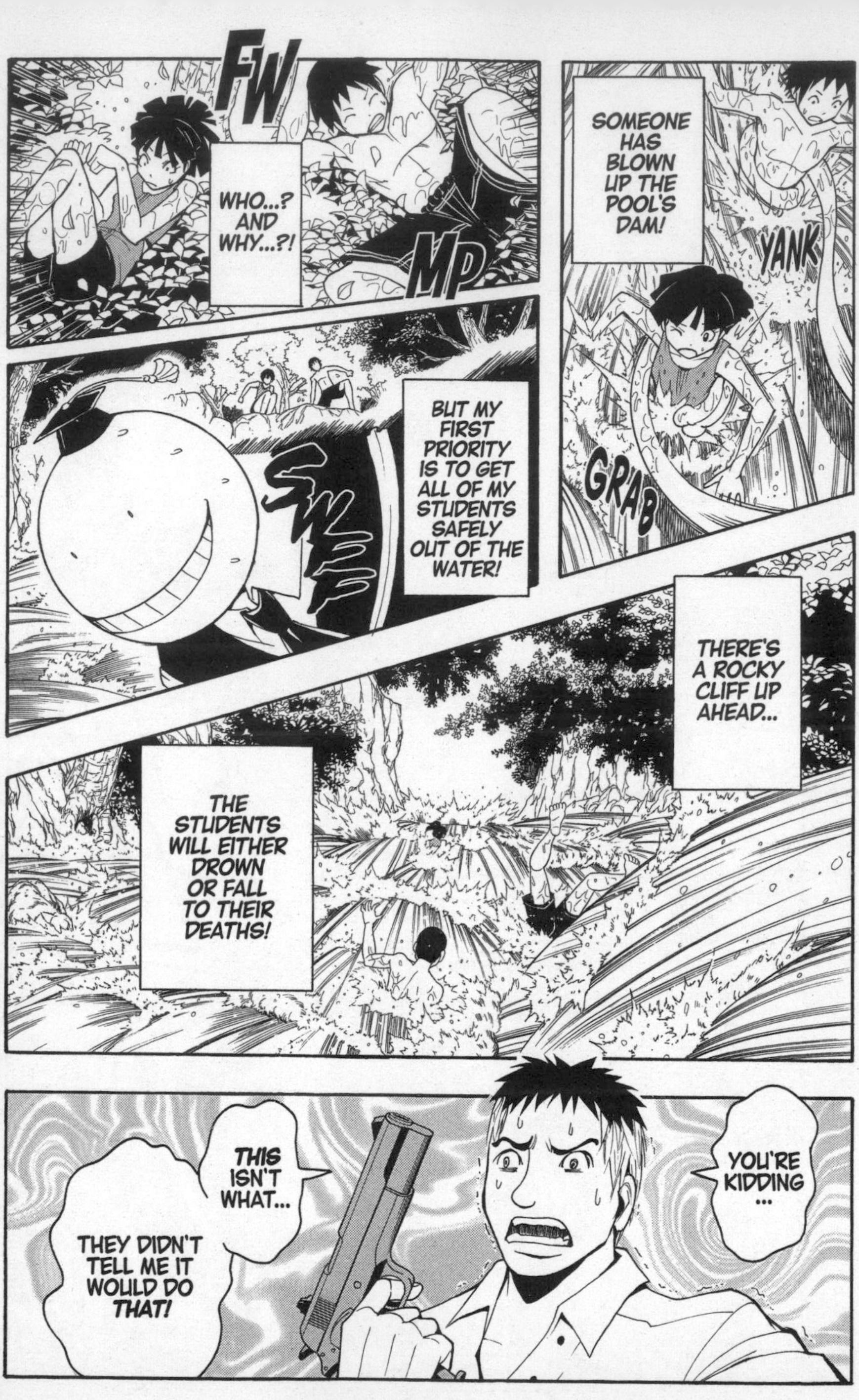
SOMEONE HAS BLOWN UP THE POOL'S DAM!
YANK
GRAB
FW
WHO...? AND WHY...?!
MP
BUT MY FIRST PRIORITY IS TO GET ALL OF MY STUDENTS SAFELY OUT OF THE WATER!
THERE'S A ROCKY CLIFF UP AHEAD...
THE STUDENTS WILL EITHER DROWN OR FALL TO THEIR DEATHS!
YOU'RE KIDDING ...
THIS ISN'T WHAT...
THEY DIDN'T TELL ME IT WOULD DO THAT!

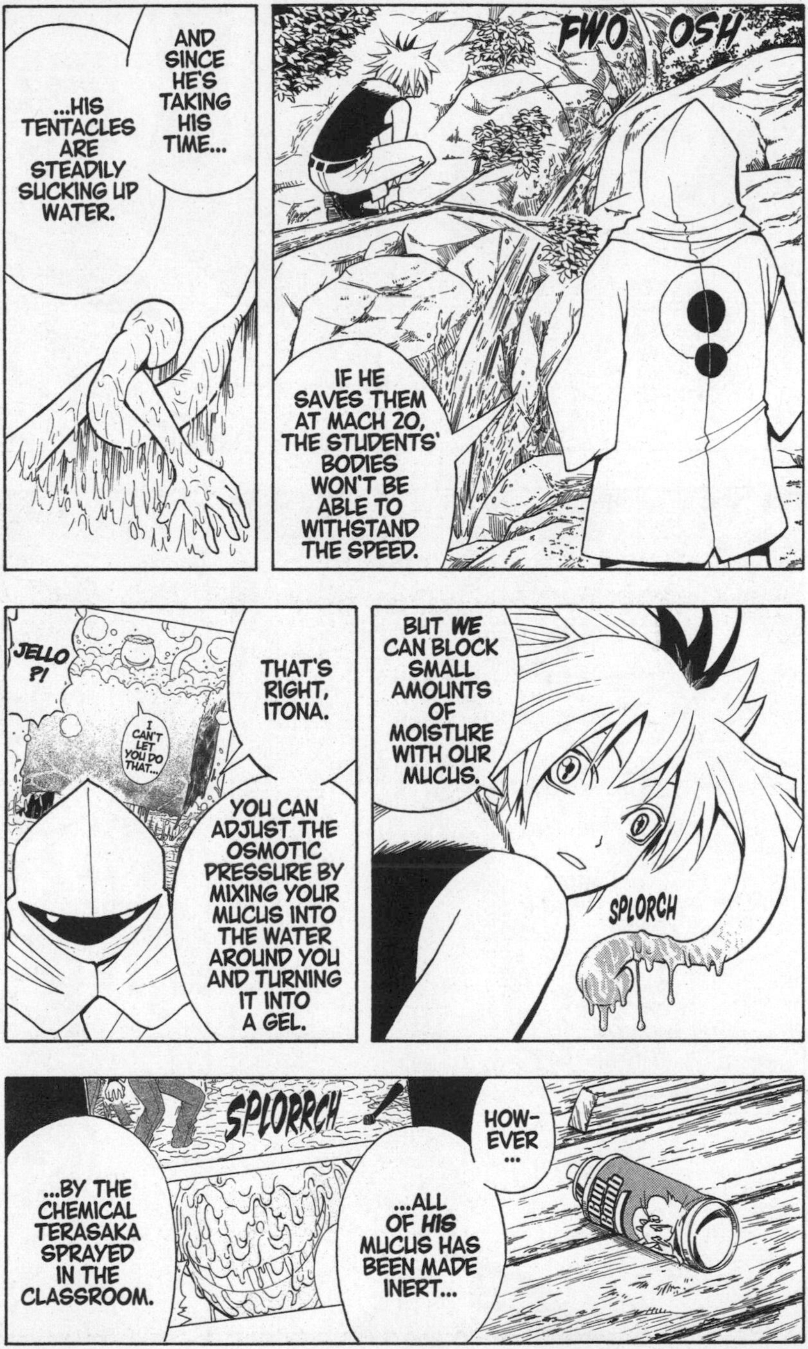
FWO OSH
IF HE SAVES THEM AT MACH 20, THE STUDENTS' BODIES WON'T BE ABLE TO WITHSTAND THE SPEED.
AND SINCE HE'S TAKING HIS TIME...
...HIS TENTACLES ARE STEADILY SUCKING UP WATER.
BUT WE CAN BLOCK SMALL AMOUNTS OF MOISTURE WITH OUR MUCUS.
SPLORCH
THAT'S RIGHT, ITONA.
JELLO ?!
I CAN'T LET YOU DO THAT...
YOU CAN ADJUST THE OSMOTIC PRESSURE BY MIXING YOUR MUCUS INTO THE WATER AROUND YOU AND TURNING IT INTO A GEL.
HOW-EVER ...
SPLORRCH
...ALL OF HIS MUCUS HAS BEEN MADE INERT...
...BY THE CHEMICAL TERASAKA SPRAYED IN THE CLASSROOM.

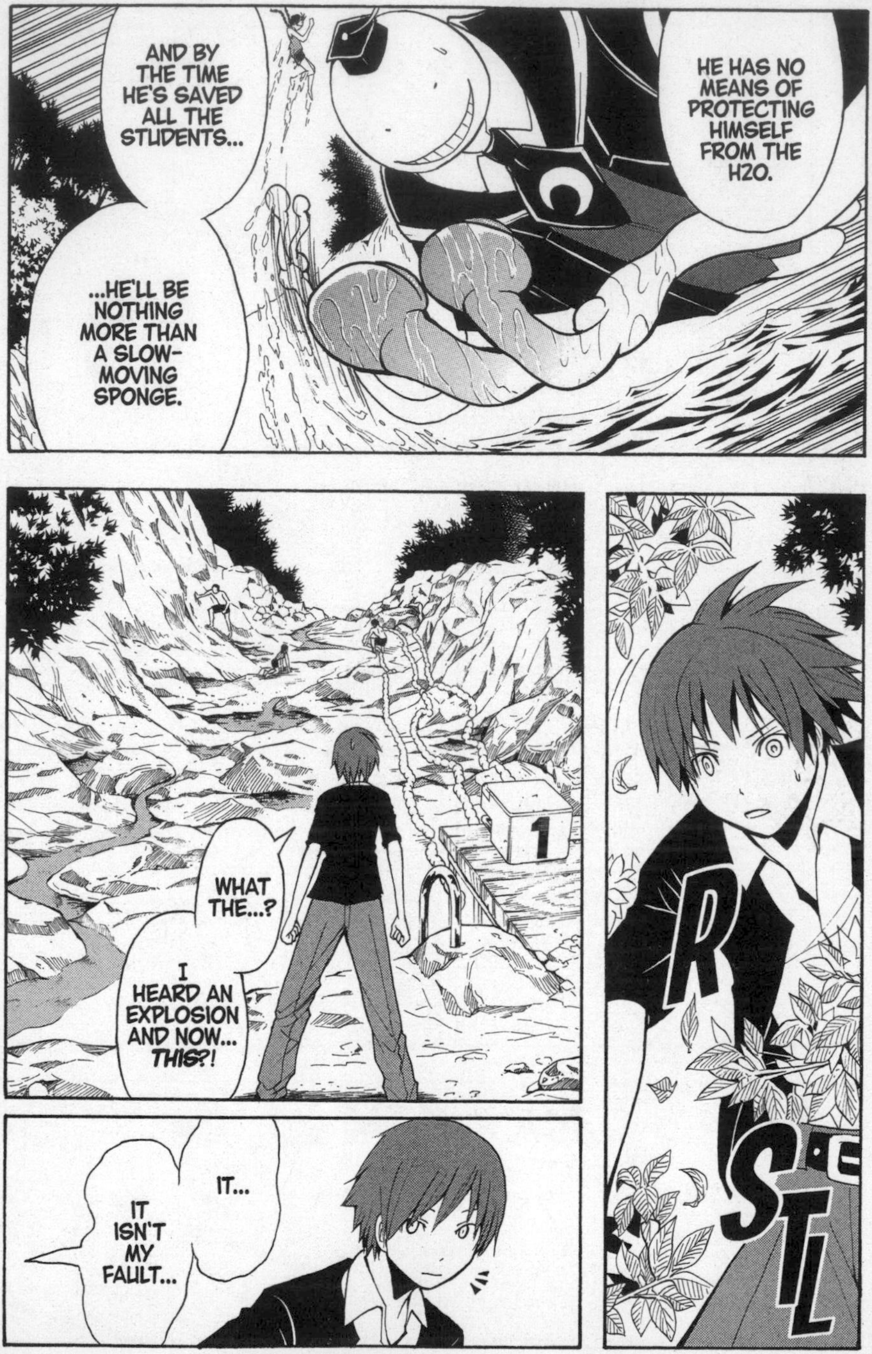
HE HAS NO MEANS OF PROTECTING HIMSELF FROM THE H2O.
AND BY THE TIME HE'S SAVED ALL THE STUDENTS...
...HE'LL BE NOTHING MORE THAN A SLOW-MOVING SPONGE.
RSTL
WHAT THE...?
I HEARD AN EXPLOSION AND NOW... THIS?!
IT...
IT ISN'T MY FAULT...

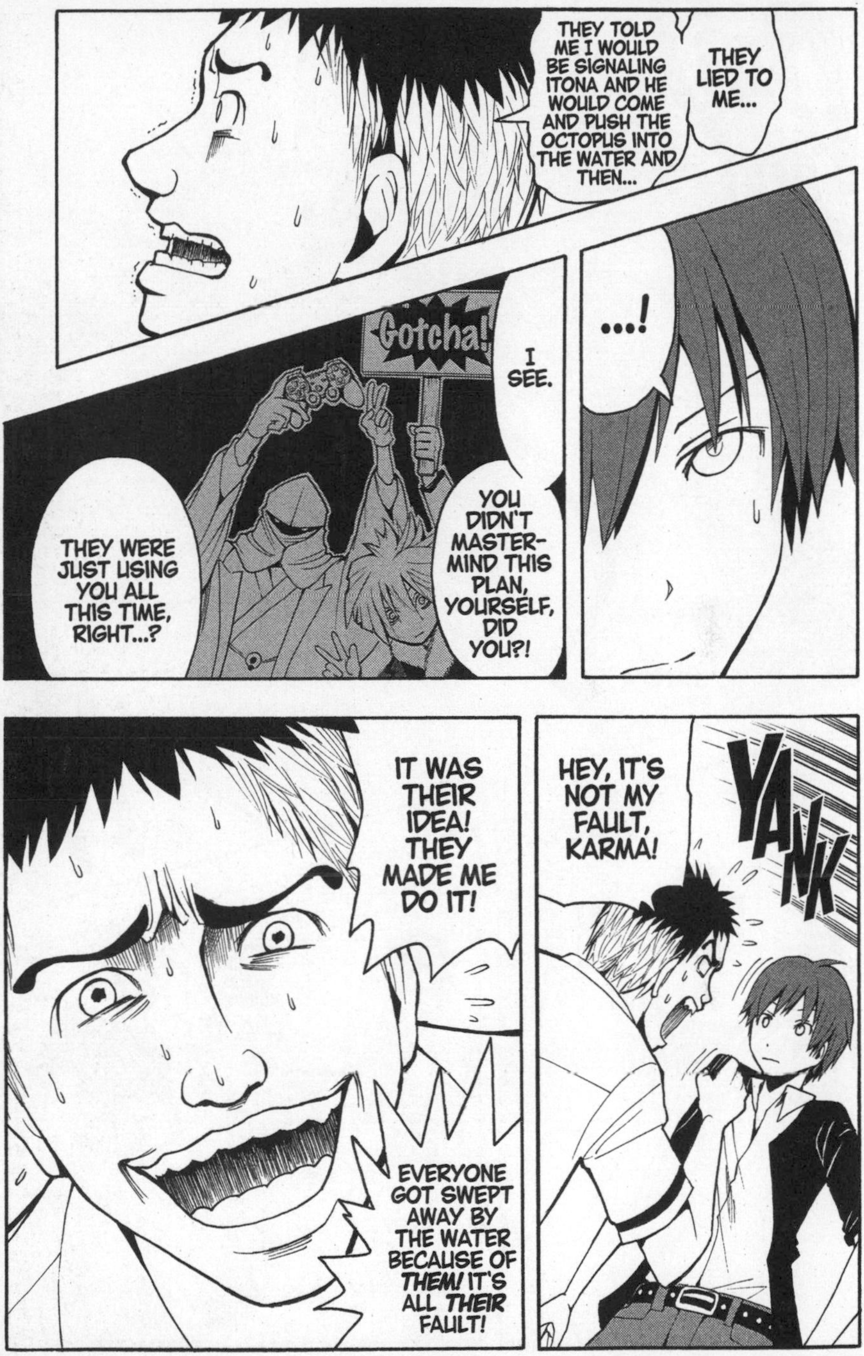
THEY TOLD ME I WOULD BE SIGNALING ITONA AND HE WOULD COME AND PUSH THE OCTOPUS INTO THE WATER AND THEN...
THEY LIED TO ME...
...!
I SEE.
YOU DIDN'T MASTER-MIND THIS PLAN, YOURSELF, DID YOU?!
Gotcha!
THEY WERE JUST USING YOU ALL THIS TIME, RIGHT...?
HEY, IT'S NOT MY FAULT, KARMA!
YANK
IT WAS THEIR IDEA! THEY MADE ME DO IT!
EVERYONE GOT SWEPT AWAY BY THE WATER BECAUSE OF *THEM!* IT'S ALL *THEIR* FAULT!

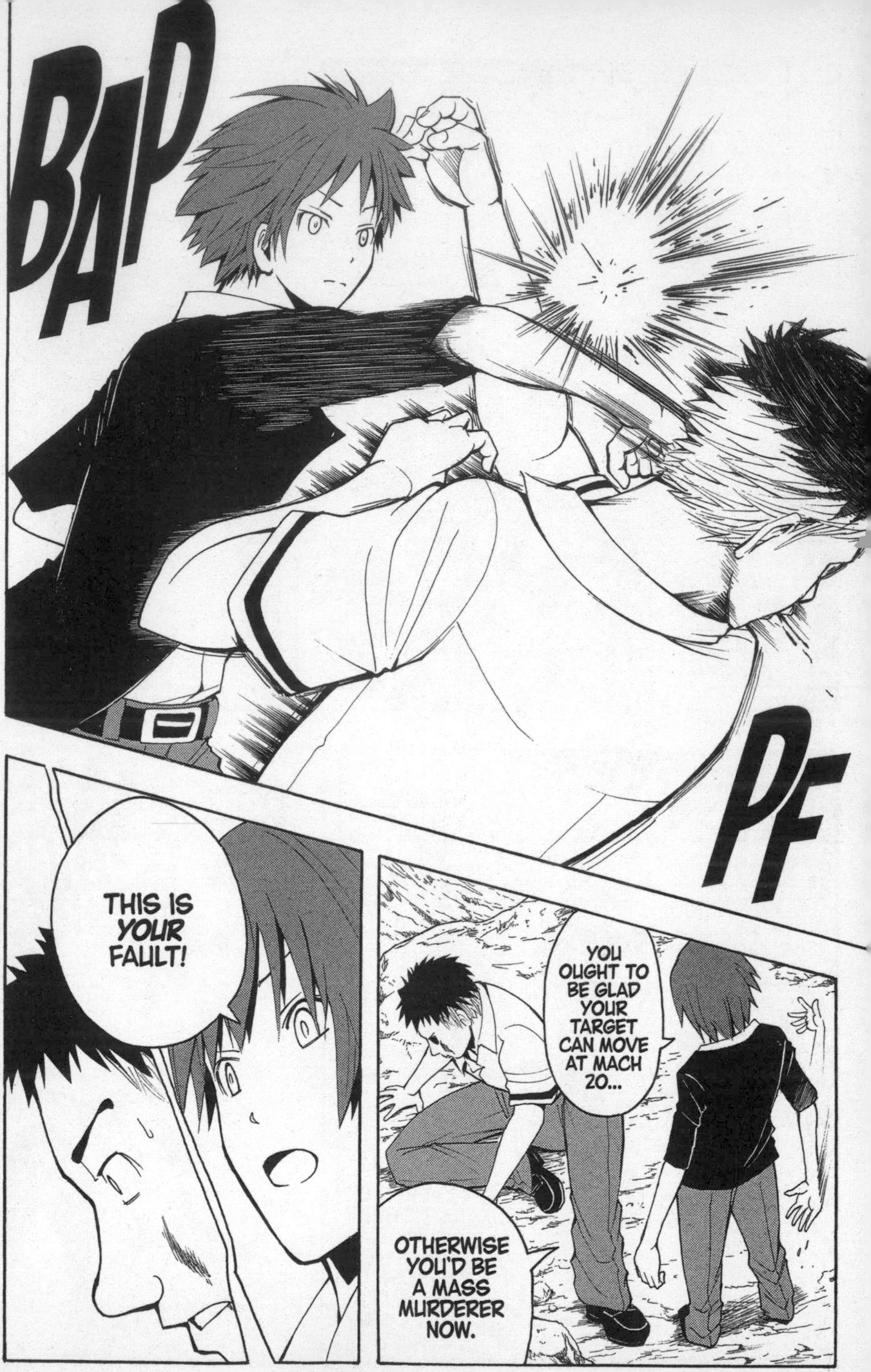
BAP
PF
YOU OUGHT TO BE GLAD YOUR TARGET CAN MOVE AT MACH 20...
OTHERWISE YOU'D BE A MASS MURDERER NOW.
THIS IS *YOUR* FAULT!

...

IF YOU'VE GOT TIME TO PLAY THE BLAME GAME...

...WHY DON'T YOU USE YOUR HEAD TO THINK ABOUT WHAT YOU SHOULD REALLY BE DOING NOW?

HE'S THE LAST ONE! I'VE SAVED EVERY-BODY!

TOSS

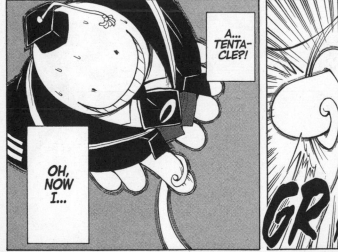

A... TENTA-CLE?!

OH, NOW I...

GRAB

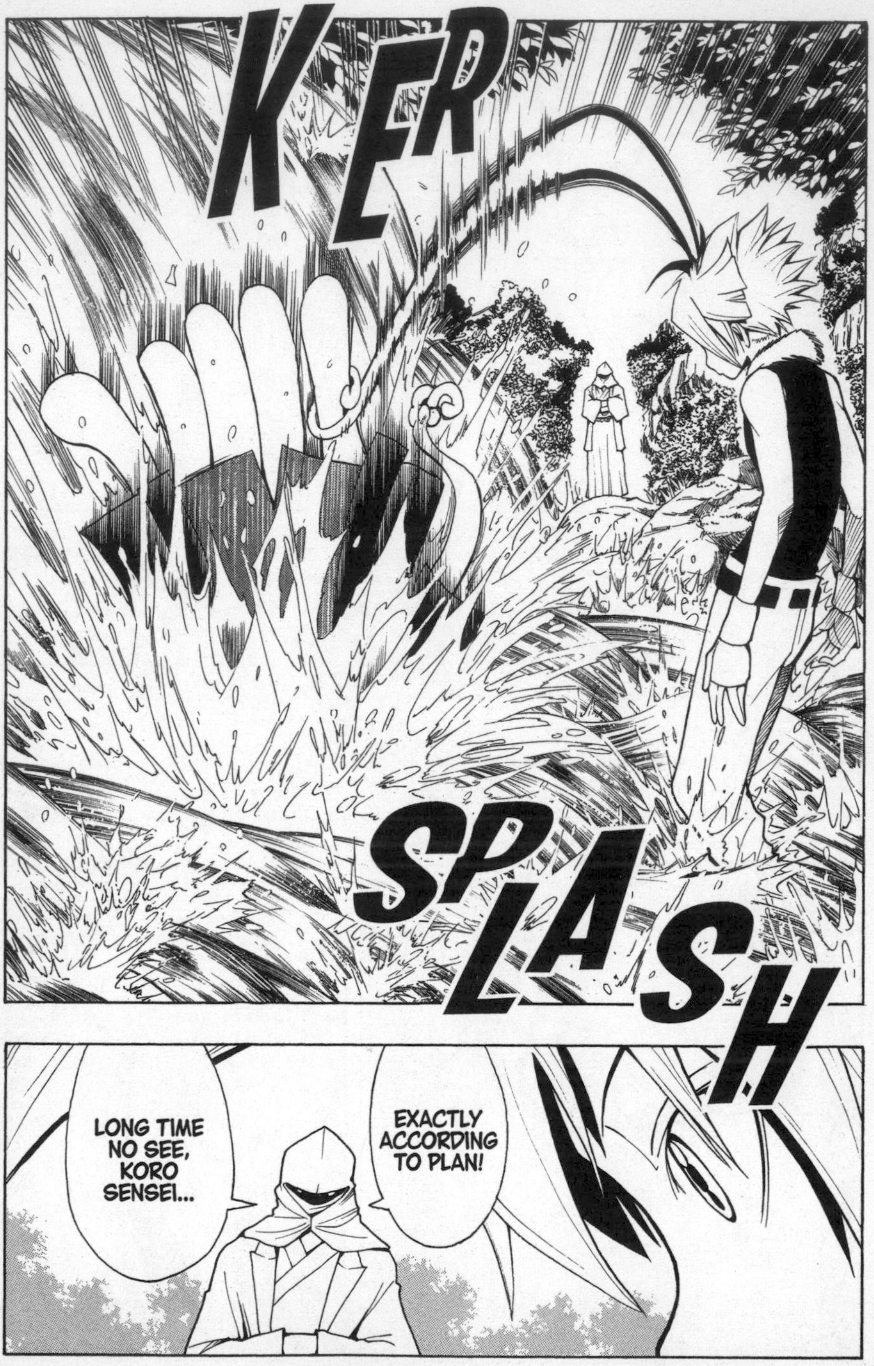
KER
SPLASH
EXACTLY ACCORDING TO PLAN!
LONG TIME NO SEE, KORO SENSEI...

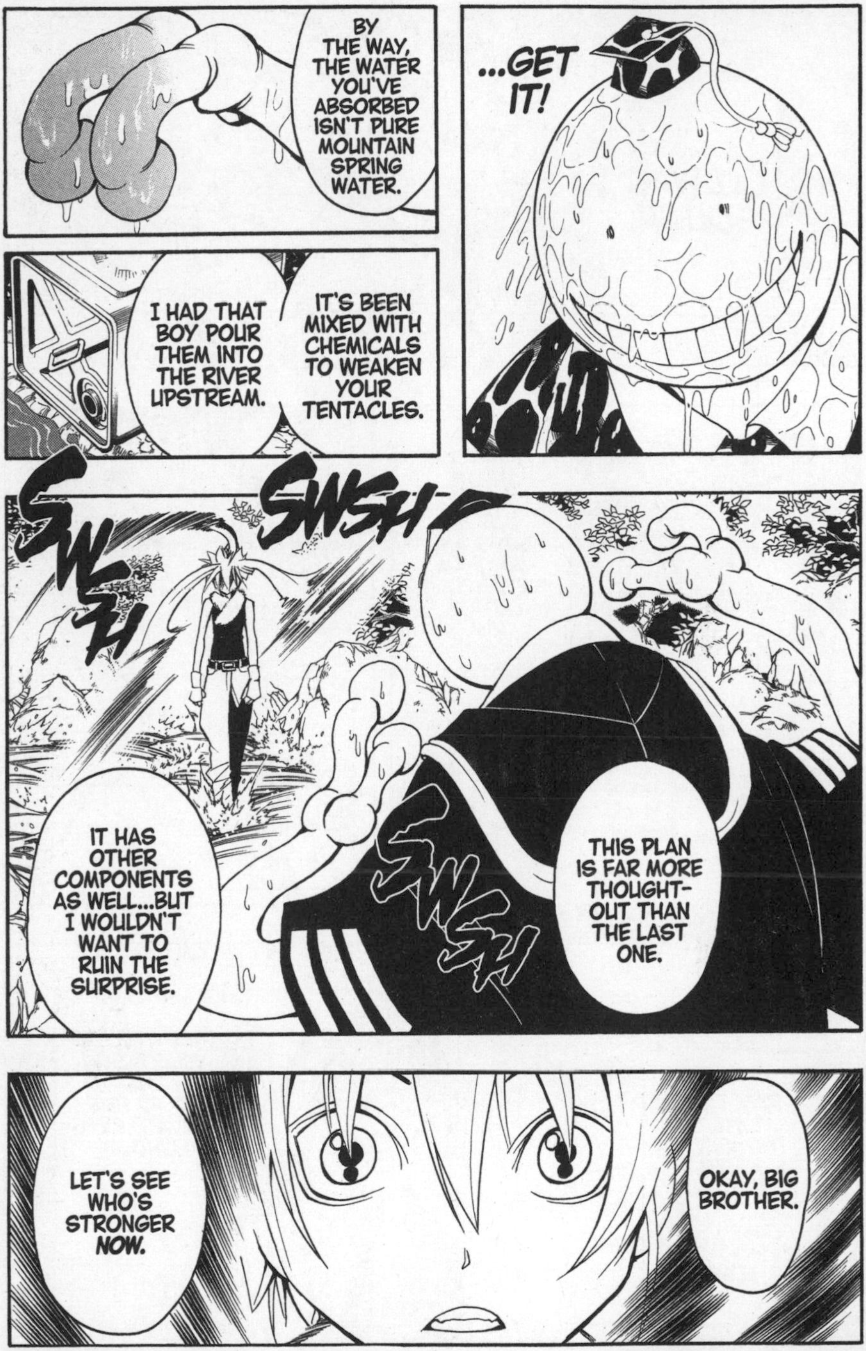
...GET IT!
BY THE WAY, THE WATER YOU'VE ABSORBED ISN'T PURE MOUNTAIN SPRING WATER.
IT'S BEEN MIXED WITH CHEMICALS TO WEAKEN YOUR TENTACLES.
I HAD THAT BOY POUR THEM INTO THE RIVER UPSTREAM.
SWSH
SWSH
THIS PLAN IS FAR MORE THOUGHT-OUT THAN THE LAST ONE.
SWSH
IT HAS OTHER COMPONENTS AS WELL...BUT I WOULDN'T WANT TO RUIN THE SURPRISE.
OKAY, BIG BROTHER.
LET'S SEE WHO'S STRONGER NOW.

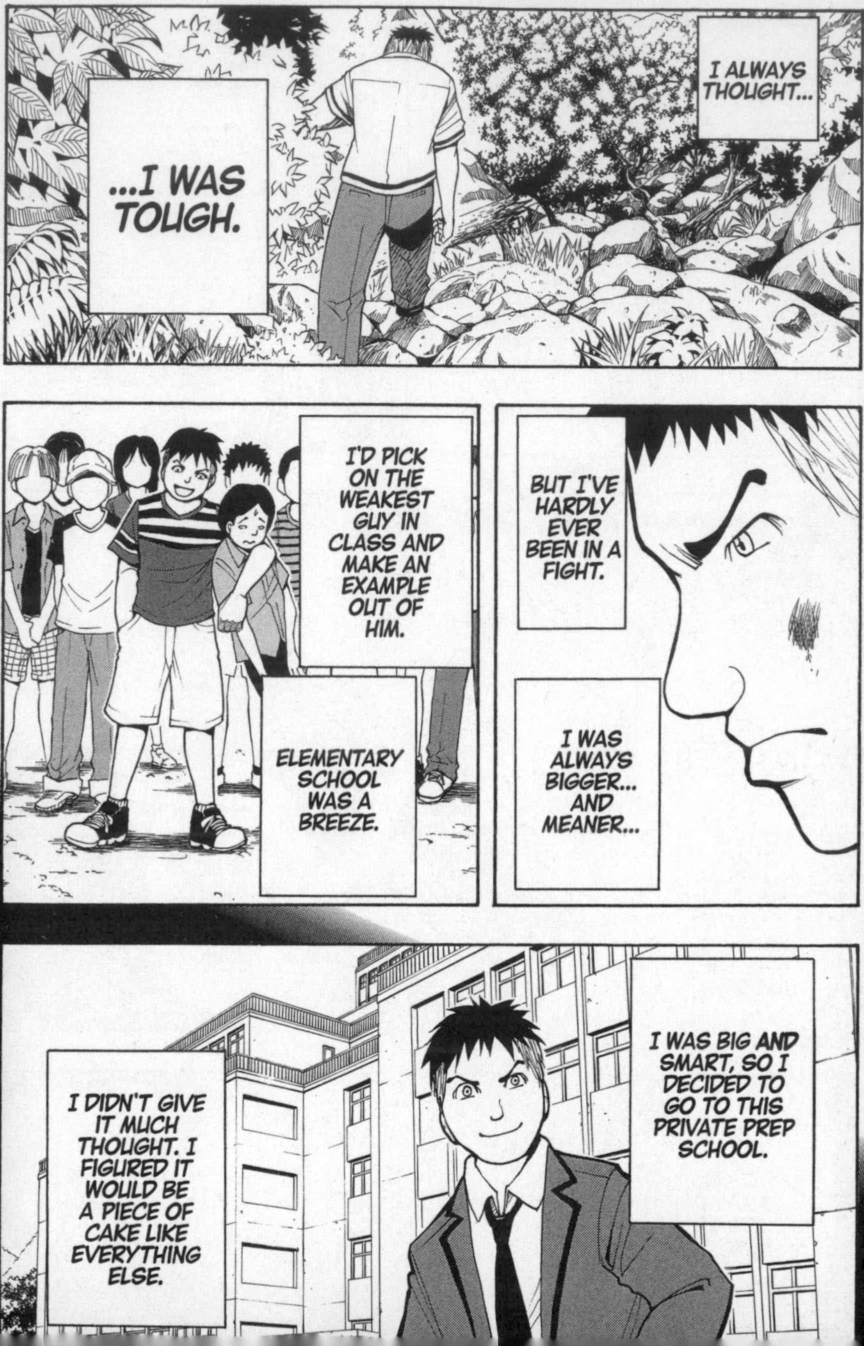
I ALWAYS THOUGHT...
...I WAS TOUGH.
BUT I'VE HARDLY EVER BEEN IN A FIGHT.
I WAS ALWAYS BIGGER... AND MEANER...
I'D PICK ON THE WEAKEST GUY IN CLASS AND MAKE AN EXAMPLE OUT OF HIM.
ELEMENTARY SCHOOL WAS A BREEZE.
I WAS BIG AND SMART, SO I DECIDED TO GO TO THIS PRIVATE PREP SCHOOL.
I DIDN'T GIVE IT MUCH THOUGHT. I FIGURED IT WOULD BE A PIECE OF CAKE LIKE EVERYTHING ELSE.

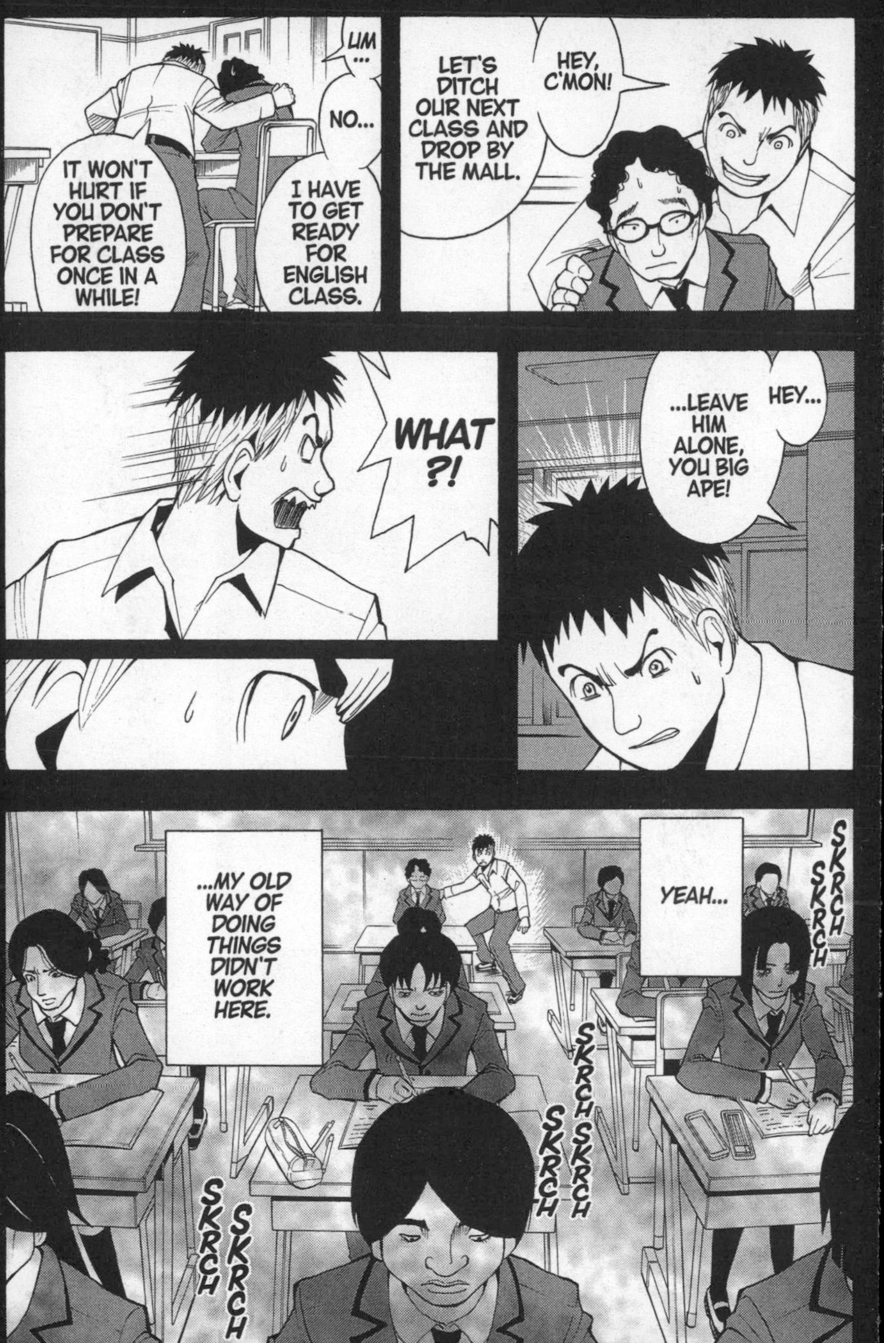
HEY, C'MON!
LET'S DITCH OUR NEXT CLASS AND DROP BY THE MALL.
UM...
NO...
I HAVE TO GET READY FOR ENGLISH CLASS.
IT WON'T HURT IF YOU DON'T PREPARE FOR CLASS ONCE IN A WHILE!
HEY...
...LEAVE HIM ALONE, YOU BIG APE!
WHAT?!
SKRCH SKRCH
YEAH...
...MY OLD WAY OF DOING THINGS DIDN'T WORK HERE.
SKRCH SKRCH
SKRCH
SKRCH SKRCH

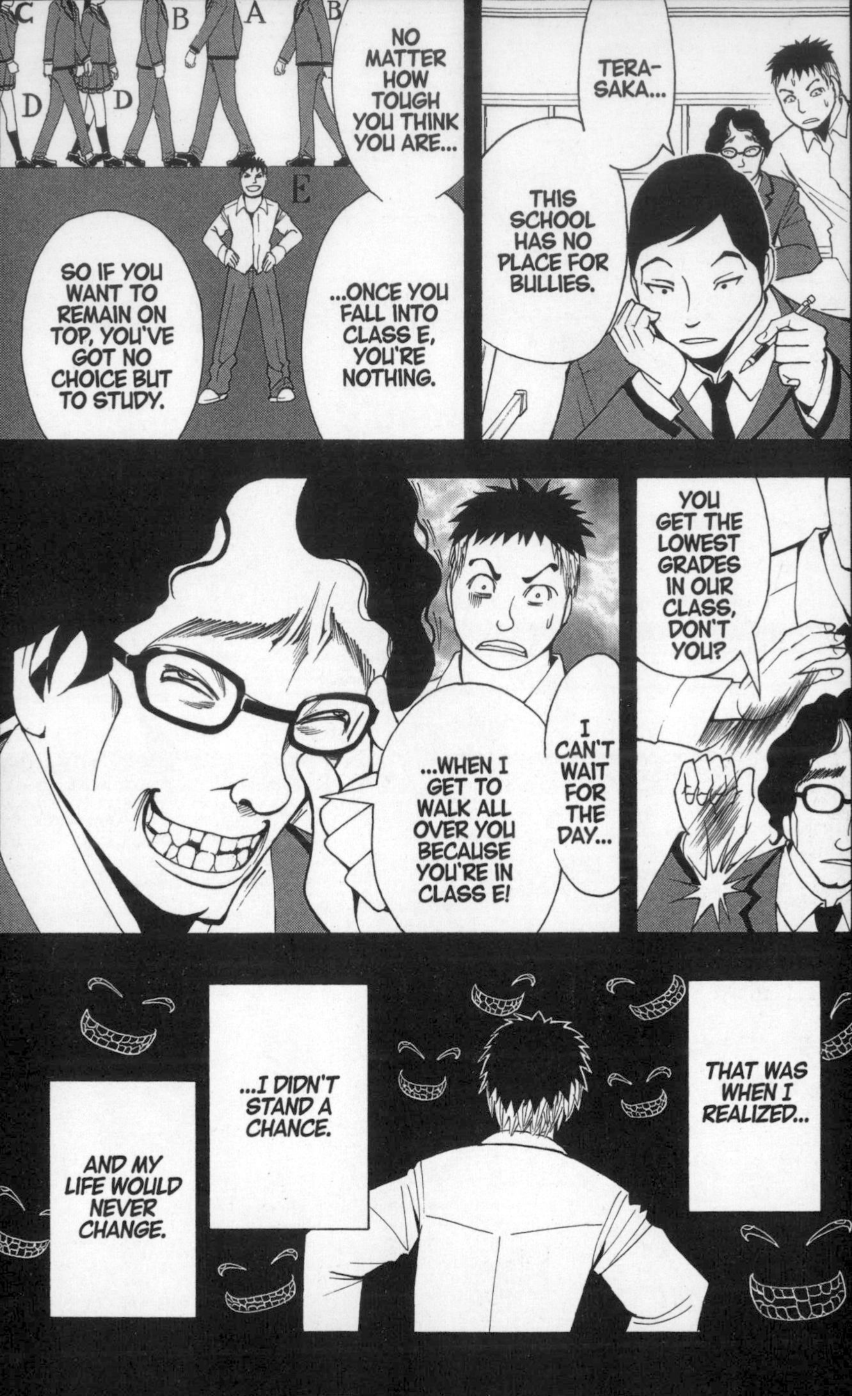
TERA-SAKA...
THIS SCHOOL HAS NO PLACE FOR BULLIES.
NO MATTER HOW TOUGH YOU THINK YOU ARE...
B A B C
D D
E
...ONCE YOU FALL INTO CLASS E, YOU'RE NOTHING.
SO IF YOU WANT TO REMAIN ON TOP, YOU'VE GOT NO CHOICE BUT TO STUDY.
YOU GET THE LOWEST GRADES IN OUR CLASS, DON'T YOU?
I CAN'T WAIT FOR THE DAY...
...WHEN I GET TO WALK ALL OVER YOU BECAUSE YOU'RE IN CLASS E!
THAT WAS WHEN I REALIZED...
...I DIDN'T STAND A CHANCE.
AND MY LIFE WOULD NEVER CHANGE.

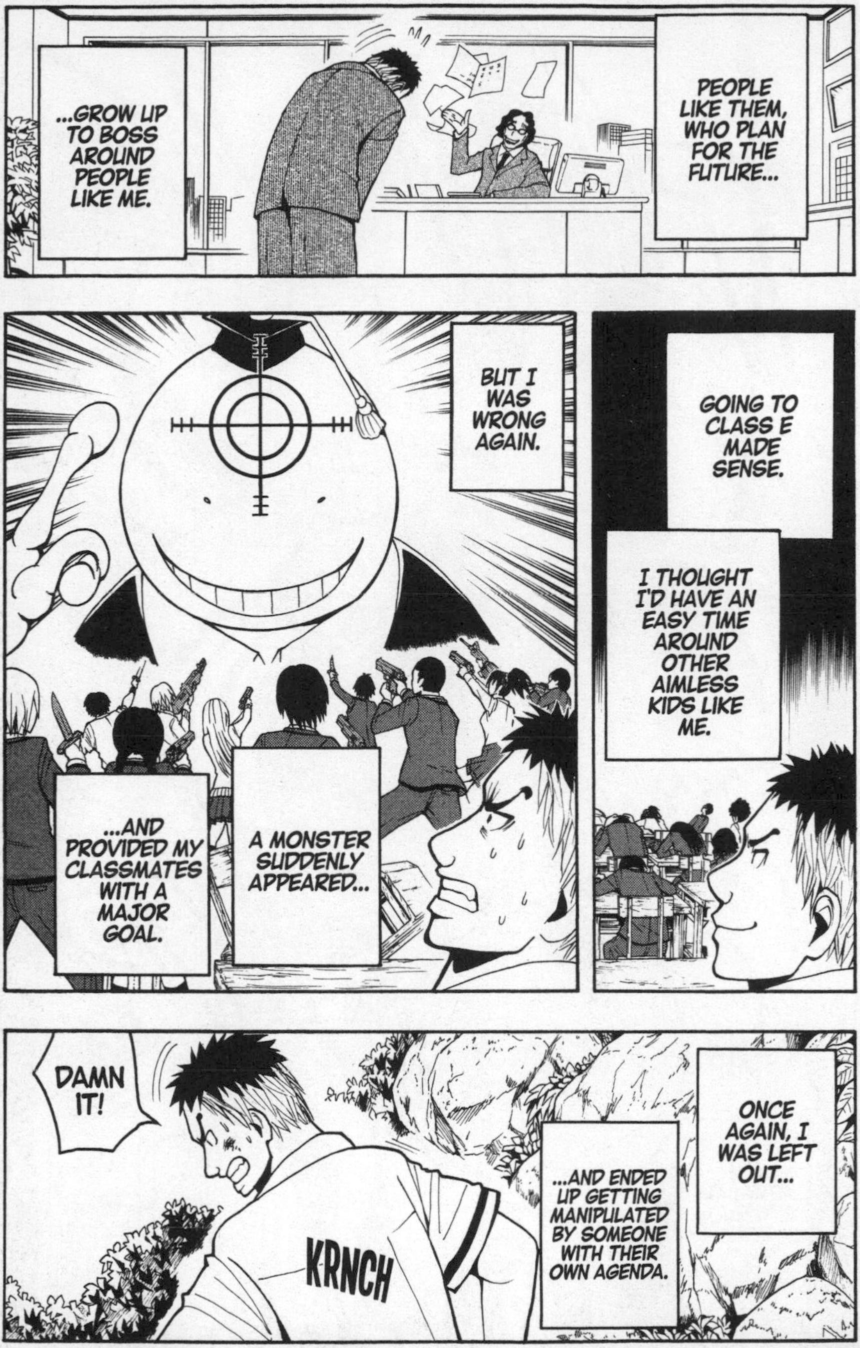
PEOPLE LIKE THEM, WHO PLAN FOR THE FUTURE...
...GROW UP TO BOSS AROUND PEOPLE LIKE ME.
GOING TO CLASS E MADE SENSE.
I THOUGHT I'D HAVE AN EASY TIME AROUND OTHER AIMLESS KIDS LIKE ME.
BUT I WAS WRONG AGAIN.
A MONSTER SUDDENLY APPEARED...
...AND PROVIDED MY CLASSMATES WITH A MAJOR GOAL.
ONCE AGAIN, I WAS LEFT OUT...
...AND ENDED UP GETTING MANIPULATED BY SOMEONE WITH THEIR OWN AGENDA.
KRNCH
DAMN IT!

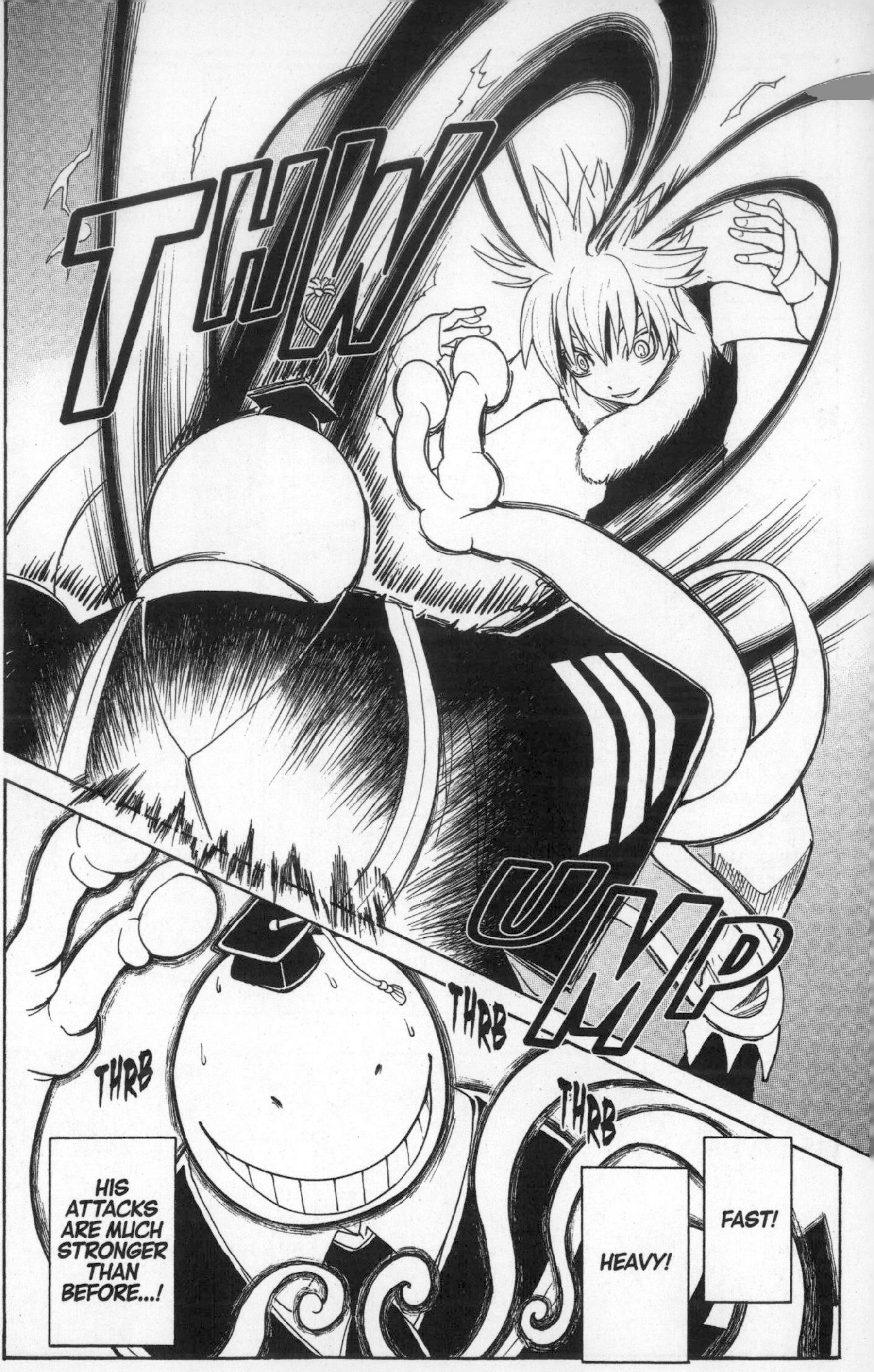
THWUMP
THRB
THRB
THRB
FAST!
HEAVY!
HIS ATTACKS ARE MUCH STRONGER THAN BEFORE...!

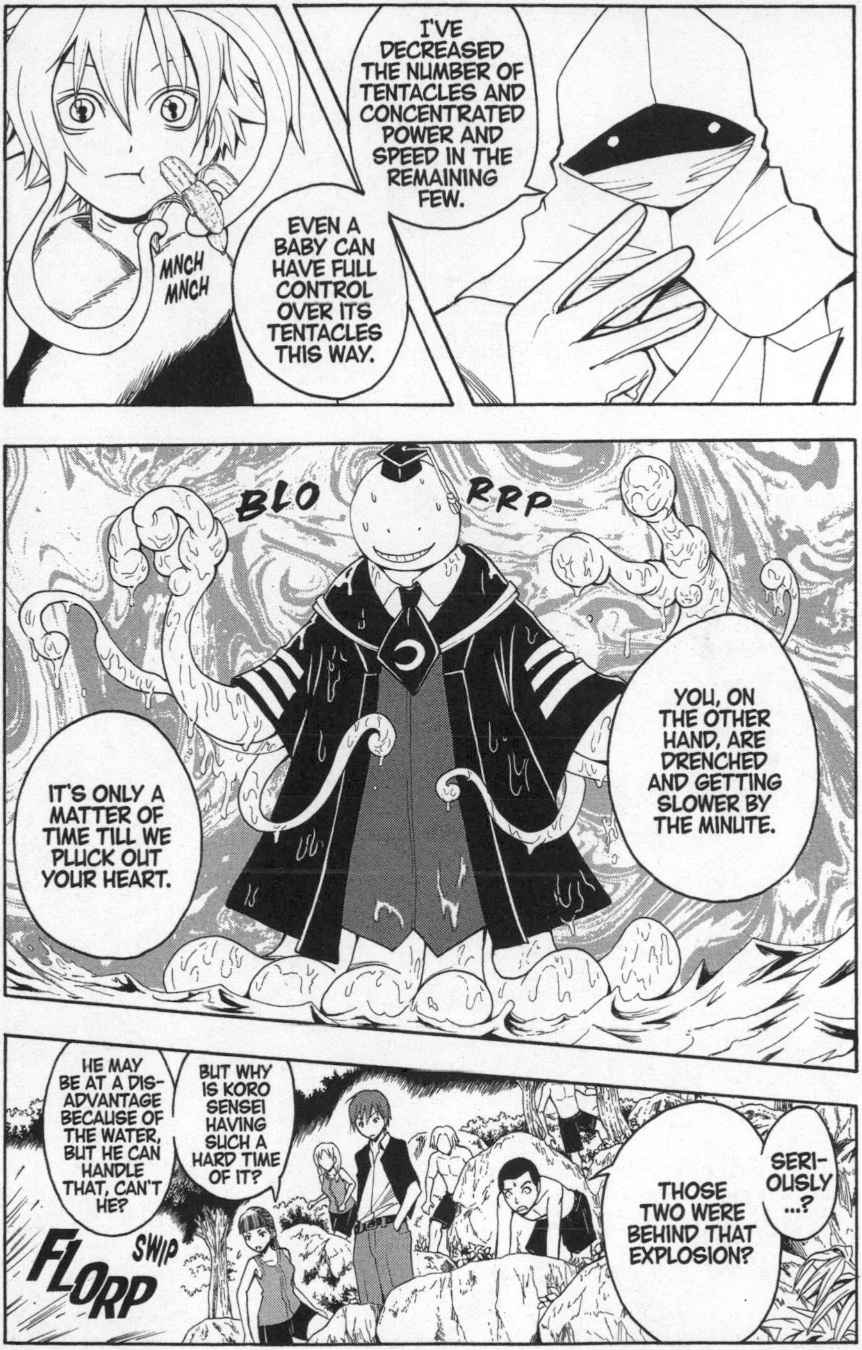
I'VE DECREASED THE NUMBER OF TENTACLES AND CONCENTRATED POWER AND SPEED IN THE REMAINING FEW.
EVEN A BABY CAN HAVE FULL CONTROL OVER ITS TENTACLES THIS WAY.
MNCH MNCH
BLO RRP
YOU, ON THE OTHER HAND, ARE DRENCHED AND GETTING SLOWER BY THE MINUTE.
IT'S ONLY A MATTER OF TIME TILL WE PLUCK OUT YOUR HEART.
SERI-OUSLY ...?
THOSE TWO WERE BEHIND THAT EXPLOSION?
BUT WHY IS KORO SENSEI HAVING SUCH A HARD TIME OF IT?
HE MAY BE AT A DIS-ADVANTAGE BECAUSE OF THE WATER, BUT HE CAN HANDLE THAT, CAN'T HE?
SWIP
FLORP

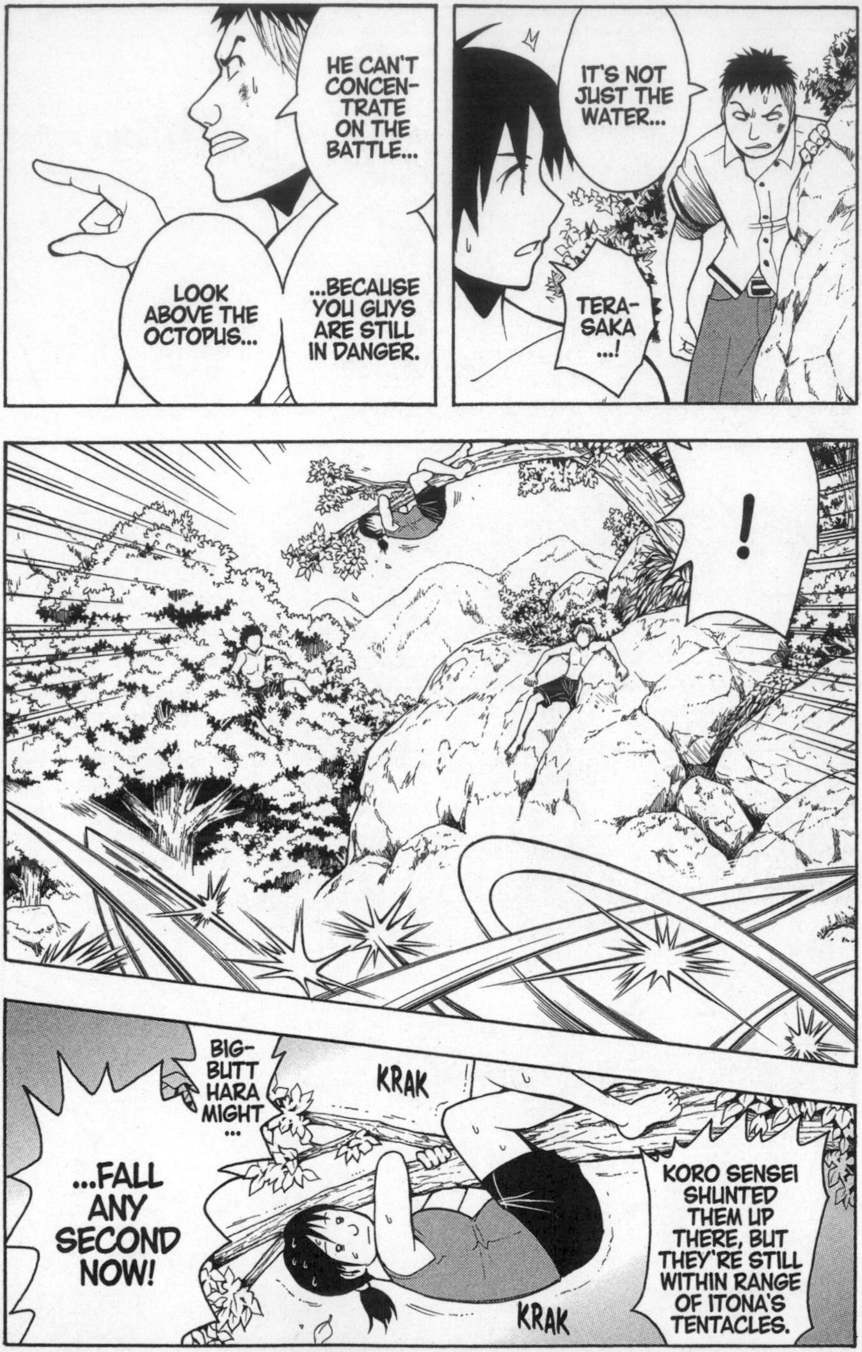
IT'S NOT JUST THE WATER...
TERA-SAKA ...!
HE CAN'T CONCEN-TRATE ON THE BATTLE...
...BECAUSE YOU GUYS ARE STILL IN DANGER.
LOOK ABOVE THE OCTOPUS...
!
KRAK
KORO SENSEI SHUNTED THEM UP THERE, BUT THEY'RE STILL WITHIN RANGE OF ITONA'S TENTACLES.
KRAK
BIG-BUTT HARA MIGHT ...
...FALL ANY SECOND NOW!

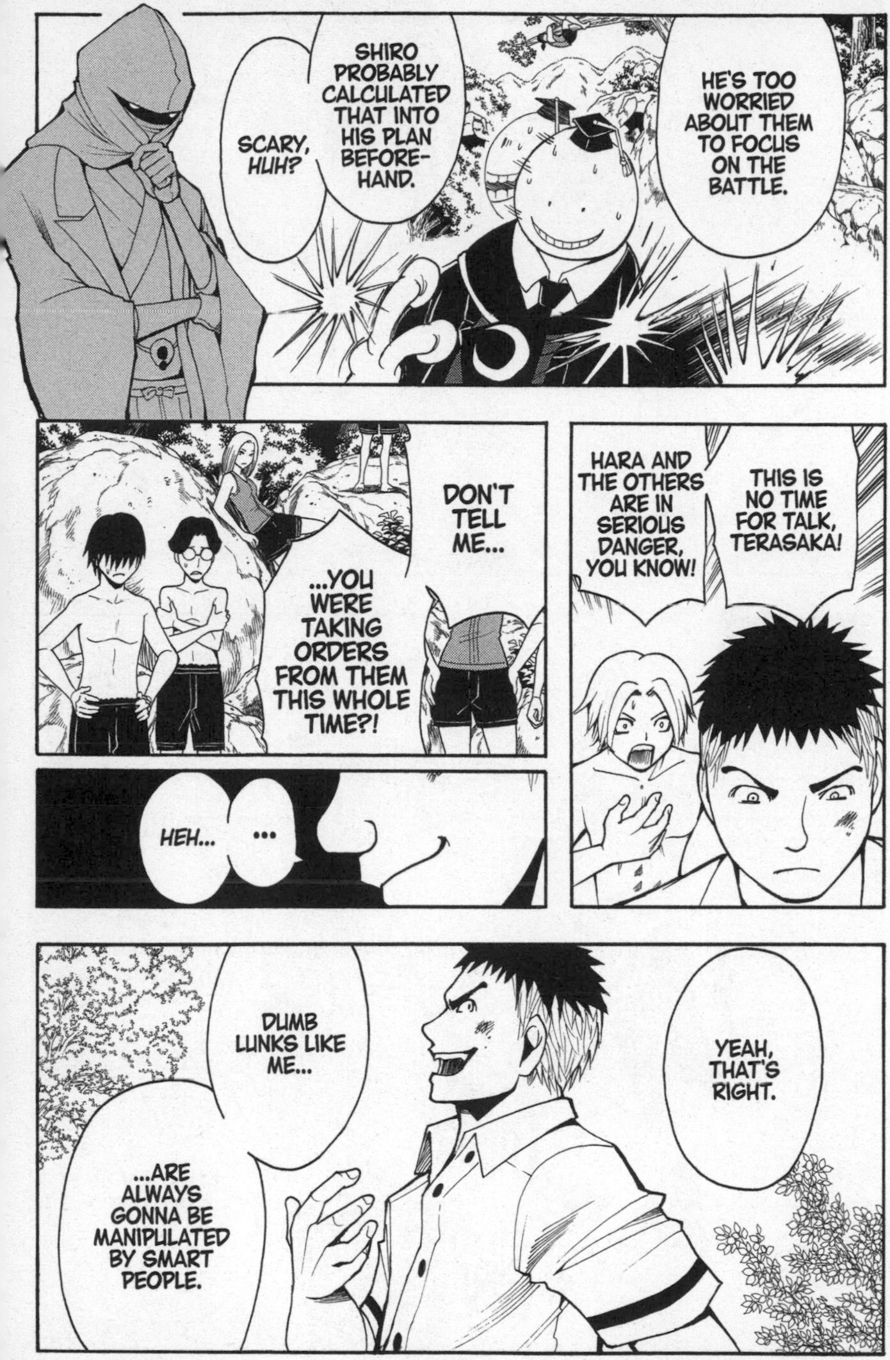
HE'S TOO WORRIED ABOUT THEM TO FOCUS ON THE BATTLE.
SHIRO PROBABLY CALCULATED THAT INTO HIS PLAN BEFORE-HAND.
SCARY, HUH?
THIS IS NO TIME FOR TALK, TERASAKA!
HARA AND THE OTHERS ARE IN SERIOUS DANGER, YOU KNOW!
DON'T TELL ME...
...YOU WERE TAKING ORDERS FROM THEM THIS WHOLE TIME?!
...
HEH...
YEAH, THAT'S RIGHT.
DUMB LUNKS LIKE ME...
...ARE ALWAYS GONNA BE MANIPULATED BY SMART PEOPLE.

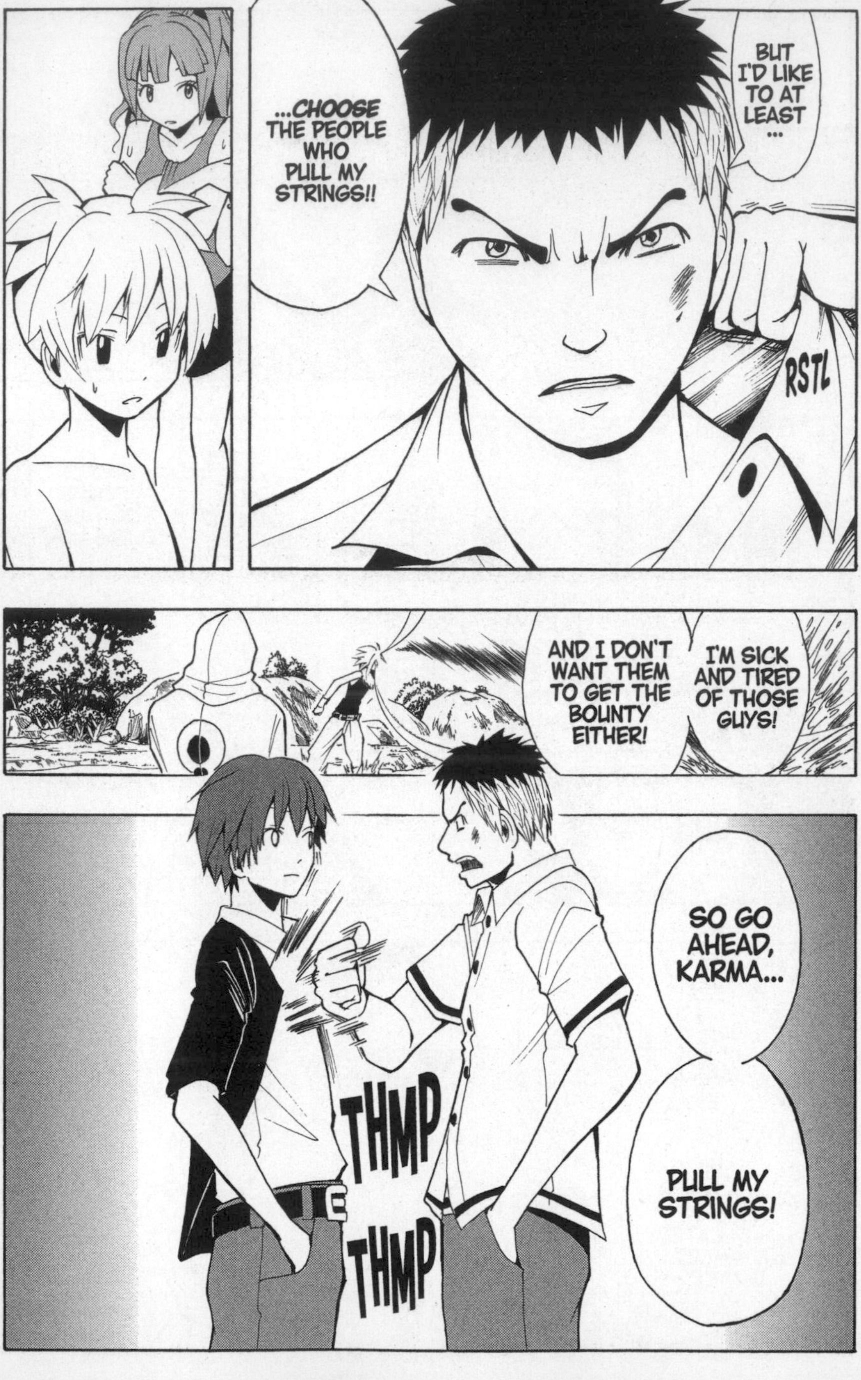
BUT I'D LIKE TO AT LEAST...
...CHOOSE THE PEOPLE WHO PULL MY STRINGS!!
RSTL
I'M SICK AND TIRED OF THOSE GUYS!
AND I DON'T WANT THEM TO GET THE BOUNTY EITHER!
SO GO AHEAD, KARMA...
PULL MY STRINGS!
THMP
THMP

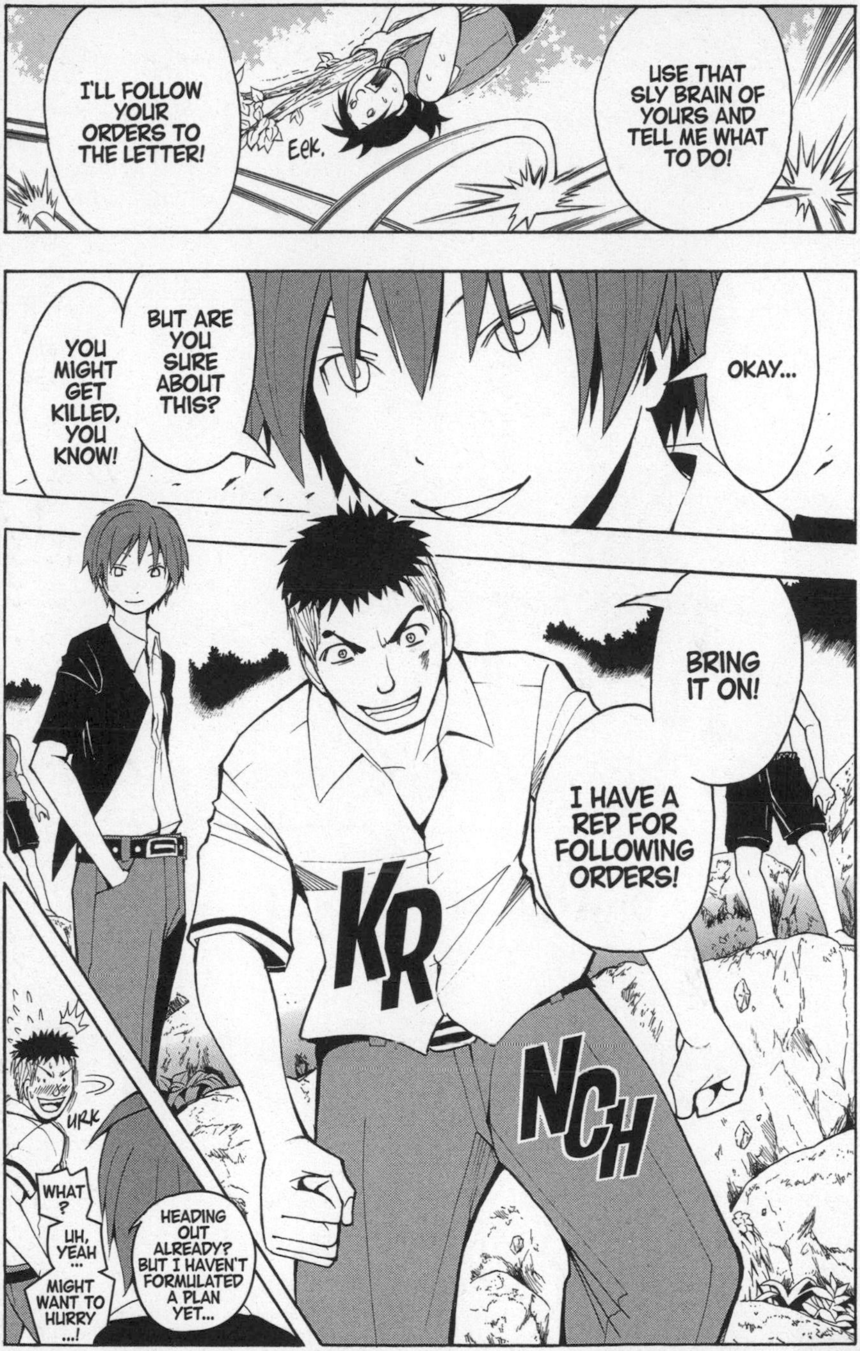
USE THAT SLY BRAIN OF YOURS AND TELL ME WHAT TO DO!
Eek.
I'LL FOLLOW YOUR ORDERS TO THE LETTER!
OKAY...
BUT ARE YOU SURE ABOUT THIS?
YOU MIGHT GET KILLED, YOU KNOW!
BRING IT ON!
I HAVE A REP FOR FOLLOWING ORDERS!
KR
NCH
URK
HEADING OUT ALREADY? BUT I HAVEN'T FORMULATED A PLAN YET...
WHAT?
UH, YEAH...
MIGHT WANT TO HURRY...!

Oh, the humidity...

Shiro Sensei's Introductory Murder Manual

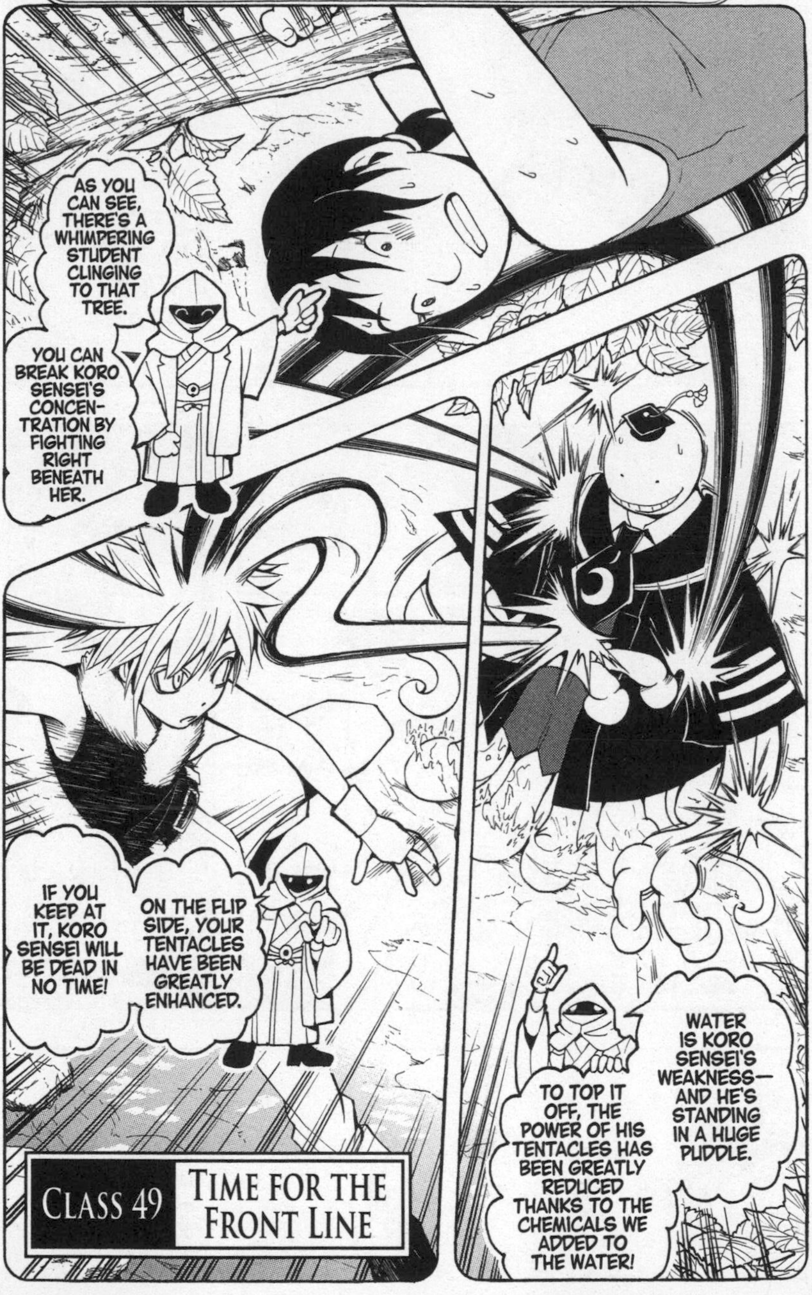
AS YOU CAN SEE, THERE'S A WHIMPERING STUDENT CLINGING TO THAT TREE.
YOU CAN BREAK KORO SENSEI'S CONCEN-TRATION BY FIGHTING RIGHT BENEATH HER.
WATER IS KORO SENSEI'S WEAKNESS— AND HE'S STANDING IN A HUGE PUDDLE.
TO TOP IT OFF, THE POWER OF HIS TENTACLES HAS BEEN GREATLY REDUCED THANKS TO THE CHEMICALS WE ADDED TO THE WATER!
ON THE FLIP SIDE, YOUR TENTACLES HAVE BEEN GREATLY ENHANCED.
IF YOU KEEP AT IT, KORO SENSEI WILL BE DEAD IN NO TIME!
CLASS 49
TIME FOR THE FRONT LINE

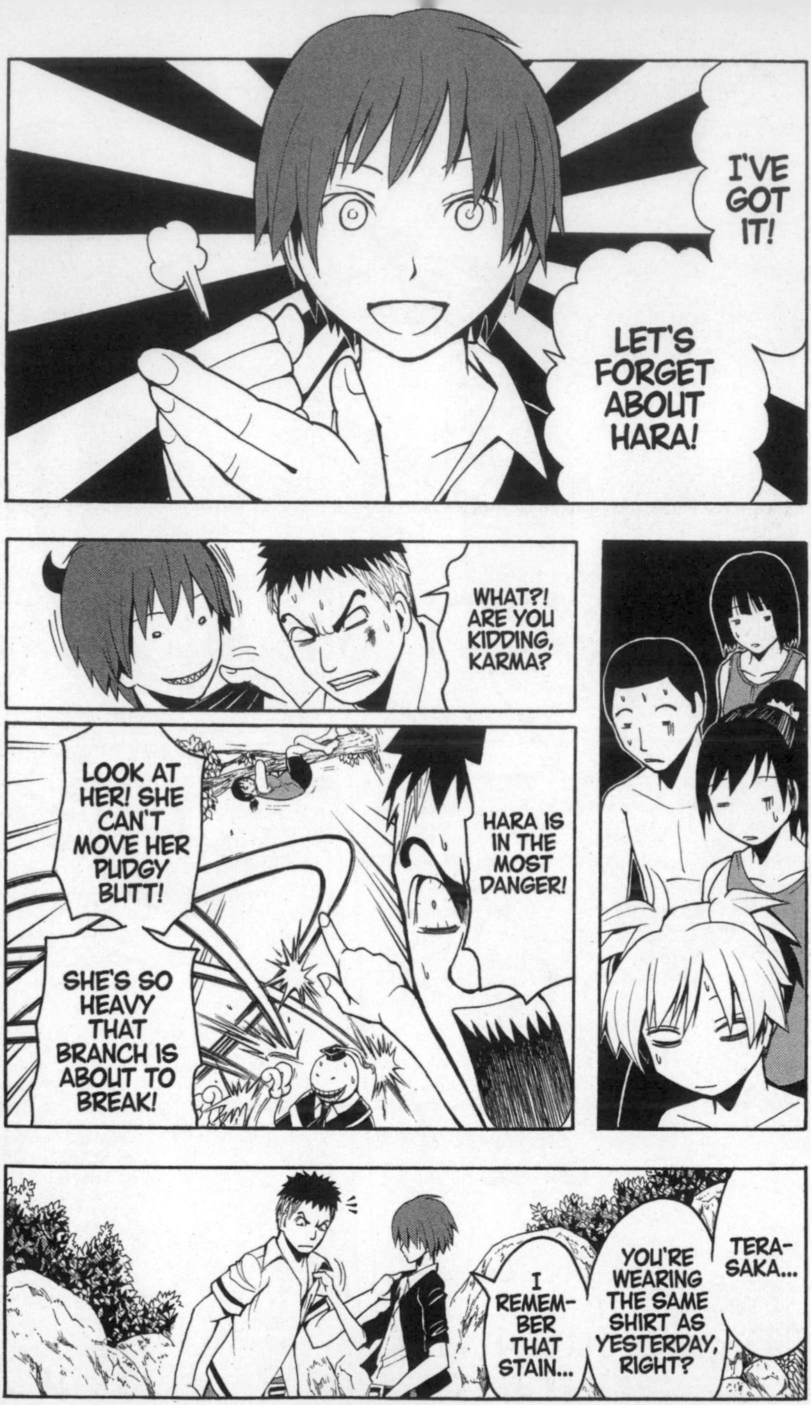
I'VE GOT IT!
LET'S FORGET ABOUT HARA!
WHAT?! ARE YOU KIDDING, KARMA?
HARA IS IN THE MOST DANGER!
LOOK AT HER! SHE CAN'T MOVE HER PUDGY BUTT!
SHE'S SO HEAVY THAT BRANCH IS ABOUT TO BREAK!
TERA-SAKA...
YOU'RE WEARING THE SAME SHIRT AS YESTERDAY, RIGHT?
I REMEM-BER THAT STAIN...

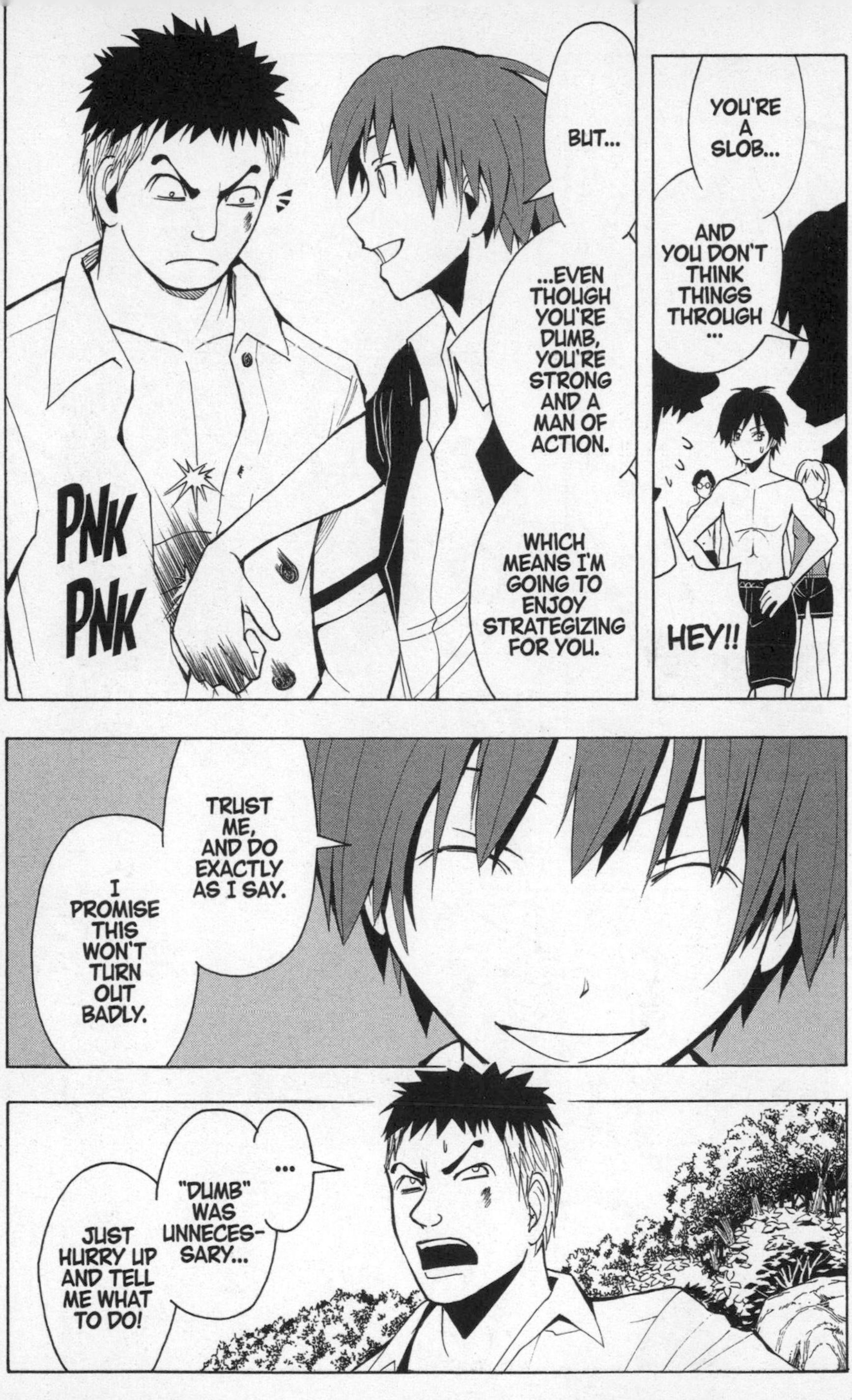
YOU'RE A SLOB...
AND YOU DON'T THINK THINGS THROUGH ...
HEY!!
BUT...
...EVEN THOUGH YOU'RE DUMB, YOU'RE STRONG AND A MAN OF ACTION.
WHICH MEANS I'M GOING TO ENJOY STRATEGIZING FOR YOU.
PNK
PNK
TRUST ME, AND DO EXACTLY AS I SAY.
I PROMISE THIS WON'T TURN OUT BADLY.
...
"DUMB" WAS UNNECES-SARY...
JUST HURRY UP AND TELL ME WHAT TO DO!

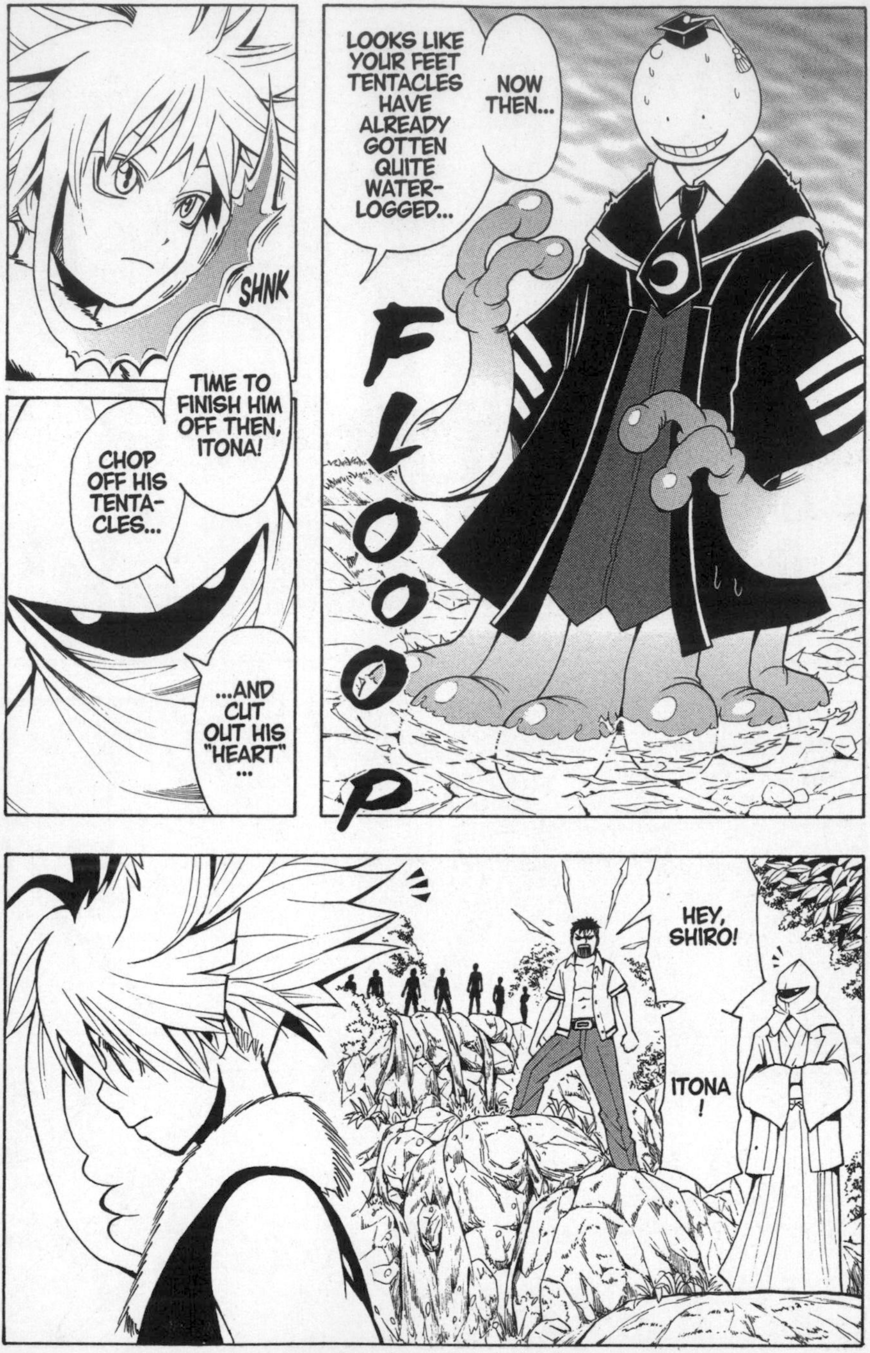
NOW THEN...
LOOKS LIKE YOUR FEET TENTACLES HAVE ALREADY GOTTEN QUITE WATER-LOGGED...
FLOOOOP
SHNK
TIME TO FINISH HIM OFF THEN, ITONA!
CHOP OFF HIS TENTACLES...
...AND CUT OUT HIS "HEART"...
HEY, SHIRO!
ITONA!

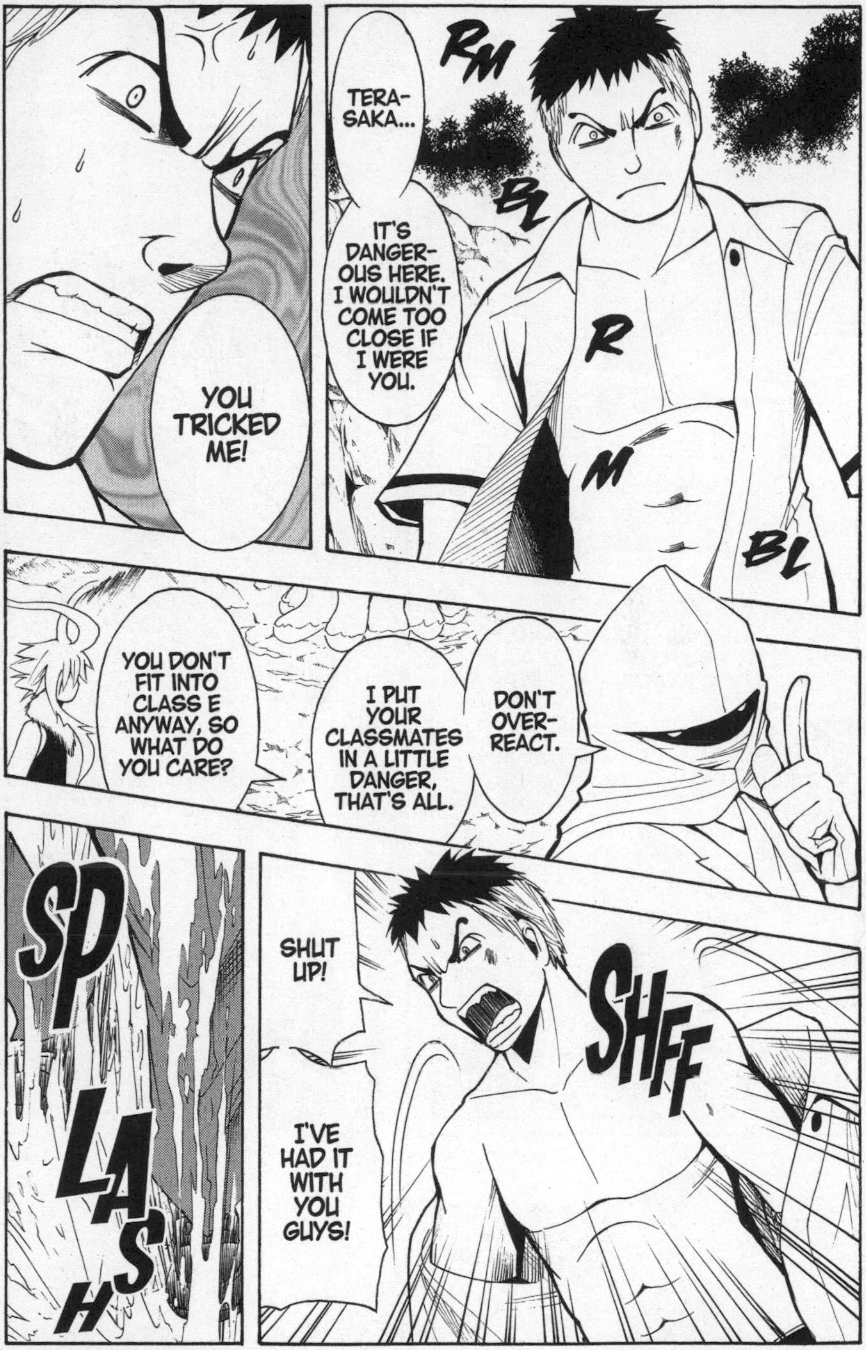
RMBL
TERA-SAKA...
IT'S DANGER-OUS HERE. I WOULDN'T COME TOO CLOSE IF I WERE YOU.
RMBL
YOU TRICKED ME!
DON'T OVER-REACT.
I PUT YOUR CLASSMATES IN A LITTLE DANGER, THAT'S ALL.
YOU DON'T FIT INTO CLASS E ANYWAY, SO WHAT DO YOU CARE?
SHFF
SHUT UP!
I'VE HAD IT WITH YOU GUYS!
SPLASH

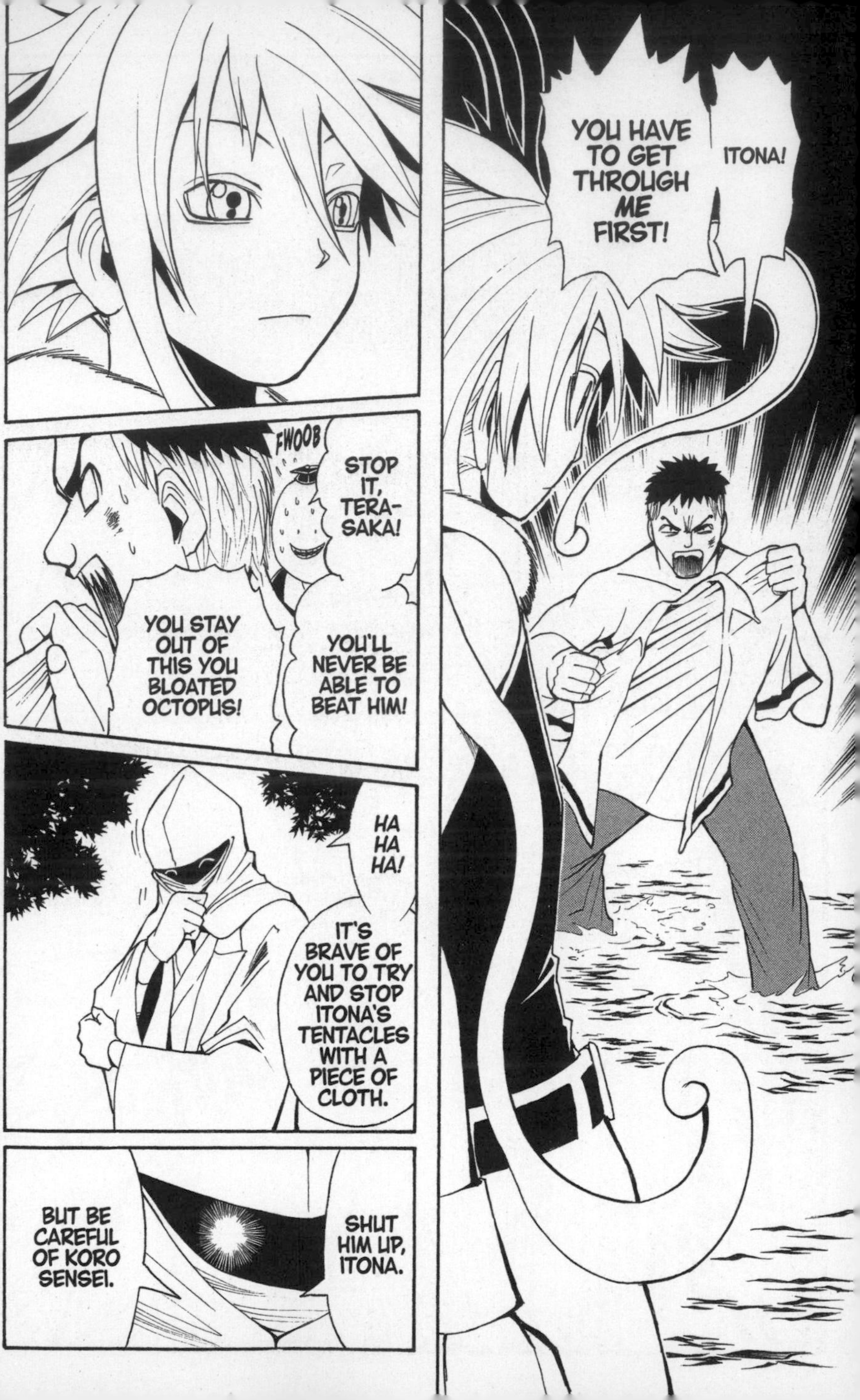
ITONA!
YOU HAVE TO GET THROUGH *ME* FIRST!
STOP IT, TERA-SAKA!
FWOOB
YOU'LL NEVER BE ABLE TO BEAT HIM!
YOU STAY OUT OF THIS YOU BLOATED OCTOPUS!
HA HA HA!
IT'S BRAVE OF YOU TO TRY AND STOP ITONA'S TENTACLES WITH A PIECE OF CLOTH.
SHUT HIM UP, ITONA.
BUT BE CAREFUL OF KORO SENSEI.

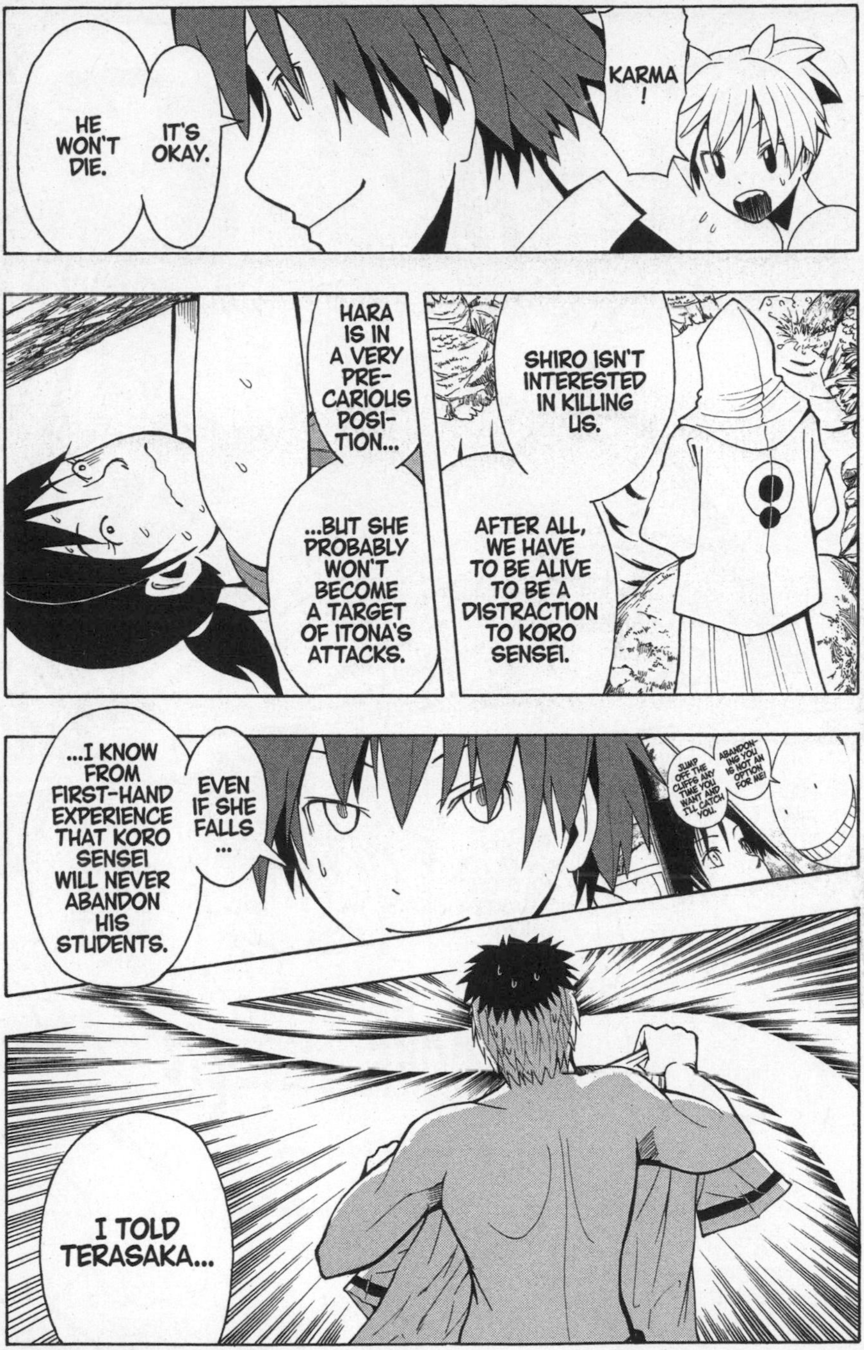
KARMA!
IT'S OKAY.
HE WON'T DIE.
SHIRO ISN'T INTERESTED IN KILLING US.
AFTER ALL, WE HAVE TO BE ALIVE TO BE A DISTRACTION TO KORO SENSEI.
HARA IS IN A VERY PRE-CARIOUS POSI-TION...
...BUT SHE PROBABLY WON'T BECOME A TARGET OF ITONA'S ATTACKS.
ABANDONING YOU IS NOT AN OPTION FOR ME!
JUMP OFF THE CLIFFS ANY TIME YOU WANT AND I'LL CATCH YOU.
EVEN IF SHE FALLS...
...I KNOW FROM FIRST-HAND EXPERIENCE THAT KORO SENSEI WILL NEVER ABANDON HIS STUDENTS.
I TOLD TERASAKA...

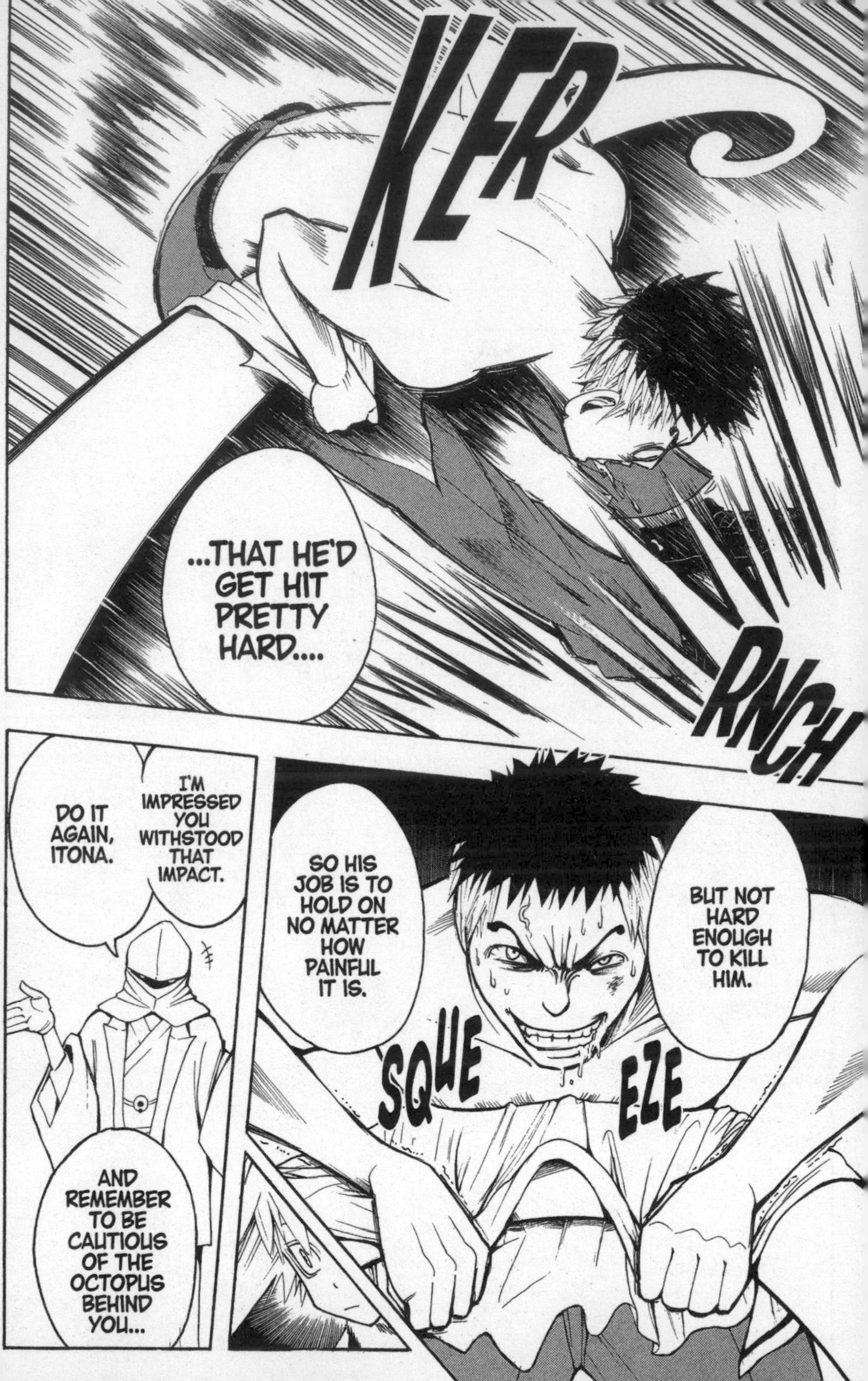
KER
...THAT HE'D GET HIT PRETTY HARD....
RNCH
BUT NOT HARD ENOUGH TO KILL HIM.
SO HIS JOB IS TO HOLD ON NO MATTER HOW PAINFUL IT IS.
SQUE
EZE
I'M IMPRESSED YOU WITHSTOOD THAT IMPACT.
DO IT AGAIN, ITONA.
AND REMEMBER TO BE CAUTIOUS OF THE OCTOPUS BEHIND YOU...

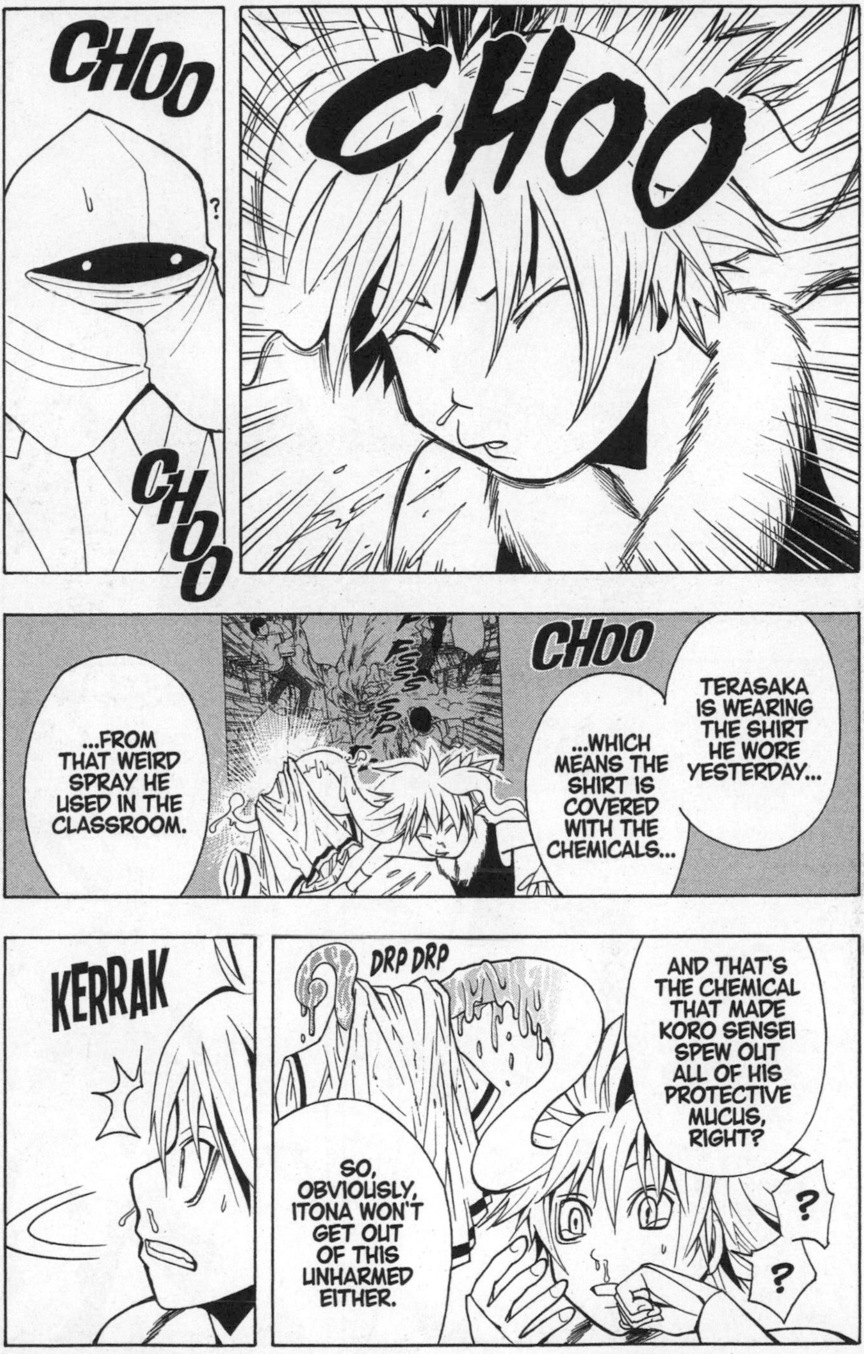
CHOO
CHOO
?
CHOO
CHOO
TERASAKA IS WEARING THE SHIRT HE WORE YESTERDAY...
...WHICH MEANS THE SHIRT IS COVERED WITH THE CHEMICALS...
...FROM THAT WEIRD SPRAY HE USED IN THE CLASSROOM.
DRP DRP
AND THAT'S THE CHEMICAL THAT MADE KORO SENSEI SPEW OUT ALL OF HIS PROTECTIVE MUCUS, RIGHT?
SO, OBVIOUSLY, ITONA WON'T GET OUT OF THIS UNHARMED EITHER.
?
?
KERRAK

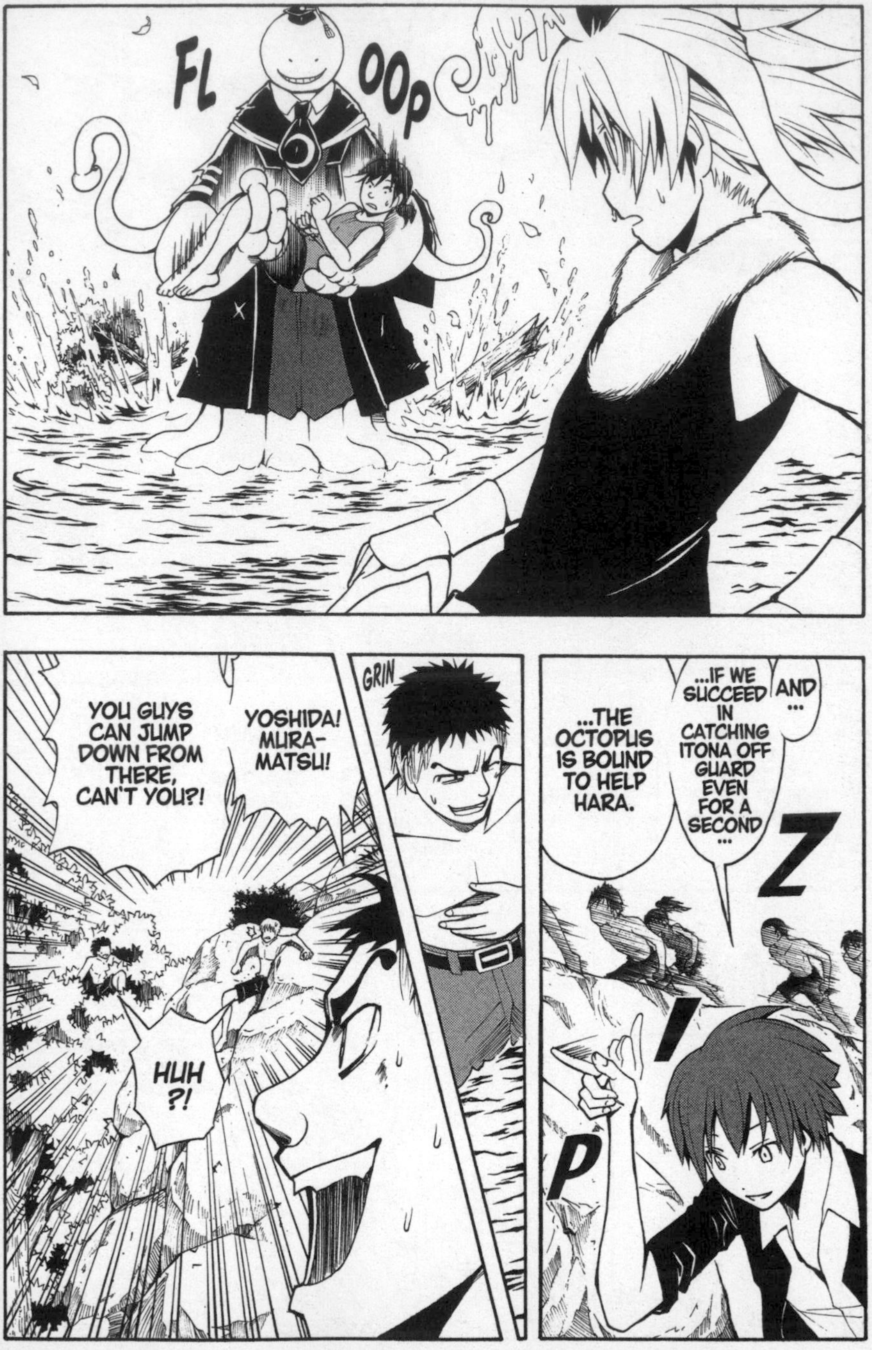
FL OOP
AND ...
...IF WE SUCCEED IN CATCHING ITONA OFF GUARD EVEN FOR A SECOND ...
...THE OCTOPUS IS BOUND TO HELP HARA.
ZIP
GRIN
YOSHIDA! MURA-MATSU!
YOU GUYS CAN JUMP DOWN FROM THERE, CAN'T YOU?!
HUH ?!

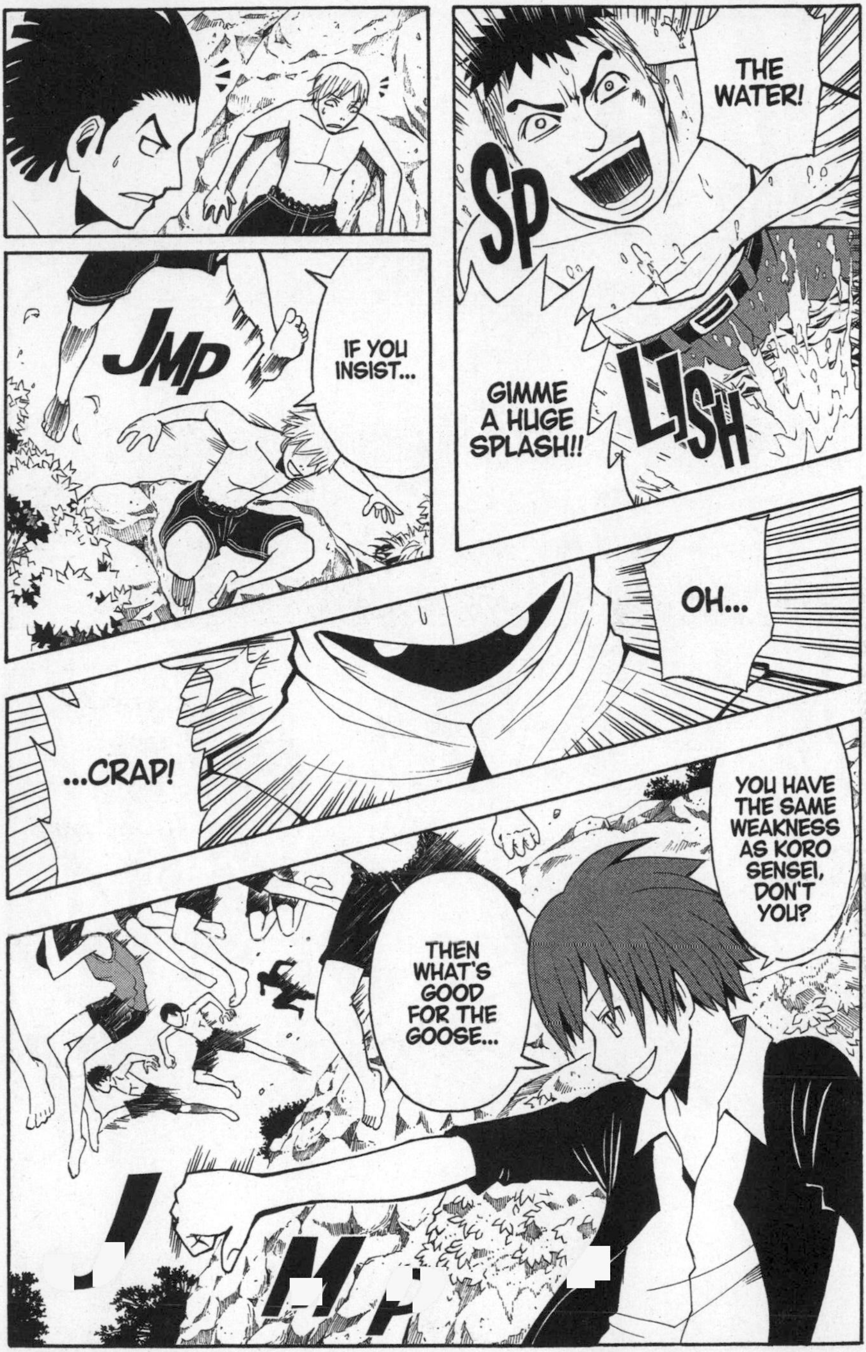
THE WATER!
SP
LISH
GIMME A HUGE SPLASH!!
JMP
IF YOU INSIST...
OH...
...CRAP!
YOU HAVE THE SAME WEAKNESS AS KORO SENSEI, DON'T YOU?
THEN WHAT'S GOOD FOR THE GOOSE...
JMP

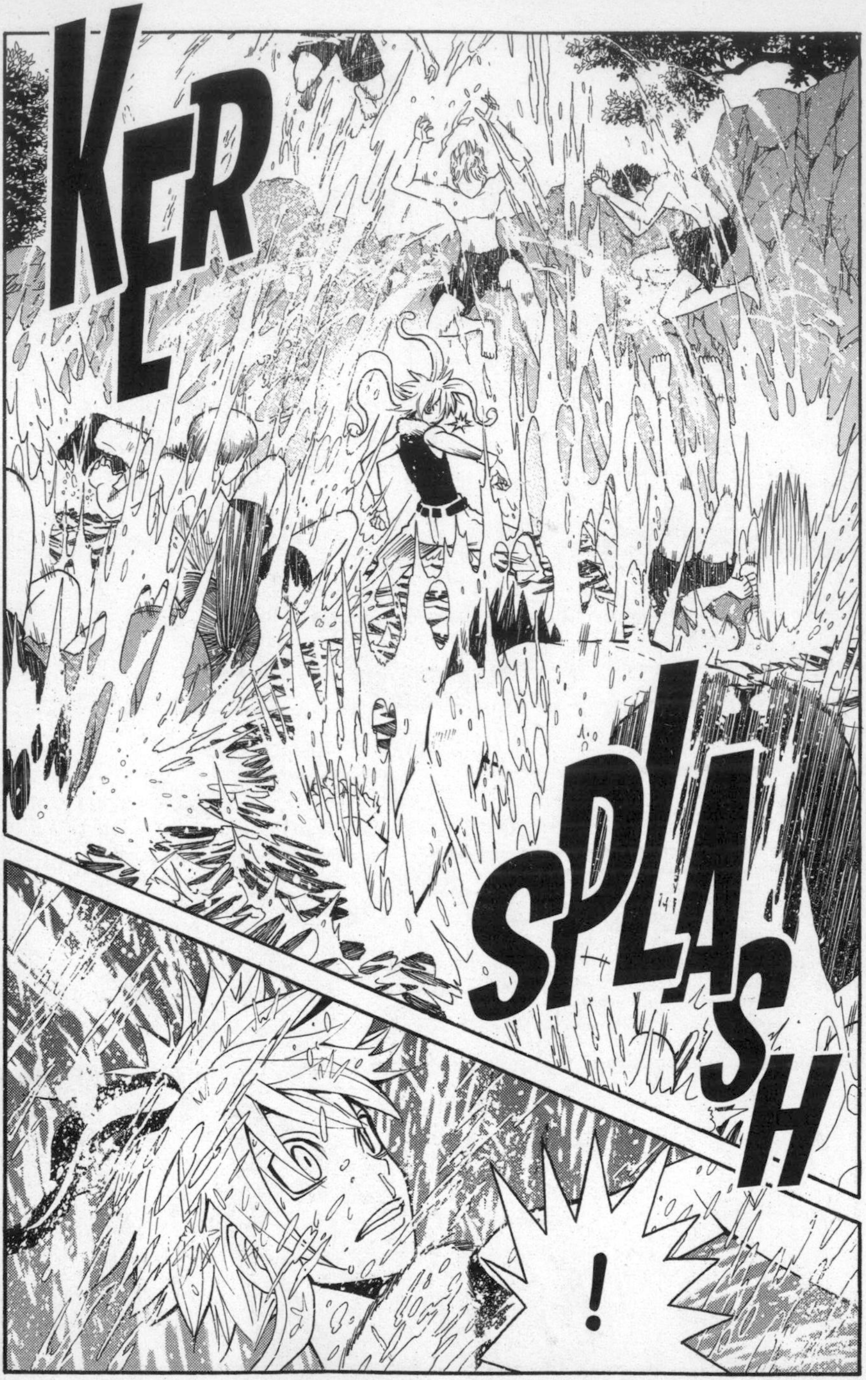
KERSPLASH
!

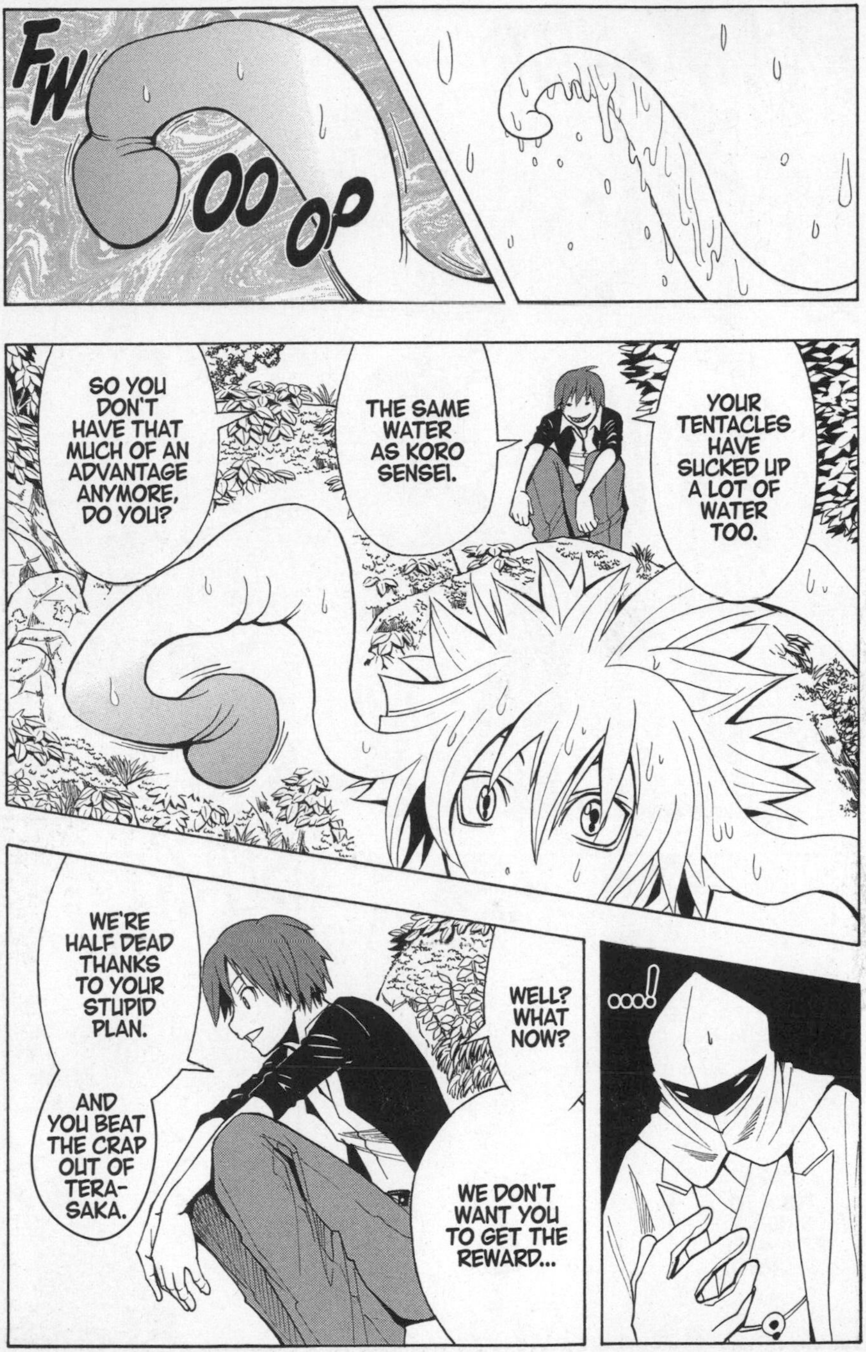
FWOOOP
YOUR TENTACLES HAVE SUCKED UP A LOT OF WATER TOO.
THE SAME WATER AS KORO SENSEI.
SO YOU DON'T HAVE THAT MUCH OF AN ADVANTAGE ANYMORE, DO YOU?
...!
WELL? WHAT NOW?
WE DON'T WANT YOU TO GET THE REWARD...
WE'RE HALF DEAD THANKS TO YOUR STUPID PLAN.
AND YOU BEAT THE CRAP OUT OF TERA-SAKA.

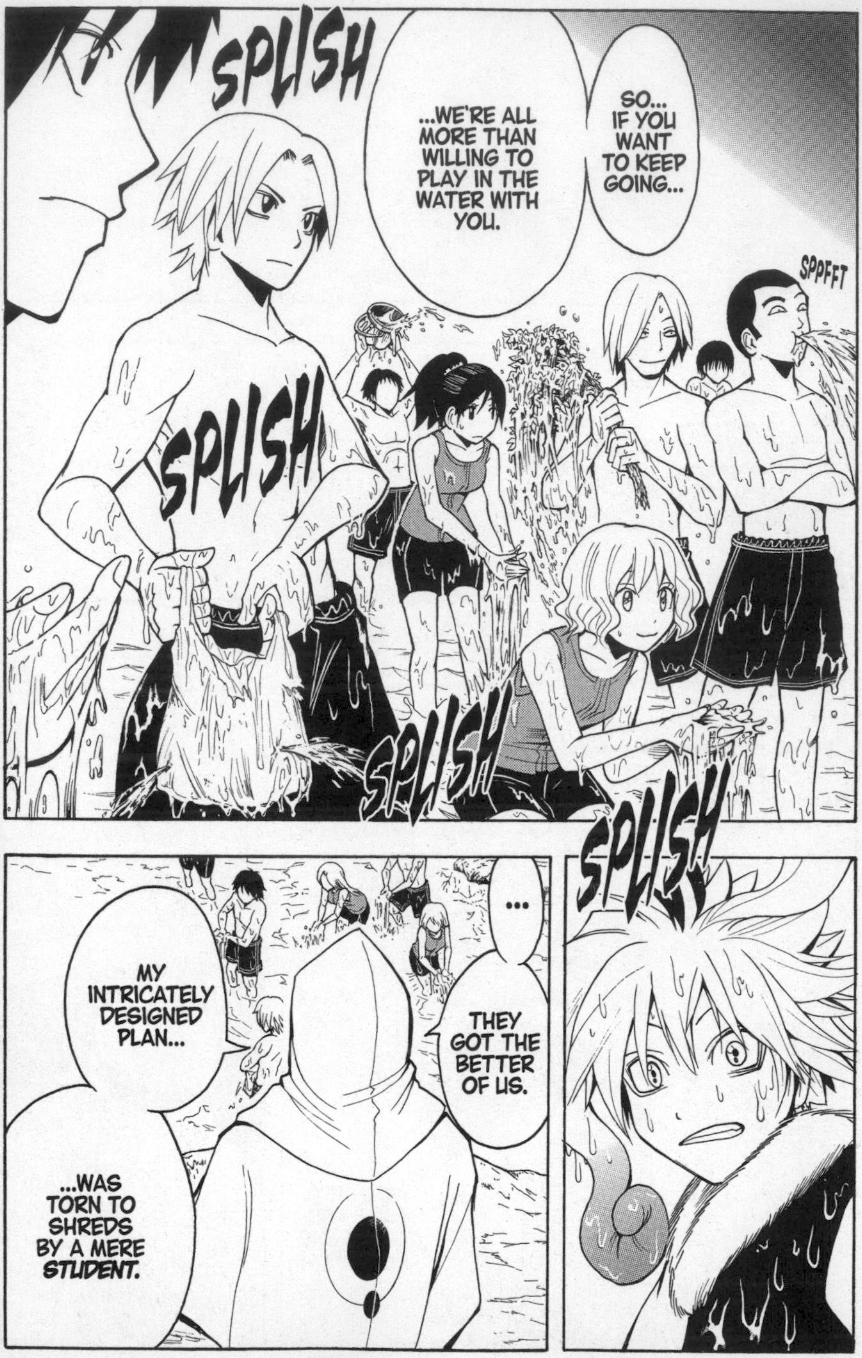
SPPFFT
SO... IF YOU WANT TO KEEP GOING...
...WE'RE ALL MORE THAN WILLING TO PLAY IN THE WATER WITH YOU.
SPLISH
SPLISH
SPLISH
SPLISH
...
THEY GOT THE BETTER OF US.
MY INTRICATELY DESIGNED PLAN...
...WAS TORN TO SHREDS BY A MERE STUDENT.

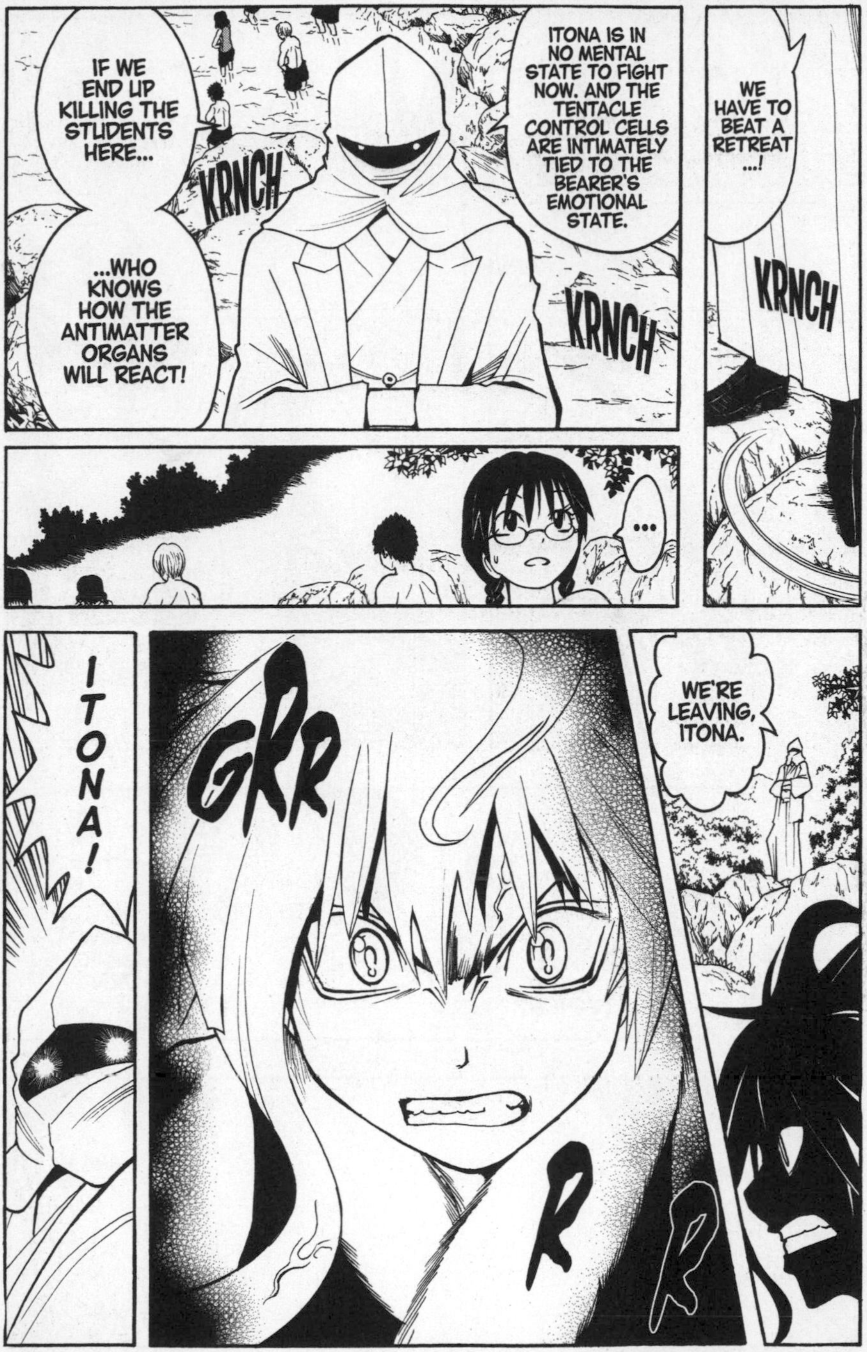
WE HAVE TO BEAT A RETREAT ...!
KRNCH
ITONA IS IN NO MENTAL STATE TO FIGHT NOW. AND THE TENTACLE CONTROL CELLS ARE INTIMATELY TIED TO THE BEARER'S EMOTIONAL STATE.
KRNCH
IF WE END UP KILLING THE STUDENTS HERE...
KRNCH
...WHO KNOWS HOW THE ANTIMATTER ORGANS WILL REACT!
...
WE'RE LEAVING, ITONA.
GRR
RRR
ITONA!

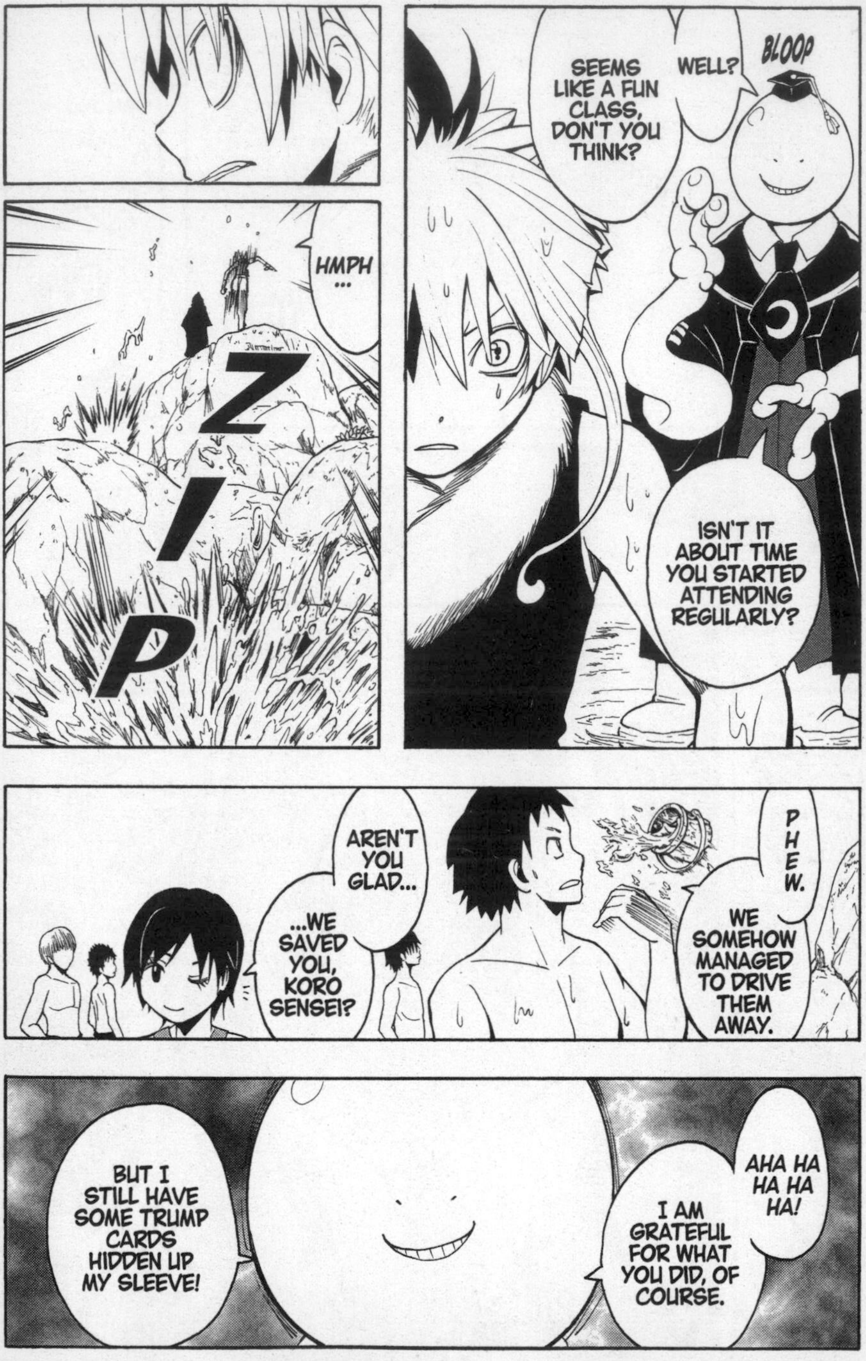
BLOOP
WELL?
SEEMS LIKE A FUN CLASS, DON'T YOU THINK?
ISN'T IT ABOUT TIME YOU STARTED ATTENDING REGULARLY?
HMPH...
ZIP
PHEW.
WE SOMEHOW MANAGED TO DRIVE THEM AWAY.
AREN'T YOU GLAD...
...WE SAVED YOU, KORO SENSEI?
AHA HA HA HA HA!
I AM GRATEFUL FOR WHAT YOU DID, OF COURSE.
BUT I STILL HAVE SOME TRUMP CARDS HIDDEN UP MY SLEEVE!

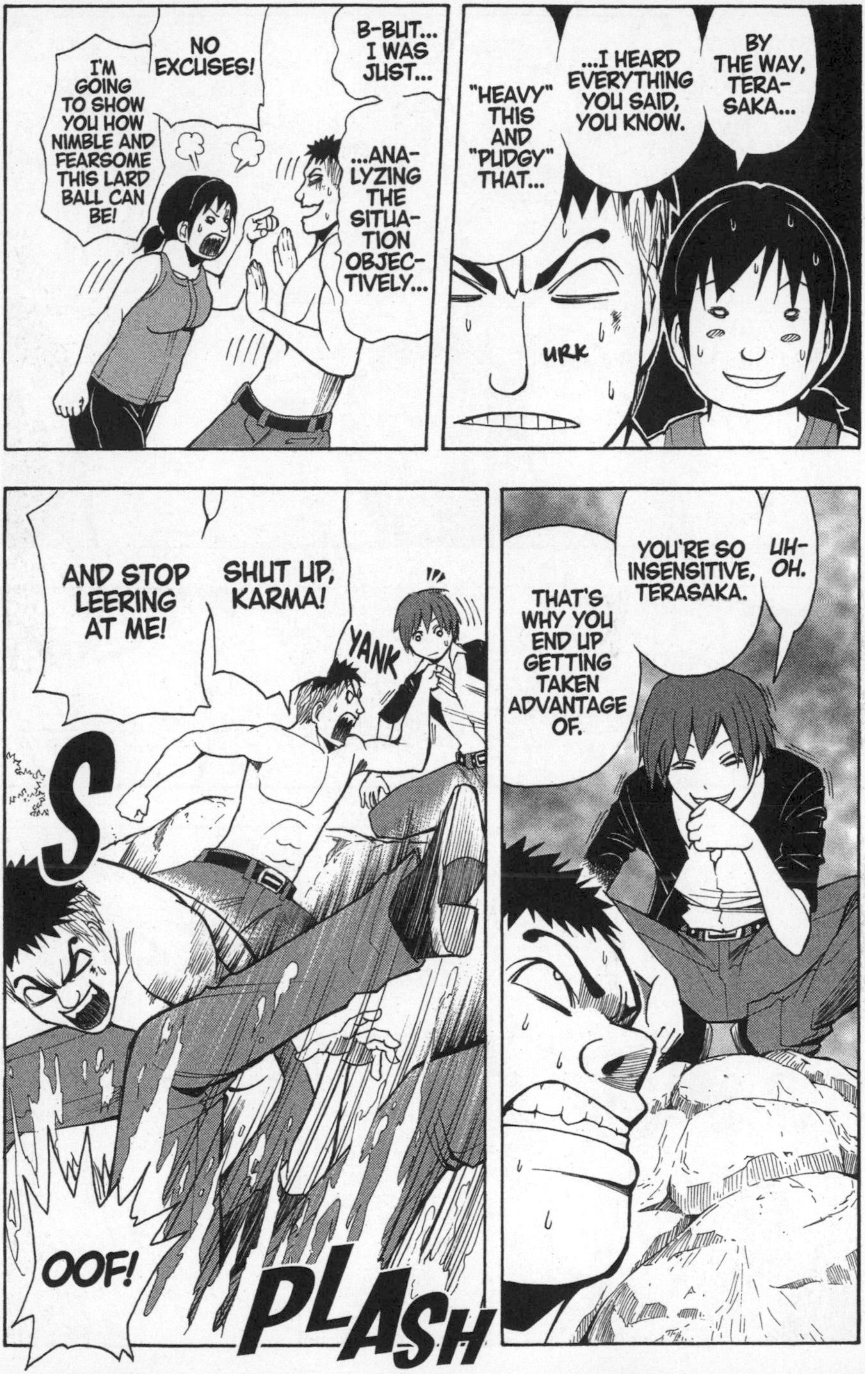
BY THE WAY, TERASAKA...
...I HEARD EVERYTHING YOU SAID, YOU KNOW.
"HEAVY" THIS AND "PUDGY" THAT...
URK
B-BUT... I WAS JUST...
...ANALYZING THE SITUATION OBJECTIVELY...
NO EXCUSES!
I'M GOING TO SHOW YOU HOW NIMBLE AND FEARSOME THIS LARD BALL CAN BE!
UH-OH.
YOU'RE SO INSENSITIVE, TERASAKA.
THAT'S WHY YOU END UP GETTING TAKEN ADVANTAGE OF.
SHUT UP, KARMA!
AND STOP LEERING AT ME!
YANK
S
OOF!
PLASH

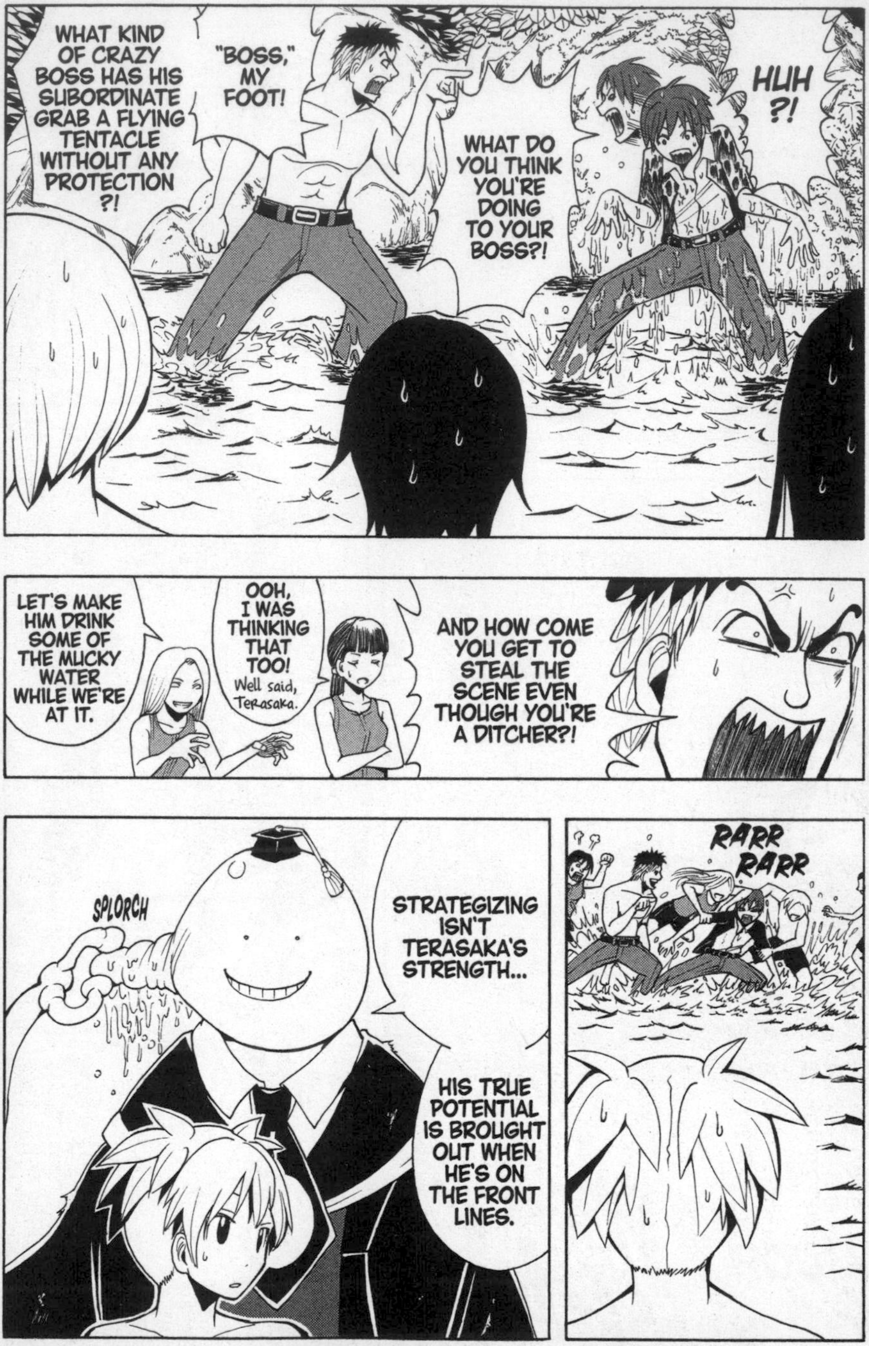
HUH ?!
WHAT DO YOU THINK YOU'RE DOING TO YOUR BOSS?!
"BOSS," MY FOOT!
WHAT KIND OF CRAZY BOSS HAS HIS SUBORDINATE GRAB A FLYING TENTACLE WITHOUT ANY PROTECTION ?!
AND HOW COME YOU GET TO STEAL THE SCENE EVEN THOUGH YOU'RE A DITCHER?!
OOH, I WAS THINKING THAT TOO!
Well said, Terasaka.
LET'S MAKE HIM DRINK SOME OF THE MUCKY WATER WHILE WE'RE AT IT.
RARR
RARR
STRATEGIZING ISN'T TERASAKA'S STRENGTH...
HIS TRUE POTENTIAL IS BROUGHT OUT WHEN HE'S ON THE FRONT LINES.
SPLORCH

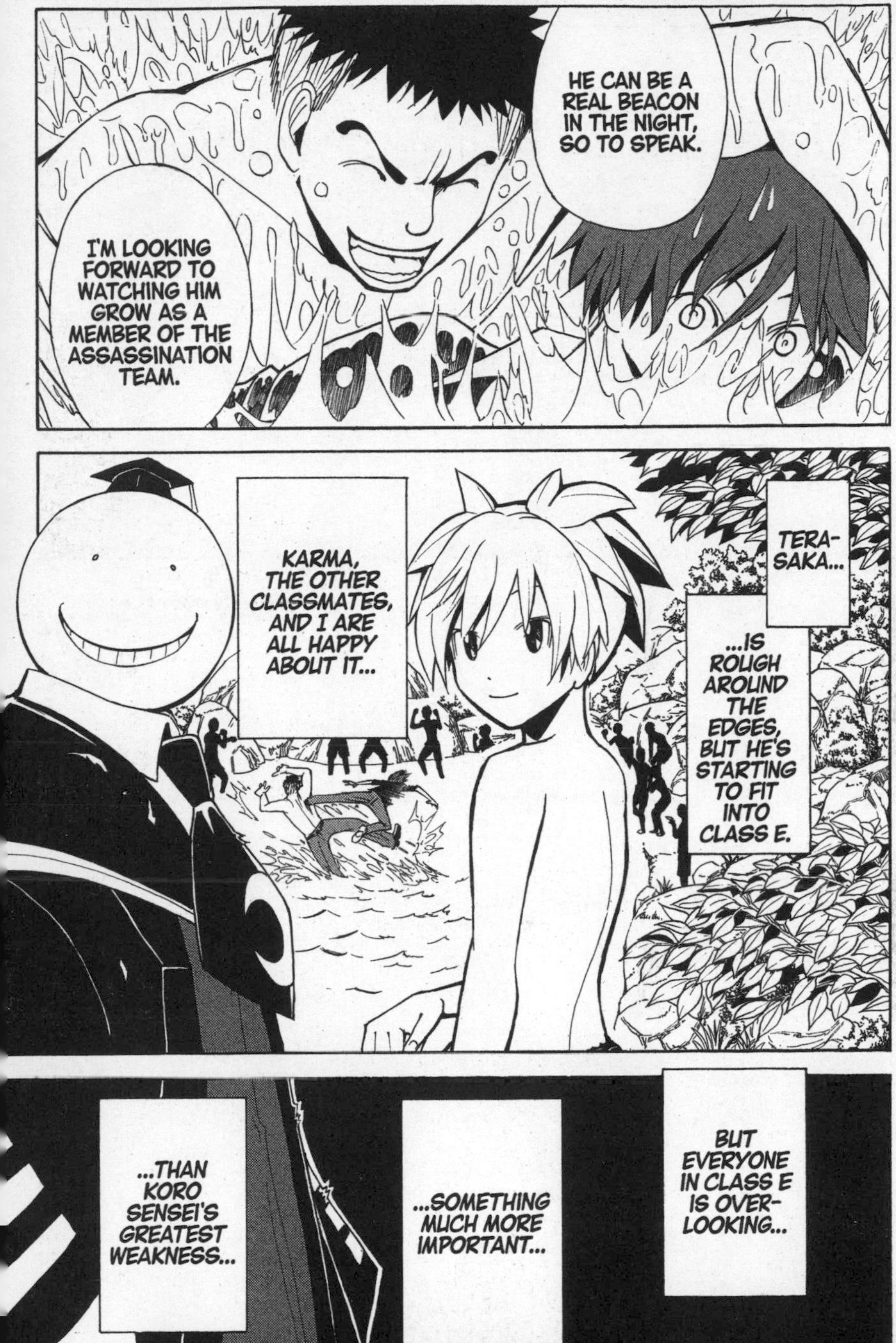
HE CAN BE A REAL BEACON IN THE NIGHT, SO TO SPEAK.
I'M LOOKING FORWARD TO WATCHING HIM GROW AS A MEMBER OF THE ASSASSINATION TEAM.
TERA-SAKA...
...IS ROUGH AROUND THE EDGES, BUT HE'S STARTING TO FIT INTO CLASS E.
KARMA, THE OTHER CLASSMATES, AND I ARE ALL HAPPY ABOUT IT...
BUT EVERYONE IN CLASS E IS OVER-LOOKING...
...SOMETHING MUCH MORE IMPORTANT...
...THAN KORO SENSEI'S GREATEST WEAKNESS...

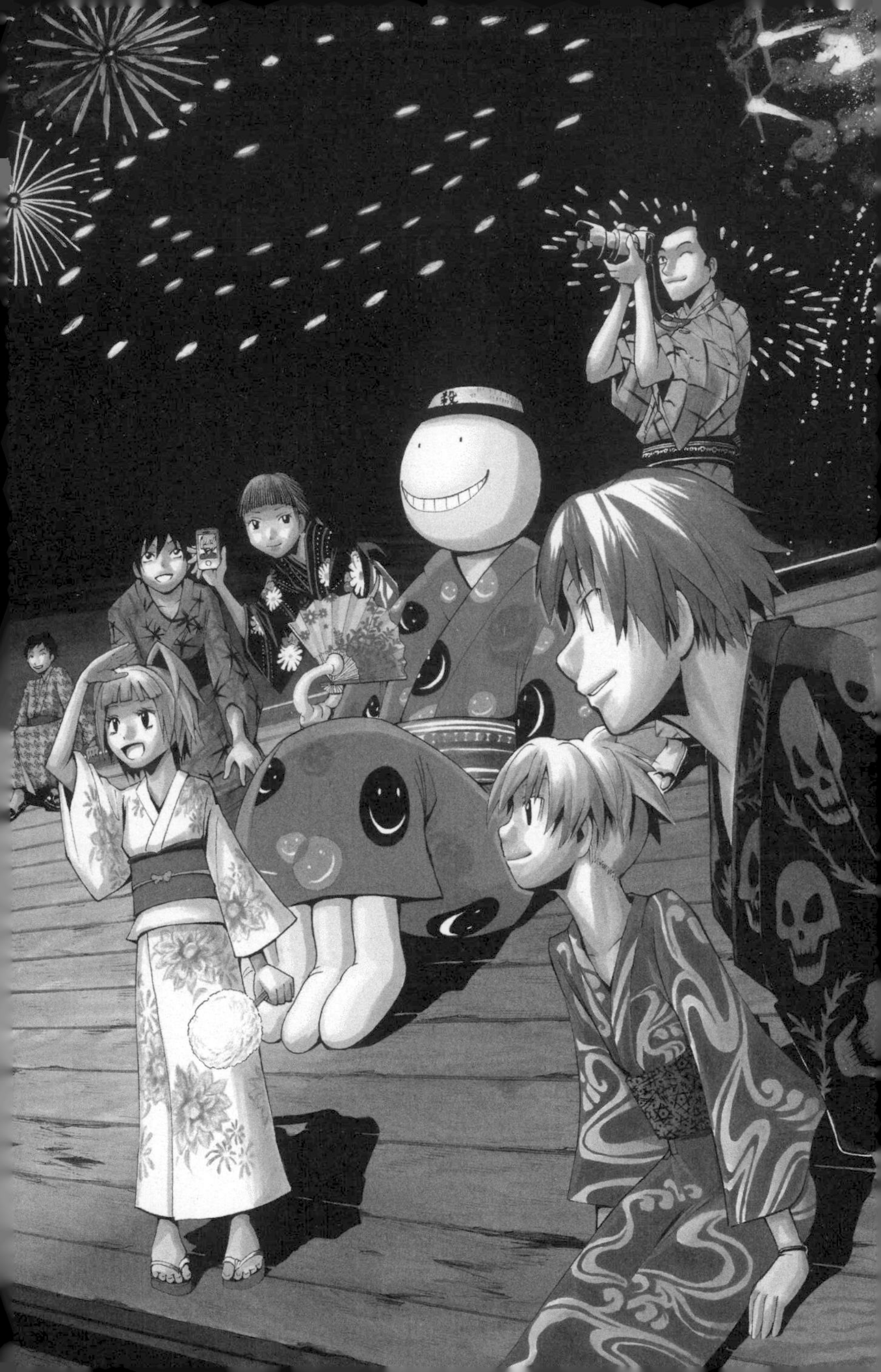

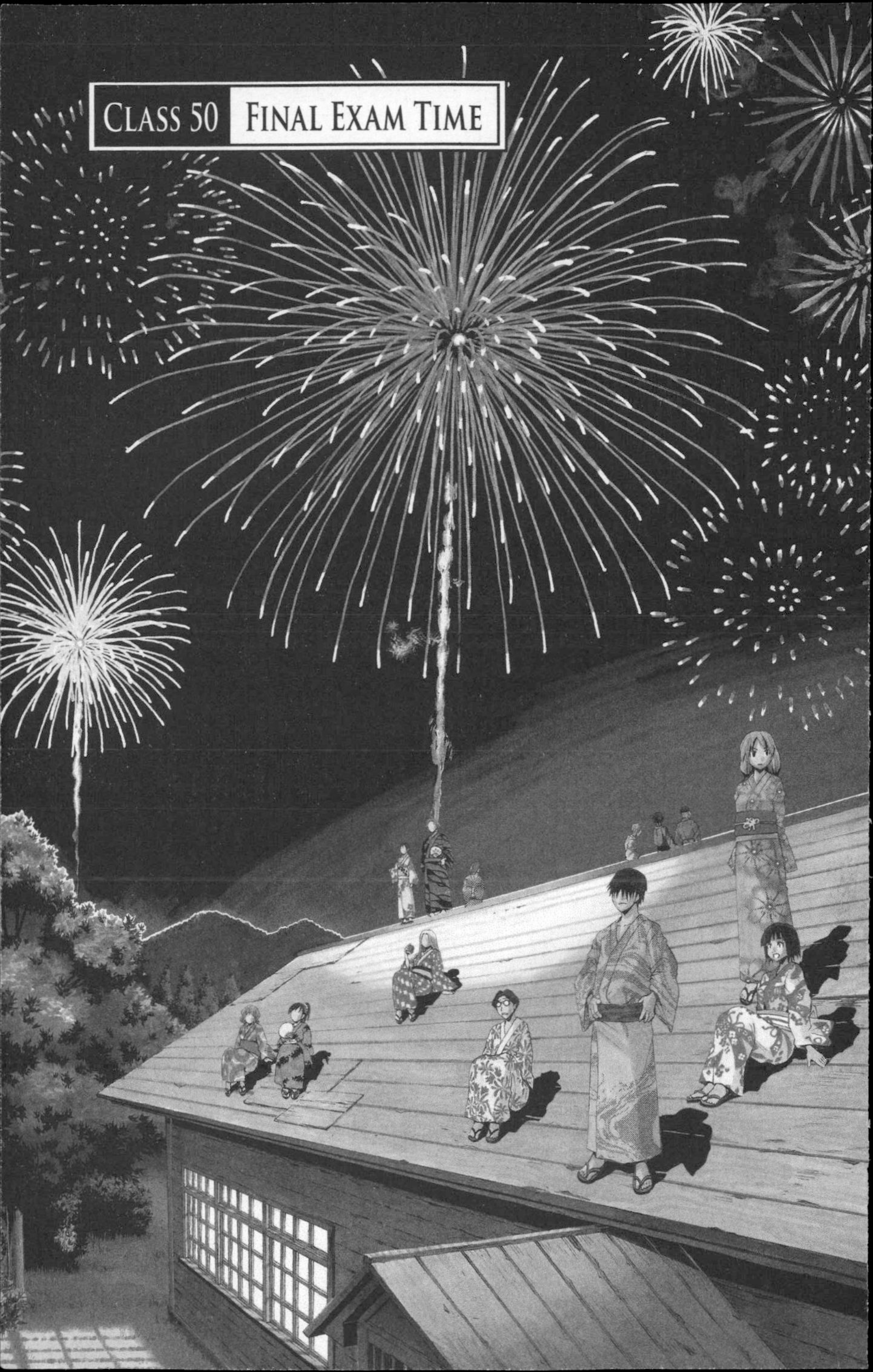
CLASS 50
FINAL EXAM TIME

E-16 RYOMA TERASAKA

- 😊 BIRTHDAY: APRIL 10
- 😊 HEIGHT: 5' 11"
- 😊 WEIGHT: 170 LBS.
- 😊 FAVORITE SUBJECT: PHYSICAL EDUCATION
- 😊 LEAST FAVORITE SUBJECT: LITERATURE AND HUMANITIES
- 😊 HOBBY/SKILL: WATCHING MARTIAL ARTS COMPETITIONS
- 😊 FUTURE GOAL: NOTHING SPECIFIC
- 😊 VAGUE FUTURE GOAL: TO BECOME A COMPETENT COMPANY EMPLOYEE WHO CEOs LIKE KARMA WILL KISS UP TO

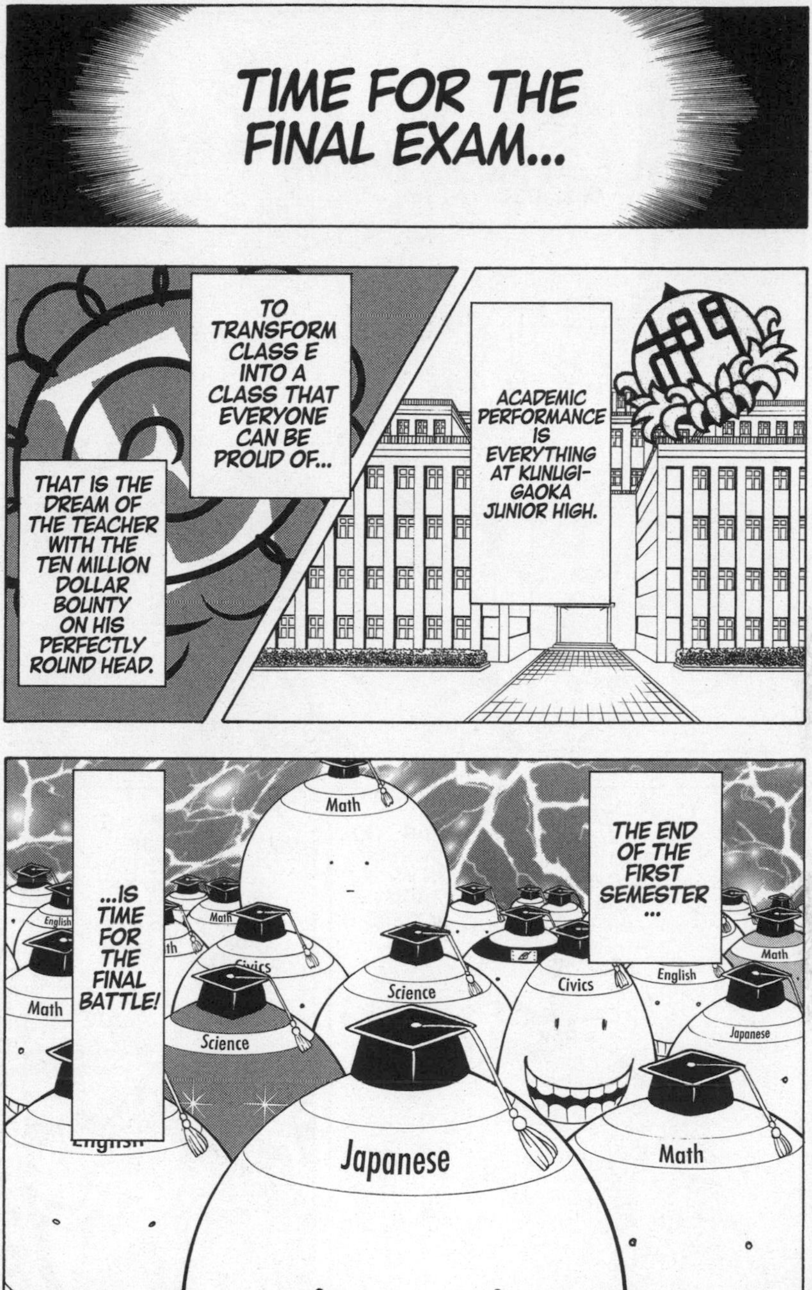
TIME FOR THE FINAL EXAM...
ACADEMIC PERFORMANCE IS EVERYTHING AT KUNUGIGAOKA JUNIOR HIGH.
TO TRANSFORM CLASS E INTO A CLASS THAT EVERYONE CAN BE PROUD OF...
THAT IS THE DREAM OF THE TEACHER WITH THE TEN MILLION DOLLAR BOUNTY ON HIS PERFECTLY ROUND HEAD.
THE END OF THE FIRST SEMESTER...
...IS TIME FOR THE FINAL BATTLE!
Math
English
Math
Civics
Science
Civics
Math
English
Japanese
Math
Science
Japanese
Math

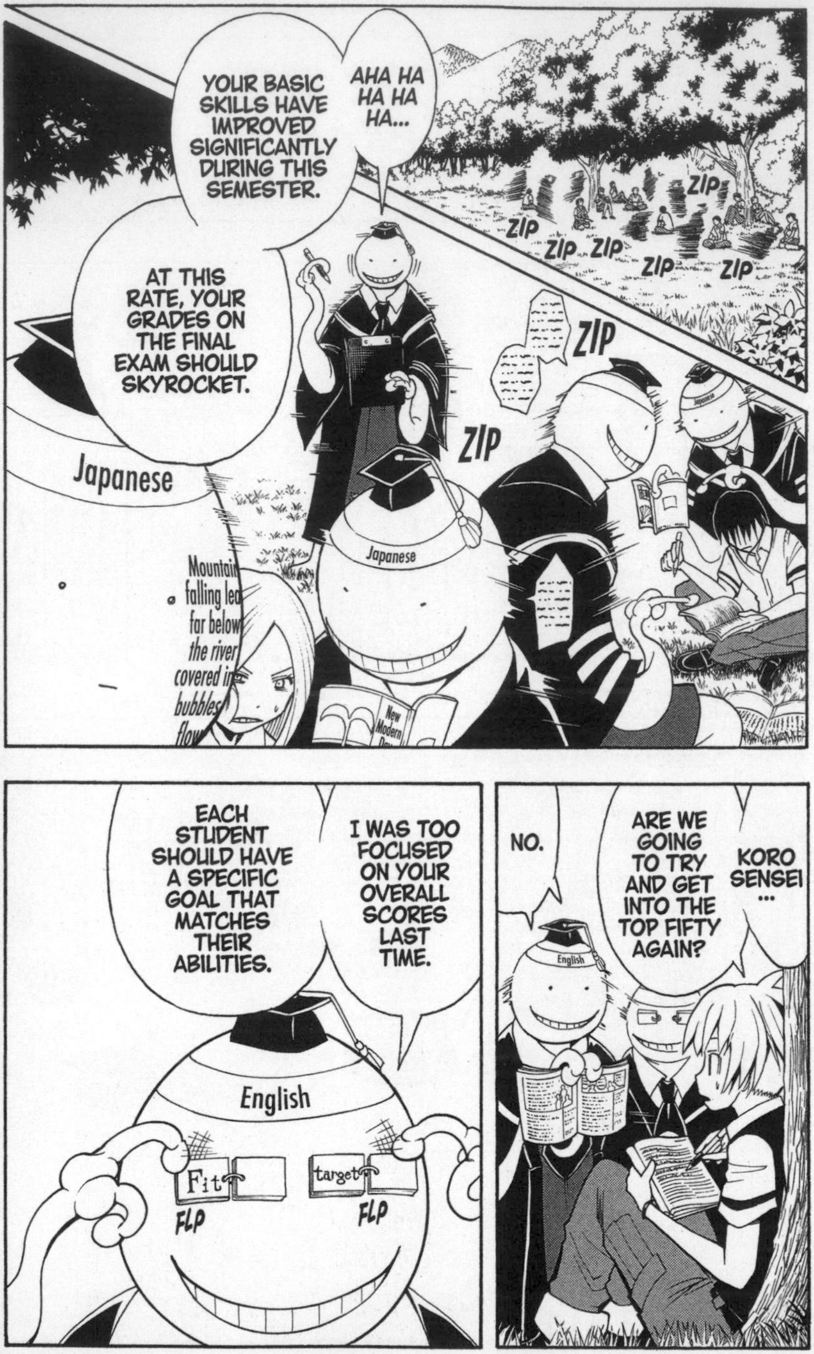
AHA HA HA HA HA...
YOUR BASIC SKILLS HAVE IMPROVED SIGNIFICANTLY DURING THIS SEMESTER.
ZIP
ZIP ZIP ZIP ZIP ZIP
AT THIS RATE, YOUR GRADES ON THE FINAL EXAM SHOULD SKYROCKET.
ZIP
ZIP
Japanese
Japanese
Japanese
Mountain
falling
far below
the river
covered in
bubbles
New Modern
KORO SENSEI ...
ARE WE GOING TO TRY AND GET INTO THE TOP FIFTY AGAIN?
NO.
English
I WAS TOO FOCUSED ON YOUR OVERALL SCORES LAST TIME.
EACH STUDENT SHOULD HAVE A SPECIFIC GOAL THAT MATCHES THEIR ABILITIES.
English
target
FLP
Fit
FLP

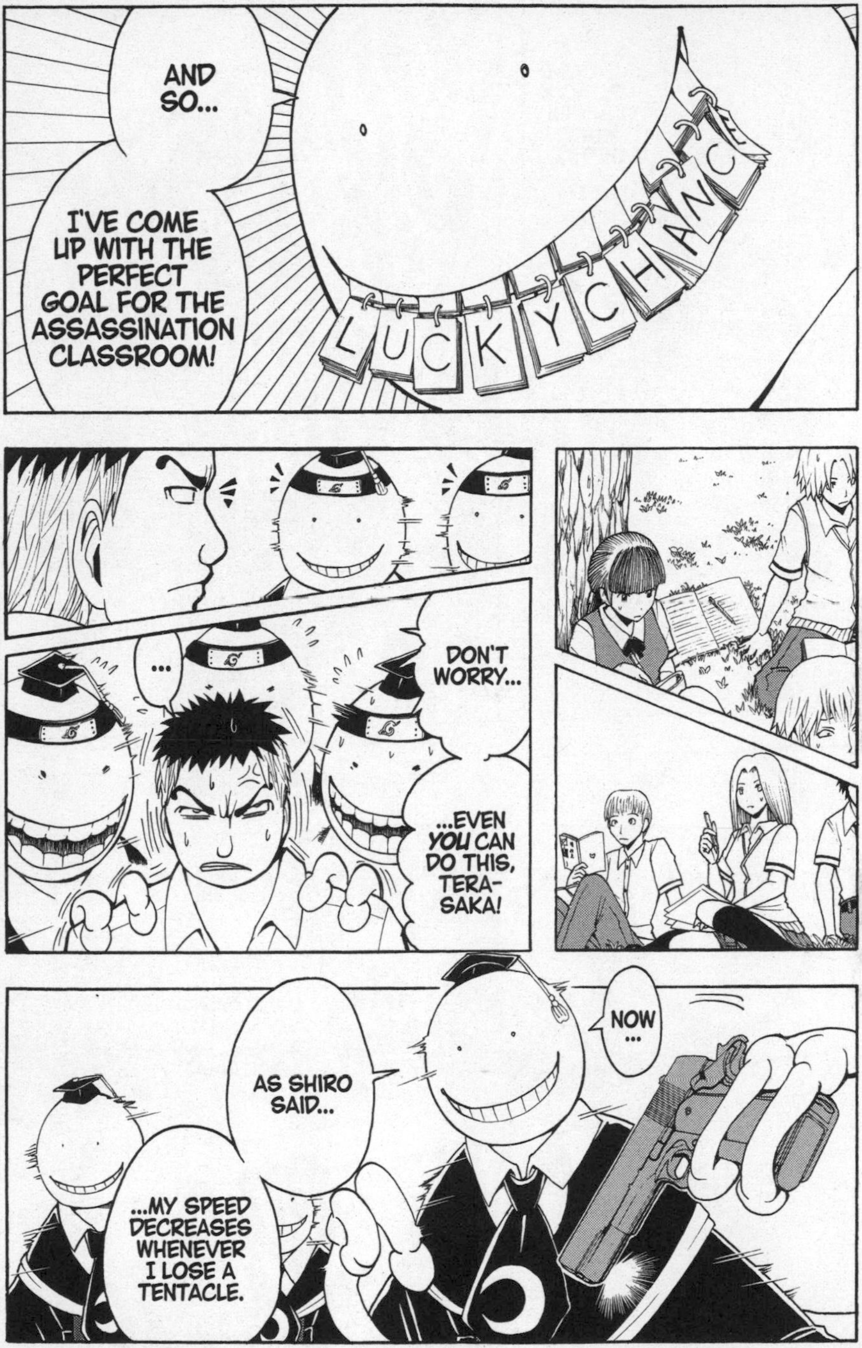
AND SO...
I'VE COME UP WITH THE PERFECT GOAL FOR THE ASSASSINATION CLASSROOM!
LUCKYCHANC
...
DON'T WORRY...
...EVEN *YOU* CAN DO THIS, TERA-SAKA!
NOW...
AS SHIRO SAID...
...MY SPEED DECREASES WHENEVER I LOSE A TENTACLE.

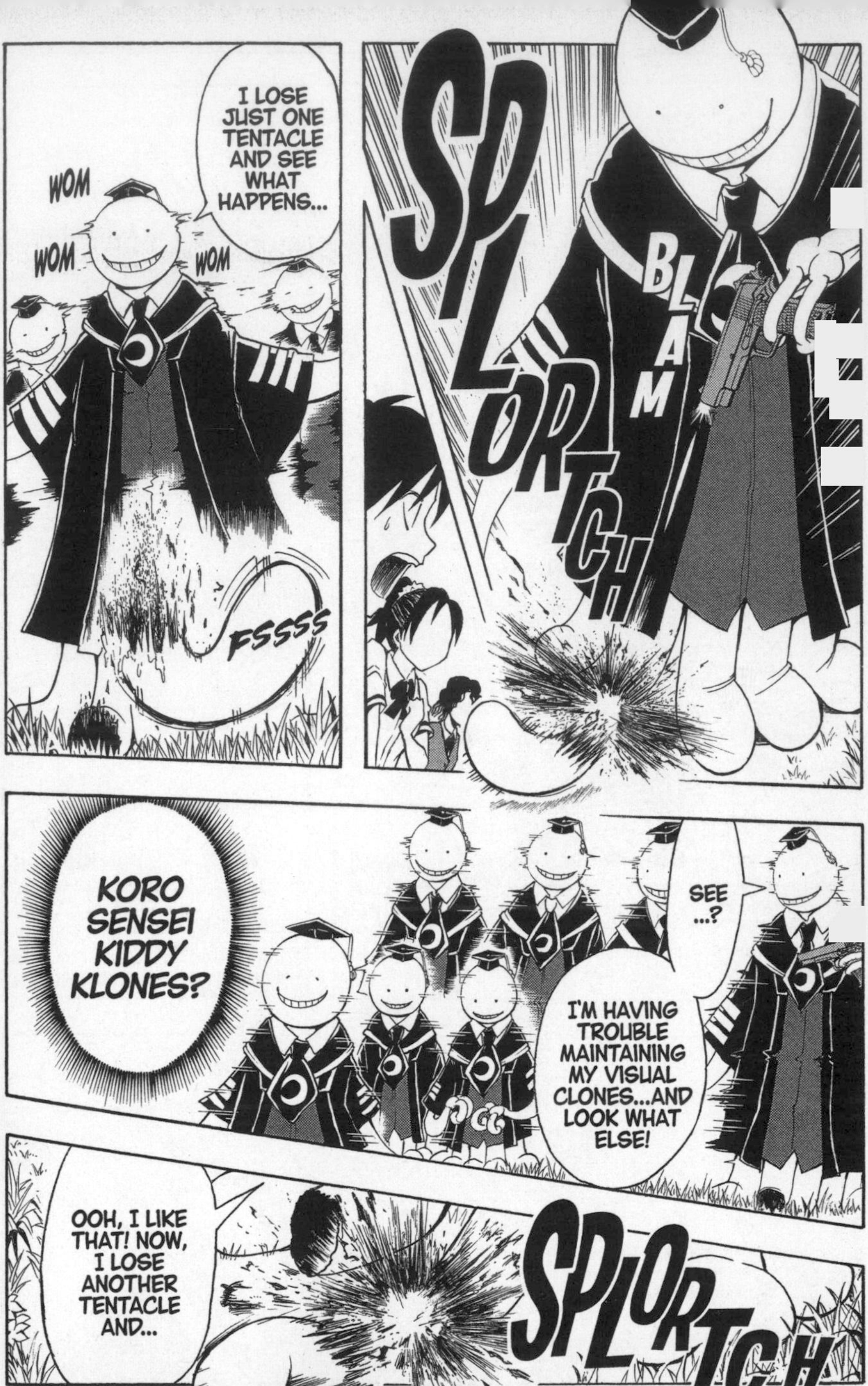
BLAM
SPLORTCH
I LOSE JUST ONE TENTACLE AND SEE WHAT HAPPENS...
WOM
WOM
WOM
FSSSS
SEE ...?
I'M HAVING TROUBLE MAINTAINING MY VISUAL CLONES...AND LOOK WHAT ELSE!
KORO SENSEI KIDDY KLONES?
OOH, I LIKE THAT! NOW, I LOSE ANOTHER TENTACLE AND...
SPLORTCH

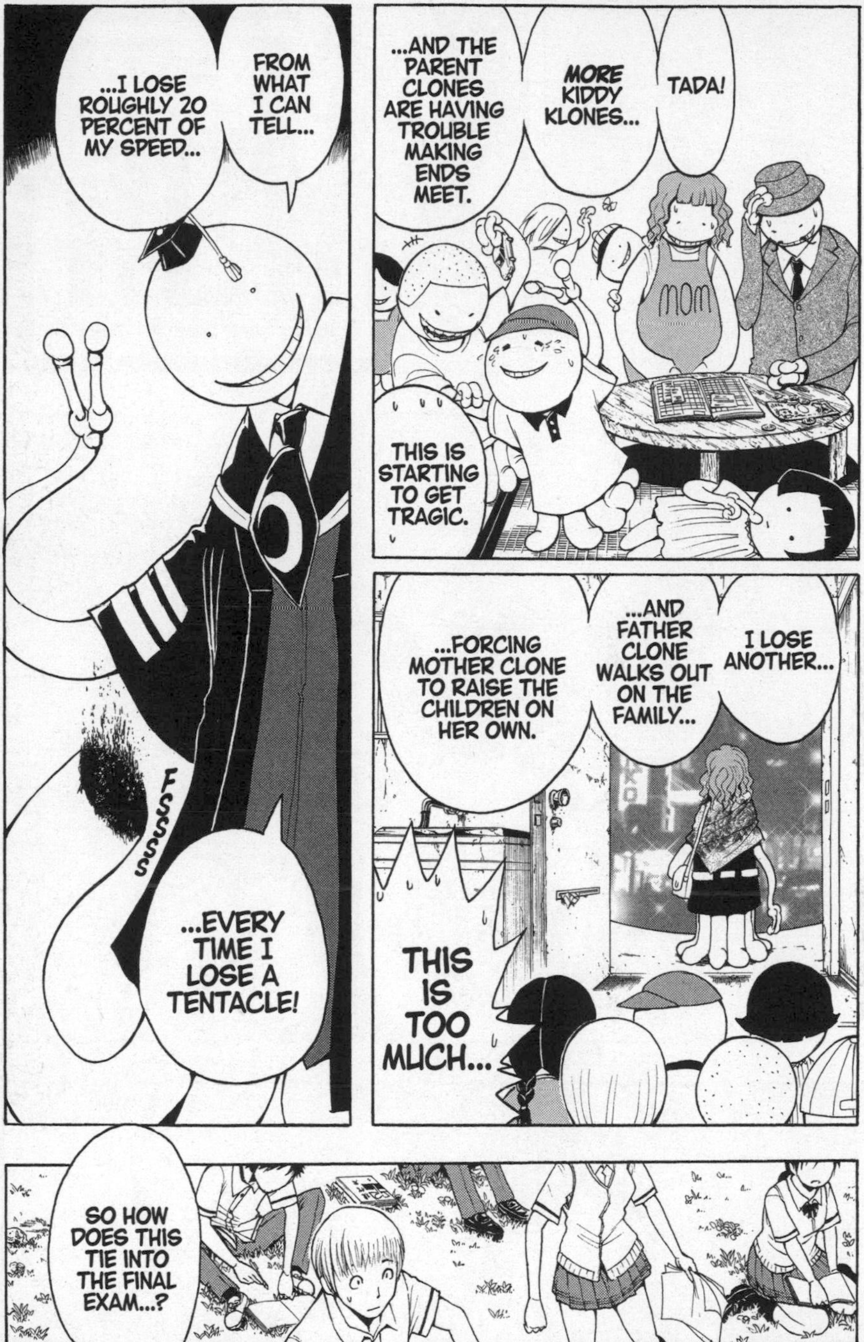
TADA!
MORE KIDDY KLONES...
...AND THE PARENT CLONES ARE HAVING TROUBLE MAKING ENDS MEET.
THIS IS STARTING TO GET TRAGIC.
I LOSE ANOTHER...
...AND FATHER CLONE WALKS OUT ON THE FAMILY...
...FORCING MOTHER CLONE TO RAISE THE CHILDREN ON HER OWN.
THIS IS TOO MUCH...
FROM WHAT I CAN TELL...
...I LOSE ROUGHLY 20 PERCENT OF MY SPEED...
FSSSSS
...EVERY TIME I LOSE A TENTACLE!
SO HOW DOES THIS TIE INTO THE FINAL EXAM...?

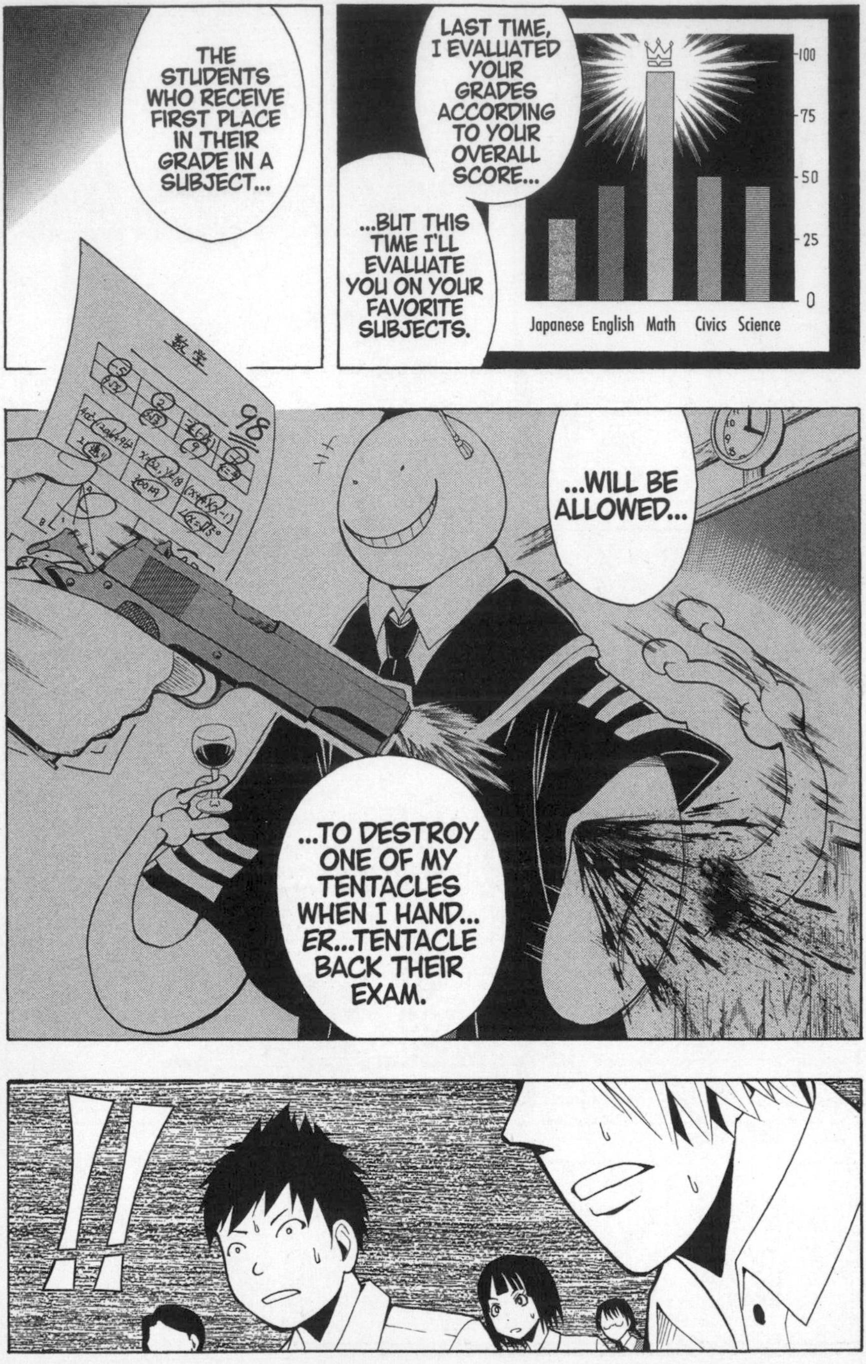
LAST TIME, I EVALUATED YOUR GRADES ACCORDING TO YOUR OVERALL SCORE...
...BUT THIS TIME I'LL EVALUATE YOU ON YOUR FAVORITE SUBJECTS.
100
75
50
25
0
Japanese English Math Civics Science
THE STUDENTS WHO RECEIVE FIRST PLACE IN THEIR GRADE IN A SUBJECT...
...WILL BE ALLOWED...
...TO DESTROY ONE OF MY TENTACLES WHEN I HAND... ER...TENTACLE BACK THEIR EXAM.
!!

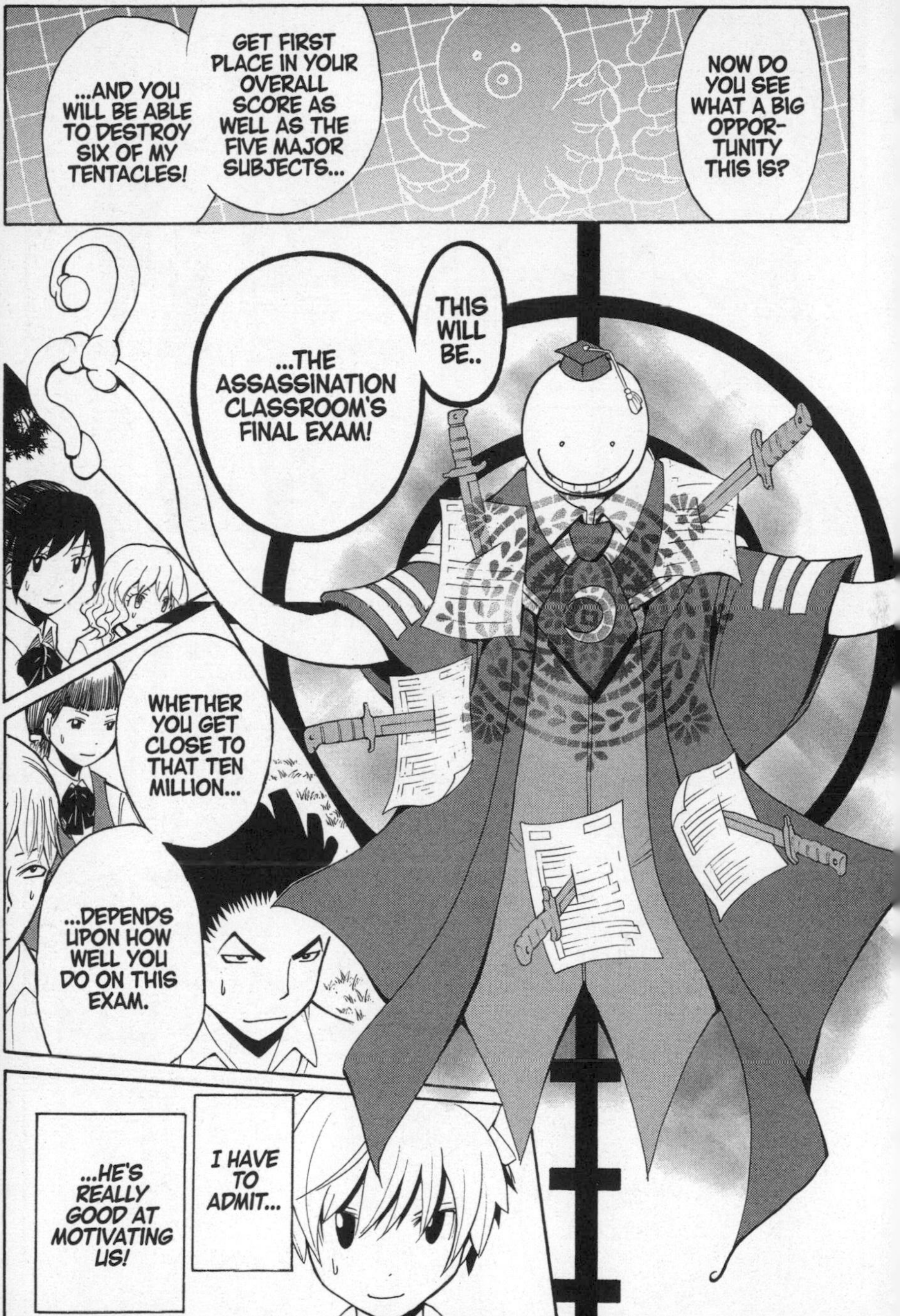
NOW DO YOU SEE WHAT A BIG OPPOR-TUNITY THIS IS?
GET FIRST PLACE IN YOUR OVERALL SCORE AS WELL AS THE FIVE MAJOR SUBJECTS...
...AND YOU WILL BE ABLE TO DESTROY SIX OF MY TENTACLES!
THIS WILL BE..
...THE ASSASSINATION CLASSROOM'S FINAL EXAM!
WHETHER YOU GET CLOSE TO THAT TEN MILLION...
...DEPENDS UPON HOW WELL YOU DO ON THIS EXAM.
I HAVE TO ADMIT...
...HE'S REALLY GOOD AT MOTIVATING US!

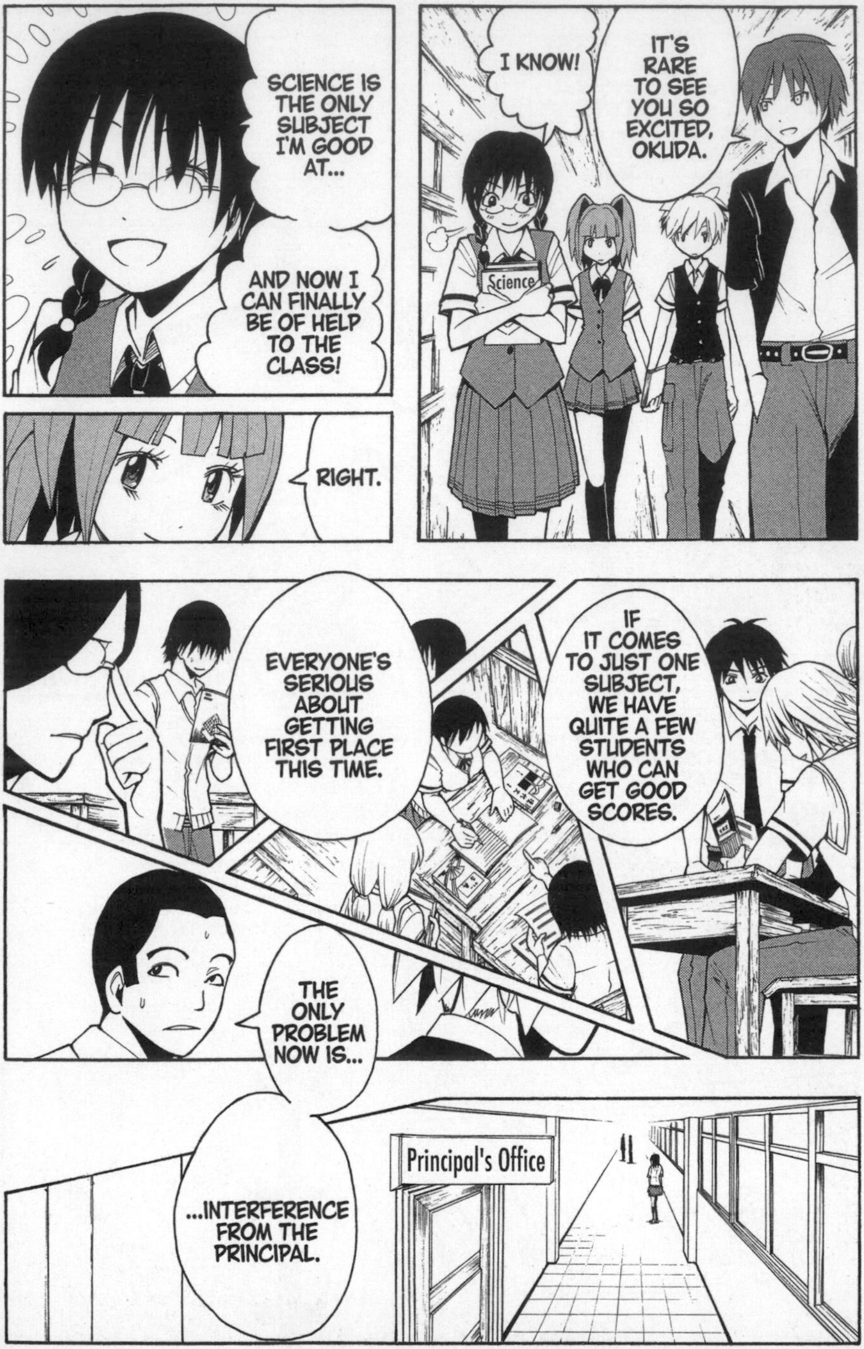
IT'S RARE TO SEE YOU SO EXCITED, OKUDA.
I KNOW!
Science
SCIENCE IS THE ONLY SUBJECT I'M GOOD AT...
AND NOW I CAN FINALLY BE OF HELP TO THE CLASS!
RIGHT.
IF IT COMES TO JUST ONE SUBJECT, WE HAVE QUITE A FEW STUDENTS WHO CAN GET GOOD SCORES.
EVERYONE'S SERIOUS ABOUT GETTING FIRST PLACE THIS TIME.
THE ONLY PROBLEM NOW IS...
Principal's Office
...INTERFERENCE FROM THE PRINCIPAL.

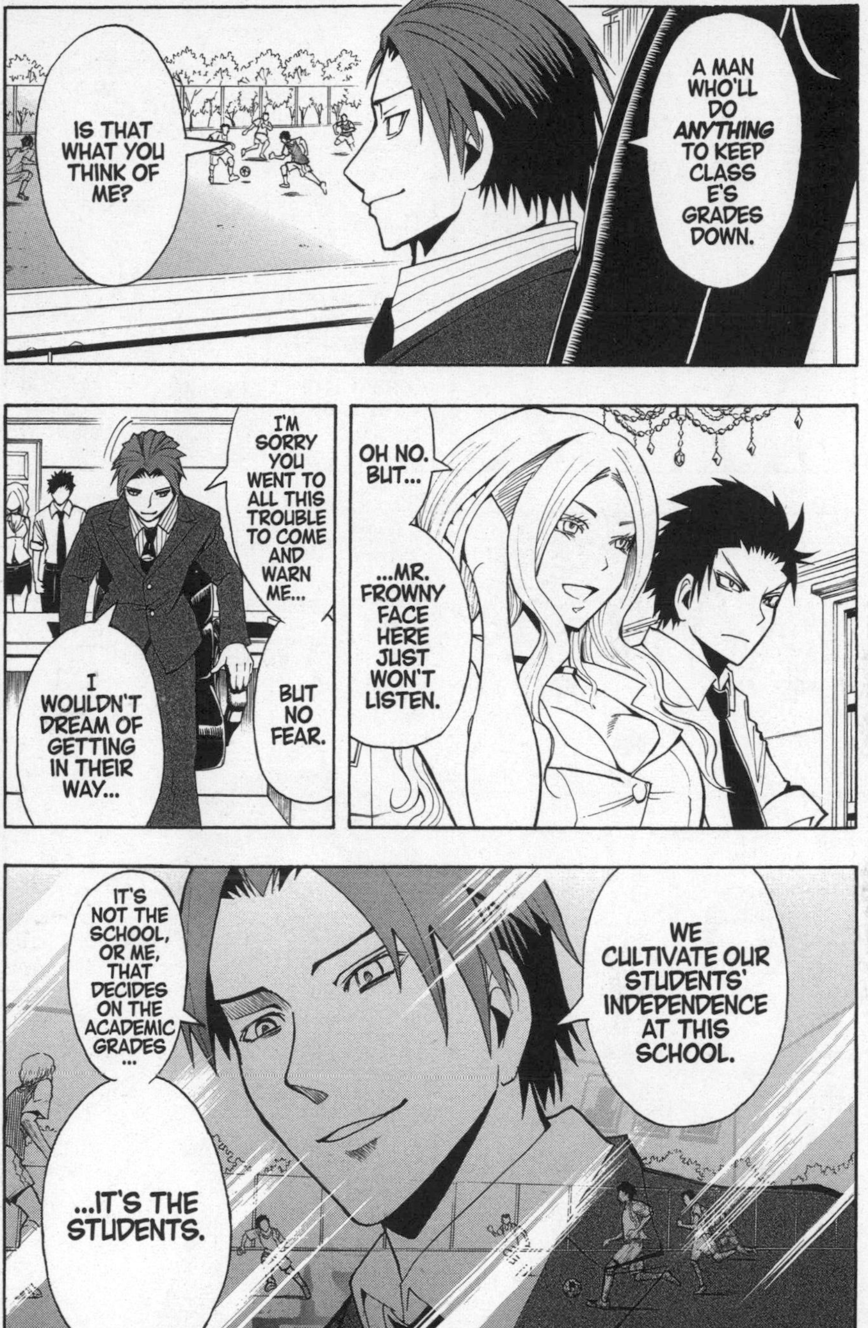
A MAN WHO'LL DO ANYTHING TO KEEP CLASS E'S GRADES DOWN.
IS THAT WHAT YOU THINK OF ME?
OH NO. BUT...
...MR. FROWNY FACE HERE JUST WON'T LISTEN.
I'M SORRY YOU WENT TO ALL THIS TROUBLE TO COME AND WARN ME...
BUT NO FEAR.
I WOULDN'T DREAM OF GETTING IN THEIR WAY...
WE CULTIVATE OUR STUDENTS' INDEPENDENCE AT THIS SCHOOL.
IT'S NOT THE SCHOOL, OR ME, THAT DECIDES ON THE ACADEMIC GRADES...
...IT'S THE STUDENTS.

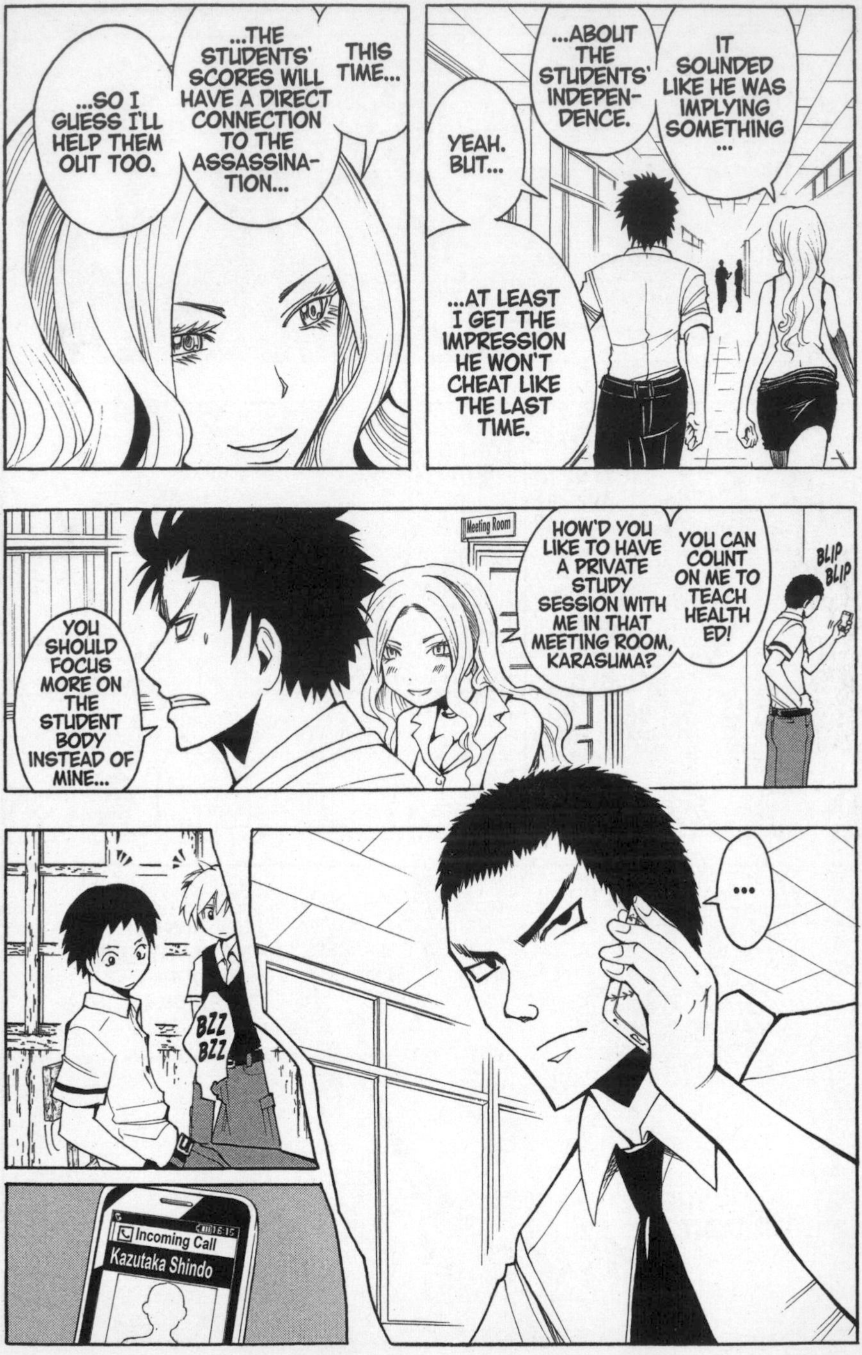
IT SOUNDED LIKE HE WAS IMPLYING SOMETHING...
...ABOUT THE STUDENTS' INDEPENDENCE.
YEAH. BUT...
...AT LEAST I GET THE IMPRESSION HE WON'T CHEAT LIKE THE LAST TIME.
THIS TIME...
...THE STUDENTS' SCORES WILL HAVE A DIRECT CONNECTION TO THE ASSASSINATION...
...SO I GUESS I'LL HELP THEM OUT TOO.
BLIP BLIP
Meeting Room
YOU CAN COUNT ON ME TO TEACH HEALTH ED!
HOW'D YOU LIKE TO HAVE A PRIVATE STUDY SESSION WITH ME IN THAT MEETING ROOM, KARASUMA?
YOU SHOULD FOCUS MORE ON THE STUDENT BODY INSTEAD OF MINE...
...
BZZ BZZ
16:15
Incoming Call
Kazutaka Shindo

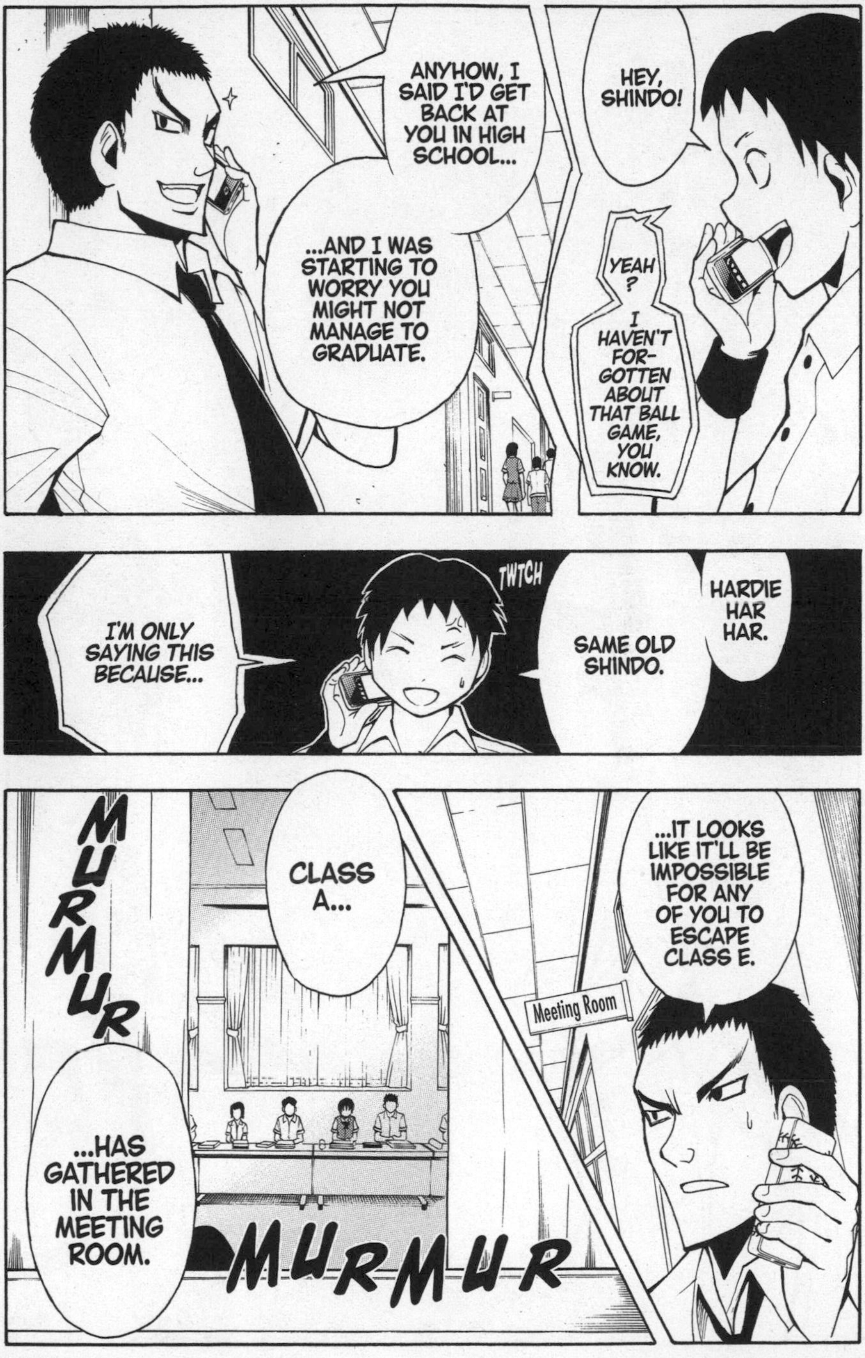
HEY, SHINDO!
YEAH? I HAVEN'T FORGOTTEN ABOUT THAT BALL GAME, YOU KNOW.
ANYHOW, I SAID I'D GET BACK AT YOU IN HIGH SCHOOL...
...AND I WAS STARTING TO WORRY YOU MIGHT NOT MANAGE TO GRADUATE.
HARDIE HAR HAR.
TWTCH
SAME OLD SHINDO.
I'M ONLY SAYING THIS BECAUSE...
...IT LOOKS LIKE IT'LL BE IMPOSSIBLE FOR ANY OF YOU TO ESCAPE CLASS E.
Meeting Room
CLASS A...
MURMUR
...HAS GATHERED IN THE MEETING ROOM.
MURMUR

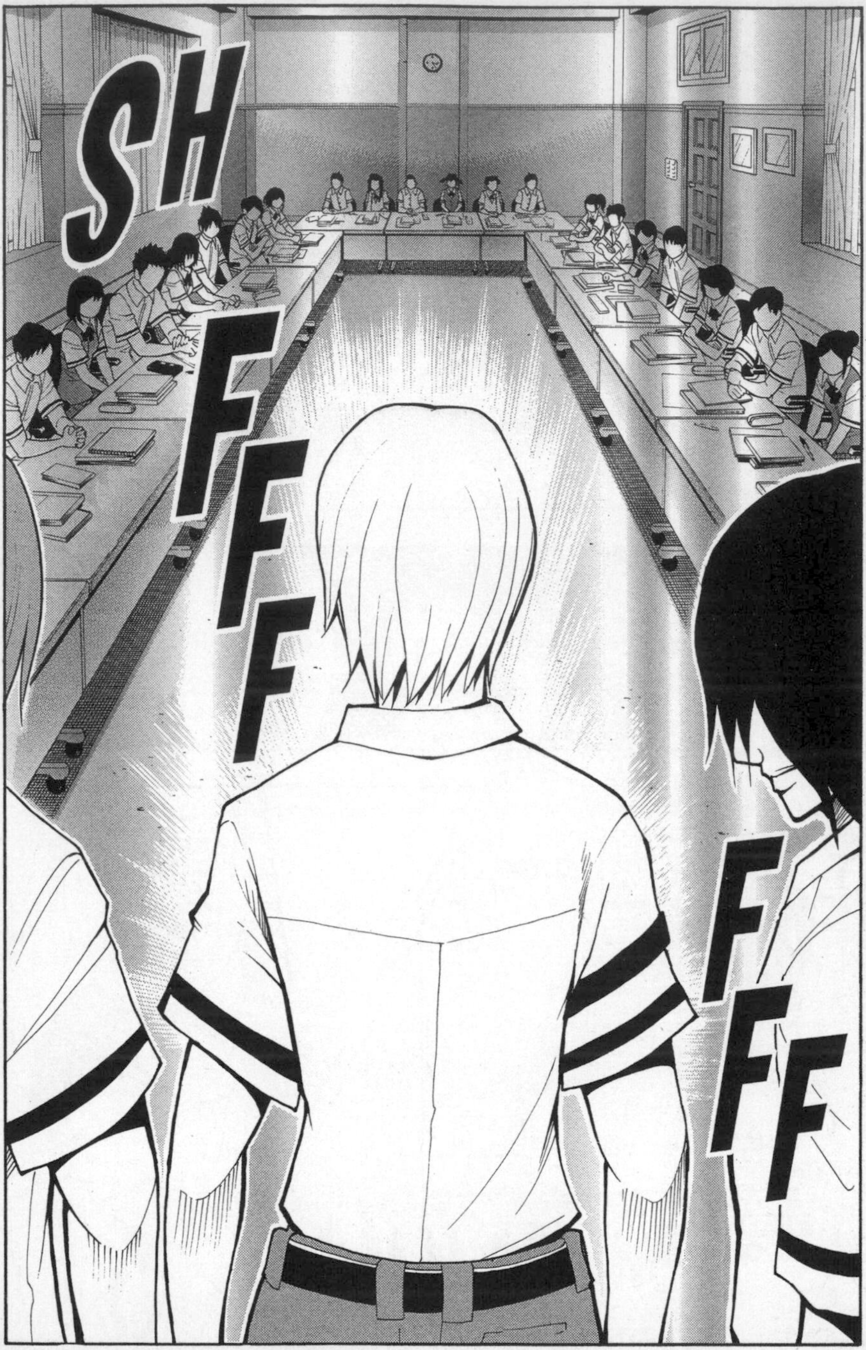
SHFFFF
FFFF

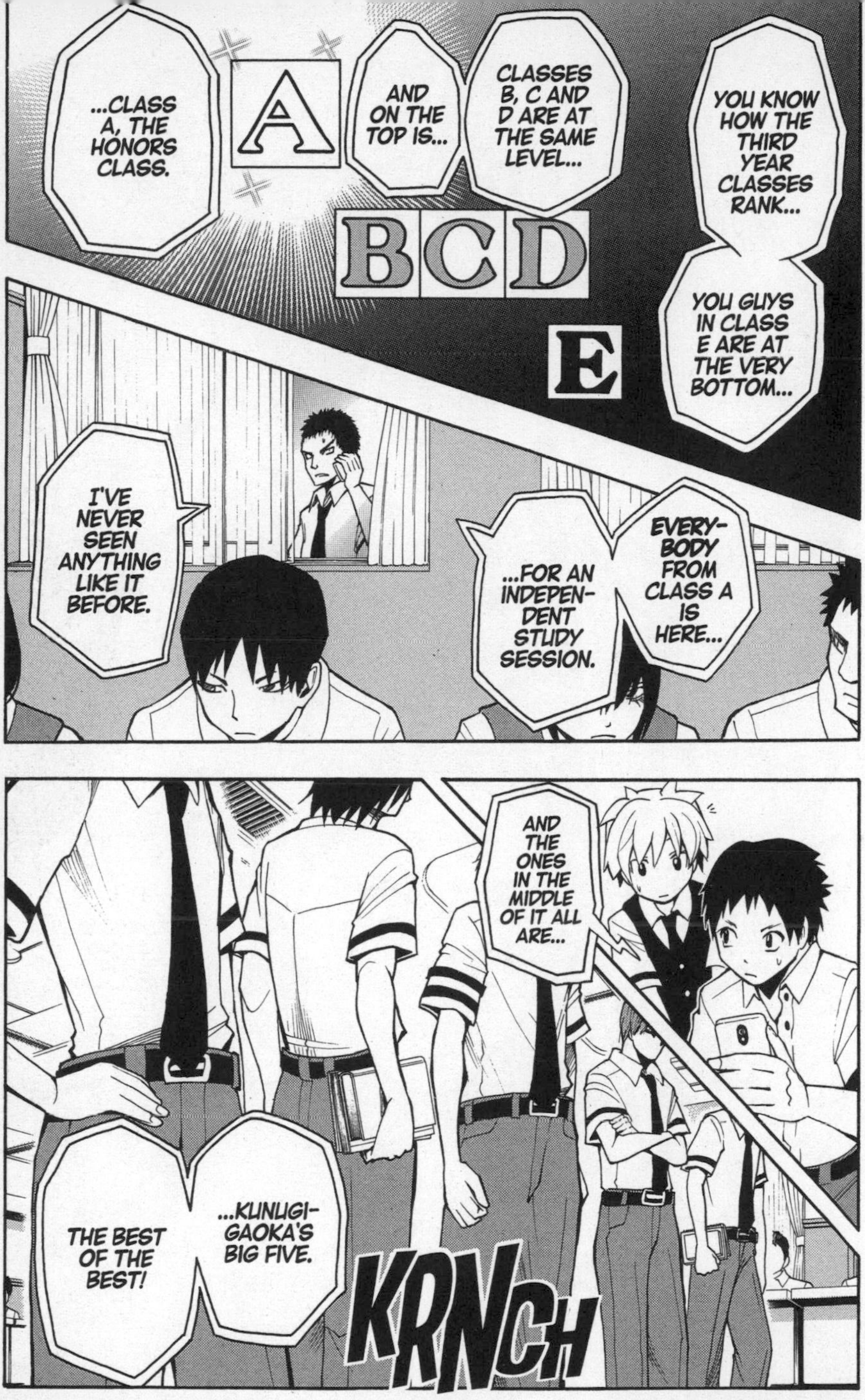
YOU KNOW HOW THE THIRD YEAR CLASSES RANK...
YOU GUYS IN CLASS E ARE AT THE VERY BOTTOM...
E
CLASSES B, C AND D ARE AT THE SAME LEVEL...
BCD
AND ON THE TOP IS...
A
...CLASS A, THE HONORS CLASS.
EVERY-BODY FROM CLASS A IS HERE...
...FOR AN INDEPEN-DENT STUDY SESSION.
I'VE NEVER SEEN ANYTHING LIKE IT BEFORE.
AND THE ONES IN THE MIDDLE OF IT ALL ARE...
...KUNUGI-GAOKA'S BIG FIVE.
THE BEST OF THE BEST!
KRNCH

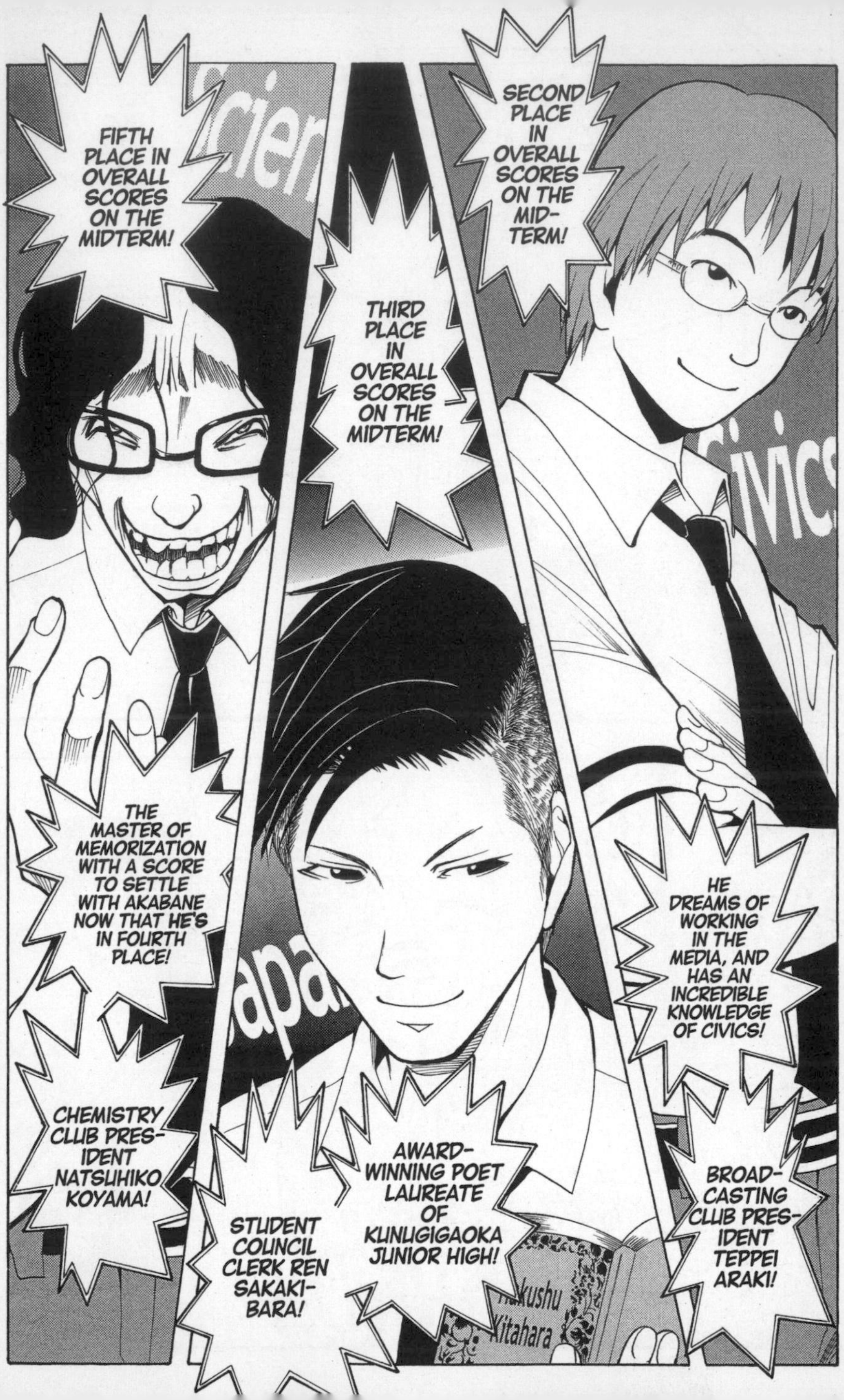
SECOND PLACE IN OVERALL SCORES ON THE MID-TERM!
Civics
HE DREAMS OF WORKING IN THE MEDIA, AND HAS AN INCREDIBLE KNOWLEDGE OF CIVICS!
BROAD-CASTING CLUB PRES-IDENT TEPPEI ARAKI!
THIRD PLACE IN OVERALL SCORES ON THE MIDTERM!
AWARD-WINNING POET LAUREATE OF KUNUGIGAOKA JUNIOR HIGH!
STUDENT COUNCIL CLERK REN SAKAKI-BARA!
Kitahara
FIFTH PLACE IN OVERALL SCORES ON THE MIDTERM!
THE MASTER OF MEMORIZATION WITH A SCORE TO SETTLE WITH AKABANE NOW THAT HE'S IN FOURTH PLACE!
CHEMISTRY CLUB PRES-IDENT NATSUHIKO KOYAMA!

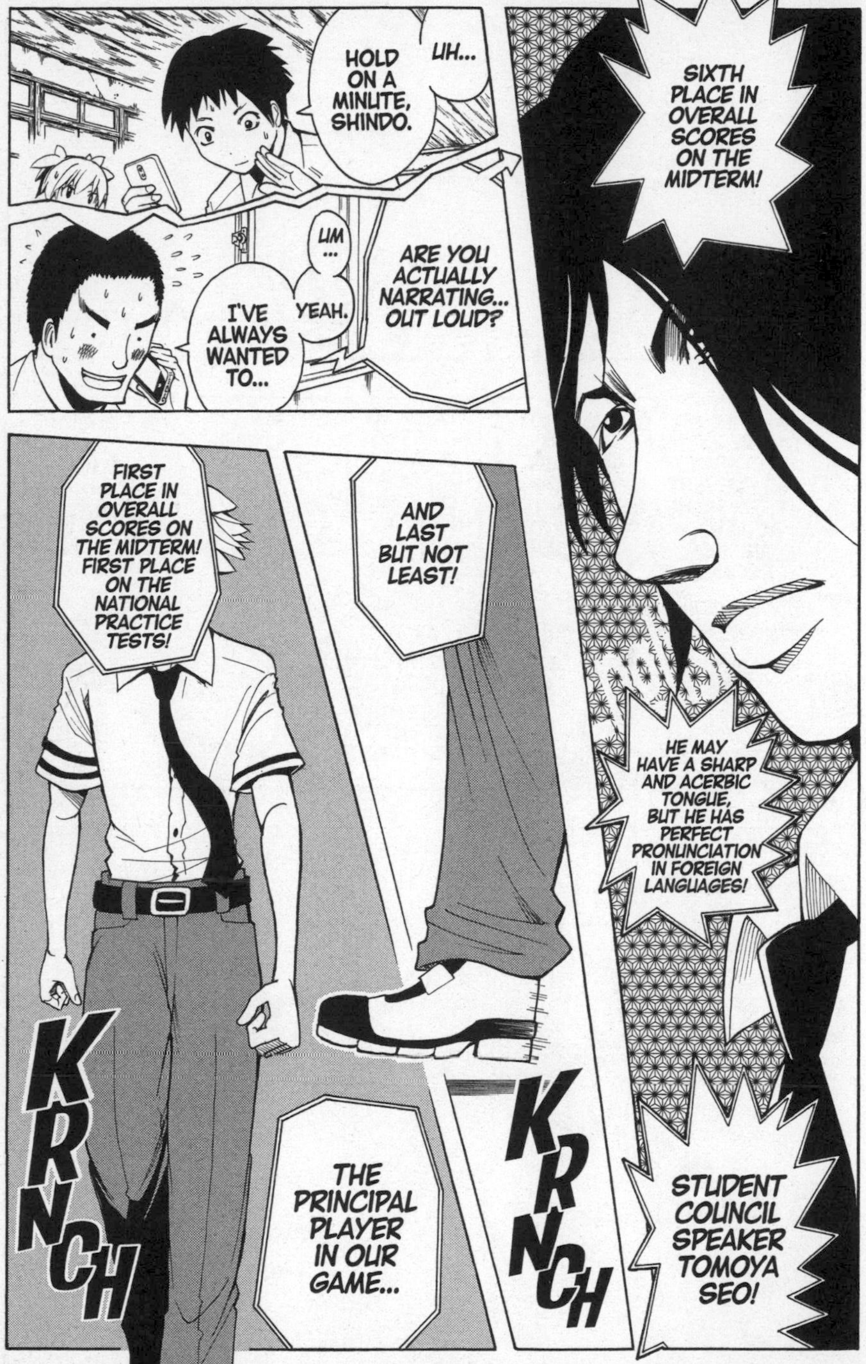
SIXTH PLACE IN OVERALL SCORES ON THE MIDTERM!
HE MAY HAVE A SHARP AND ACERBIC TONGUE, BUT HE HAS PERFECT PRONUNCIATION IN FOREIGN LANGUAGES!
STUDENT COUNCIL SPEAKER TOMOYA SEO!
UH...
HOLD ON A MINUTE, SHINDO.
ARE YOU ACTUALLY NARRATING... OUT LOUD?
UM...
YEAH.
I'VE ALWAYS WANTED TO...
AND LAST BUT NOT LEAST!
THE PRINCIPAL PLAYER IN OUR GAME...
KRNCH
FIRST PLACE IN OVERALL SCORES ON THE MIDTERM! FIRST PLACE ON THE NATIONAL PRACTICE TESTS!
KRNCH

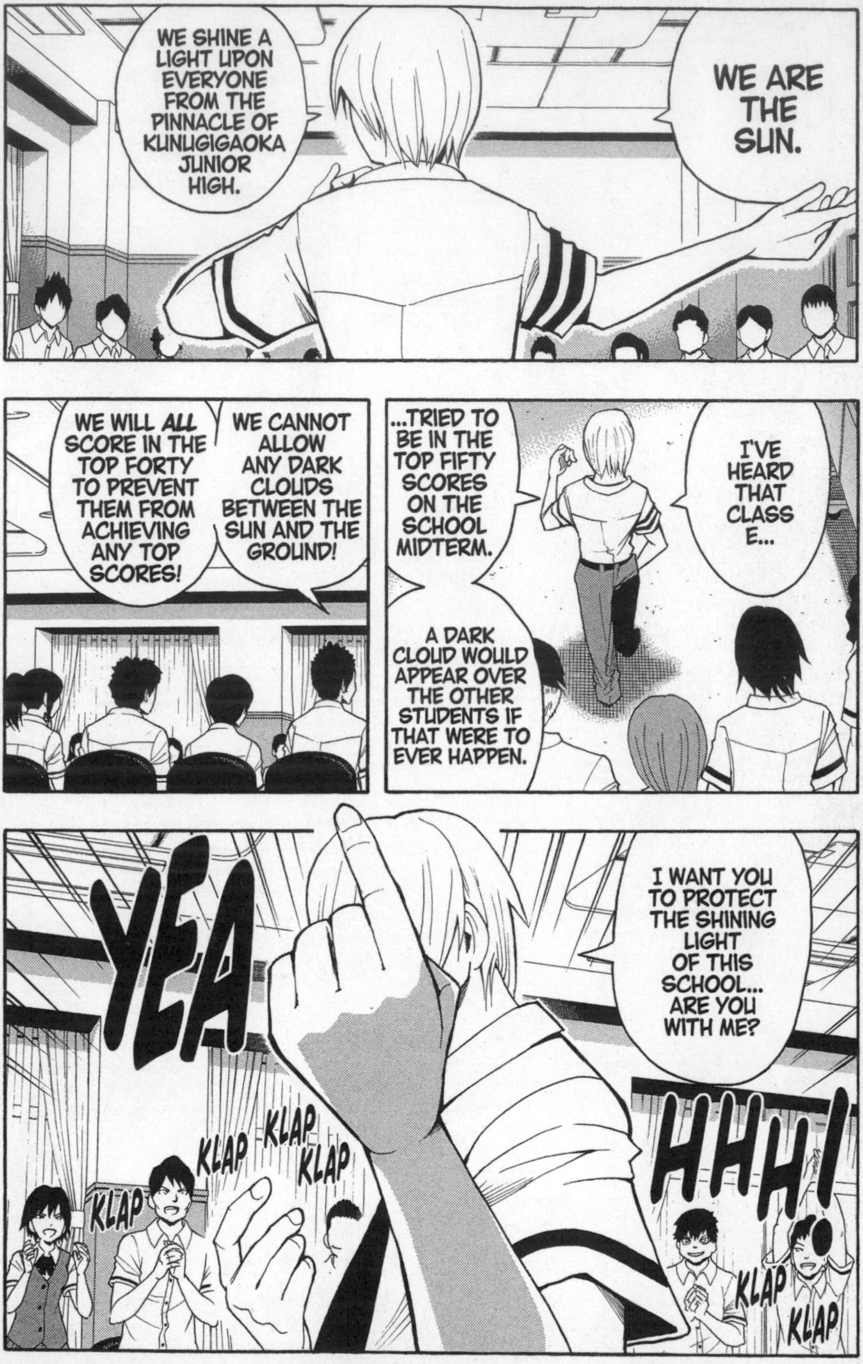
WE ARE THE SUN.
WE SHINE A LIGHT UPON EVERYONE FROM THE PINNACLE OF KUNUGIGAOKA JUNIOR HIGH.
I'VE HEARD THAT CLASS E...
...TRIED TO BE IN THE TOP FIFTY SCORES ON THE SCHOOL MIDTERM.
A DARK CLOUD WOULD APPEAR OVER THE OTHER STUDENTS IF THAT WERE TO EVER HAPPEN.
WE CANNOT ALLOW ANY DARK CLOUDS BETWEEN THE SUN AND THE GROUND!
WE WILL ALL SCORE IN THE TOP FORTY TO PREVENT THEM FROM ACHIEVING ANY TOP SCORES!
I WANT YOU TO PROTECT THE SHINING LIGHT OF THIS SCHOOL... ARE YOU WITH ME?
HHH!
YEA
KLAP KLAP
KLAP KLAP
KLAP KLAP

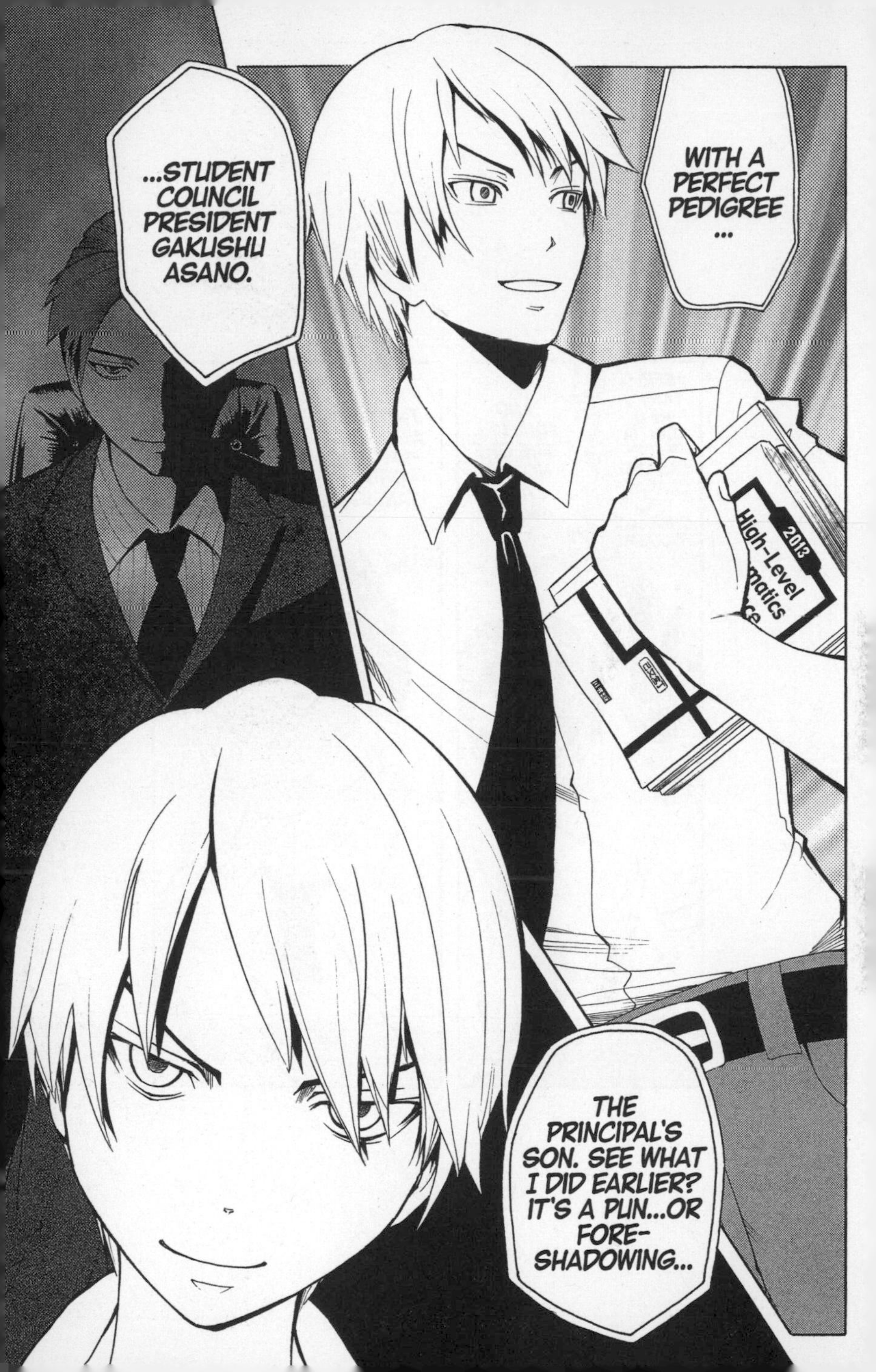
WITH A PERFECT PEDIGREE...
...STUDENT COUNCIL PRESIDENT GAKUSHU ASANO.
2013
High-Level
THE PRINCIPAL'S SON. SEE WHAT I DID EARLIER? IT'S A PUN...OR FORE-SHADOWING...

AND YOU CAN'T FORGET THIS GUY WHEN TALKING ABOUT TOADIES!
THE GUY WITH THE PIMPLES, NOBUTA TANAKA!
AND FINALLY... THE ONE NO ONE CARES ABOUT...
SERIOUSLY, HE'S JUST A BACKGROUND CHARACTER... CHOSUKE TAKADA!

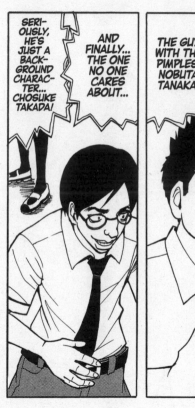

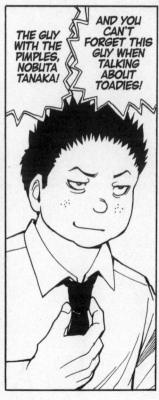

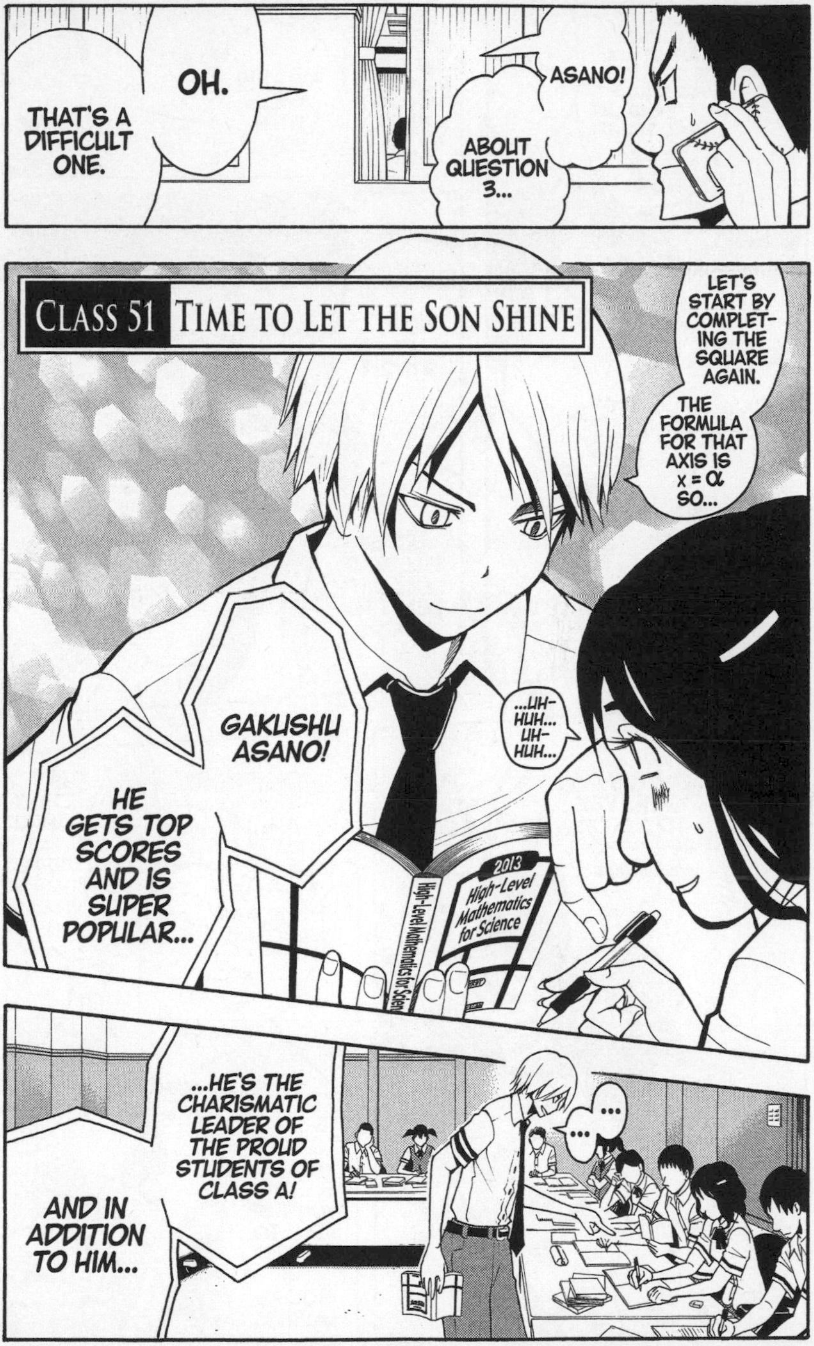
ASANO!
ABOUT QUESTION 3...
OH.
THAT'S A DIFFICULT ONE.
CLASS 51 TIME TO LET THE SON SHINE
LET'S START BY COMPLETING THE SQUARE AGAIN.
THE FORMULA FOR THAT AXIS IS x = α SO...
...UH-HUH... UH-HUH...
GAKUSHU ASANO!
HE GETS TOP SCORES AND IS SUPER POPULAR...
2013 High-Level Mathematics for Science
...
...
...HE'S THE CHARISMATIC LEADER OF THE PROUD STUDENTS OF CLASS A!
AND IN ADDITION TO HIM...

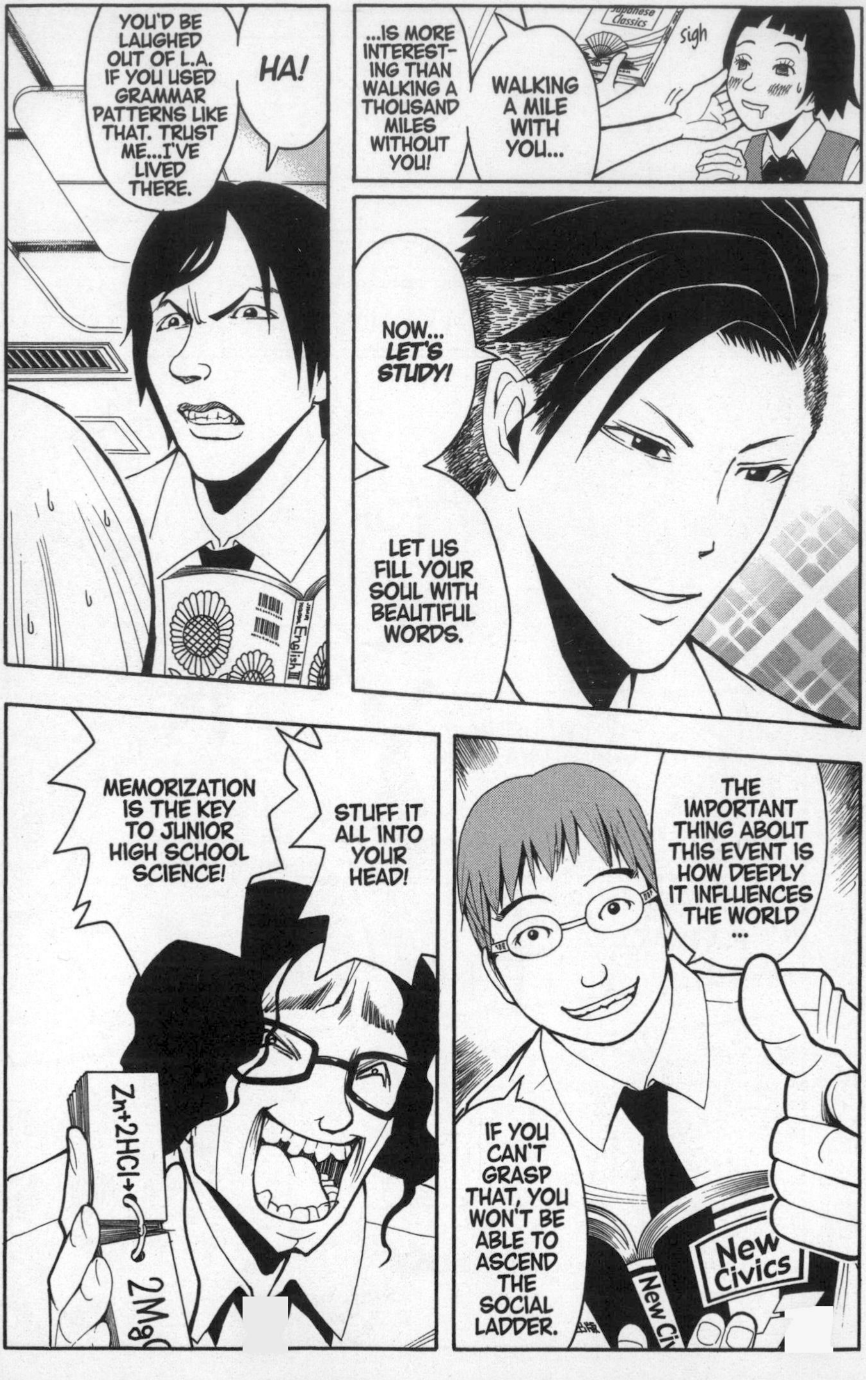
WALKING A MILE WITH YOU...
...IS MORE INTERESTING THAN WALKING A THOUSAND MILES WITHOUT YOU!
Japanese Classics
sigh
NOW... LET'S STUDY!
LET US FILL YOUR SOUL WITH BEAUTIFUL WORDS.
HA!
YOU'D BE LAUGHED OUT OF L.A. IF YOU USED GRAMMAR PATTERNS LIKE THAT. TRUST ME...I'VE LIVED THERE.
English III
THE IMPORTANT THING ABOUT THIS EVENT IS HOW DEEPLY IT INFLUENCES THE WORLD ...
IF YOU CAN'T GRASP THAT, YOU WON'T BE ABLE TO ASCEND THE SOCIAL LADDER.
New Civics
STUFF IT ALL INTO YOUR HEAD!
MEMORIZATION IS THE KEY TO JUNIOR HIGH SCHOOL SCIENCE!
Zn+2HCl→
2Mg

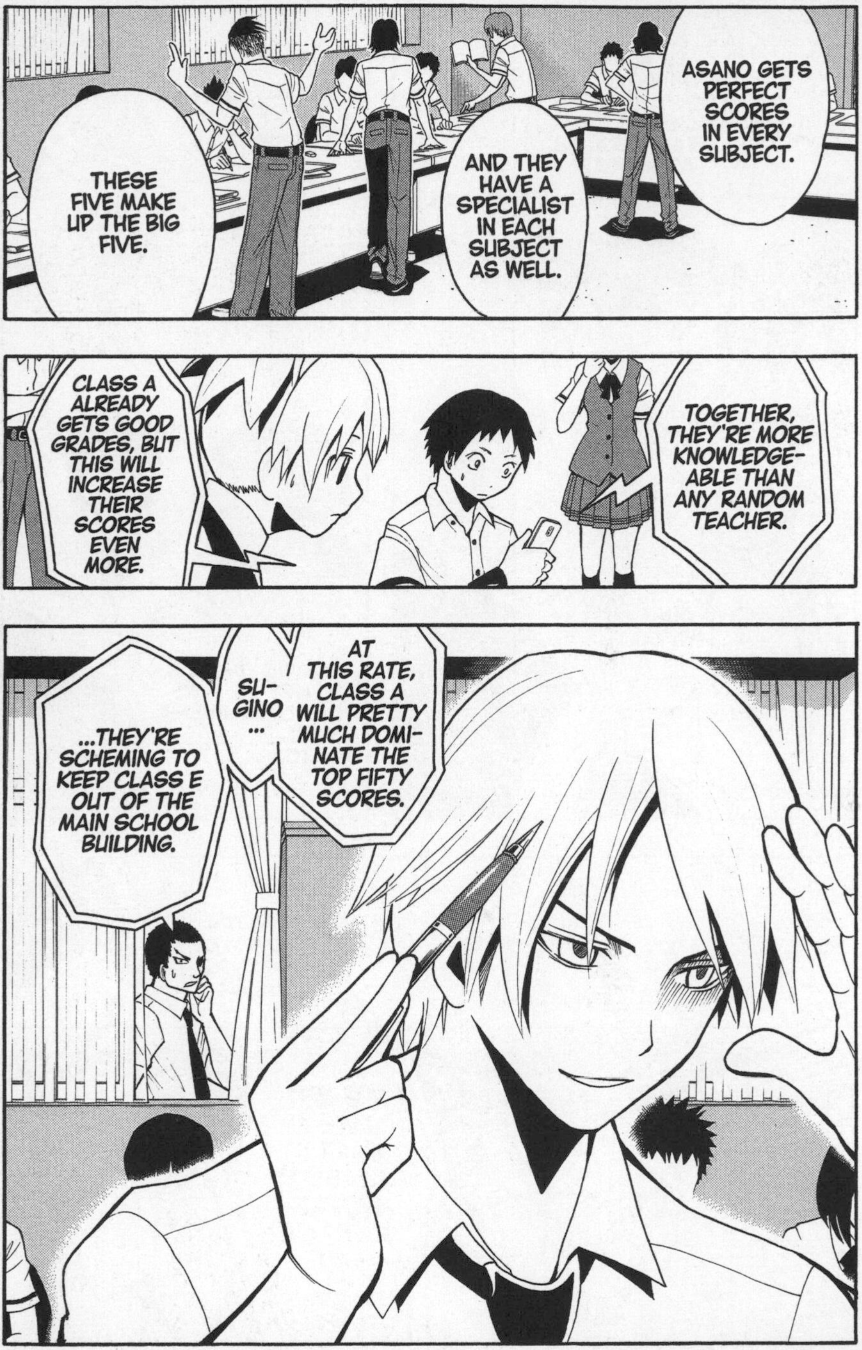
ASANO GETS PERFECT SCORES IN EVERY SUBJECT.
AND THEY HAVE A SPECIALIST IN EACH SUBJECT AS WELL.
THESE FIVE MAKE UP THE BIG FIVE.
TOGETHER, THEY'RE MORE KNOWLEDGE-ABLE THAN ANY RANDOM TEACHER.
CLASS A ALREADY GETS GOOD GRADES, BUT THIS WILL INCREASE THEIR SCORES EVEN MORE.
AT THIS RATE, CLASS A WILL PRETTY MUCH DOMINATE THE TOP FIFTY SCORES.
SUGINO...
...THEY'RE SCHEMING TO KEEP CLASS E OUT OF THE MAIN SCHOOL BUILDING.

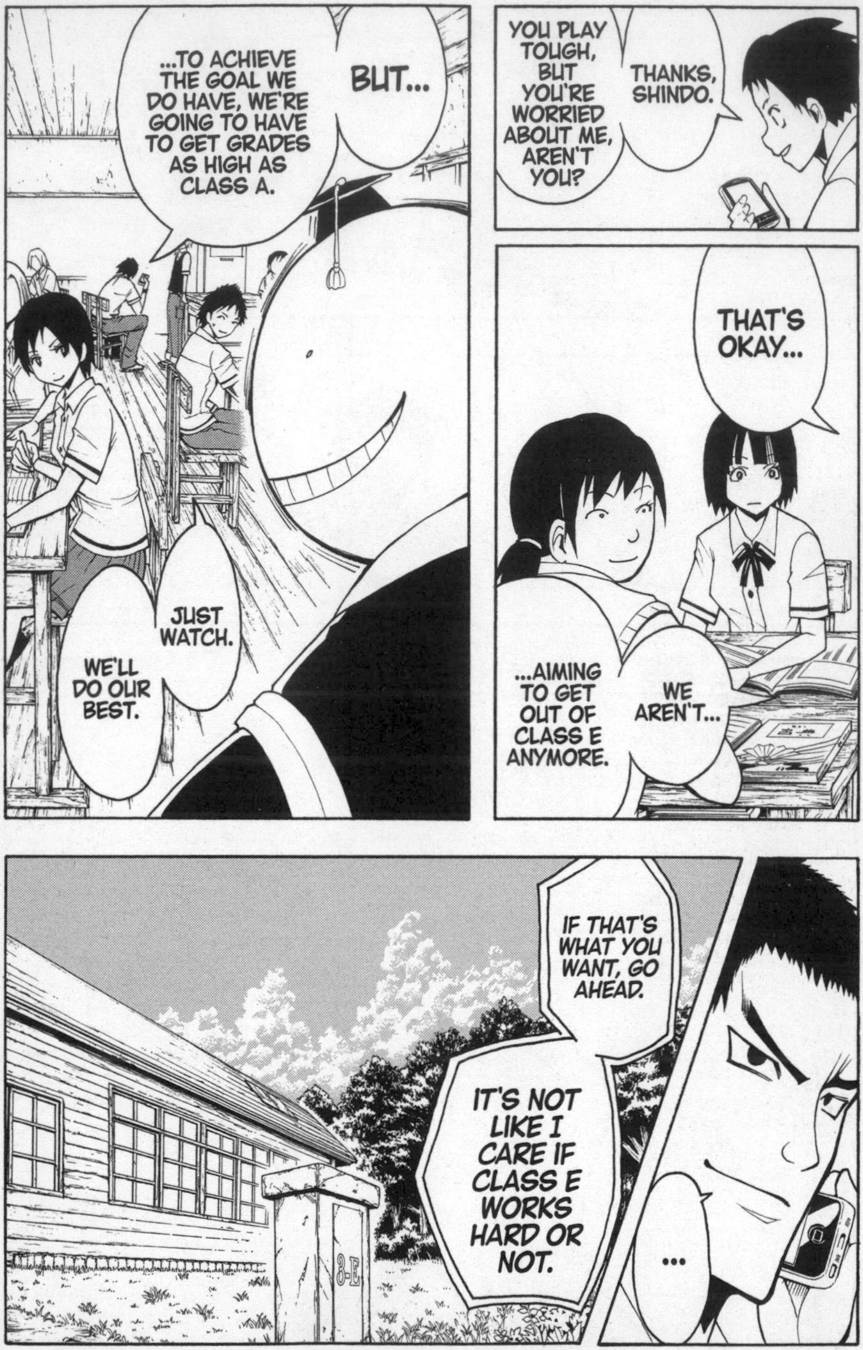
THANKS, SHINDO.
YOU PLAY TOUGH, BUT YOU'RE WORRIED ABOUT ME, AREN'T YOU?
THAT'S OKAY...
WE AREN'T...
...AIMING TO GET OUT OF CLASS E ANYMORE.
BUT...
...TO ACHIEVE THE GOAL WE DO HAVE, WE'RE GOING TO HAVE TO GET GRADES AS HIGH AS CLASS A.
JUST WATCH.
WE'LL DO OUR BEST.
...
IF THAT'S WHAT YOU WANT, GO AHEAD.
IT'S NOT LIKE I CARE IF CLASS E WORKS HARD OR NOT.
3-E

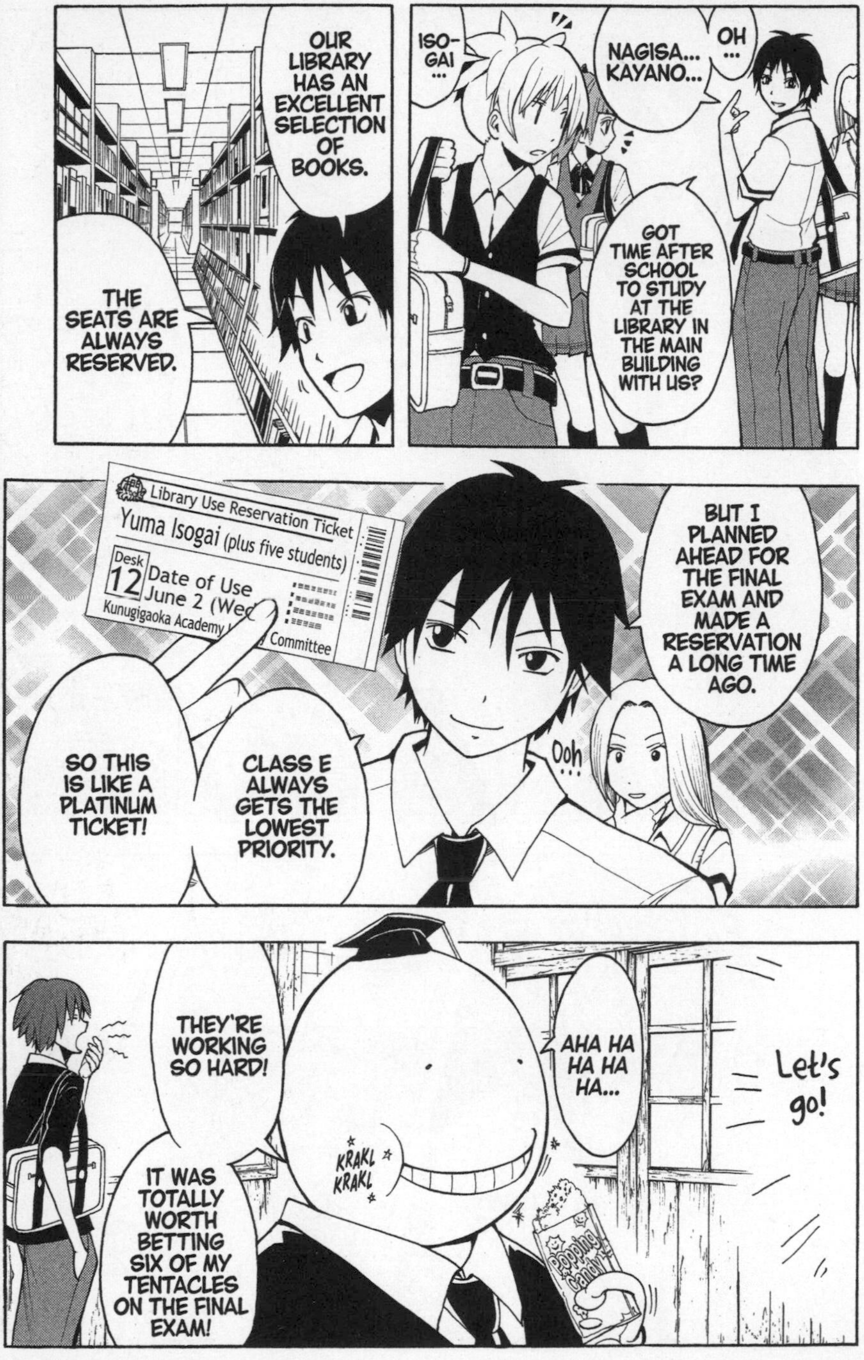
OH ...
NAGISA... KAYANO...
ISO-GAI ...
GOT TIME AFTER SCHOOL TO STUDY AT THE LIBRARY IN THE MAIN BUILDING WITH US?
OUR LIBRARY HAS AN EXCELLENT SELECTION OF BOOKS.
THE SEATS ARE ALWAYS RESERVED.
BUT I PLANNED AHEAD FOR THE FINAL EXAM AND MADE A RESERVATION A LONG TIME AGO.
Library Use Reservation Ticket
Yuma Isogai (plus five students)
Desk 12
Date of Use
June 2 (Wed
Kunugigaoka Academy
Committee
Ooh ...
CLASS E ALWAYS GETS THE LOWEST PRIORITY.
SO THIS IS LIKE A PLATINUM TICKET!
Let's go!
AHA HA HA HA HA...
THEY'RE WORKING SO HARD!
KRAKL KRAKL
Popping Candy
IT WAS TOTALLY WORTH BETTING SIX OF MY TENTACLES ON THE FINAL EXAM!

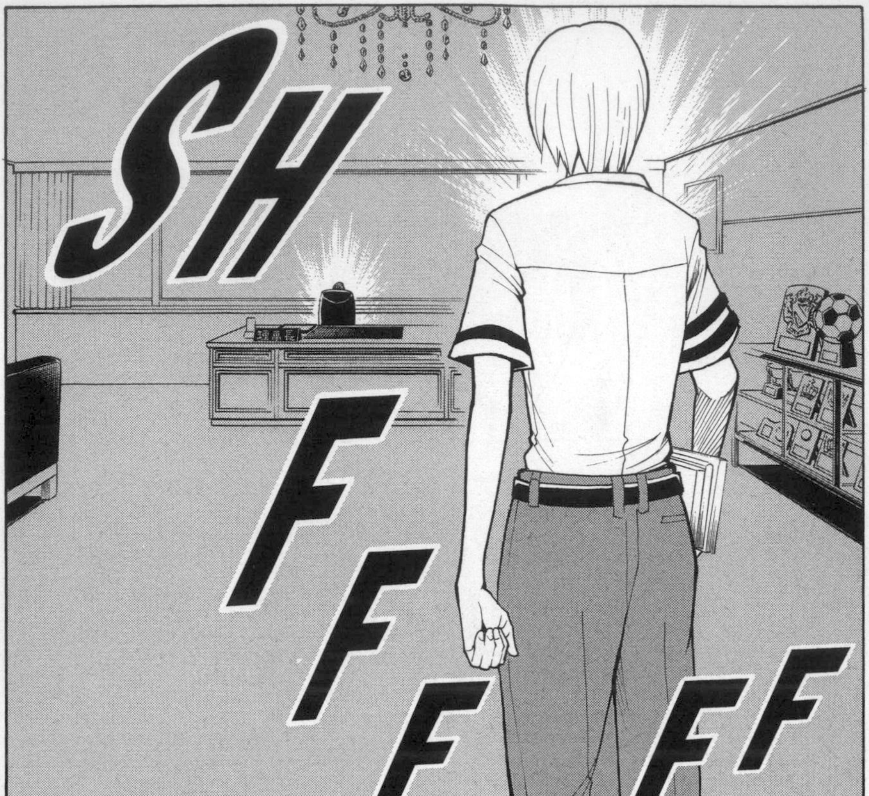
SHFFFFFF

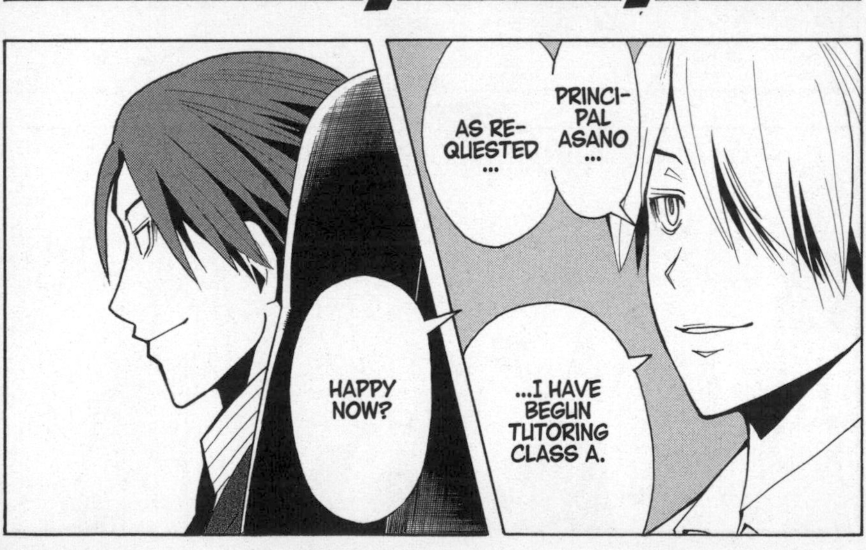
PRINCI-PAL ASANO...
AS RE-QUESTED...
...I HAVE BEGUN TUTORING CLASS A.
HAPPY NOW?

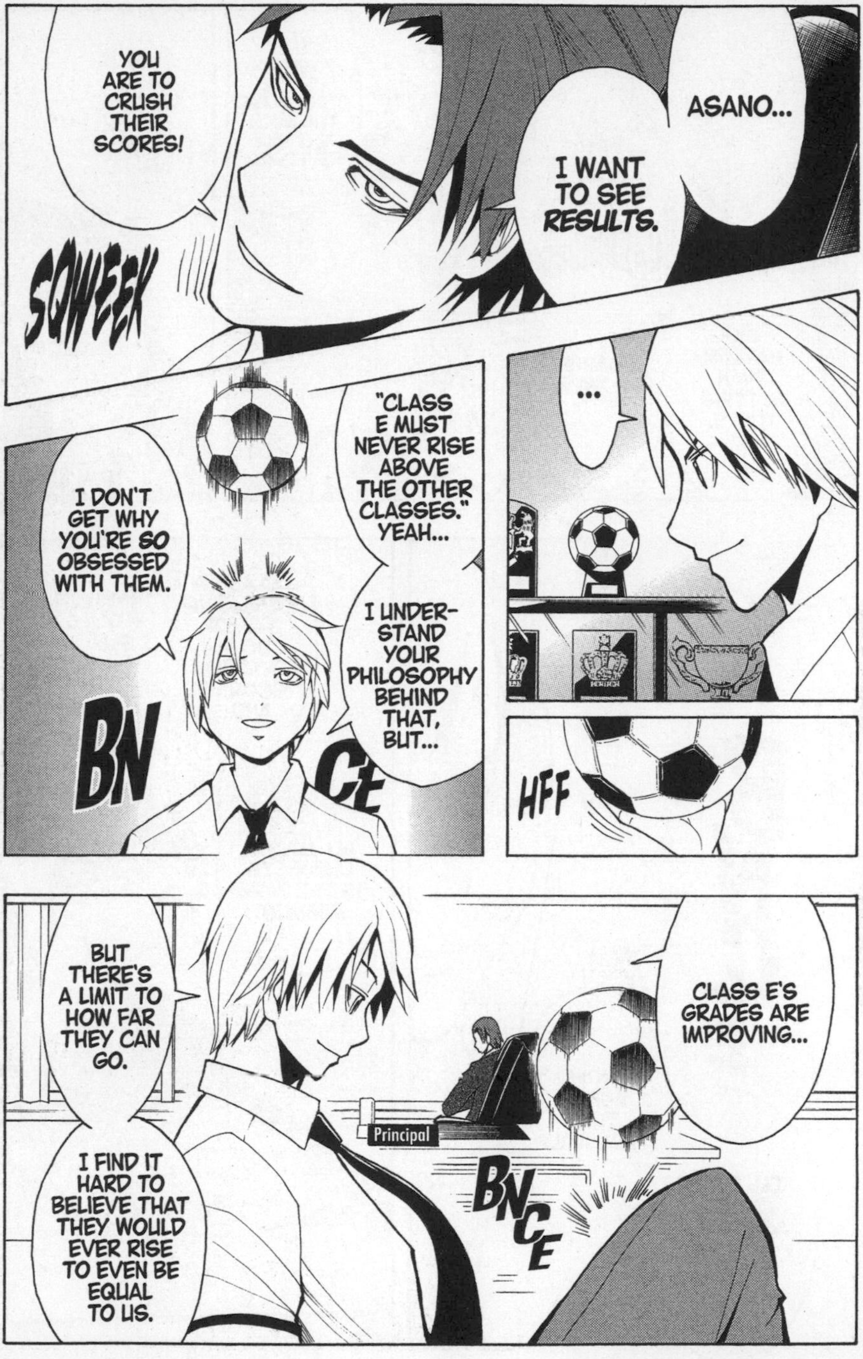
ASANO... I WANT TO SEE RESULTS.
YOU ARE TO CRUSH THEIR SCORES!
SQWEEK
...
HFF
"CLASS E MUST NEVER RISE ABOVE THE OTHER CLASSES." YEAH...
I UNDER-STAND YOUR PHILOSOPHY BEHIND THAT, BUT...
I DON'T GET WHY YOU'RE SO OBSESSED WITH THEM.
BNCE
CLASS E'S GRADES ARE IMPROVING...
Principal
BNCE
BUT THERE'S A LIMIT TO HOW FAR THEY CAN GO.
I FIND IT HARD TO BELIEVE THAT THEY WOULD EVER RISE TO EVEN BE EQUAL TO US.

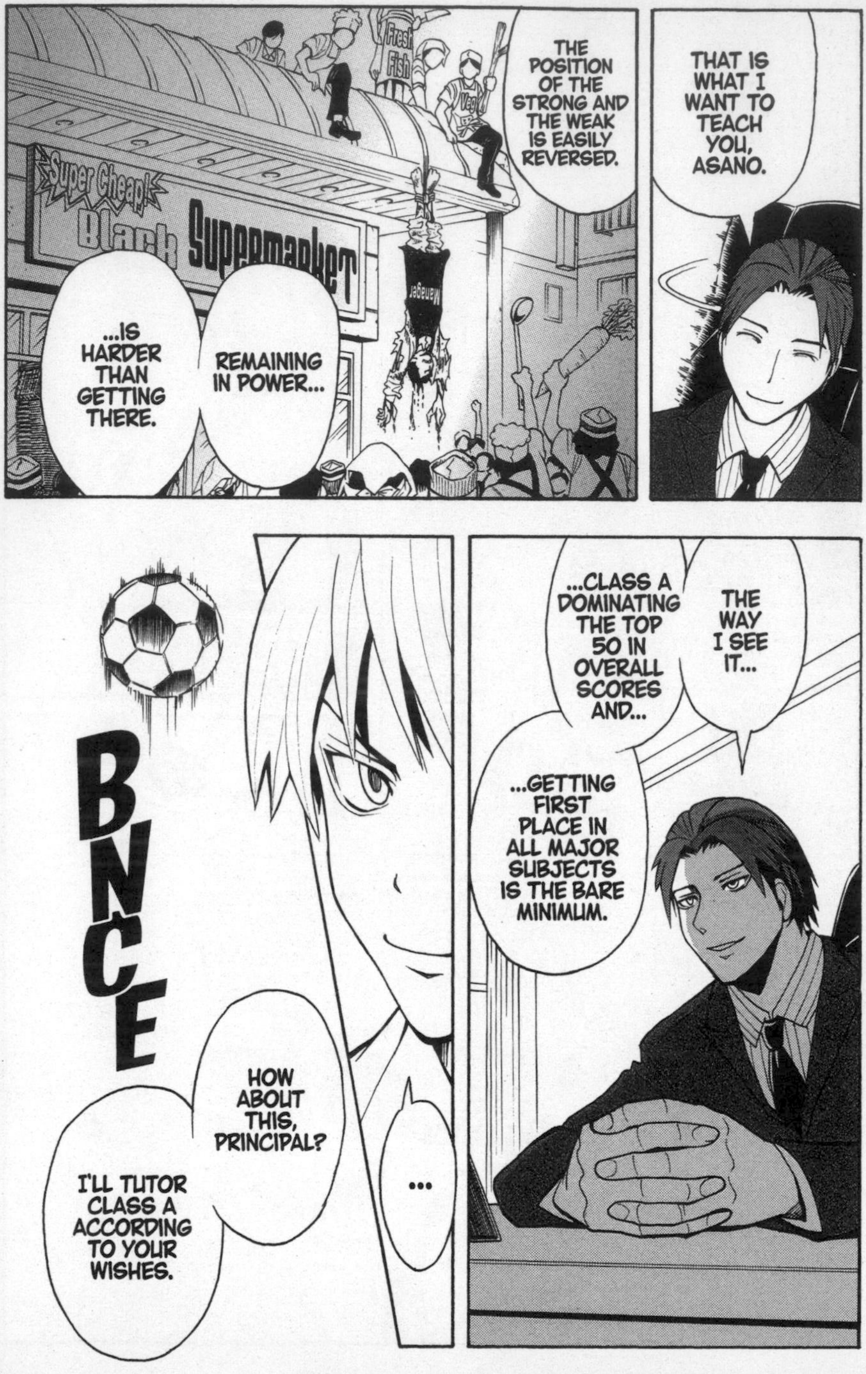
THAT IS WHAT I WANT TO TEACH YOU, ASANO.
THE POSITION OF THE STRONG AND THE WEAK IS EASILY REVERSED.
Fresh Fish
Veg
Super Cheap! Black Supermarket
Manager
REMAINING IN POWER...
...IS HARDER THAN GETTING THERE.
THE WAY I SEE IT...
...CLASS A DOMINATING THE TOP 50 IN OVERALL SCORES AND...
...GETTING FIRST PLACE IN ALL MAJOR SUBJECTS IS THE BARE MINIMUM.
...
HOW ABOUT THIS, PRINCIPAL?
I'LL TUTOR CLASS A ACCORDING TO YOUR WISHES.
BNCE

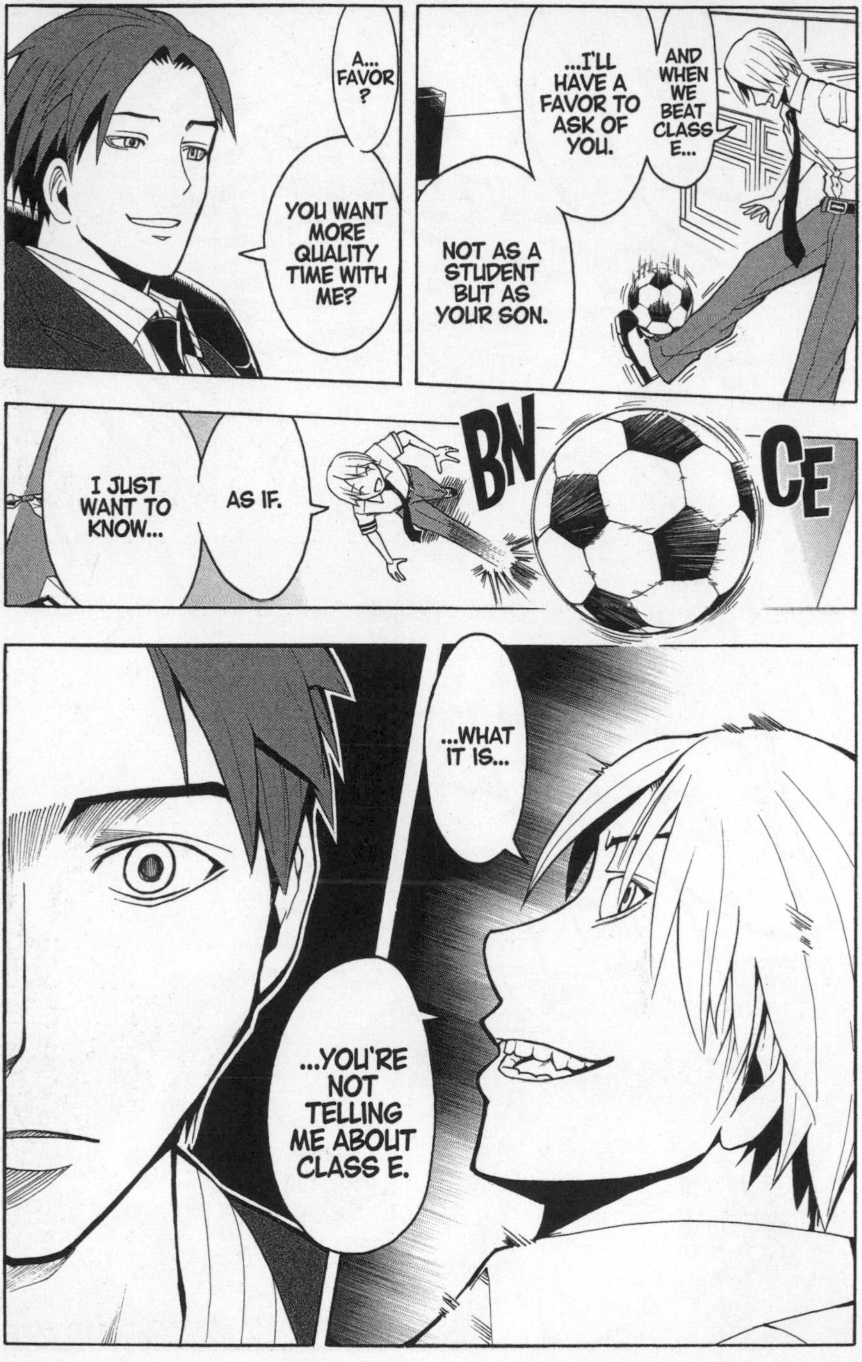
AND WHEN WE BEAT CLASS E...
...I'LL HAVE A FAVOR TO ASK OF YOU.
NOT AS A STUDENT BUT AS YOUR SON.
A... FAVOR?
YOU WANT MORE QUALITY TIME WITH ME?
BN CE
AS IF.
I JUST WANT TO KNOW...
...WHAT IT IS...
...YOU'RE NOT TELLING ME ABOUT CLASS E.

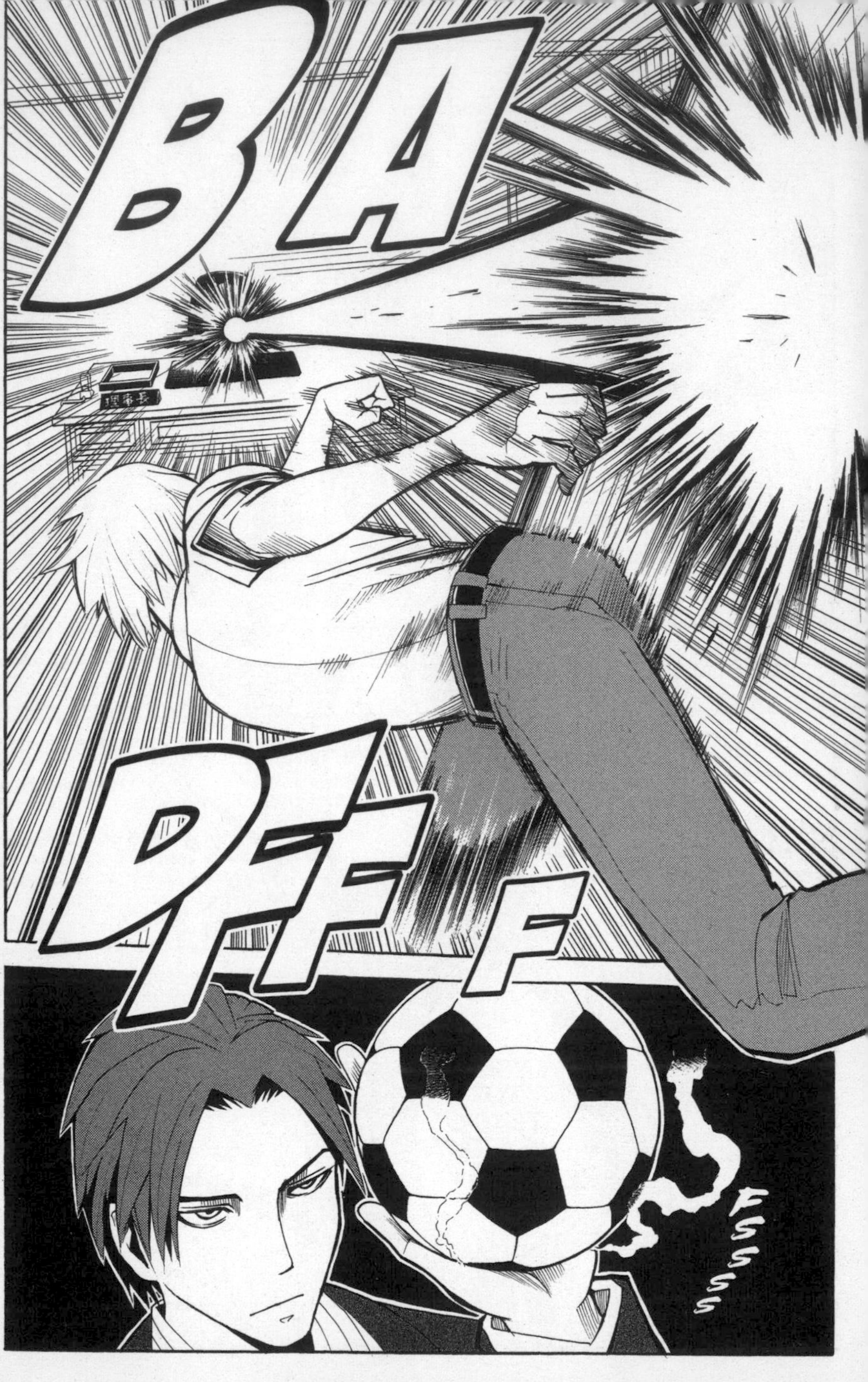
BA
DFFF
FSSSS

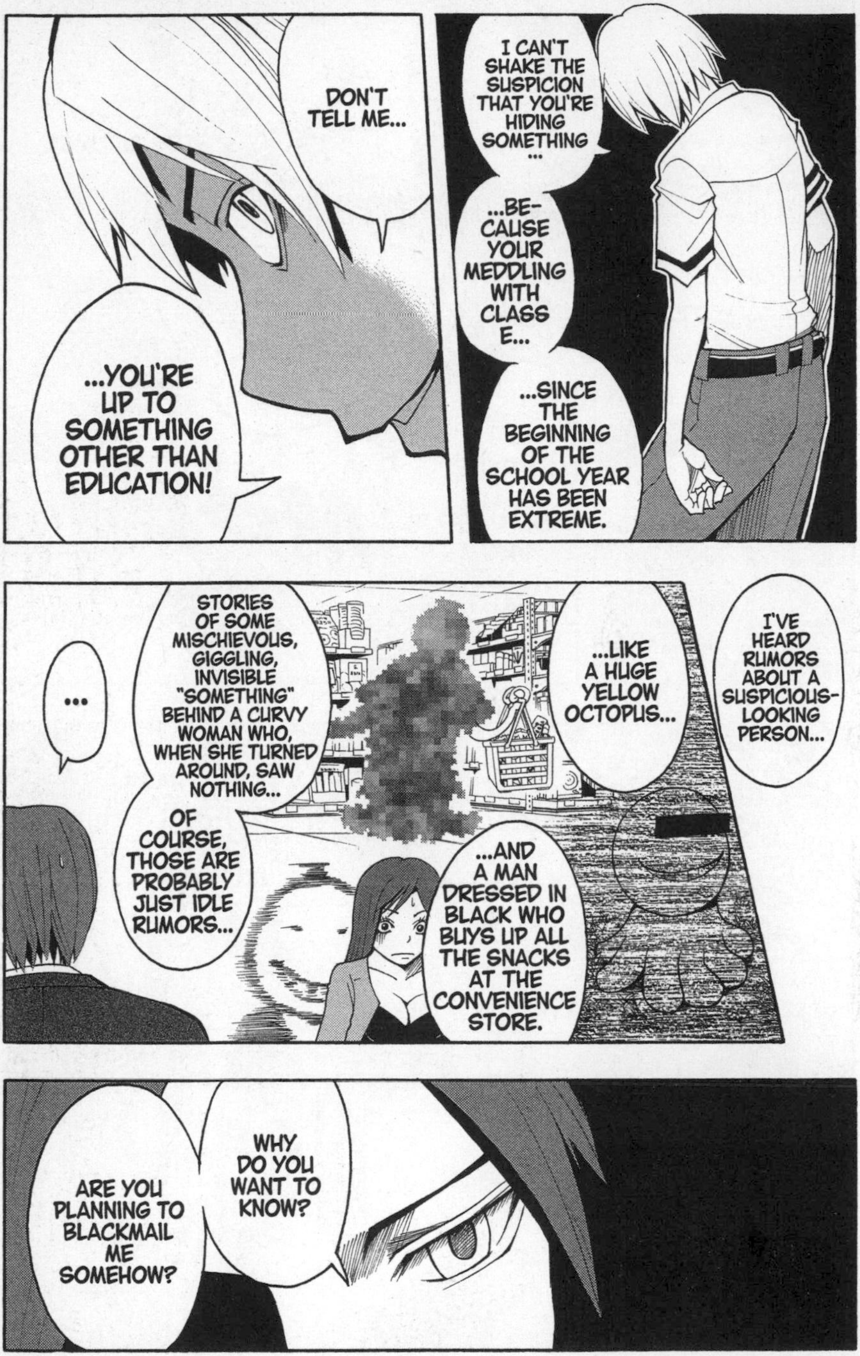
I CAN'T SHAKE THE SUSPICION THAT YOU'RE HIDING SOMETHING...
...BE-CAUSE YOUR MEDDLING WITH CLASS E...
...SINCE THE BEGINNING OF THE SCHOOL YEAR HAS BEEN EXTREME.
DON'T TELL ME...
...YOU'RE UP TO SOMETHING OTHER THAN EDUCATION!
I'VE HEARD RUMORS ABOUT A SUSPICIOUS-LOOKING PERSON...
...LIKE A HUGE YELLOW OCTOPUS...
...AND A MAN DRESSED IN BLACK WHO BUYS UP ALL THE SNACKS AT THE CONVENIENCE STORE.
STORIES OF SOME MISCHIEVOUS, GIGGLING, INVISIBLE "SOMETHING" BEHIND A CURVY WOMAN WHO, WHEN SHE TURNED AROUND, SAW NOTHING...
OF COURSE, THOSE ARE PROBABLY JUST IDLE RUMORS...
...
WHY DO YOU WANT TO KNOW?
ARE YOU PLANNING TO BLACKMAIL ME SOMEHOW?

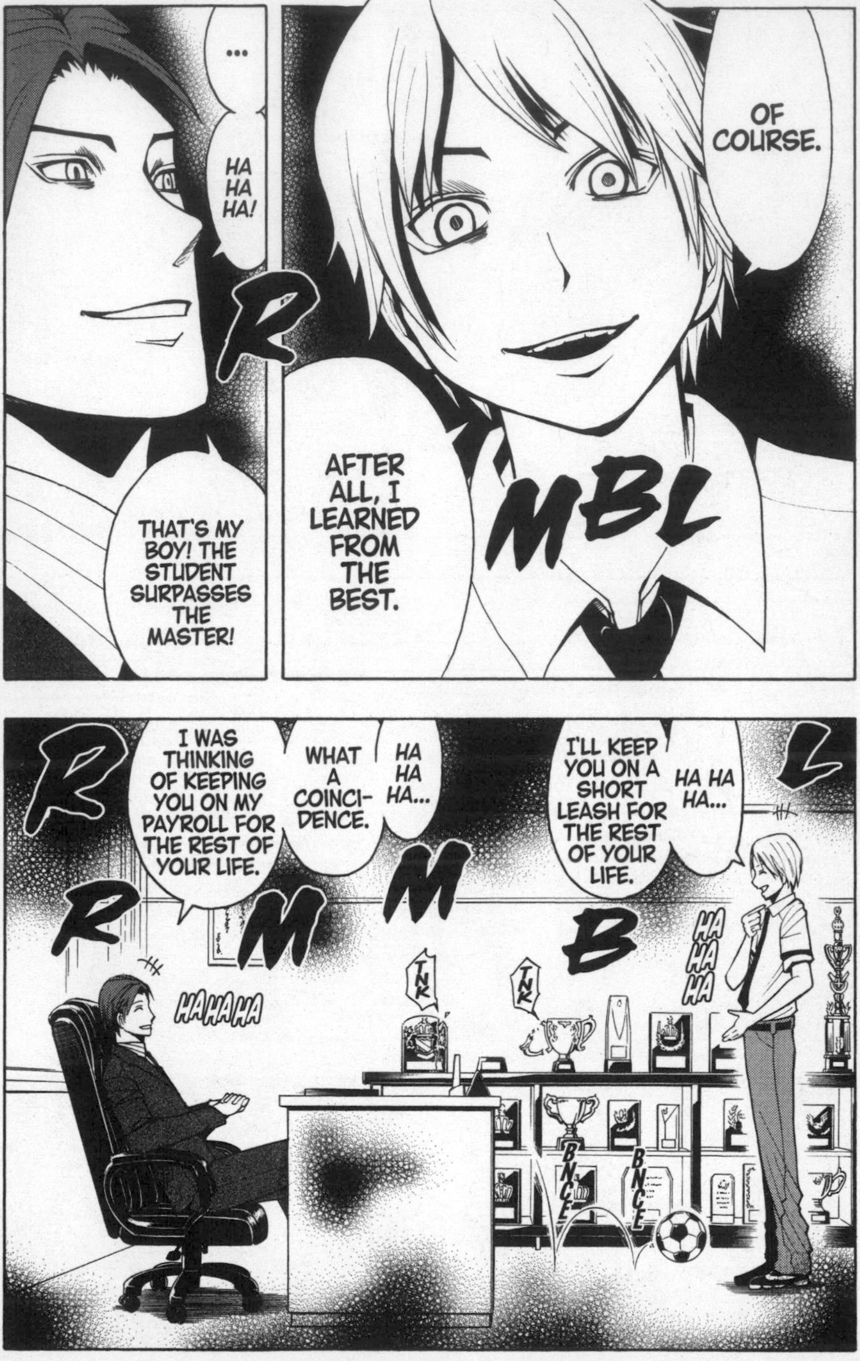
OF COURSE.
AFTER ALL, I LEARNED FROM THE BEST.
MBL
...
HA HA HA!
R
THAT'S MY BOY! THE STUDENT SURPASSES THE MASTER!
L
HA HA HA...
I'LL KEEP YOU ON A SHORT LEASH FOR THE REST OF YOUR LIFE.
HA HA HA...
WHAT A COINCIDENCE.
I WAS THINKING OF KEEPING YOU ON MY PAYROLL FOR THE REST OF YOUR LIFE.
R
HA HA HA
B
M
M
R
TNK
TNK
BNCE
BNCE
HAHAHA

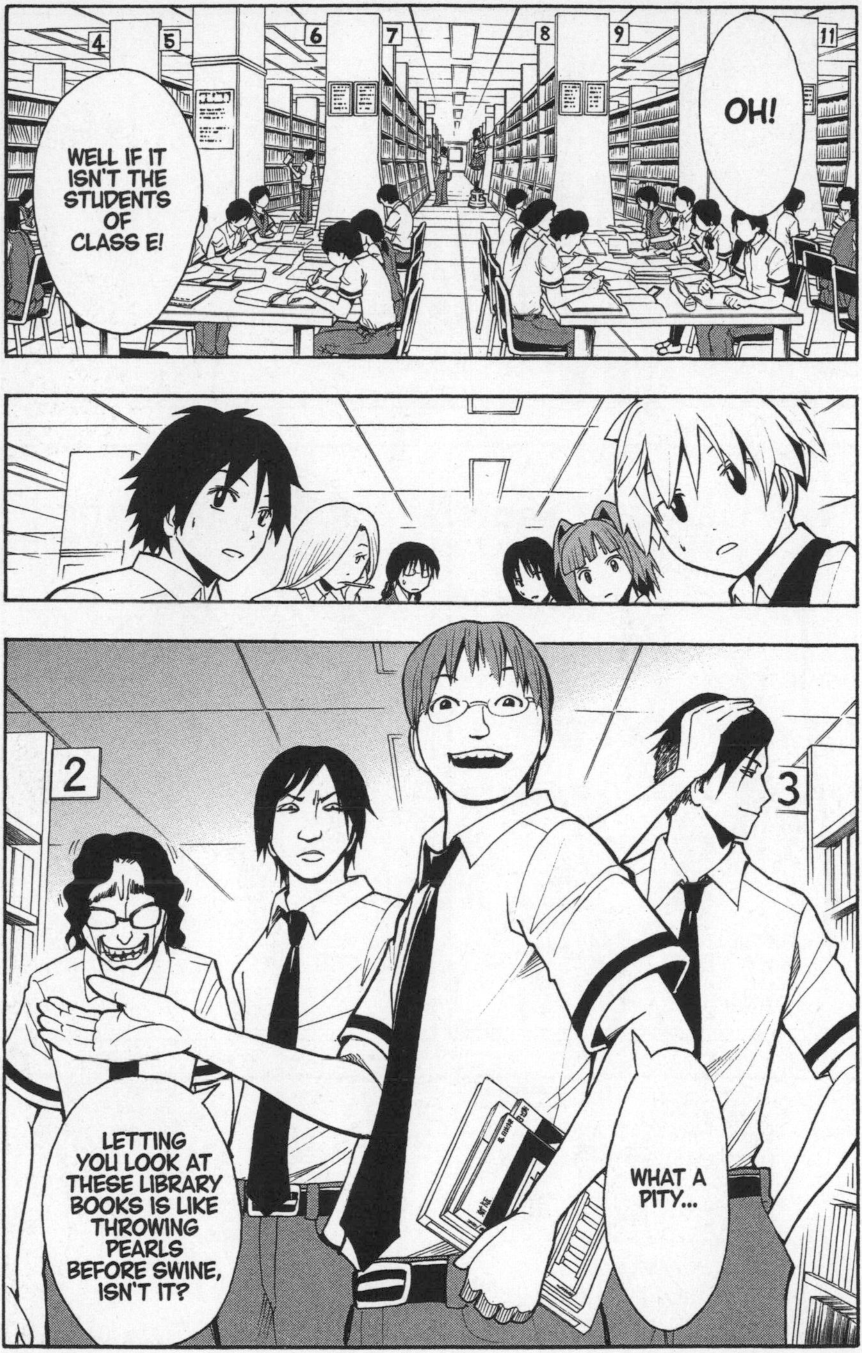
OH!
WELL IF IT ISN'T THE STUDENTS OF CLASS E!
WHAT A PITY...
LETTING YOU LOOK AT THESE LIBRARY BOOKS IS LIKE THROWING PEARLS BEFORE SWINE, ISN'T IT?

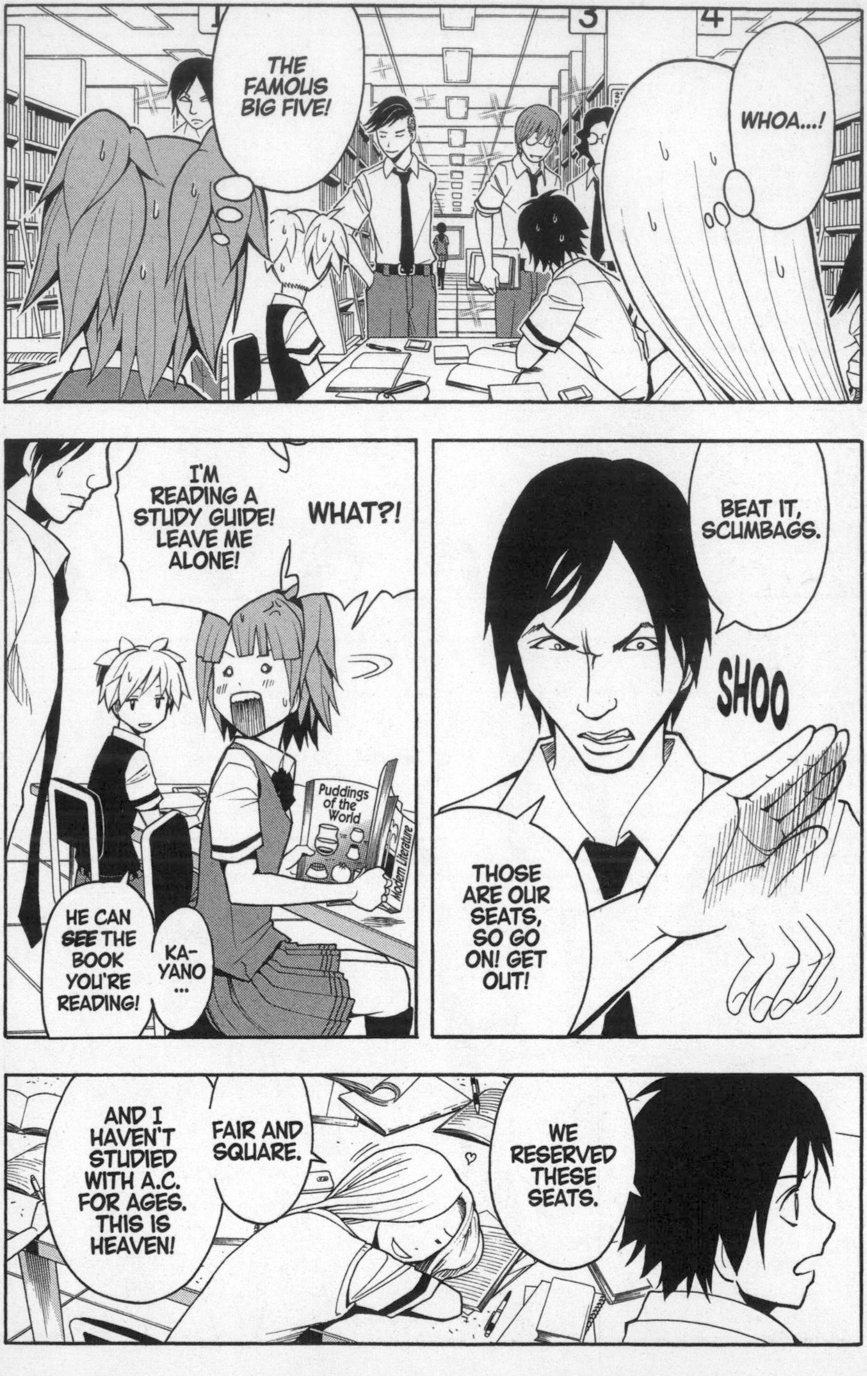
WHOA...!
THE FAMOUS BIG FIVE!
BEAT IT, SCUMBAGS.
SHOO
THOSE ARE OUR SEATS, SO GO ON! GET OUT!
WHAT?!
I'M READING A STUDY GUIDE! LEAVE ME ALONE!
Puddings of the World
Modern Literature
KA-YANO...
HE CAN SEE THE BOOK YOU'RE READING!
WE RESERVED THESE SEATS.
FAIR AND SQUARE.
AND I HAVEN'T STUDIED WITH A.C. FOR AGES. THIS IS HEAVEN!

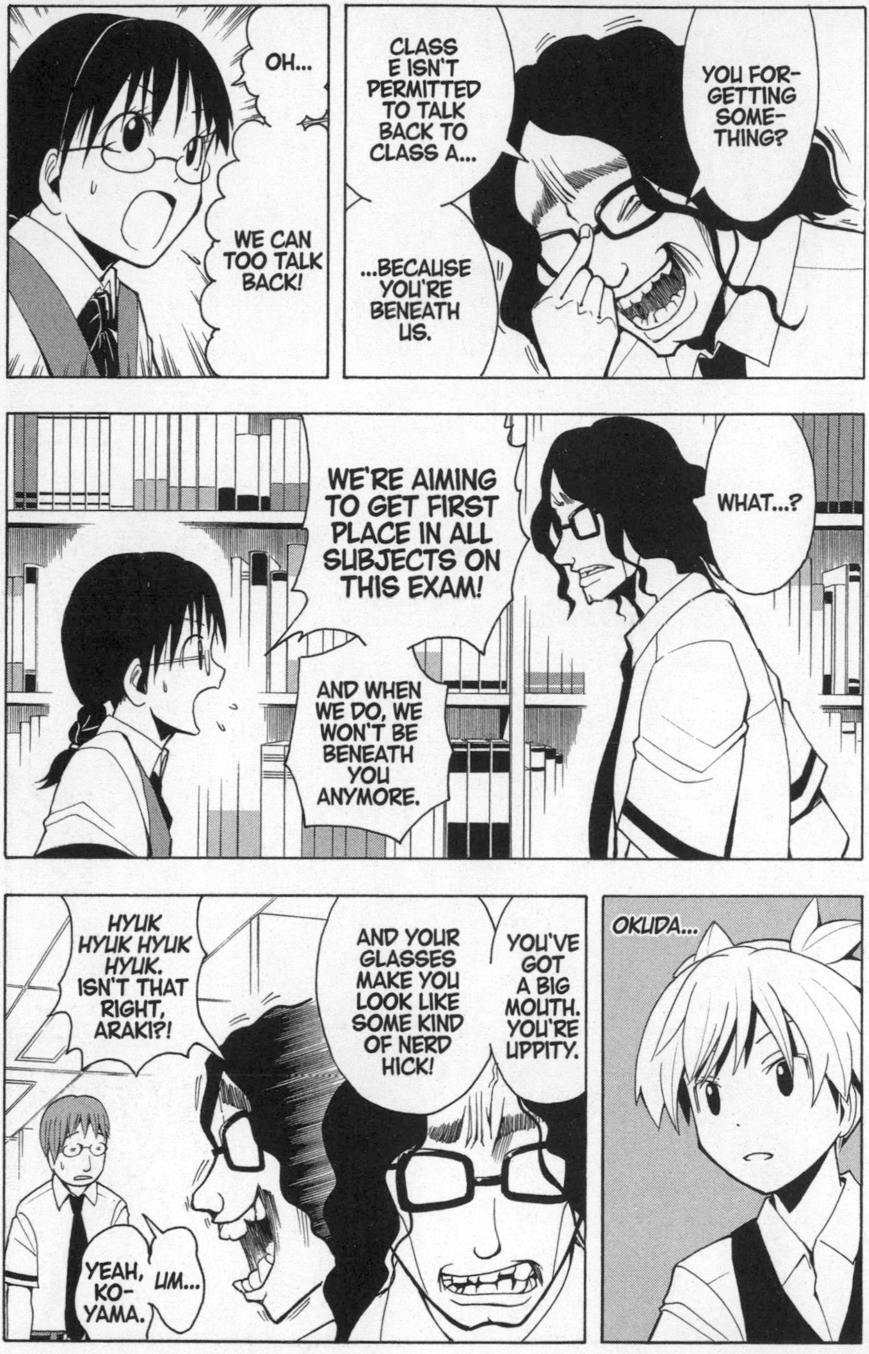
YOU FOR-GETTING SOME-THING?
CLASS E ISN'T PERMITTED TO TALK BACK TO CLASS A...
...BECAUSE YOU'RE BENEATH US.
OH...
WE CAN TOO TALK BACK!
WHAT...?
WE'RE AIMING TO GET FIRST PLACE IN ALL SUBJECTS ON THIS EXAM!
AND WHEN WE DO, WE WON'T BE BENEATH YOU ANYMORE.
OKUDA...
YOU'VE GOT A BIG MOUTH. YOU'RE UPPITY.
AND YOUR GLASSES MAKE YOU LOOK LIKE SOME KIND OF NERD HICK!
HYUK HYUK HYUK HYUK. ISN'T THAT RIGHT, ARAKI?!
UM...
YEAH, KO-YAMA.

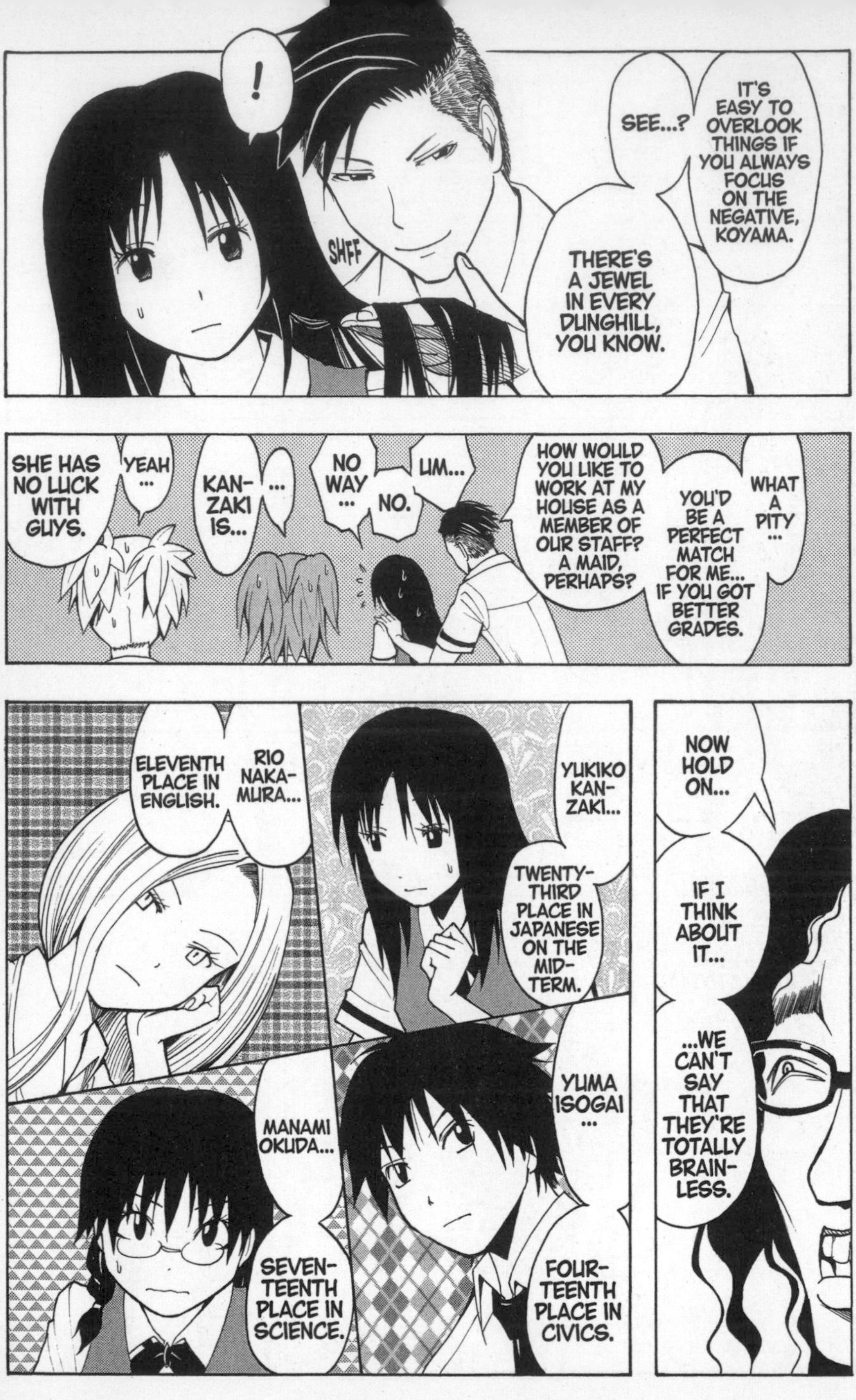
IT'S EASY TO OVERLOOK THINGS IF YOU ALWAYS FOCUS ON THE NEGATIVE, KOYAMA.
SEE...?
THERE'S A JEWEL IN EVERY DUNGHILL, YOU KNOW.
SHFF
!
WHAT A PITY ...
YOU'D BE A PERFECT MATCH FOR ME... IF YOU GOT BETTER GRADES.
HOW WOULD YOU LIKE TO WORK AT MY HOUSE AS A MEMBER OF OUR STAFF? A MAID, PERHAPS?
UM...
NO.
NO WAY ...
...
KANZAKI IS...
YEAH ...
SHE HAS NO LUCK WITH GUYS.
NOW HOLD ON...
IF I THINK ABOUT IT...
...WE CAN'T SAY THAT THEY'RE TOTALLY BRAINLESS.
YUKIKO KANZAKI...
TWENTY-THIRD PLACE IN JAPANESE ON THE MIDTERM.
RIO NAKAMURA...
ELEVENTH PLACE IN ENGLISH.
YUMA ISOGAI ...
FOURTEENTH PLACE IN CIVICS.
MANAMI OKUDA...
SEVENTEENTH PLACE IN SCIENCE.

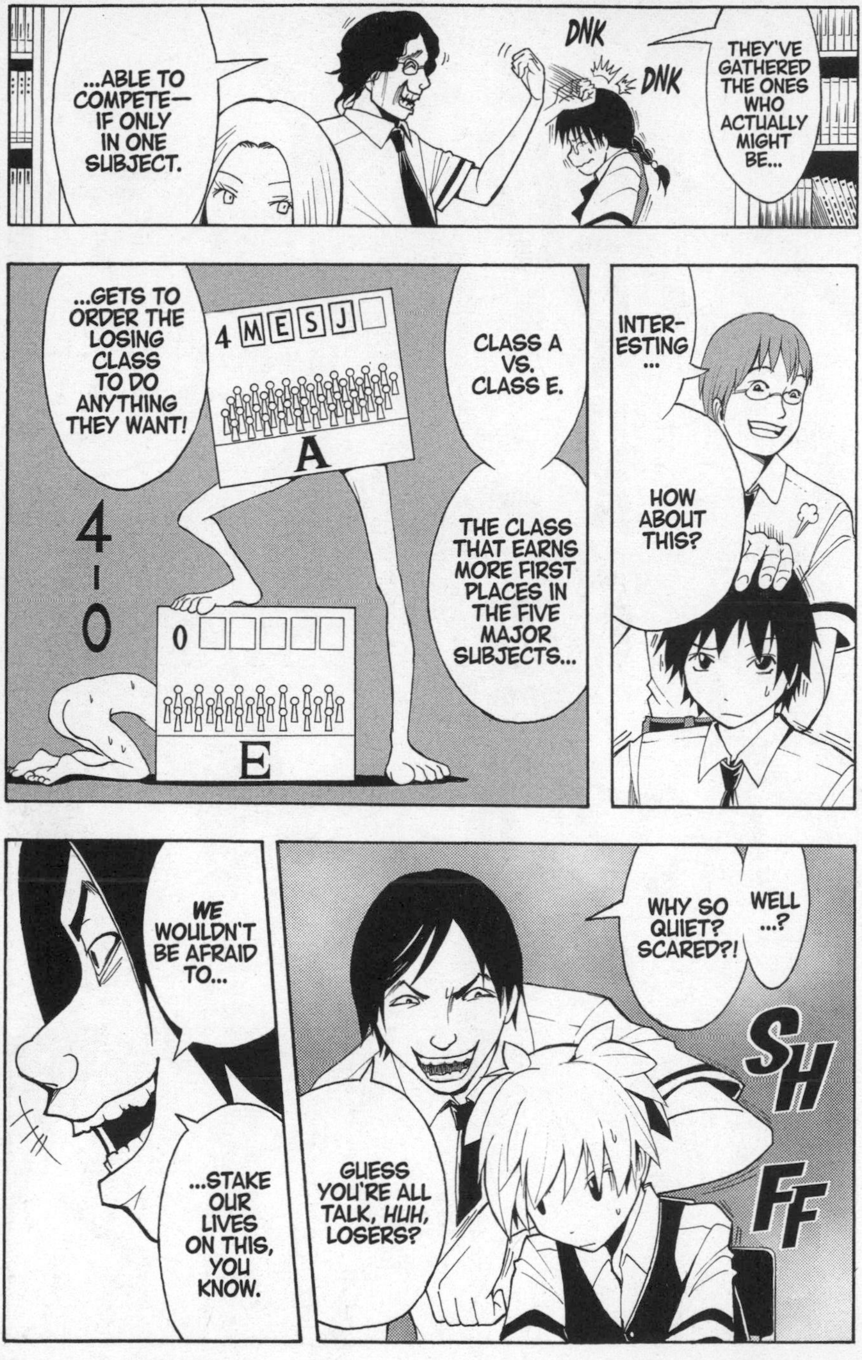
THEY'VE GATHERED THE ONES WHO ACTUALLY MIGHT BE...
DNK
DNK
...ABLE TO COMPETE—IF ONLY IN ONE SUBJECT.
INTER-ESTING ...
HOW ABOUT THIS?
CLASS A VS. CLASS E.
THE CLASS THAT EARNS MORE FIRST PLACES IN THE FIVE MAJOR SUBJECTS...
...GETS TO ORDER THE LOSING CLASS TO DO ANYTHING THEY WANT!
4 M E S J
A
4-0
0
E
WELL ...?
WHY SO QUIET? SCARED?!
SHFF
GUESS YOU'RE ALL TALK, HUH, LOSERS?
WE WOULDN'T BE AFRAID TO...
...STAKE OUR LIVES ON THIS, YOU KNOW.

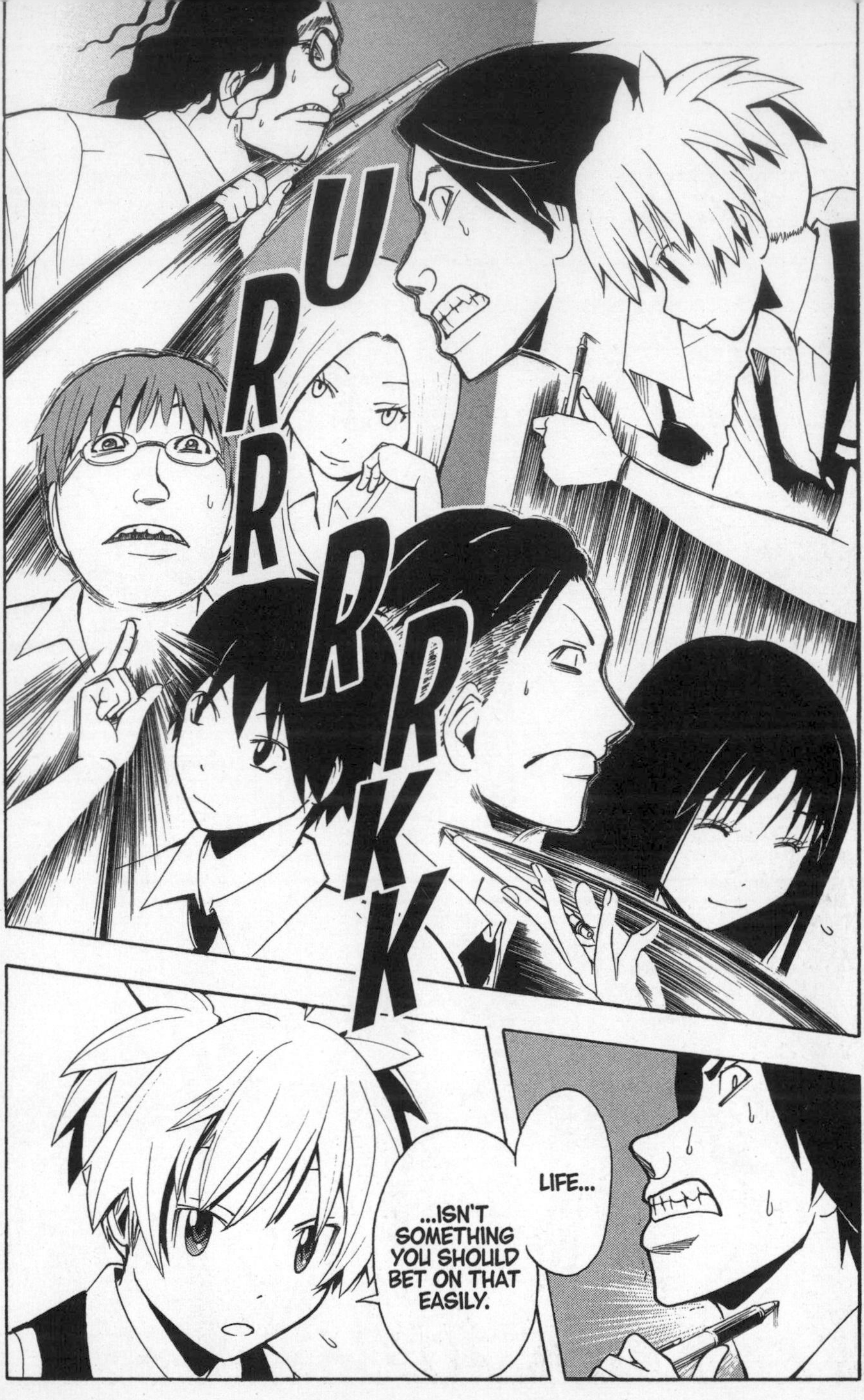
URRRRRK
LIFE...
...ISN'T SOMETHING YOU SHOULD BET ON THAT EASILY.

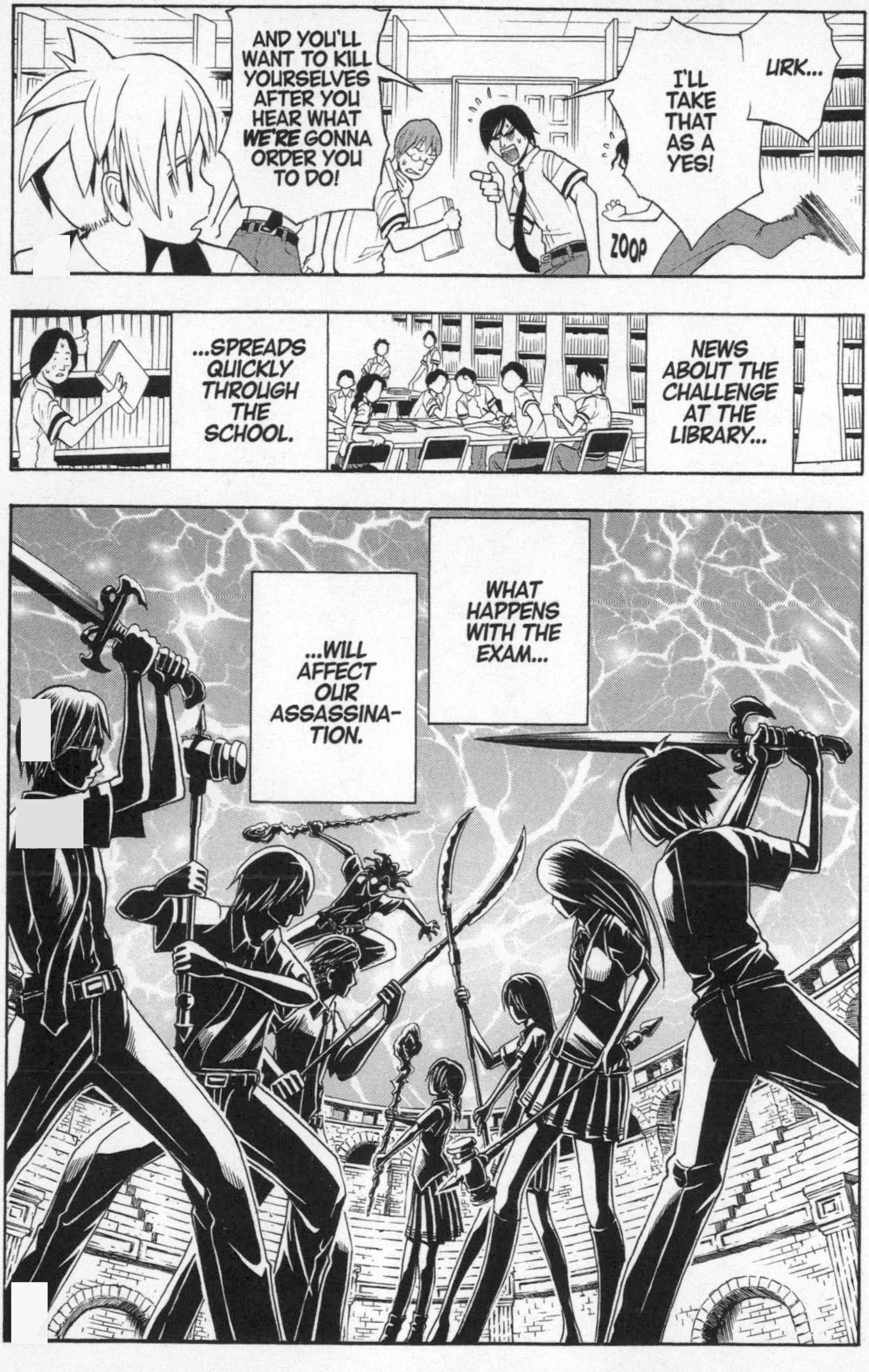
URK...
I'LL TAKE THAT AS A YES!
ZOOP
AND YOU'LL WANT TO KILL YOURSELVES AFTER YOU HEAR WHAT WE'RE GONNA ORDER YOU TO DO!
NEWS ABOUT THE CHALLENGE AT THE LIBRARY...
...SPREADS QUICKLY THROUGH THE SCHOOL.
WHAT HAPPENS WITH THE EXAM...
...WILL AFFECT OUR ASSASSINA-TION.

Father's Day

Think of it
more as a tie...

...and less of a
leash.

–Gakushu

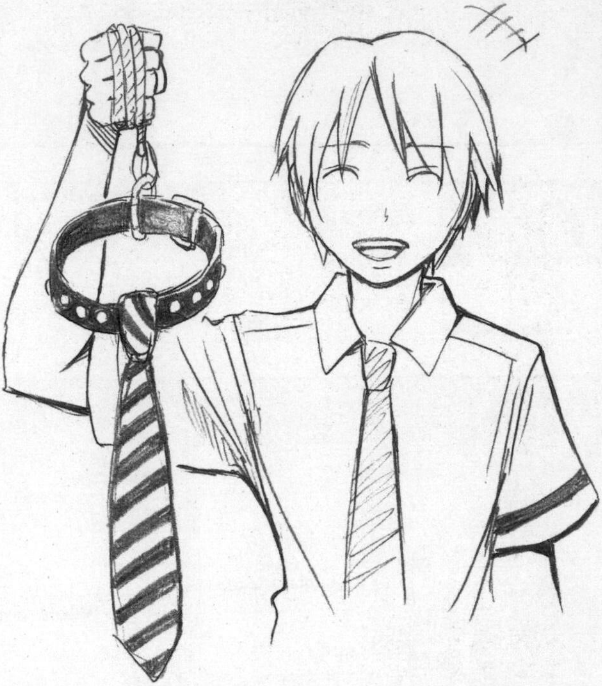

CLASS 52 TIME FOR THE ACE

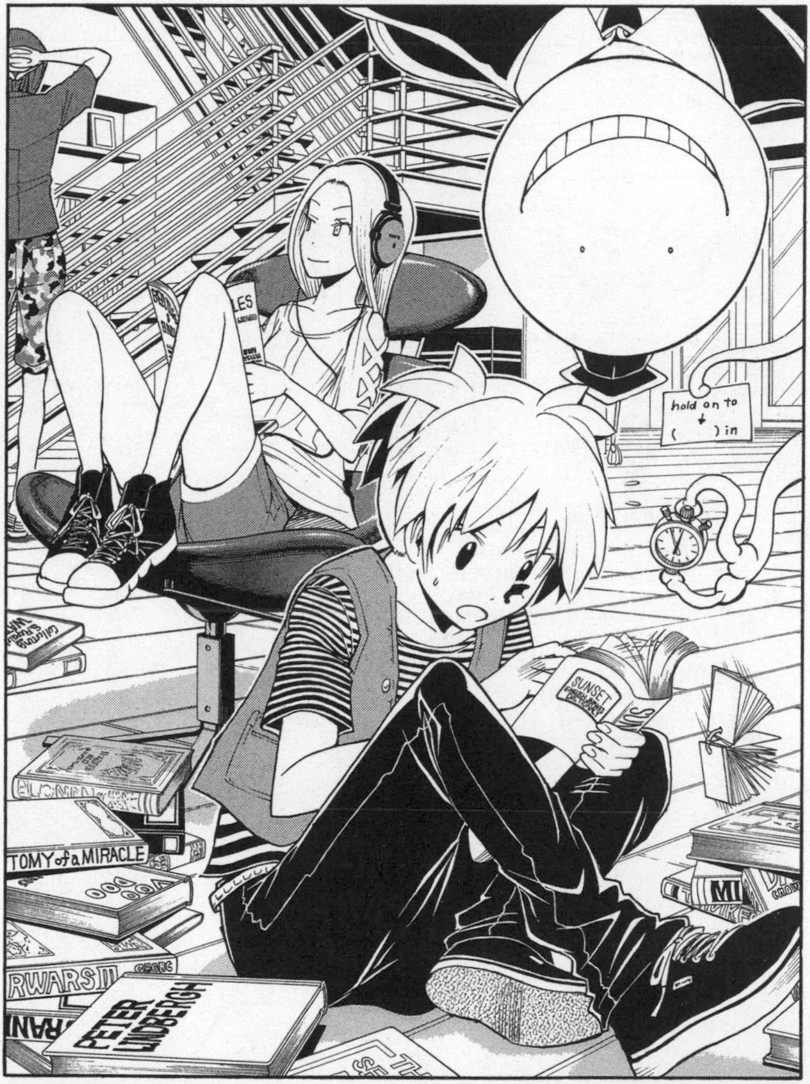
hold on to
( ) in
SUNSET
TOMY of a MIRACLE
RWARS III
PETER LINDBERGH

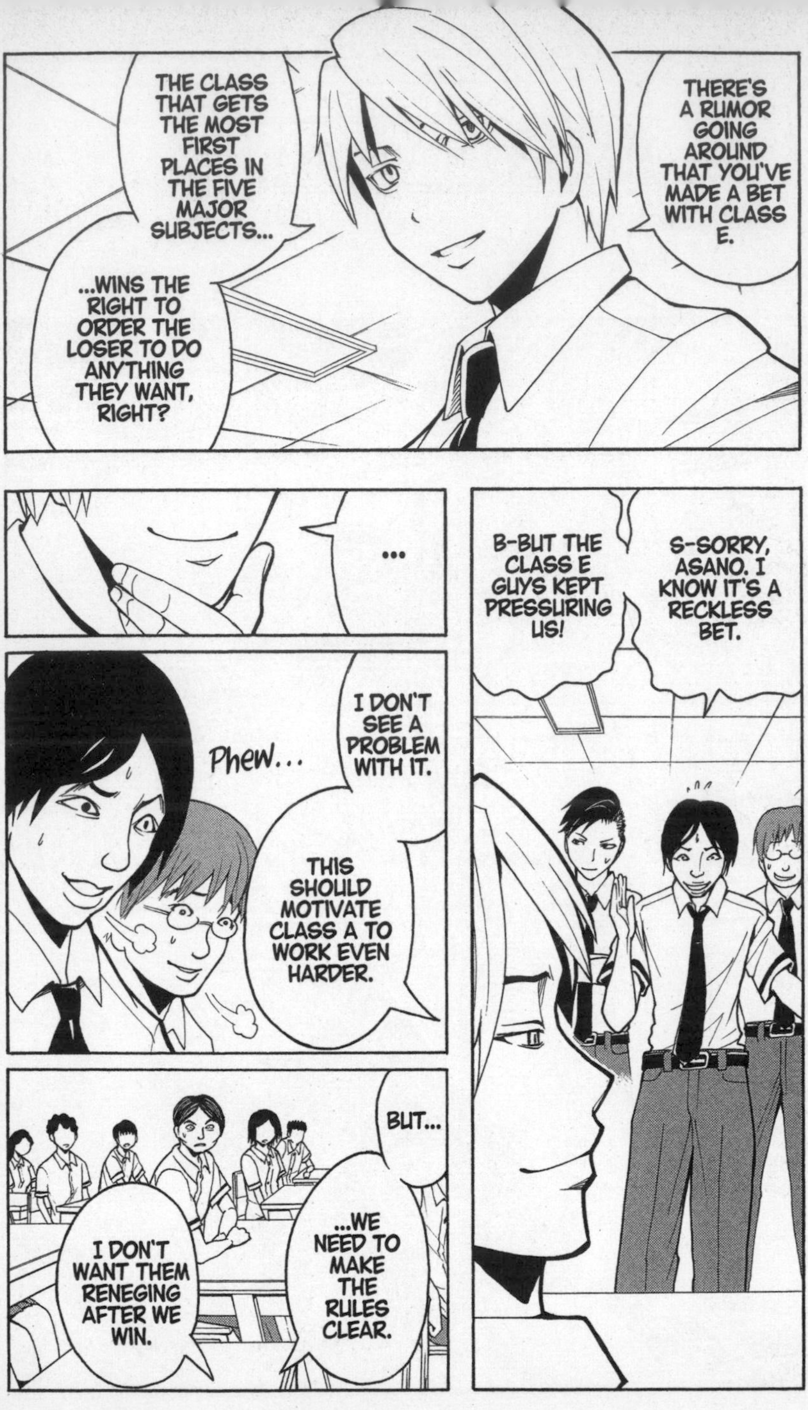
THERE'S A RUMOR GOING AROUND THAT YOU'VE MADE A BET WITH CLASS E.
THE CLASS THAT GETS THE MOST FIRST PLACES IN THE FIVE MAJOR SUBJECTS...
...WINS THE RIGHT TO ORDER THE LOSER TO DO ANYTHING THEY WANT, RIGHT?
S-SORRY, ASANO. I KNOW IT'S A RECKLESS BET.
B-BUT THE CLASS E GUYS KEPT PRESSURING US!
...
I DON'T SEE A PROBLEM WITH IT.
Phew...
THIS SHOULD MOTIVATE CLASS A TO WORK EVEN HARDER.
BUT...
...WE NEED TO MAKE THE RULES CLEAR.
I DON'T WANT THEM RENEGING AFTER WE WIN.

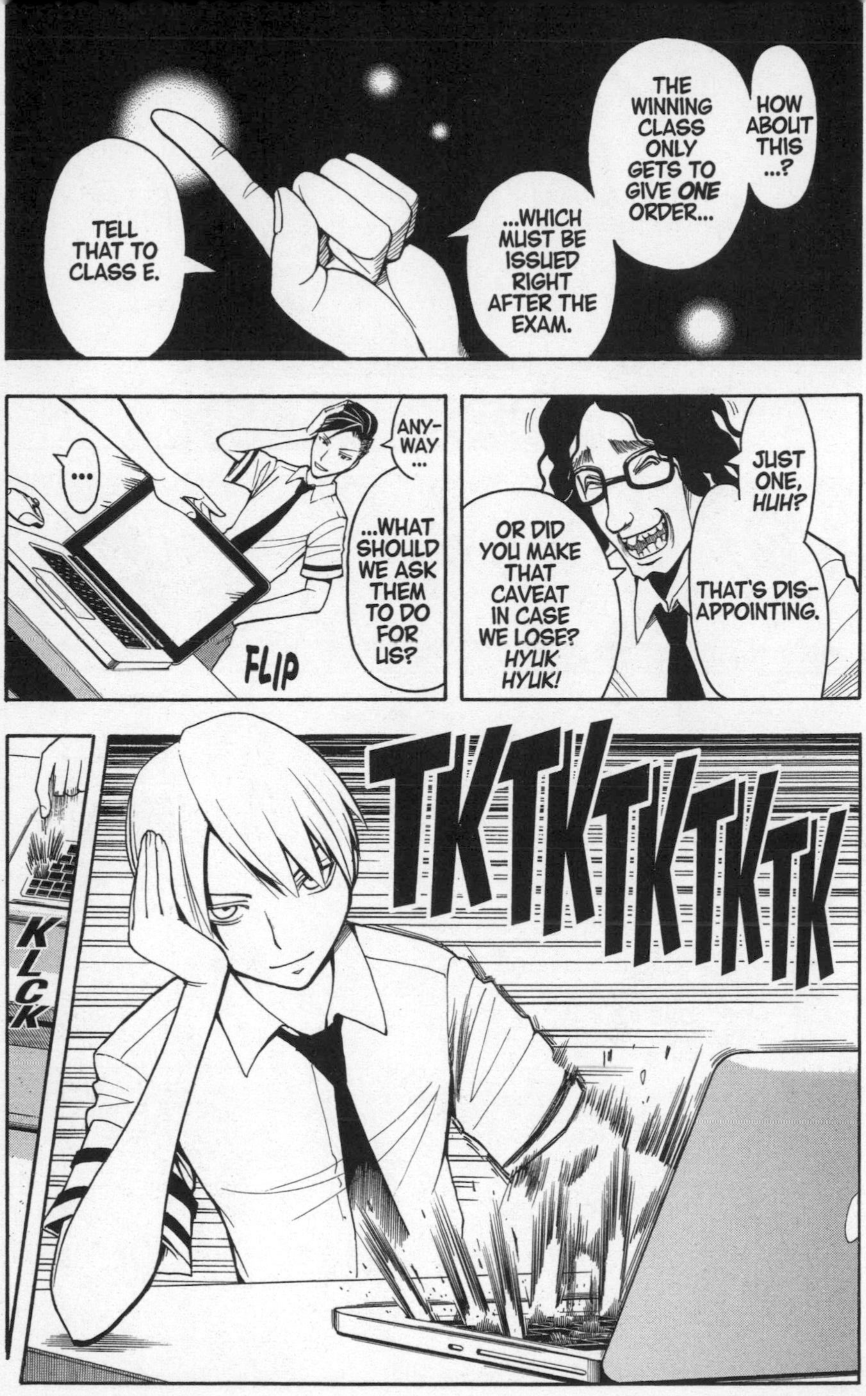
HOW ABOUT THIS ...?
THE WINNING CLASS ONLY GETS TO GIVE ONE ORDER...
...WHICH MUST BE ISSUED RIGHT AFTER THE EXAM.
TELL THAT TO CLASS E.
JUST ONE, HUH?
THAT'S DIS-APPOINTING.
OR DID YOU MAKE THAT CAVEAT IN CASE WE LOSE? HYUK HYUK!
ANY-WAY ...
...WHAT SHOULD WE ASK THEM TO DO FOR US?
FLIP
...
TKTKTKTKTKTK
KLCK

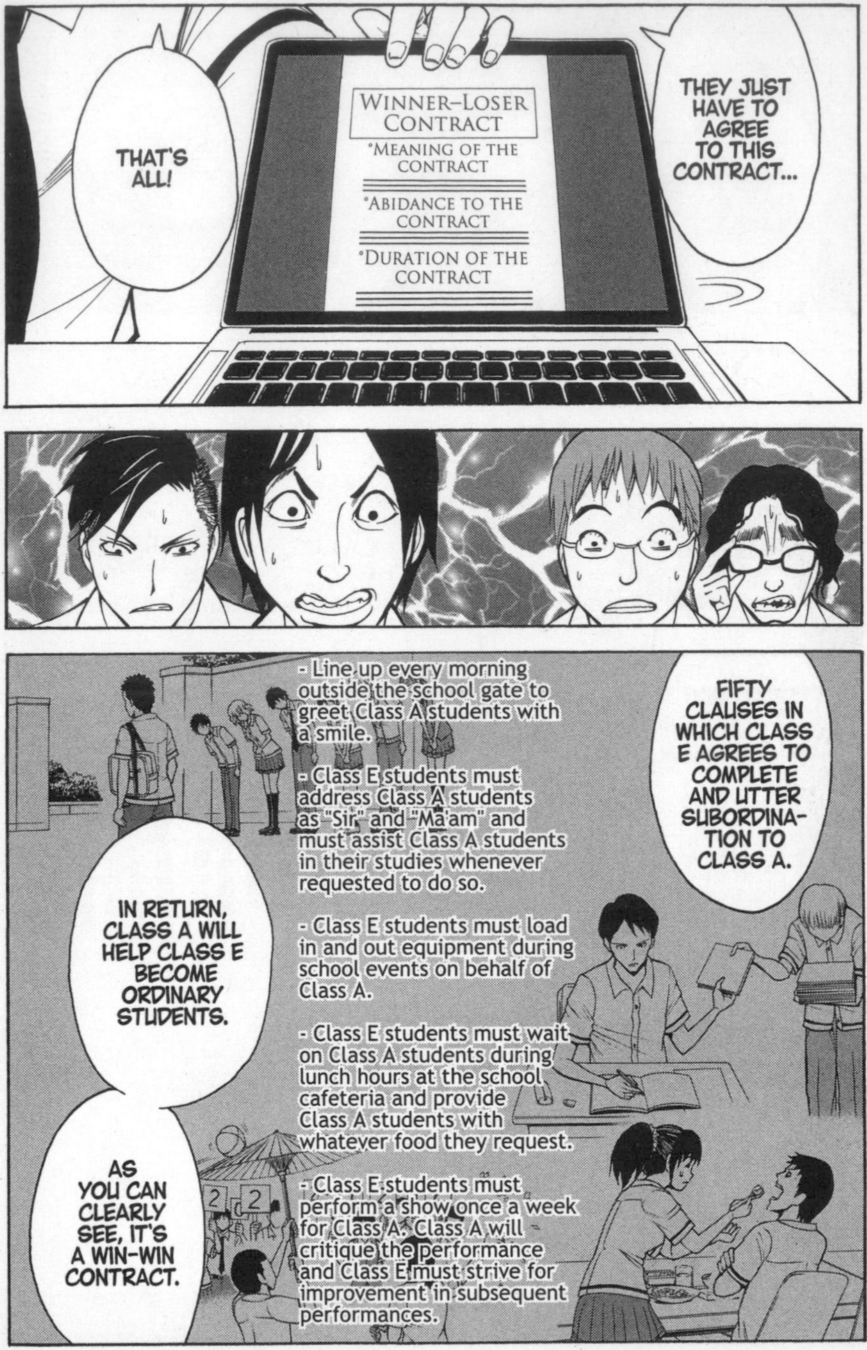
THEY JUST HAVE TO AGREE TO THIS CONTRACT...
WINNER–LOSER CONTRACT
°MEANING OF THE CONTRACT
°ABIDANCE TO THE CONTRACT
°DURATION OF THE CONTRACT
THAT'S ALL!
FIFTY CLAUSES IN WHICH CLASS E AGREES TO COMPLETE AND UTTER SUBORDINATION TO CLASS A.
- Line up every morning outside the school gate to greet Class A students with a smile.
- Class E students must address Class A students as "Sir" and "Ma'am" and must assist Class A students in their studies whenever requested to do so.
- Class E students must load in and out equipment during school events on behalf of Class A.
- Class E students must wait on Class A students during lunch hours at the school cafeteria and provide Class A students with whatever food they request.
- Class E students must perform a show once a week for Class A. Class A will critique the performance and Class E must strive for improvement in subsequent performances.
IN RETURN, CLASS A WILL HELP CLASS E BECOME ORDINARY STUDENTS.
AS YOU CAN CLEARLY SEE, IT'S A WIN-WIN CONTRACT.

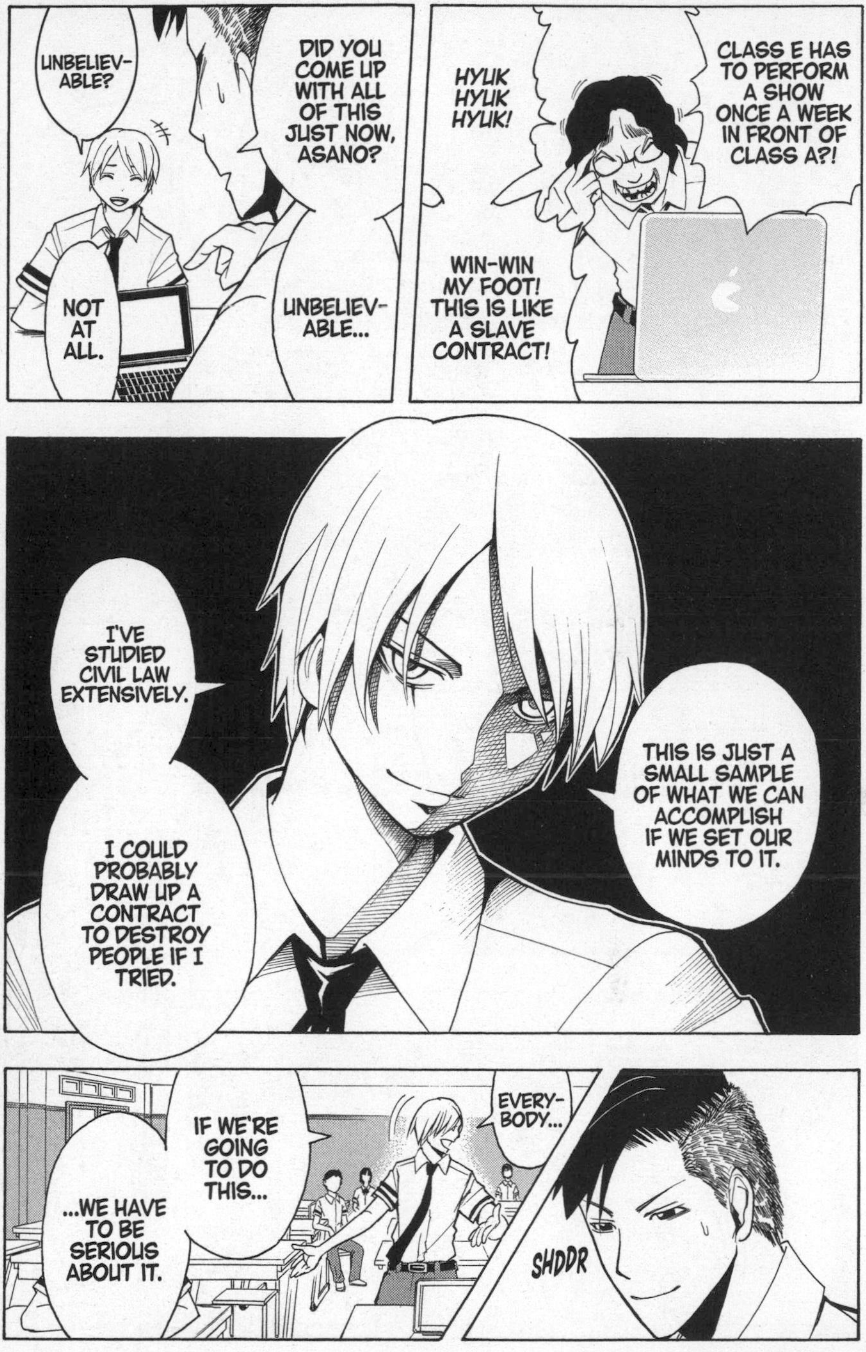
CLASS E HAS TO PERFORM A SHOW ONCE A WEEK IN FRONT OF CLASS A?!
HYUK HYUK HYUK!
WIN-WIN MY FOOT! THIS IS LIKE A SLAVE CONTRACT!
DID YOU COME UP WITH ALL OF THIS JUST NOW, ASANO?
UNBELIEVABLE?
UNBELIEVABLE...
NOT AT ALL.
THIS IS JUST A SMALL SAMPLE OF WHAT WE CAN ACCOMPLISH IF WE SET OUR MINDS TO IT.
I'VE STUDIED CIVIL LAW EXTENSIVELY.
I COULD PROBABLY DRAW UP A CONTRACT TO DESTROY PEOPLE IF I TRIED.
SHDDR
EVERYBODY...
IF WE'RE GOING TO DO THIS...
...WE HAVE TO BE SERIOUS ABOUT IT.

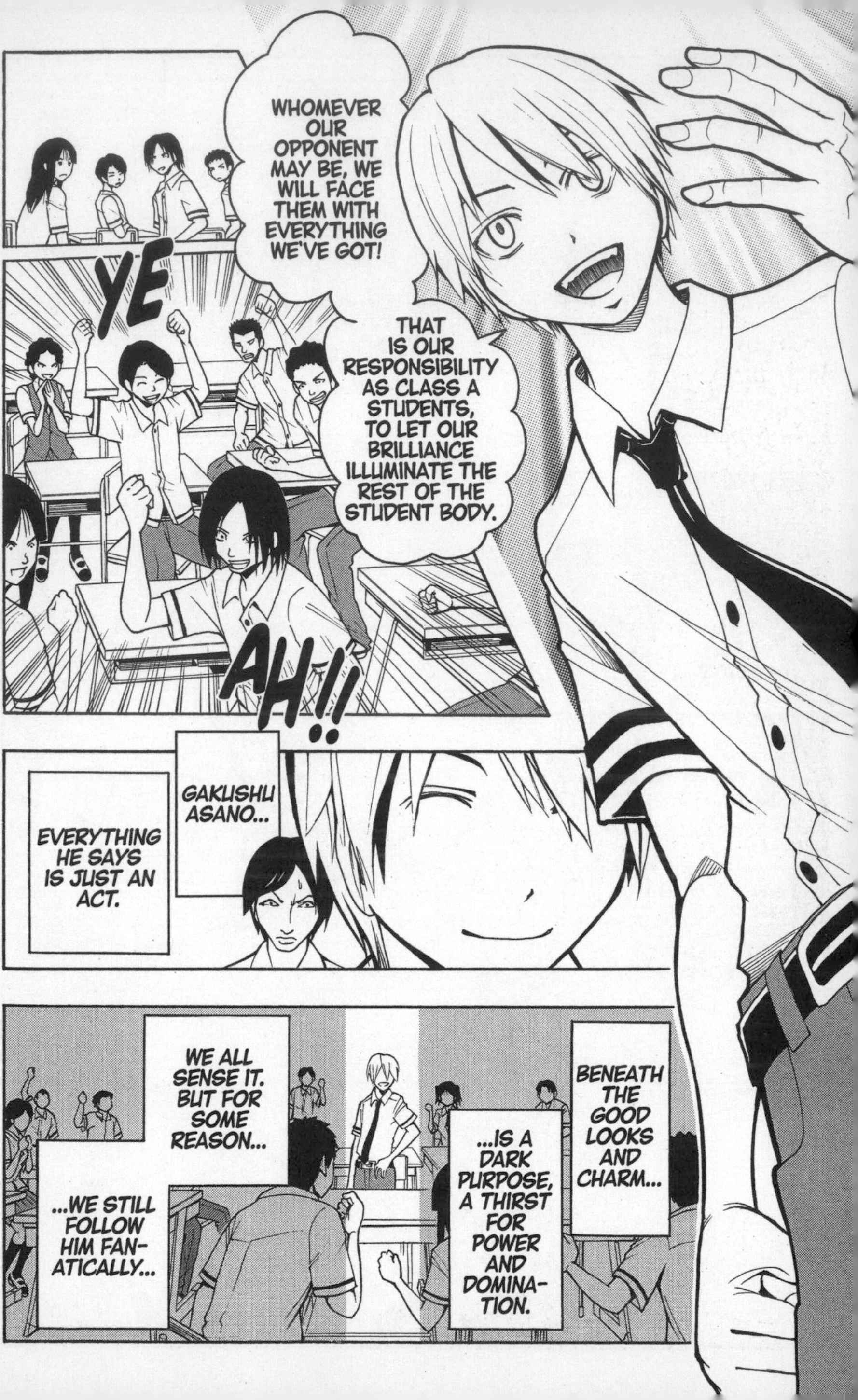
WHOMEVER OUR OPPONENT MAY BE, WE WILL FACE THEM WITH EVERYTHING WE'VE GOT!
THAT IS OUR RESPONSIBILITY AS CLASS A STUDENTS, TO LET OUR BRILLIANCE ILLUMINATE THE REST OF THE STUDENT BODY.
YE
AH!!
GAKUSHU ASANO...
EVERYTHING HE SAYS IS JUST AN ACT.
BENEATH THE GOOD LOOKS AND CHARM...
...IS A DARK PURPOSE, A THIRST FOR POWER AND DOMINATION.
WE ALL SENSE IT. BUT FOR SOME REASON...
...WE STILL FOLLOW HIM FAN-ATICALLY...

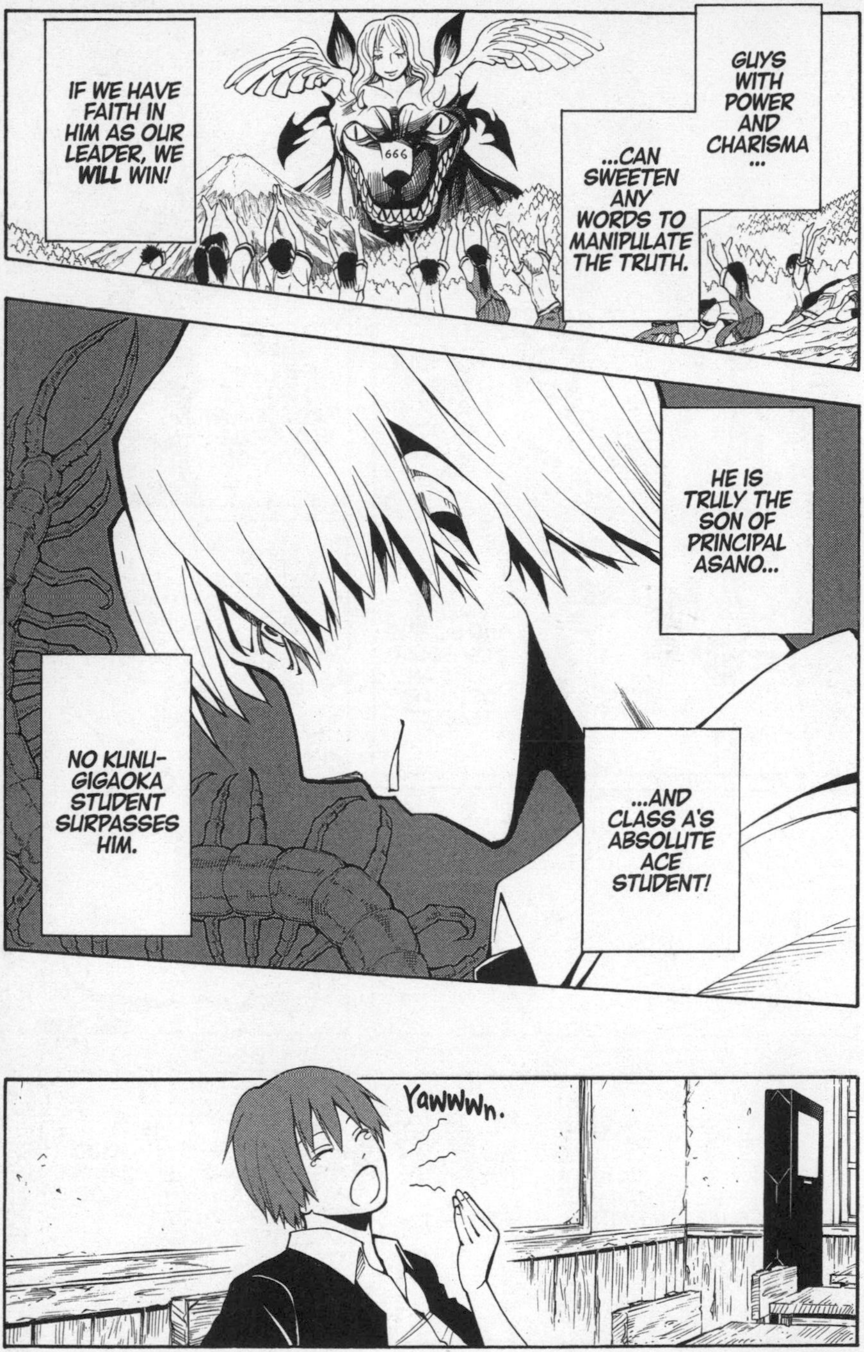
GUYS WITH POWER AND CHARISMA...
...CAN SWEETEN ANY WORDS TO MANIPULATE THE TRUTH.
666
IF WE HAVE FAITH IN HIM AS OUR LEADER, WE WILL WIN!
HE IS TRULY THE SON OF PRINCIPAL ASANO...
...AND CLASS A'S ABSOLUTE ACE STUDENT!
NO KUNU-GIGAOKA STUDENT SURPASSES HIM.
Yawwwn.

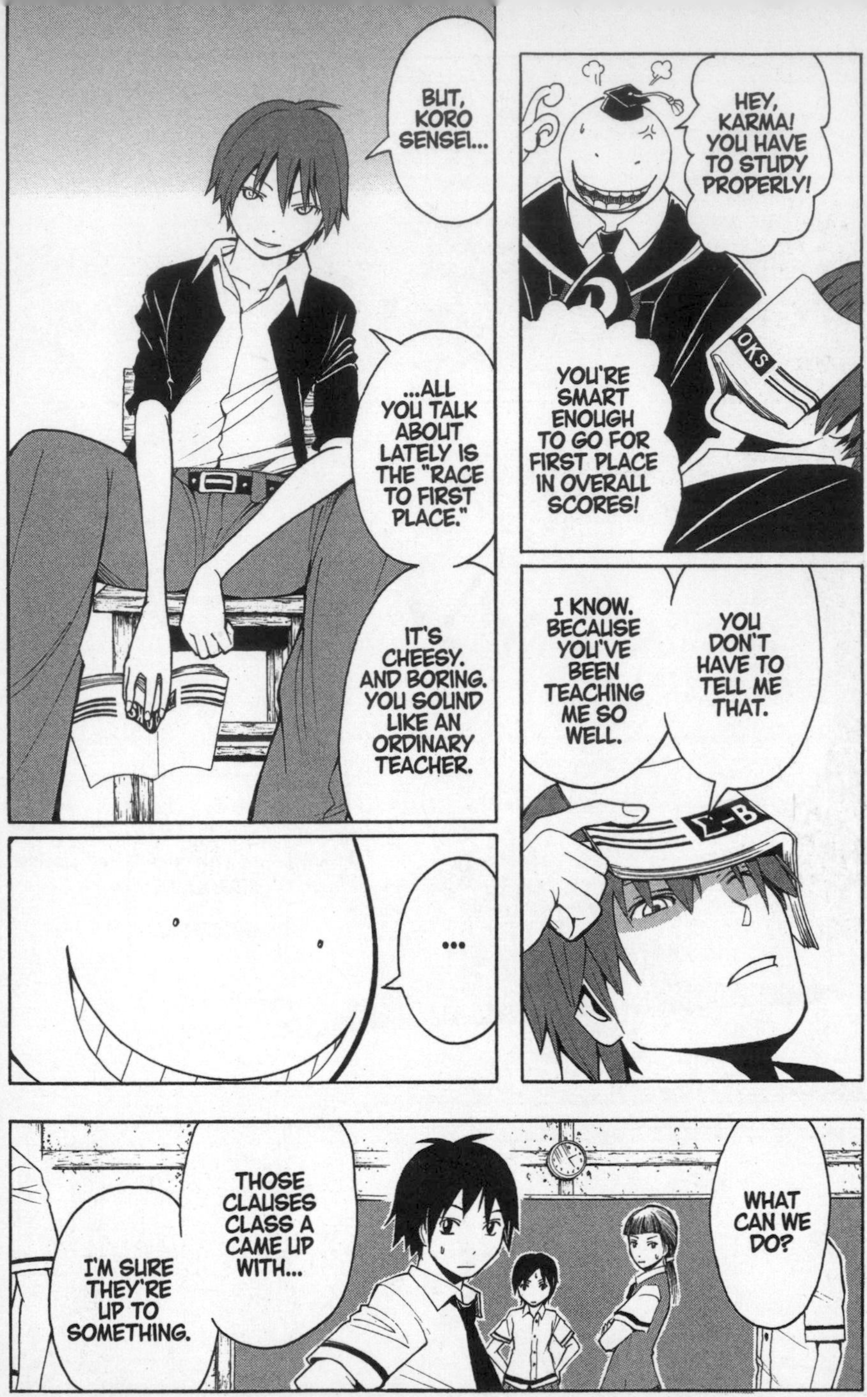
HEY, KARMA! YOU HAVE TO STUDY PROPERLY!
YOU'RE SMART ENOUGH TO GO FOR FIRST PLACE IN OVERALL SCORES!
BUT, KORO SENSEI...
...ALL YOU TALK ABOUT LATELY IS THE "RACE TO FIRST PLACE."
IT'S CHEESY. AND BORING. YOU SOUND LIKE AN ORDINARY TEACHER.
YOU DON'T HAVE TO TELL ME THAT.
I KNOW. BECAUSE YOU'VE BEEN TEACHING ME SO WELL.
...
WHAT CAN WE DO?
THOSE CLAUSES CLASS A CAME UP WITH...
I'M SURE THEY'RE UP TO SOMETHING.

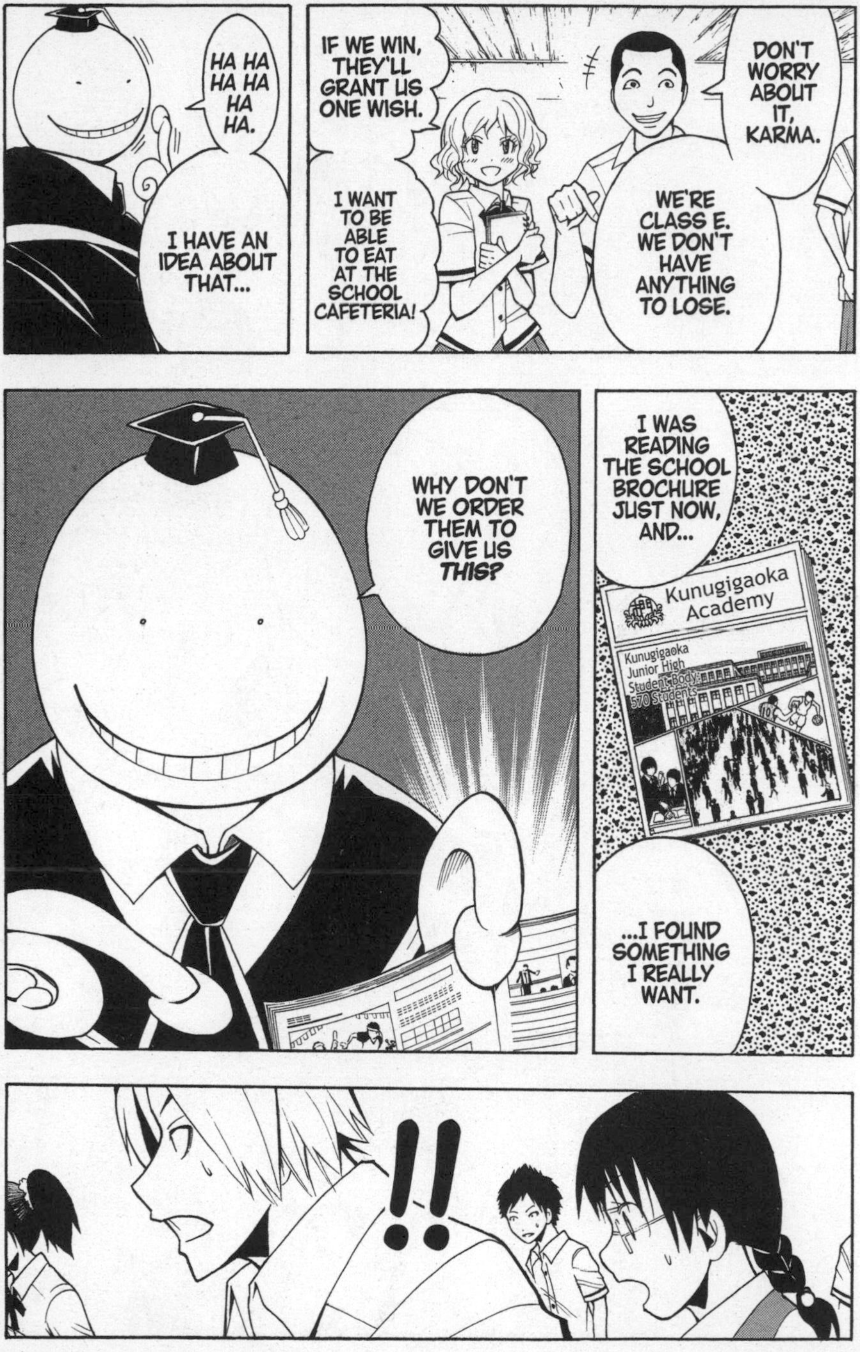
DON'T WORRY ABOUT IT, KARMA.
WE'RE CLASS E. WE DON'T HAVE ANYTHING TO LOSE.
IF WE WIN, THEY'LL GRANT US ONE WISH.
I WANT TO BE ABLE TO EAT AT THE SCHOOL CAFETERIA!
HA HA HA HA HA HA.
I HAVE AN IDEA ABOUT THAT...
I WAS READING THE SCHOOL BROCHURE JUST NOW, AND...
Kunugigaoka Academy
Kunugigaoka Junior High Student Body 570 Students
...I FOUND SOMETHING I REALLY WANT.
WHY DON'T WE ORDER THEM TO GIVE US *THIS?*
!!

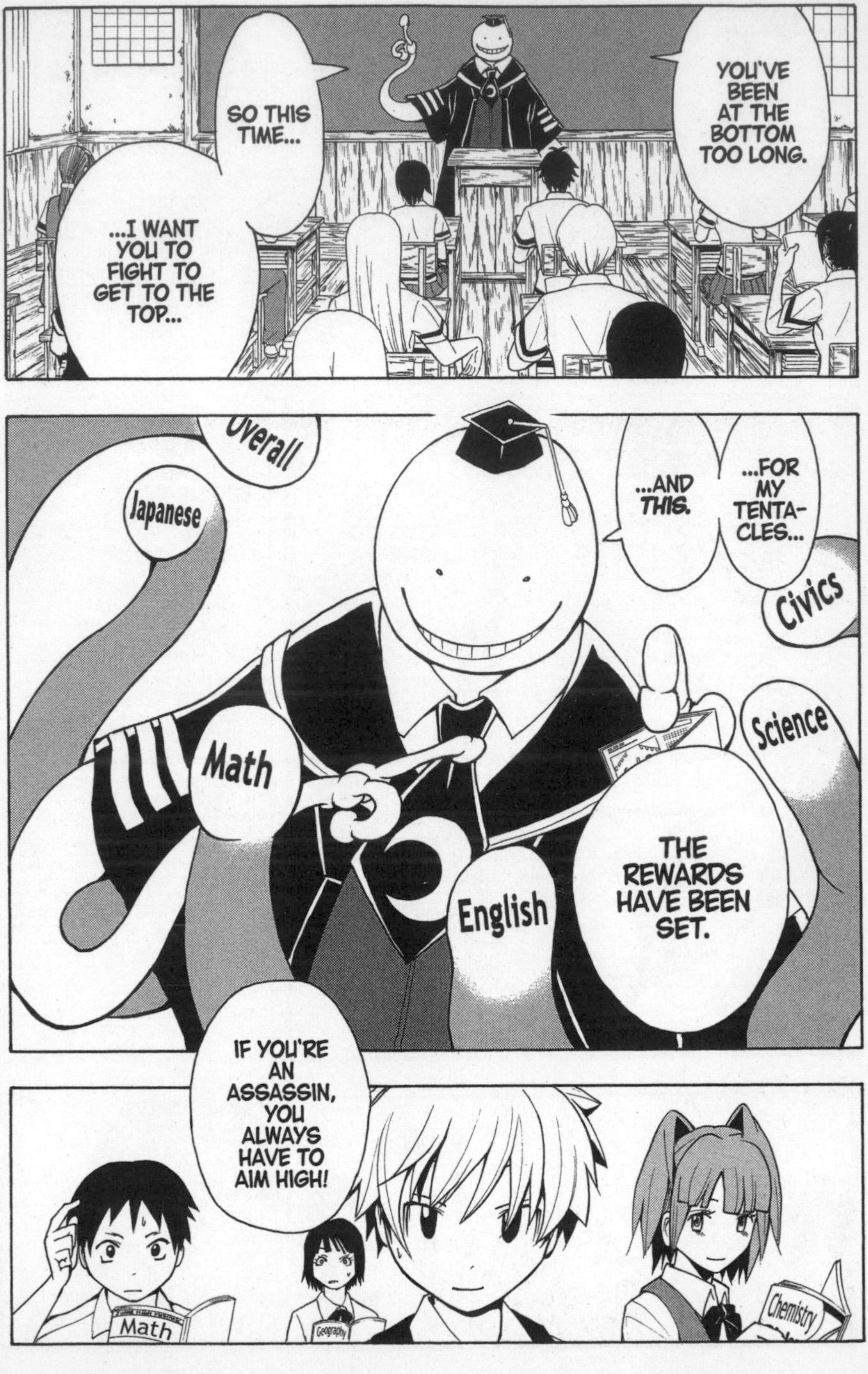
YOU'VE BEEN AT THE BOTTOM TOO LONG.
SO THIS TIME...
...I WANT YOU TO FIGHT TO GET TO THE TOP...
...FOR MY TENTACLES...
...AND THIS.
Civics
Overall
Japanese
Science
Math
THE REWARDS HAVE BEEN SET.
English
IF YOU'RE AN ASSASSIN, YOU ALWAYS HAVE TO AIM HIGH!
Chemistry
Geography
Math

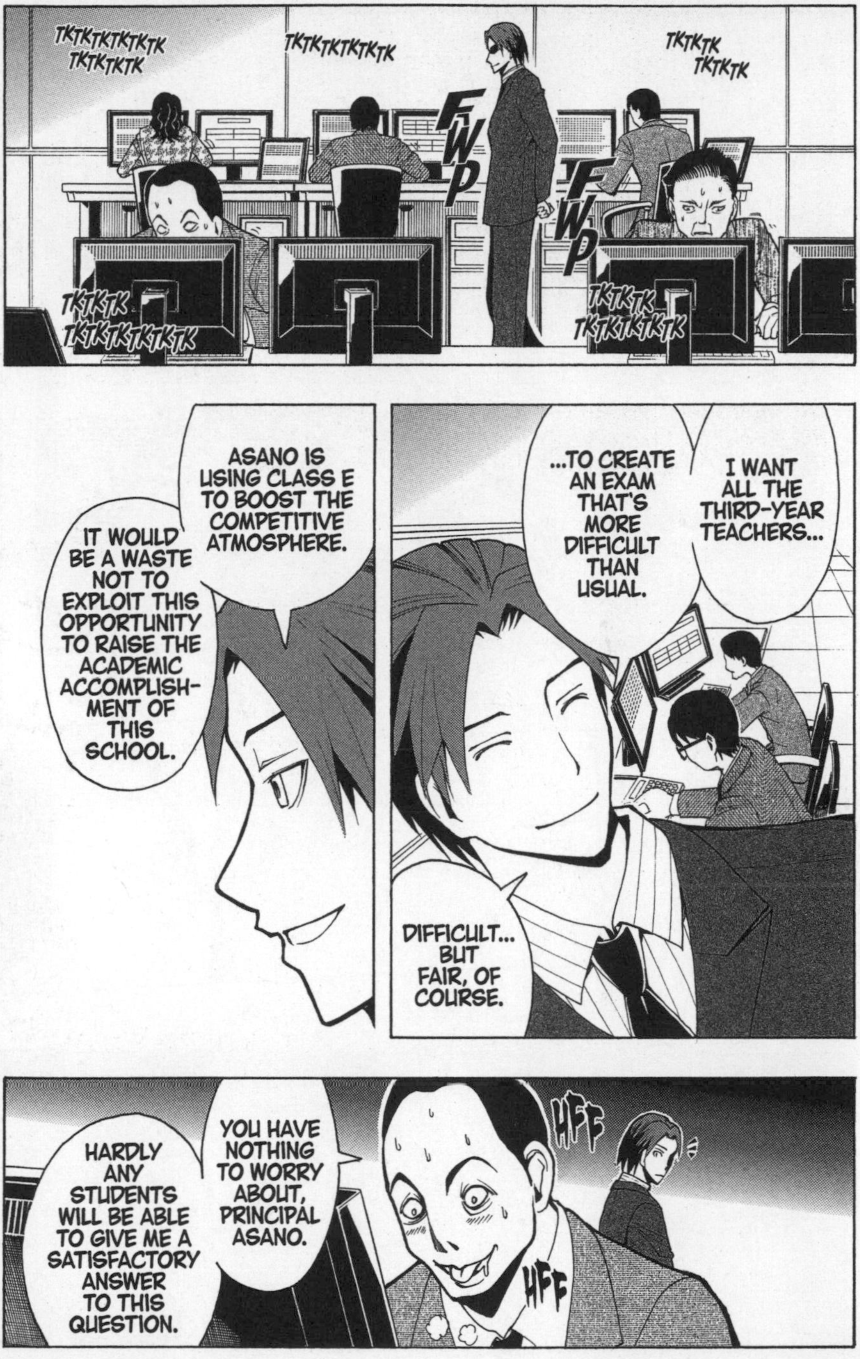
TKTKTK TKTKTK
FWP
FWP
TKTKTK TKTKTKTKTK
TKTKTKTKTK
TKTKTKTKTKTK TKTKTKTK
TKTKTK TKTKTKTKTKTK
I WANT ALL THE THIRD-YEAR TEACHERS...
...TO CREATE AN EXAM THAT'S MORE DIFFICULT THAN USUAL.
DIFFICULT... BUT FAIR, OF COURSE.
ASANO IS USING CLASS E TO BOOST THE COMPETITIVE ATMOSPHERE.
IT WOULD BE A WASTE NOT TO EXPLOIT THIS OPPORTUNITY TO RAISE THE ACADEMIC ACCOMPLISHMENT OF THIS SCHOOL.
HFF
HFF
YOU HAVE NOTHING TO WORRY ABOUT, PRINCIPAL ASANO.
HARDLY ANY STUDENTS WILL BE ABLE TO GIVE ME A SATISFACTORY ANSWER TO THIS QUESTION.

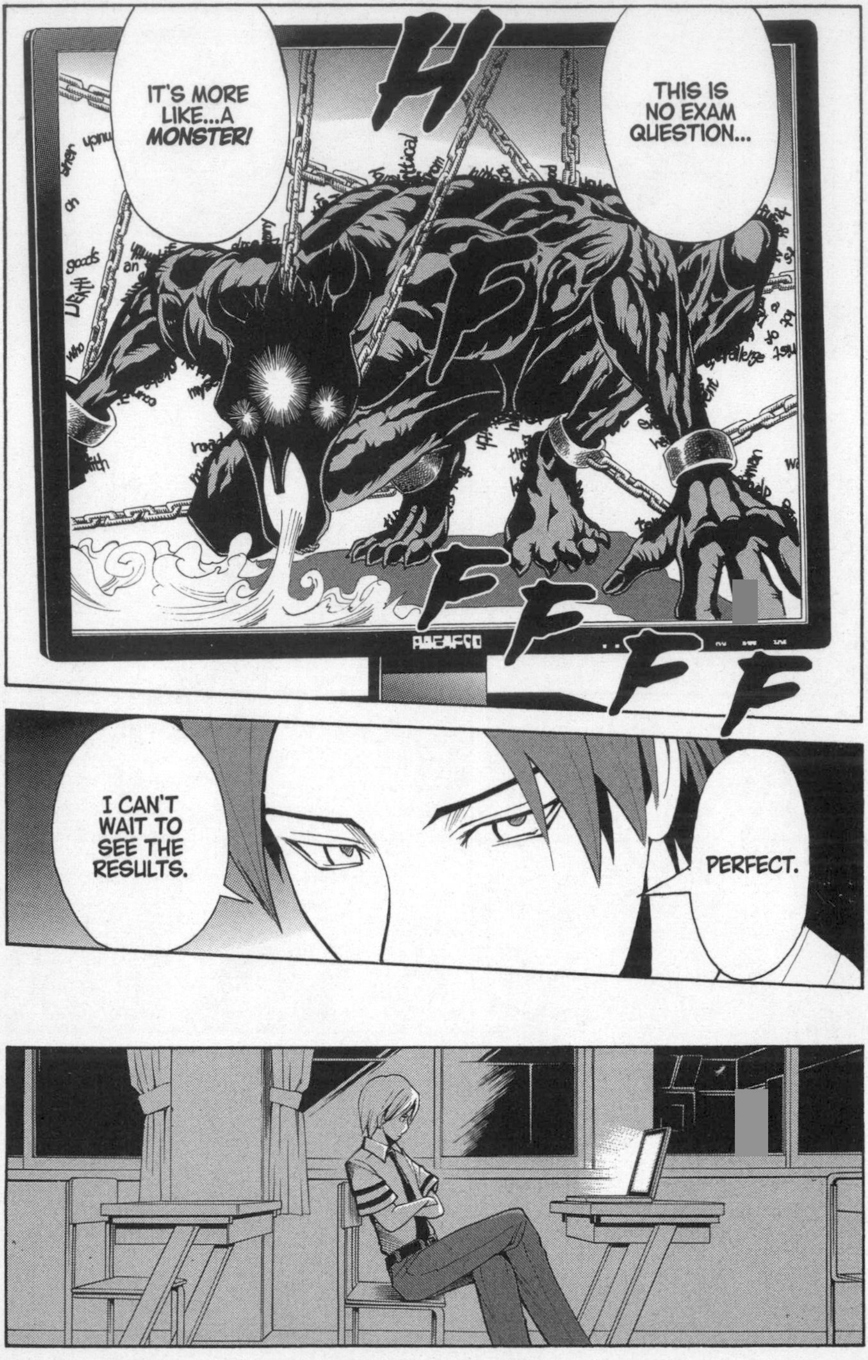
THIS IS NO EXAM QUESTION...
IT'S MORE LIKE...A MONSTER!
HSFFFF
PERFECT.
I CAN'T WAIT TO SEE THE RESULTS.

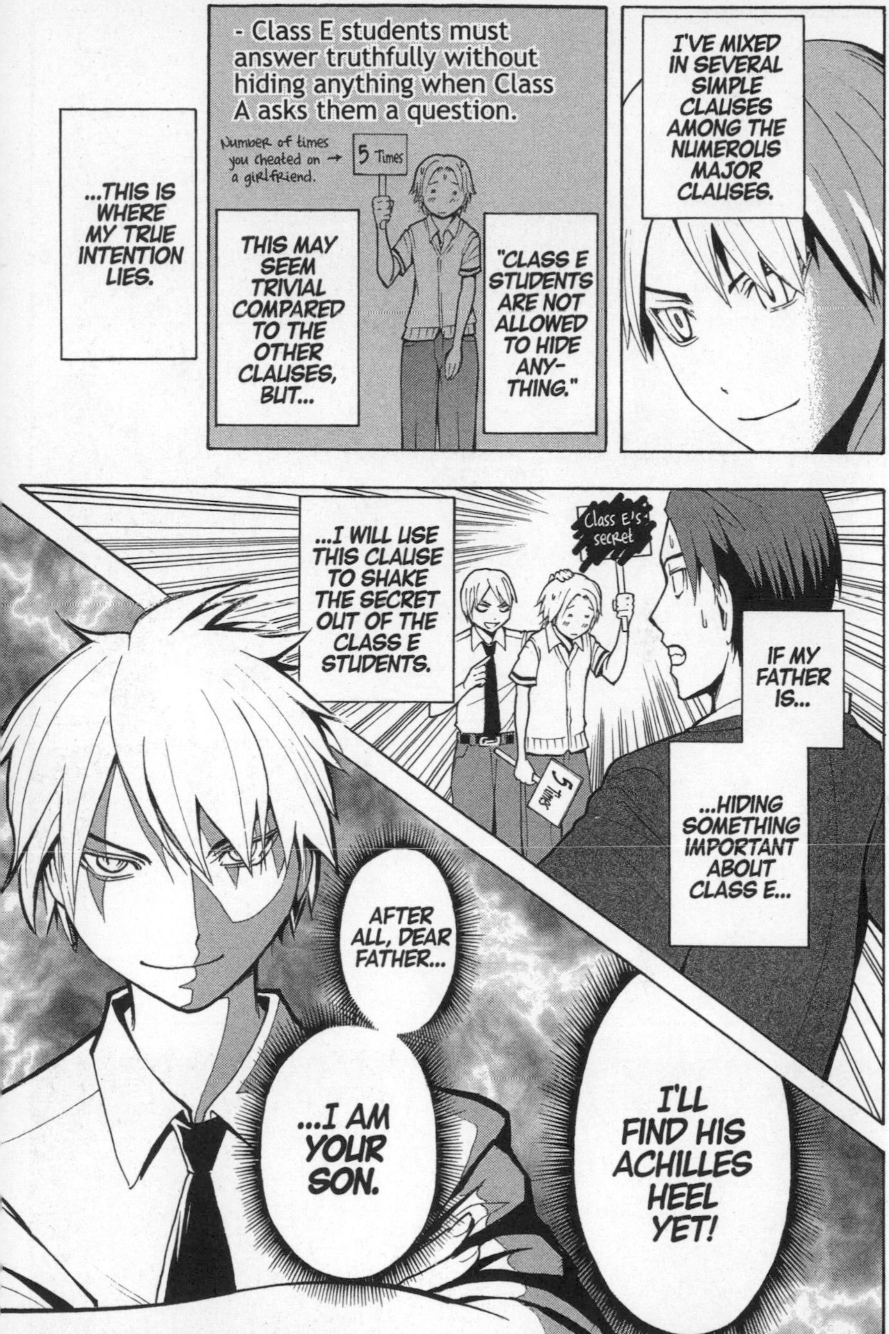
I'VE MIXED IN SEVERAL SIMPLE CLAUSES AMONG THE NUMEROUS MAJOR CLAUSES.
- Class E students must answer truthfully without hiding anything when Class A asks them a question.
"CLASS E STUDENTS ARE NOT ALLOWED TO HIDE ANY-THING."
Number of times you cheated on a girlfriend.
5 Times
THIS MAY SEEM TRIVIAL COMPARED TO THE OTHER CLAUSES, BUT...
...THIS IS WHERE MY TRUE INTENTION LIES.
IF MY FATHER IS...
...HIDING SOMETHING IMPORTANT ABOUT CLASS E...
Class E's secret
5 Times
...I WILL USE THIS CLAUSE TO SHAKE THE SECRET OUT OF THE CLASS E STUDENTS.
I'LL FIND HIS ACHILLES HEEL YET!
AFTER ALL, DEAR FATHER...
...I AM YOUR SON.

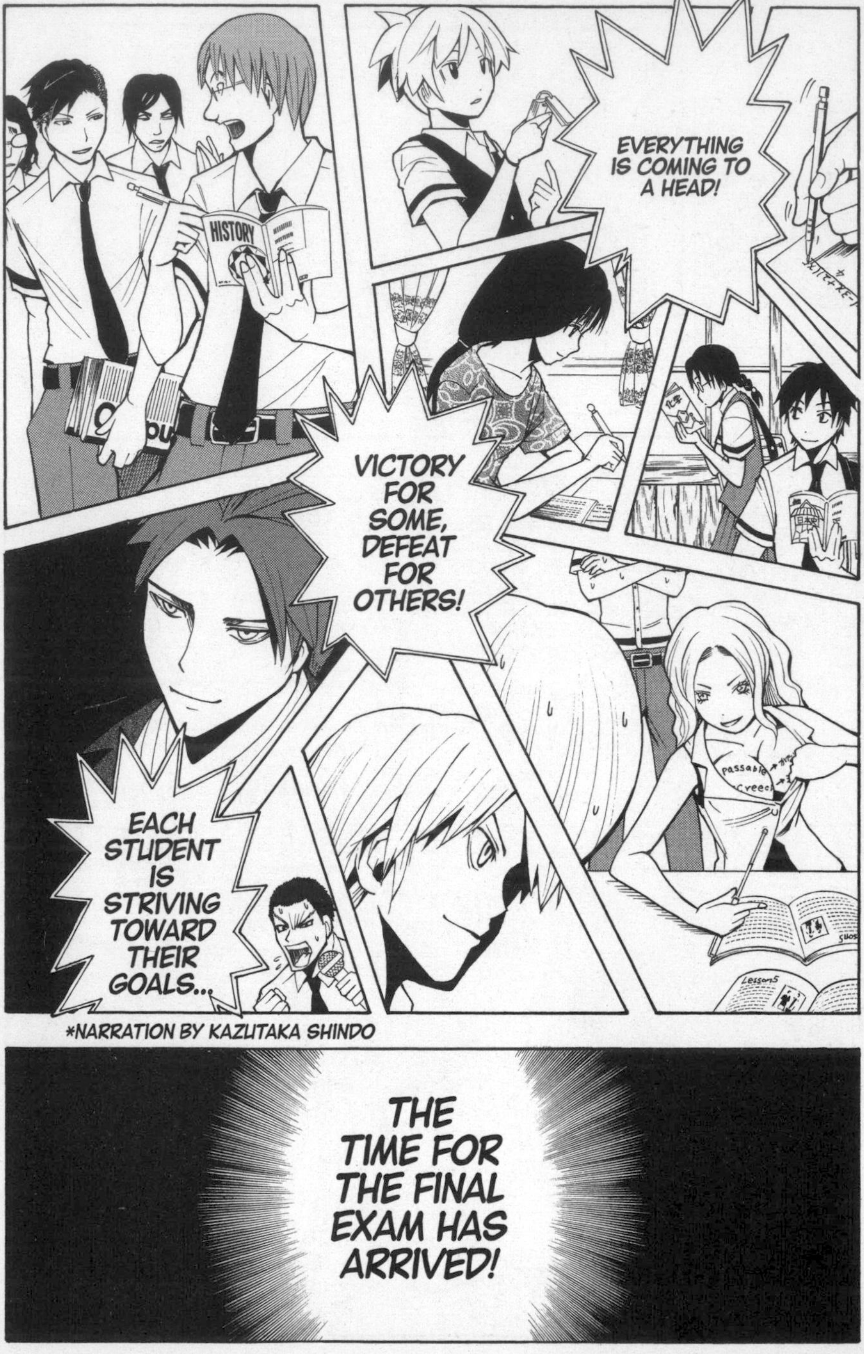
EVERYTHING IS COMING TO A HEAD!
HISTORY
VICTORY FOR SOME, DEFEAT FOR OTHERS!
EACH STUDENT IS STRIVING TOWARD THEIR GOALS...
*NARRATION BY KAZUTAKA SHINDO
THE TIME FOR THE FINAL EXAM HAS ARRIVED!

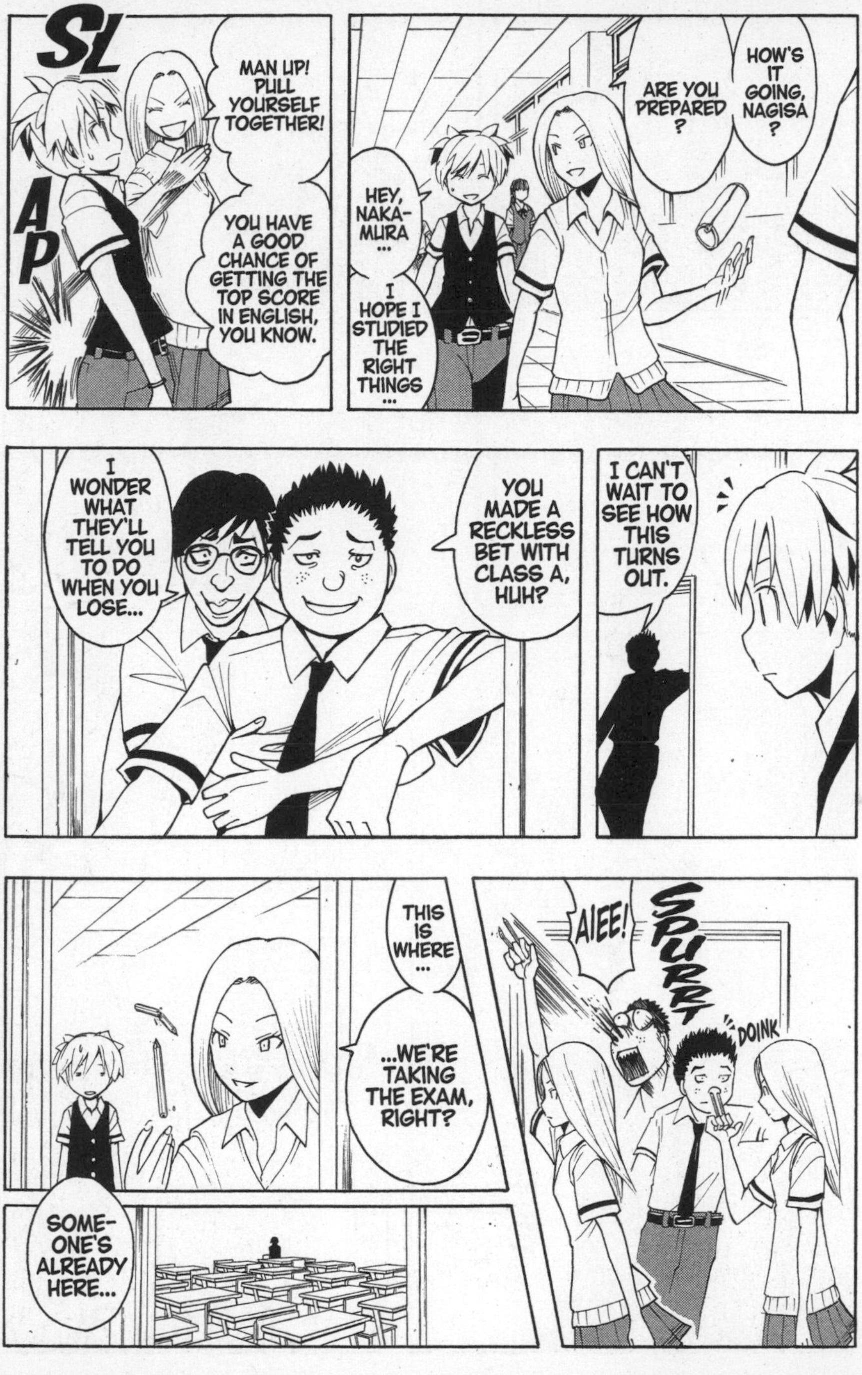
HOW'S IT GOING, NAGISA?
ARE YOU PREPARED?
HEY, NAKAMURA...
I HOPE I STUDIED THE RIGHT THINGS...
SLAP
MAN UP! PULL YOURSELF TOGETHER!
YOU HAVE A GOOD CHANCE OF GETTING THE TOP SCORE IN ENGLISH, YOU KNOW.
I CAN'T WAIT TO SEE HOW THIS TURNS OUT.
YOU MADE A RECKLESS BET WITH CLASS A, HUH?
I WONDER WHAT THEY'LL TELL YOU TO DO WHEN YOU LOSE...
AIEE!
SPURT
DOINK
THIS IS WHERE...
...WE'RE TAKING THE EXAM, RIGHT?
SOME-ONE'S ALREADY HERE...

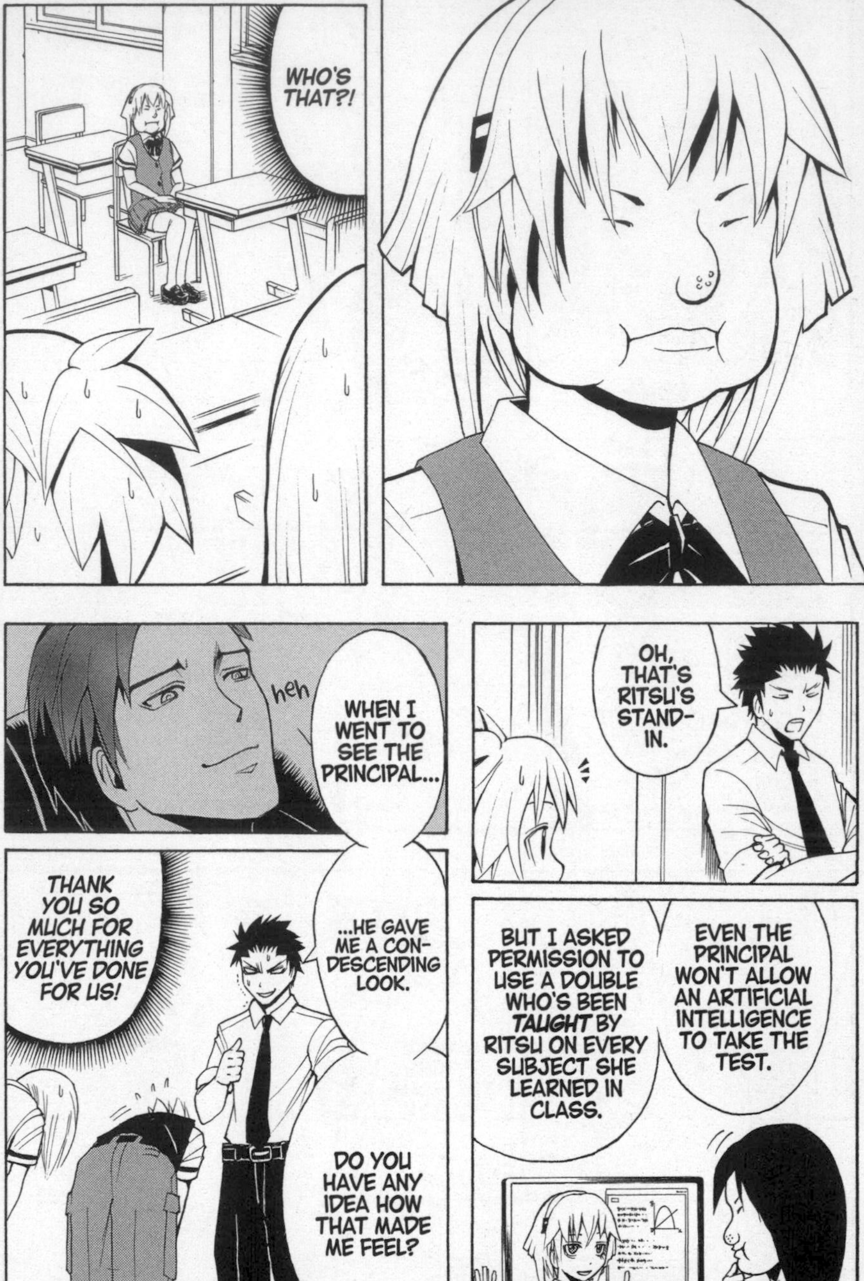
WHO'S THAT?!
OH, THAT'S RITSU'S STAND-IN.
EVEN THE PRINCIPAL WON'T ALLOW AN ARTIFICIAL INTELLIGENCE TO TAKE THE TEST.
BUT I ASKED PERMISSION TO USE A DOUBLE WHO'S BEEN *TAUGHT* BY RITSU ON EVERY SUBJECT SHE LEARNED IN CLASS.
heh
WHEN I WENT TO SEE THE PRINCIPAL...
...HE GAVE ME A CON-DESCENDING LOOK.
THANK YOU SO MUCH FOR EVERYTHING YOU'VE DONE FOR US!
DO YOU HAVE ANY IDEA HOW THAT MADE ME FEEL?

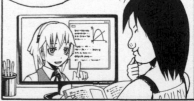

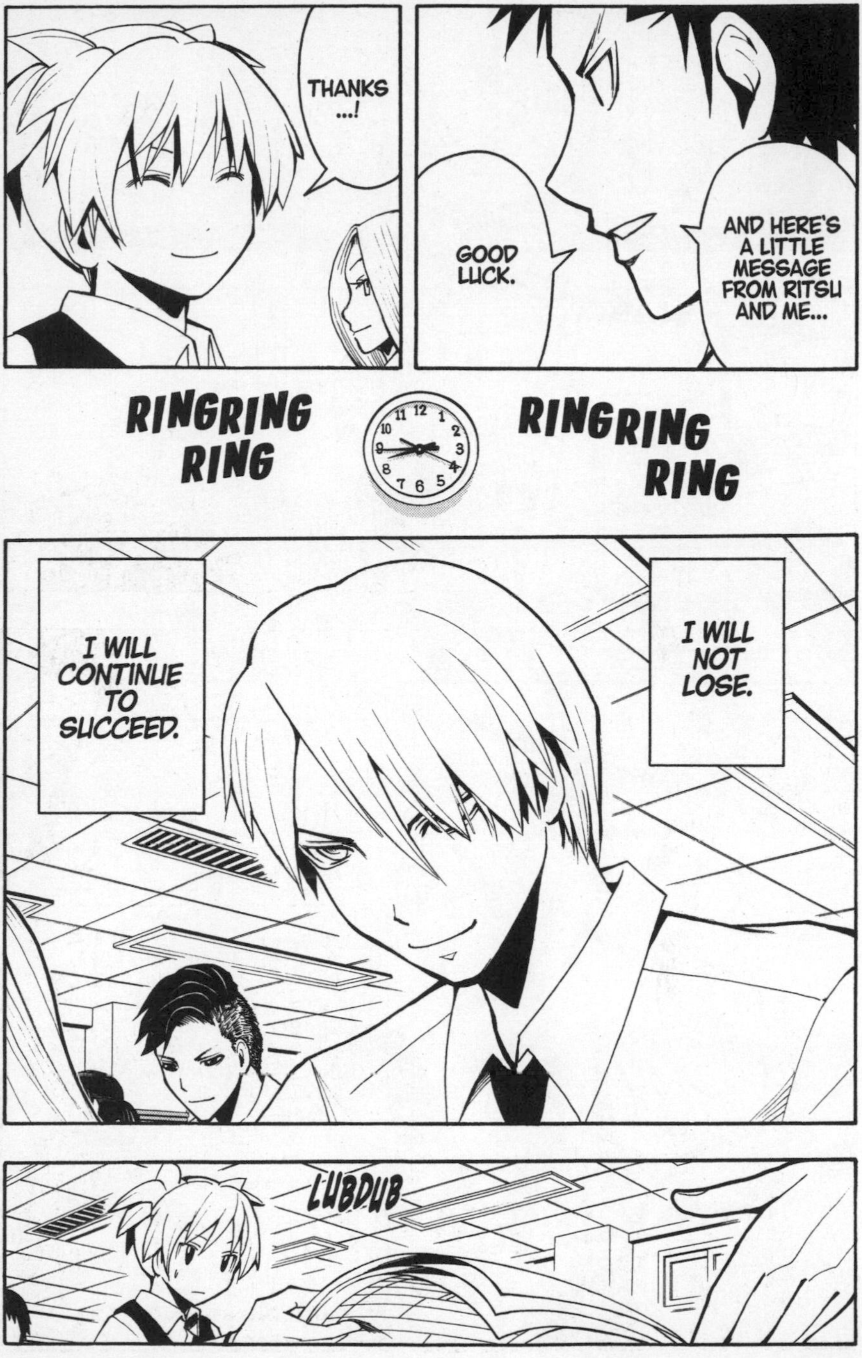
AND HERE'S A LITTLE MESSAGE FROM RITSU AND ME...
GOOD LUCK.
THANKS ...!
RINGRING RING
RINGRING RING
I WILL NOT LOSE.
I WILL CONTINUE TO SUCCEED.
LUBDUB

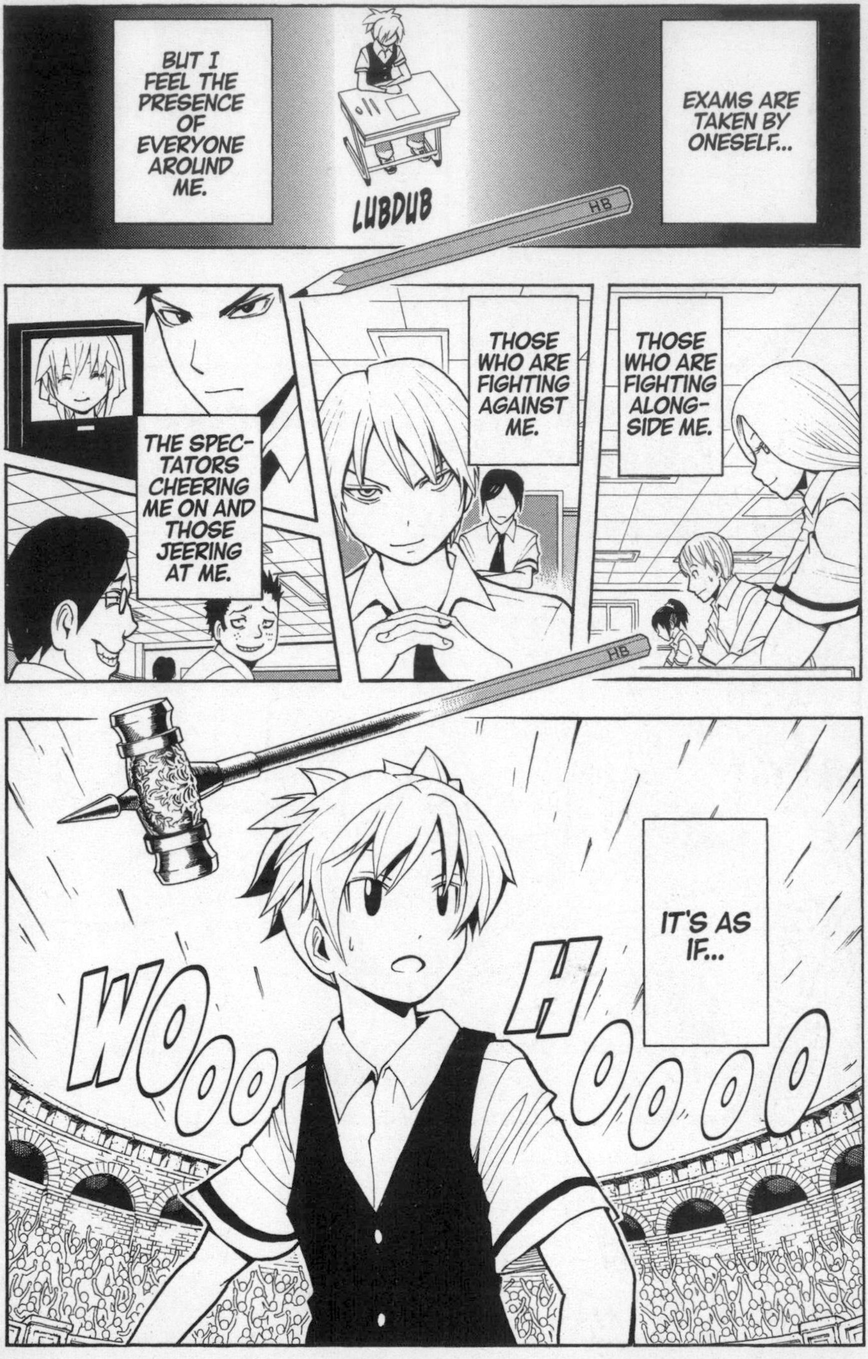
EXAMS ARE TAKEN BY ONESELF...
LUBDUB
BUT I FEEL THE PRESENCE OF EVERYONE AROUND ME.
HB
THOSE WHO ARE FIGHTING ALONG-SIDE ME.
THOSE WHO ARE FIGHTING AGAINST ME.
THE SPEC-TATORS CHEERING ME ON AND THOSE JEERING AT ME.
HB
IT'S AS IF...
WOOOH OOOO

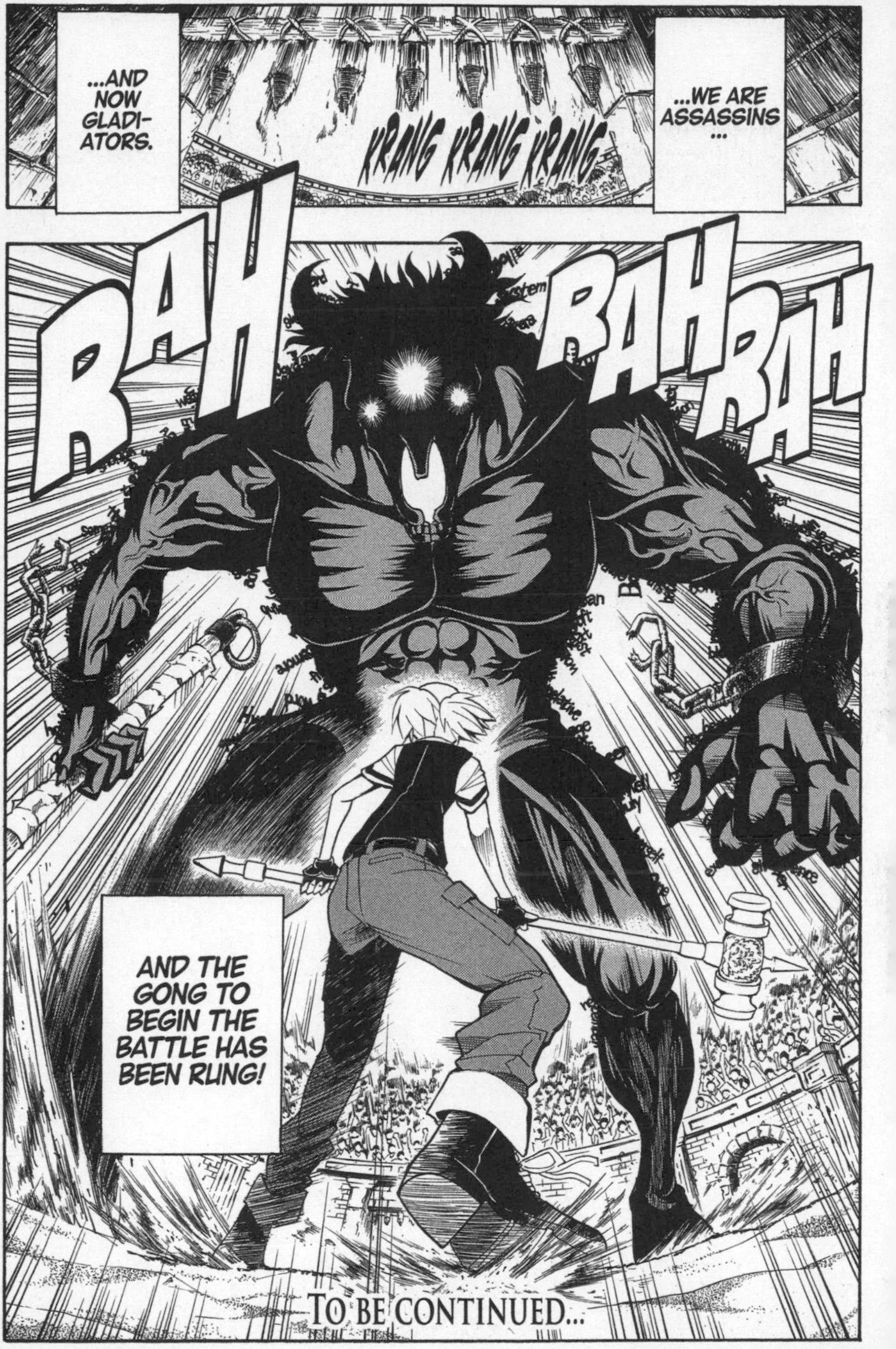
...WE ARE ASSASSINS ...
KRANG KRANG KRANG
...AND NOW GLADI-ATORS.
RAH RAH RAH
AND THE GONG TO BEGIN THE BATTLE HAS BEEN RUNG!
TO BE CONTINUED...

I often use current events and parody in my manga, but that's become a lot more difficult than it used to be.

One major reason is the lack of subjects everyone has in common, due to the decline in TV viewership. Parodies aren't funny if you use subjects that only a handful of people can relate to.

The diversity of culture is a fine thing, but every now and again, I would like to see the outbreak of a social phenomenon that every Tom, Dick and Harry knows about. For that to happen, I believe TV needs to make a comeback...

—Yusei Matsui

Yusei Matsui was born on the last day of January in Saitama Prefecture, Japan. He has been drawing manga since elementary school. Some of his favorite manga series are *Bobobo-bo Bo-bobo*, *JoJo's Bizarre Adventure* and *Ultimate Muscle*. Matsui learned his trade working as an assistant to manga artist Yoshio Sawai, creator of *Bobobo-bo Bo-bobo*. In 2005, Matsui debuted his original manga *Neuro: Supernatural Detective* in *Weekly Shonen Jump*. In 2007, *Neuro* was adapted into an anime. In 2012, *Assassination Classroom* began serialization in *Weekly Shonen Jump*.

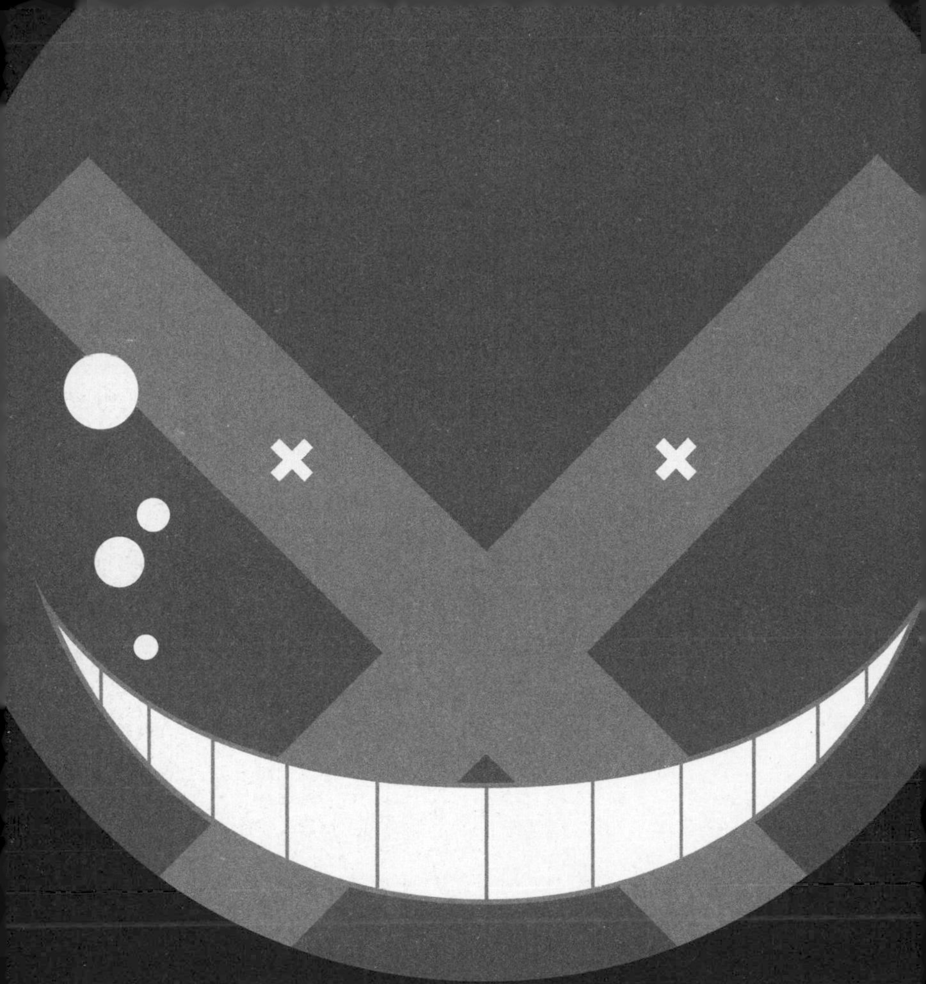

A purple ✕ is a sign that you're wrong, in case him yelling "Impossible," "Not allowed" and "Absolutely not!!" didn't give it away.

ASSASSINATION CLASSROOM

YUSEI MATSUI

6

SWIM TIME

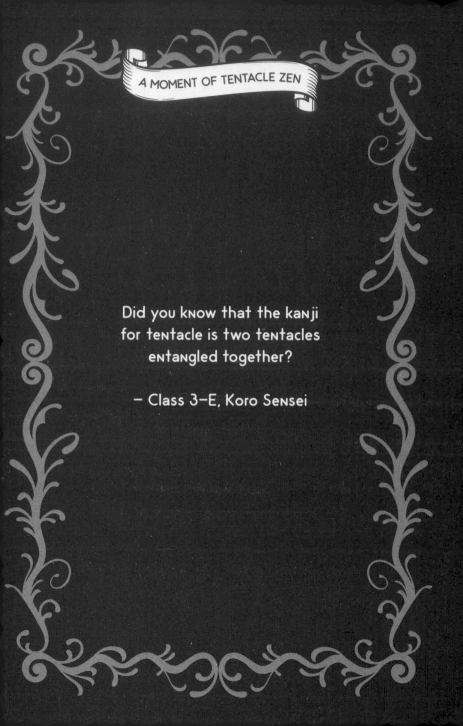

A MOMENT OF TENTACLE ZEN

Did you know that the kanji
for tentacle is two tentacles
entangled together?

– Class 3–E, Koro Sensei

ASSASSINATION CLASSROOM

Volume 6
SHONEN JUMP ADVANCED Manga Edition

Story and Art by YUSEI MATSUI

Translation/Tetsuichiro Miyaki
English Adaptation/Bryant Turnage
Touch-up Art & Lettering/Stephen Dutro
Cover & Interior Design/Sam Elzway
Editor/Annette Roman

ANSATSU KYOSHITSU © 2012 by Yusei Matsui
All rights reserved.
First published in Japan in 2012 by SHUEISHA Inc., Tokyo.
English translation rights arranged by SHUEISHA Inc.

The stories, characters and incidents mentioned in this publication are entirely fictional.

Printed in the U.S.A.

Published by VIZ Media, LLC
P.O. Box 77010
San Francisco, CA 94107

10 9 8 7 6 5 4 3 2 1
First printing, October 2015

www.viz.com
www.shonenjump.com

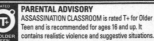

The 3-E students hope to kill on their final exams to win not only respect but a special reward. Over summer break, Nagisa, Sugino and Maehara play amateur entomologist with...a girl? After rigorous training with the greatest assassin of all, the class launches their best assassination plan yet! But in the nick of time, Koro Sensei transforms into an invulnerable form—which completely disables him. Now who will save our would-be assassins from a mysterious biological weapon...?

Available December 2015!

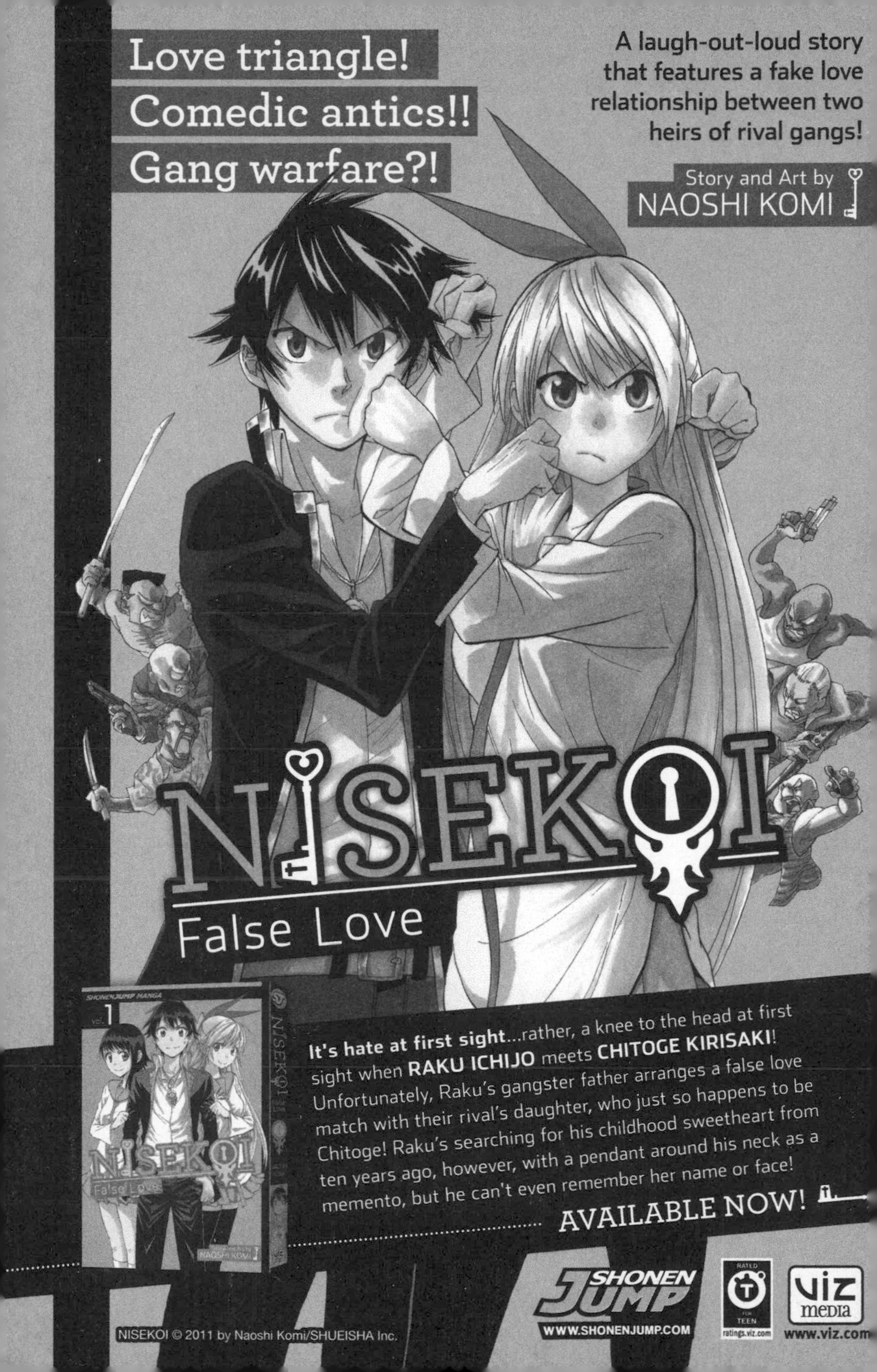
Love triangle!
Comedic antics!!
Gang warfare?!
A laugh-out-loud story that features a fake love relationship between two heirs of rival gangs!
Story and Art by
NAOSHI KOMI
NISEKOI
False Love
SHONENJUMP MANGA
vol. 1
It's hate at first sight...rather, a knee to the head at first sight when RAKU ICHIJO meets CHITOGE KIRISAKI! Unfortunately, Raku's gangster father arranges a false love match with their rival's daughter, who just so happens to be Chitoge! Raku's searching for his childhood sweetheart from ten years ago, however, with a pendant around his neck as a memento, but he can't even remember her name or face!
AVAILABLE NOW!
SHONEN JUMP
WWW.SHONENJUMP.COM
RATED T FOR TEEN
ratings.viz.com
viz media
www.viz.com
NISEKOI © 2011 by Naoshi Komi/SHUEISHA Inc.

You're Reading in the Wrong Direction!!

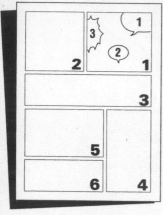

Whoops! Guess what? You're starting at the wrong end of the comic!

...It's true! In keeping with the original Japanese format, **Assassination Classroom** is meant to be read from right to left, starting in the upper-right corner.

Unlike English, which is read from left to right, Japanese is read from right to left, meaning that action, sound effects and word-balloon order are completely reversed... something which can make readers unfamiliar with Japanese feel pretty backwards themselves. For this reason, manga or Japanese comics published in the U.S. in English have sometimes been published "flopped"—that is, printed in exact reverse order, as though seen from the other side of a mirror.

By flopping pages, U.S. publishers can avoid confusing readers, but the compromise is not without its downside. For one thing, a character in a flopped manga series who once wore in the original Japanese version a T-shirt emblazoned with "M A Y" (as in "the merry month of") now wears one which reads "Y A M"! Additionally, many manga creators in Japan are themselves unhappy with the process, as some feel the mirror-imaging of their art skews their original intentions.

We are proud to bring you Yusei Matsui's **Assasssination Classroom** in the original unflopped format.

For now, though, turn to the other side of the book and let the adventure begin...!

—Editor